OECD/G20 Base Erosion and Profit Shifting Project

Harmful Tax Practices – 2019 Peer Review Reports on the Exchange of Information on Tax Rulings

INCLUSIVE FRAMEWORK ON BEPS: ACTION 5

OECD
BETTER POLICIES FOR BETTER LIVES

Please cite this publication as:
OECD (2020), *Harmful Tax Practices – 2019 Peer Review Reports on the Exchange of Information on Tax Rulings: Inclusive Framework on BEPS: Action 5* , OECD/G20 Base Erosion and Profit Shifting Project, OECD Publishing, Paris, *https://doi.org/10.1787/afd1bf8c-en*.

ISBN 978-92-64-70564-7 (print)
ISBN 978-92-64-53805-4 (pdf)

OECD/G20 Base Erosion and Profit Shifting Project
ISSN 2313-2604 (print)
ISSN 2313-2612 (online)

Photo credits: Cover © ninog-Fotolia.com.

Corrigenda to publications may be found on line at: *www.oecd.org/about/publishing/corrigenda.htm*.

Foreword

The integration of national economies and markets has increased substantially in recent years, putting a strain on the international tax rules, which were designed more than a century ago. Weaknesses in the current rules create opportunities for base erosion and profit shifting (BEPS), requiring bold moves by policy makers to restore confidence in the system and ensure that profits are taxed where economic activities take place and value is created.

Following the release of the report Addressing Base Erosion and Profit Shifting in February 2013, OECD and G20 countries adopted a 15-point Action Plan to address BEPS in September 2013. The Action Plan identified 15 actions along three key pillars: introducing coherence in the domestic rules that affect cross-border activities, reinforcing substance requirements in the existing international standards, and improving transparency as well as certainty.

After two years of work, measures in response to the 15 actions were delivered to G20 Leaders in Antalya in November 2015. All the different outputs, including those delivered in an interim form in 2014, were consolidated into a comprehensive package. The BEPS package of measures represents the first substantial renovation of the international tax rules in almost a century. Once the new measures become applicable, it is expected that profits will be reported where the economic activities that generate them are carried out and where value is created. BEPS planning strategies that rely on outdated rules or on poorly co-ordinated domestic measures will be rendered ineffective.

Implementation is now the focus of this work. The BEPS package is designed to be implemented via changes in domestic law and practices, and in tax treaties. With the negotiation of a multilateral instrument (MLI) having been finalised in 2016 to facilitate the implementation of the treaty related BEPS measures, over 85 jurisdictions are covered by the MLI. The entry into force of the MLI on 1 July 2018 paves the way for swift implementation of the treaty related measures. OECD and G20 countries also agreed to continue to work together to ensure a consistent and co-ordinated implementation of the BEPS recommendations and to make the project more inclusive. Globalisation requires that global solutions and a global dialogue be established which go beyond OECD and G20 countries.

A better understanding of how the BEPS recommendations are implemented in practice could reduce misunderstandings and disputes between governments. Greater focus on implementation and tax administration should therefore be mutually beneficial to governments and business. Proposed improvements to data and analysis will help support ongoing evaluation of the quantitative impact of BEPS, as well as evaluating the impact of the countermeasures developed under the BEPS Project.

As a result, the OECD established the OECD/G20 Inclusive Framework on BEPS (Inclusive Framework), bringing all interested and committed countries and jurisdictions on an equal footing in the Committee on Fiscal Affairs and all its subsidiary bodies. The Inclusive Framework, which already has more than 130 members, is monitoring and peer reviewing the implementation of the minimum standards as well as completing the work on standard setting to address BEPS issues. In addition to BEPS members, other international organisations and regional tax bodies are involved in the work of the Inclusive Framework, which also consults business and the civil society on its different work streams.

This report was approved by the Inclusive Framework on 16 November 2020 and prepared for publication by the OECD Secretariat.

Abbreviations and acronyms

AMPD	Administration Methodology and Procedures Department (Armenia)
APA	Advance pricing arrangement
ATR	Advance tax ruling
BEPS	Base Erosion and Profit Shifting
CLO	Central Liaison Office (San Marino)
EOI	Exchange of Information
ETA	Egyptian tax administration
EU	European Union
FHTP	Forum on Harmful Tax Practice
ICD	International Cooperation Department (Armenia)
IP	Intellectual Property
ISTD	Income and Sales Tax Department (Jordan)
IRD	Inland Revenue Department (Antigua and Barbuda)
JIC	Jordan Investment Commission
MNE	Multinational Enterprise
OECD	Organization for Economic Co-operation and Development
PE	Permanent Establishment
R&D	Research and Development
SAARC	South Asian Association for Regional Cooperation
SRC	Seychelles Revenue Commission
SRC	State Revenue Committee (Armenia)
STA	Swedish Tax Agency
TAPA	Tax Administration and Procedures Act (Antigua and Barbuda)
ToR	Terms of reference
TRNC	Turkish Republic of Northern Cyprus
XML	Extensible Mark-Up Language

Table of contents

TABLES

Executive summary

Context for the exchange of information on tax rulings (the "transparency framework")

The BEPS Action 5 minimum standard on the compulsory spontaneous exchange of information on tax rulings (the "transparency framework") provides tax administrations with timely information on rulings that have been granted to a foreign related party of their resident taxpayer or a permanent establishment, which can be used in conducting risk assessments and which, in the absence of exchange, could give rise to BEPS concerns.

The transparency framework requires spontaneous exchange of information on five categories of taxpayer-specific rulings: (i) rulings related to certain preferential regimes, (ii) unilateral advance pricing arrangements (APAs) or other cross-border unilateral rulings in respect of transfer pricing, (iii) rulings providing for a downward adjustment of taxable profits, (iv) permanent establishment (PE) rulings; and (v) related party conduit rulings.[1] The requirement to exchange information on the rulings in the above categories includes certain past rulings as well as future rulings, pursuant to pre-defined periods which are outlined in each jurisdiction's report and that varies according to the time when a certain jurisdiction has joined the Inclusive Framework or has been identified as a Jurisdiction of Relevance. The exchanges occur pursuant to international exchange of information agreements, which provide the legal conditions under which exchanges take place, including the need to ensure taxpayer confidentiality.

The inclusion of the above categories of rulings in the scope of the transparency framework is not intended to suggest that the issuance of such rulings constitutes a preferential regime or a harmful tax practice. In practice, tax rulings can be an effective way to provide certainty to taxpayers and reduce the risk of disputes. Rather, the need for transparency on rulings is that a tax administration's lack of knowledge or information on the tax treatment of a taxpayer in another jurisdiction can impact the treatment of transactions or arrangements undertaken with a related taxpayer resident in their own jurisdiction and thus lead to BEPS concerns. The availability of timely and targeted information about such rulings, as agreed in the template in Annex C of the Action 5 Report, Countering Harmful Tax Practices More Effectively, Taking Into Account Transparency and Substance (OECD, 2015[1]), is intended to better equip tax authorities to quickly identify risk areas.

This framework was designed with a view to finding a balance between ensuring that the information exchanged is relevant to other tax administrations and that it does not impose an unnecessary administrative burden on either the country exchanging the information or the country receiving it.

Scope of this review

This is the fourth annual peer review of the transparency framework, and covers 124 Inclusive Framework member jurisdictions. This comprises all Inclusive Framework members that joined prior to 30 June 2019 and Jurisdictions of Relevance identified by the Inclusive Framework prior to 30 June 2019. Of these 124 jurisdictions, there were 30 jurisdictions which are not able to legally, or in practice, issue rulings in scope of the transparency framework, and therefore no separate peer review report is included for these jurisdictions.[2]

Eight other members of the Inclusive Framework have not been assessed under the transparency framework, namely Anguilla, the Bahamas, Bahrain, Bermuda, the British Virgin Islands, the Cayman Islands, the Turks and Caicos Islands and the United Arab Emirates. These jurisdictions do not impose any corporate income tax, and therefore cannot legally issue rulings within scope of the transparency framework and nor do Inclusive Framework members exchange information on rulings with them. Therefore, these jurisdictions are considered to be outside the scope of the transparency framework.

The reviews contained in this annual report cover the steps jurisdictions have taken to implement the transparency framework during the calendar year 2019. The reviews have been prepared using information from each reviewed jurisdiction, input from peers who received exchanges of information under the transparency framework, and input from the delegates of the Forum on Harmful Tax Practices ("FHTP").

Key findings

Key findings from this fourth annual peer review include:

- As at 31 December 2019, almost 20 000 tax rulings in the scope of the transparency framework had been issued by the jurisdictions being reviewed. This is the cumulative figure, including certain past rulings issued since 2010. Over 2 000 tax rulings in scope of the transparency framework were issued in 2019 by the 124 jurisdictions reviewed.
- Over 36 000 exchanges of information took place by 31 December 2019, with approximately 7 000 exchanges undertaken during 2019, 9 000 exchanges undertaken during 2018, 14 000 exchanges undertaken during 2017 and 6 000 exchanges during 2016.
- Out of the 94 reviewed jurisdictions, 62 jurisdictions did not receive any recommendations, as they have met all the terms of reference. A further 12 jurisdictions received only one recommendation.
- 58 recommendations for improvement have been made for the year in review.
- 68 peer input questionnaires were submitted providing feedback on the conduct of the exchanges by Inclusive Framework members. Peer input is not mandatory, but in cases where it was provided it has in a number of cases allowed jurisdictions to revise their processes and improve the clarity and quality of information exchanged.
- In a number of cases, the peer review process has assisted jurisdictions in identifying areas where improvement is required, and jurisdictions have been able to take action to implement changes over 2020 while the peer review was ongoing. Where these changes were implemented in 2020, they are generally not taken into account in the recommendations issued for the year 2019. However, these changes would be reviewed in a subsequent peer review.

Table 1. Compilation of recommendations

Aspect of the implementation of the transparency framework that should be improved	Recommendation for improvement
Andorra	
Andorra experienced difficulties in identifying all potential exchange jurisdictions for future rulings.	Andorra is recommended to continue its efforts to ensure that all potential exchange jurisdictions are identified swiftly for all future rulings. This recommendation remains unchanged since the 2017 and 2018 peer review reports.
Andorra is still developing a process to ensure that the information is completed in the required form and exchanges are performed in accordance with the timelines.	Andorra is recommended to continue its efforts to put in place the necessary process to complete the information in the form of Annex C of the BEPS Action 5 Report, to ensure that information is submitted to the

	Competent Authority without undue delay and exchanges are performed in accordance with the timelines. These recommendations remain unchanged since the 2017 and 2018 peer review reports but they are now targeted to specific aspects of the ToR that still need to be put in place.
Angola	
Angola has not yet finalised the steps to have in place its necessary information and gathering process.	Angola is recommended to finalise its information gathering process for identifying all past and future rulings and all potential exchange jurisdictions, with a review and supervision mechanism, as soon as possible. This recommendation remains unchanged since the 2017 and 2018 peer review reports.
Angola has not yet finalised the steps to have effective compulsory spontaneous exchange of information on the tax rulings within the scope of the transparency framework.	Angola is recommended to continue to put in place a domestic legal framework allowing spontaneous exchange of information on rulings and to continue its efforts to complete the templates for all relevant rulings and to ensure that the exchanges of information on rulings occur as soon as possible. This recommendation remains unchanged since the 2017 and 2018 peer review reports.
Antigua and Barbuda	
	No recommendations are made.
Argentina	
Argentina experienced some delays in exchanging information on one future ruling.	No recommendation is made because Argentina completed exchanges on the delayed future ruling quickly after the issues were identified and resolved, and this is not a recurring issue.
Armenia	
Armenia is in the process to put in place an information gathering process and a review and supervision mechanism.	Armenia is recommended to finalise its information gathering process for identifying all future rulings and potential exchange jurisdictions, with a review and supervision mechanism, as soon as possible.
Armenia does not have a process to complete the templates on relevant rulings, to make them available to the Competent Authority for exchange of information, and to exchange them with relevant jurisdictions.	Armenia is recommended to develop a process to complete the templates on relevant rulings and to ensure that the exchanges of information on rulings occur in accordance with the form and timelines under the transparency framework.
Aruba	
	No recommendations are made.
Australia	
	No recommendations are made.
Austria	
	No recommendations are made.
Barbados	
Barbados did not identify or exchange information on new entrants to the grandfathered IP regime.	Barbados is recommended to identify and exchange information on all new entrants to the grandfathered IP regime as soon as possible. This recommendation remains unchanged since the 2017 and 2018 peer review reports.
Belgium	
	No recommendations are made.
Benin	
Benin has not yet finalised the steps to have in place its necessary information and gathering process.	Benin is recommended to finalise its information gathering process, with a review and supervision mechanism, as soon as possible. This recommendation remains unchanged since the prior year peer review report.
Benin has not yet finalised the steps to have effective compulsory spontaneous exchange of information on the tax rulings within the scope of the transparency framework.	Benin is recommended to continue to put in place a domestic legal framework allowing spontaneous exchange of information on rulings and to continue its efforts to complete the templates for all relevant rulings and to ensure that the exchanges of information on rulings occur as soon as possible. This recommendation remains unchanged since the prior year peer review report.
Botswana	
Botswana has not yet finalised the steps to have in place it necessary information gathering process.	Botswana is recommended to apply the best efforts approach to identify all potential exchange jurisdictions for APA and PE rulings and to put in place a review and supervision mechanism, as soon as possible. This recommendation remains unchanged since the prior year peer review

	report.
Botswana does not yet have the necessary legal framework in place for exchanging information on rulings and a process in place to ensure the timely exchange of information on rulings in the form required by the transparency framework.	Botswana is recommended to continue to put in place a domestic legal framework allowing spontaneous exchange of information on rulings and to ensure the timely exchange of information on rulings in the form required by the transparency framework. This recommendation remains unchanged since the prior year peer review report.
Brazil	
	No recommendations are made.
Brunei Darussalam	
	No recommendations are made.
Cabo Verde	
Cabo Verde does not have a process to complete the templates on relevant rulings and to make them available to the Competent Authority for exchange of information.	Cabo Verde is recommended to develop a process to complete the templates on relevant rulings and to ensure that the exchanges of information on rulings occur in accordance with the form and timelines under the transparency framework going forward.
Canada	
	No recommendations are made.
Chile	
	No recommendations are made.
China (People's Republic of)	
	No recommendations are made.
Colombia	
	No recommendations are made.
Congo	
It is not known whether Congo has finalised the steps to have in place its necessary information and gathering process.	Congo is recommended to finalise its information gathering process, with a review and supervision mechanism, as soon as possible. This recommendation remains unchanged since the 2017 and 2018 peer review reports.
It is not known whether Congo has finalised the steps to have effective compulsory spontaneous exchange of information on the tax rulings within the scope of the transparency framework.	Congo is recommended to continue to put in place a domestic legal framework allowing spontaneous exchange of information on rulings and to continue its efforts to complete the templates for all relevant rulings and to ensure that the exchanges of information on rulings occur as soon as possible. This recommendation remains unchanged since the 2017 and 2018 peer review reports.
Costa Rica	
	No recommendations are made.
Croatia	
	No recommendations are made.
Curacao	
The information gathering process is still underway in Curaçao with respect to past and future rulings in scope of the transparency framework and the classification of these rulings under each category.	Curaçao is recommended to finalise its information gathering process for identifying all past and future rulings in scope of the transparency framework as soon as possible. This recommendation remains unchanged since the 2017 and 2018 peer review reports.
Curaçao experienced delays in exchanging information on past and future rulings.	Curaçao is recommended to continue its efforts to ensure that all information on past and future rulings is exchanged as soon as possible. This recommendation remains unchanged since the 2017 and 2018 peer review reports.
Czech Republic	
	No recommendations are made.
Denmark	
	No recommendations are made.
Dominican Republic	
The Dominican Republic is still in the process of ensuring the timely exchange of information on rulings.	The Dominican Republic is recommended to ensure that the exchanges of information on rulings occur as soon as possible.
Egypt	
Egypt has not yet identified all potential exchange jurisdictions for both past and future rulings and does not have a review and supervision mechanism in place to ensure that all relevant information on the	Egypt is recommended to continue its efforts to identify all potential exchange jurisdictions for both past and future rulings and to implement a review and supervision mechanism, as soon as possible. This

identification of rulings and potential exchange jurisdictions is captured adequately.	recommendation remains unchanged since the prior year peer review report.
Egypt does not have in place a process to ensure the timely exchange of information on rulings in the form required by the transparency framework.	Egypt is recommended to develop a process to complete the templates on relevant rulings and to ensure that the exchanges of information on rulings occur in accordance with the form and timelines under the transparency framework. This recommendation remains unchanged since the prior year peer review report.
Estonia	
	No recommendations are made.
Faroe Islands	
The Faroe Islands does not yet have its necessary information and gathering process in place.	The Faroe Islands is recommended to ensure that it has put in place an effective information gathering process to identify all relevant past and future rulings and all potential exchange jurisdictions and to implement a review and supervision mechanism, as soon as possible.
The Faroe Islands does not have a process to complete the templates on relevant rulings, to make them available to the Competent Authority for exchange of information, and to exchange them with relevant jurisdictions.	The Faroe Islands is recommended to develop a process to complete the templates for all relevant rulings and to ensure that the exchanges of information on rulings occur in accordance with the form and timelines under the transparency framework going forward.
Finland	
Finland experienced some delays in exchanging information on future rulings due to technical reason.	No recommendation is made because Finland completed the exchanges on the delayed future rulings quickly after the issues were identified and resolved, and this is not a recurring issue.
France	
France did not identify or exchange information on new entrants to the IP regime or taxpayers benefitting from the third category of IP asset with respect to the former IP regime.	France is recommended to identify and exchange information on all new entrants to the IP regime, and to identify and exchange information on taxpayers benefitting from the third category of IP assets. This recommendation remains unchanged since the 2016, 2017 and 2018 peer review reports.
Gabon	
It is not known whether Gabon has finalised the steps to have in place its necessary information and gathering process.	Gabon is recommended to finalise its information gathering process, with a review and supervision mechanism, as soon as possible. This recommendation remains unchanged since the prior year peer review report.
It is not known whether Gabon has finalised the steps to have effective compulsory spontaneous exchange of information on the tax rulings within the scope of the transparency framework.	Gabon is recommended to continue to put in place a domestic legal framework allowing spontaneous exchange of information on rulings and to continue its efforts to complete the templates for all relevant rulings and to ensure that the exchanges of information on rulings occur as soon as possible. This recommendation remains unchanged since the prior year peer review report.
Georgia	
	No recommendations are made.
Germany	
	No recommendations are made.
Greece	
	No recommendations are made.
Grenada	
Grenada has not put in place the necessary information gathering process.	Grenada is recommended to finalise its information gathering process for identifying all future rulings and potential exchange jurisdictions, with a review and supervision mechanism, as soon as possible.
Grenada does not have a process to complete the templates on relevant rulings, to make them available to the Competent Authority for exchange of information, and to exchange them with relevant jurisdictions.	Grenada is recommended to develop a process to complete the templates on relevant rulings and to ensure that the exchanges of information on rulings occur in accordance with the form and timelines under the transparency framework.
Guernsey	
	No recommendations are made.
Hong Kong (China)	
	No recommendations are made.
Hungary	
Hungary did not yet apply the "best efforts approach" to identify potential	Hungary is recommended to continue to apply the "best efforts approach"

exchange jurisdictions for all past rulings.	to identify potential exchange jurisdictions for all past rulings. This recommendation remains unchanged since the 2016, 2017 and 2018 peer review reports.
Hungary experienced some delays for the exchange of future rulings.	Hungary is recommended to ensure that all information on future rulings is exchanged as soon as possible.
Hungary did not identify or exchange all information on new entrants to the grandfathered IP regime.	Hungary is recommended to continue its efforts to identify and exchange information on all new entrants to the grandfathered IP regime. This recommendation remains unchanged since the 2016, 2017 and 2018 peer review reports.
Iceland	
	No recommendations are made.
India	
India experienced delays in the exchange of information on future APAs.	India is recommended to continue its efforts to ensure that all information on future APAs is exchanged as soon as possible. This recommendation remains unchanged since the 2017 and 2018 peer review reports.
Indonesia	
	No recommendations are made.
Ireland	
	No recommendations are made.
Isle of Man	
	No recommendations are made.
Israel	
During the year in review, concerns were raised regarding the existence of a process for completion of templates in accordance with the form agreed under the transparency framework.	Israel is recommended to develop a process to complete the templates on future rulings, and in particular, the summary section, in accordance with the form agreed under the transparency framework.
During the year in review, Israel continued to experience delays in the provision of rulings to the Competent Authority.	Israel is recommended to continue its efforts to ensure that information is made available to the Competent Authority without undue delay. This recommendation remains unchanged since the 2017 and 2018 peer review reports.
Italy	
	No recommendations are made.
Jamaica	
	No recommendations are made.
Japan	
	No recommendations are made.
Jersey	
	No recommendations are made.
Jordan	
Jordan does not have specific mechanisms in place for identifying future rulings and potential exchange jurisdictions within the scope of the transparency framework as well as for reviewing and supervising that all relevant information is captured adequately.	Jordan is recommended to ensure that it has put in place an effective information gathering process to identify all future rulings and potential exchange jurisdictions, with a review and supervision mechanism, as soon as possible.
Jordan has not the necessary domestic legal basis to exchange information spontaneously and Jordan does not yet have a process to exchange information on rulings in the required format and timelines.	Jordan is recommended to put in place a domestic legal framework allowing spontaneous exchange of information on the relevant tax rulings and to ensure the timely exchange of information on rulings in the form required by the transparency framework.
Jordan has not identified information on new entrants to the harmful Development zone regime, and as such has not exchanged information on these taxpayers.	Jordan is recommended to identify and exchange information on all new entrants to the IP regime.
Kazakhstan	
Kazakhstan does not have in place the necessary information gathering process.	Kazakhstan is recommended to finalise its information gathering process for identifying all future rulings and potential exchange jurisdictions, with a review and supervision mechanism, as soon as possible. This recommendation remains unchanged since the prior year peer review report.
Kazakhstan does not have a domestic legal framework allowing spontaneous exchange of information on rulings and does not have in place a process for completion of templates and exchange of information on rulings.	Kazakhstan is recommended to put in place a domestic legal framework allowing spontaneous exchange of information on rulings if needed and to ensure the timely exchange of information on rulings in the form required by the transparency framework. This recommendation remains

	unchanged since the prior year peer review report
Kenya	
	No recommendations are made.
Korea	
	No recommendations are made.
Latvia	
	No recommendations are made.
Liechtenstein	
	No recommendations are made.
Lithuania	
	No recommendations are made.
Luxembourg	
	No recommendations are made.
Malaysia	
Malaysia experienced difficulties in identifying all potential exchange jurisdictions for future rulings.	Malaysia is recommended to continue its efforts to ensure that all potential exchange jurisdictions are identified swiftly for all future rulings.
Malaysia experienced delays in the provision of rulings to the Competent Authority and did not undertake spontaneous exchange of information on all tax rulings within scope of the transparency framework during the year in review.	Malaysia is recommended to continue its efforts to reduce the timelines for providing the information on rulings to the Competent Authority and to complete the templates for all relevant rulings and to ensure that the exchanges of information on rulings occur as soon as possible. This recommendation remains unchanged since the 2017 and 2018 peer review reports.
Malaysia did not identify or exchange information on new entrants to the grandfathered IP regime.	Malaysia is recommended to identify and exchange information on all new entrants to the grandfathered IP regime as soon as possible. This recommendation remains unchanged since the 2017 and 2018 peer review reports.
Malta	
	No recommendations are made.
Mauritius	
	No recommendations are made.
Mexico	
Mexico experienced one minor delay in exchanging information on future rulings.	No recommendation is made because Mexico completed the exchange on the delayed future ruling quickly after the issue was identified and resolved, and this is not a recurring issue.
Morocco	
Morocco does not have a process to complete the templates on relevant rulings, to make them available to the Competent Authority for exchange of information, and to exchange them with relevant jurisdictions.	Morocco is recommended to develop a process to complete the templates on relevant rulings and to ensure that the exchanges of information on rulings occur in accordance with the form and timelines under the transparency framework.
Netherlands	
	No recommendations are made.
New Zealand	
	No recommendations are made.
Norway	
Norway experienced some delays in exchanging information on one future ruling.	No recommendation is made because Norway completed exchanges on the delayed future ruling quickly after the issues were identified and resolved, and this is not a recurring issue.
Panama	
	No recommendations are made.
Peru	
.	No recommendations are made.
Philippines	
The Philippines does not currently collect information on all potential exchange jurisdictions, particularly the ultimate parent company for past rulings.	The Philippines is recommended to apply the "best efforts approach" to identify potential exchange jurisdictions for all past rulings. This recommendation remains unchanged since the 2017 and 2018 peer review reports.
The Philippines does not currently collect information on all potential	The Philippines is recommended to apply the "best efforts approach" to

exchange jurisdictions, particularly the ultimate parent company for past rulings.	identify potential exchange jurisdictions for all past rulings. This recommendation remains unchanged since the 2017 and 2018 peer review reports.
The Philippines does not have a review and supervision mechanism in place to ensure that all relevant information on the identification of rulings and potential exchange jurisdictions is captured adequately.	The Philippines is recommended to have in place a review and supervision mechanism to ensure that all relevant information is captured adequately. This recommendation remains unchanged since the 2017 and 2018 peer review reports.
The Philippines does not yet have the necessary domestic legal framework in place for exchanging information on rulings or a process in place to ensure the timely exchange of information on rulings in the form required by the transparency framework.	The Philippines is recommended to continue to put in place a domestic legal framework allowing spontaneous exchange of information on rulings and to ensure the timely exchange of information on rulings in the form required by the transparency framework. This recommendation remains unchanged since the 2017 and 2018 peer review reports.
Poland	
	No recommendations are made.
Portugal	
	No recommendations are made.
Qatar	
	No recommendations are made.
Romania	
Although Romania has now completed the outstanding exchanges on past ruling and future rulings issued in 2017 and 2018, Romania experienced delays in the exchange of future rulings issued in 2019.	Romania is recommended to ensure that all information on future rulings is exchanged as soon as possible. Romania also received a recommendation on timely exchange of information on rulings in the 2017 and 2018 peer review reports.
Russia	
	No recommendations are made.
Saint Kitts and Nevis	
	No recommendations are made.
Saint Lucia	
Saint Lucia has not yet finalised the steps to have in place its information gathering process.	Saint Lucia is recommended to finalise its information gathering process for identifying all future rulings and potential exchange jurisdictions, with a review and supervision mechanism, as soon as possible. This recommendation remains unchanged since the prior year peer review report.
Saint Lucia has not yet finalised a process to complete the templates on relevant rulings, to make them available to the Competent Authority for exchange of information, and to exchange them with relevant jurisdictions.	Saint Lucia is recommended to put in place a process to complete the templates on relevant rulings and to ensure that the exchanges of information on rulings occur in accordance with the form and timelines under the transparency framework. This recommendation remains unchanged since the prior year peer review report.
San Marino	
San Marino experienced difficulties in the identification of past rulings and identified one additional past ruling that was not previously captured.	No recommendations are made because San Marino has quickly taken steps to identify and remedy the issue, completed the exchanges on the one identified past ruling quickly after the issues were identified and resolved, and this is not a recurring issue.
Senegal	
	No recommendations are made.
Seychelles	
	No recommendations are made.
Singapore	
	No recommendations are made.
Sint Maarten	
	No recommendations are made.
Slovak Republic	
	No recommendations are made.
Slovenia	
Slovenia experienced some delays in exchanging information on one future ruling.	No recommendation is made because Slovenia completed the exchange on the delayed future ruling quickly after the issues were identified and resolved, and this is not a recurring issue.
South Africa	

	No recommendations are made.
Spain	
Spain has not exchanged information on new assets of existing taxpayers benefitting from the grandfathered regime, as this information was not available during the year in review. It is noted that Spain has already started to take steps to amend the tax form adopted in August 2017 to address this, but the tax form was appealed before the National Court and proceedings remained underway for the year in review.	Spain is recommended to continue its efforts to identify and exchange relevant information on new assets of existing taxpayers benefitting from the grandfathered IP regime. This recommendation remains unchanged since the 2017 and 2018 peer review reports.
Sri Lanka	
Sri Lanka has not put in place the necessary information gathering process.	Sri Lanka is recommended to finalise its information gathering process for identifying all future rulings and potential exchange jurisdictions, with a review and supervision mechanism, as soon as possible. This recommendation remains unchanged since the 2017 and 2018 peer review reports.
Sri Lanka does not have a process to complete the templates on relevant rulings, to make them available to the Competent Authority for exchange of information, and to exchange them with relevant jurisdictions.	Sri Lanka is recommended to put in place a domestic legal framework allowing spontaneous exchange of information on rulings and to develop a process to complete the templates on relevant rulings and to ensure that the exchanges of information on rulings occur in accordance with the form and timelines under the transparency framework. This recommendation remains unchanged since the 2017 and 2018 peer review reports.
Sweden	
Sweden experienced delays in identifying all potential exchange jurisdictions for future rulings.	Sweden is recommended to continue its efforts to finalise its rulings practice to require taxpayers to provide information on all potential exchange jurisdictions for future rulings as soon as possible. This recommendation remains unchanged since the 2016, 2017 and 2018 peer review reports.
Switzerland	
Switzerland identified additional past rulings that were not previously captured.	Switzerland is recommended to strengthen its information gathering process identifying all past rulings in scope of the transparency framework and its review and supervision mechanism to ensure that the information gathering process is working effectively.
Switzerland experienced delays in the provision of rulings to the Competent Authority, as additional steps were required in order to ensure the summary templates provided to the Competent Authority were complete and correct.	Switzerland is recommended to continue its efforts to strengthen its process and allocation of resources and to ensure the accurate and timely completion of the summary templates, in order to reduce the timelines for providing the information on past and future rulings to the Competent Authority.
Switzerland experienced some delays in exchanging information on past and future rulings.	Switzerland is recommended to continue to ensure that all information on past and future rulings is exchanged as soon as possible.
Thailand	
Thailand does not yet have the necessary legal framework in place for exchanging information on rulings.	Thailand is recommended to finalise the amendments to put the domestic legal basis in place to commence exchanges as soon as possible.
Thailand did not undertake spontaneous exchange of information on all tax rulings within scope of the transparency framework during the year in review.	Thailand is recommended to ensure that all information on past and future rulings is exchanged as soon as possible after the domestic legal basis is in force. This recommendation remains unchanged since the prior year's peer review report.
Turkey	
During the year in review, Turkey was not able to identify and exchange information on new entrants to the grandfathered IP regime or to exchange information on all taxpayers benefitting from the third category of assets in the IP regime.	Turkey is recommended to identify and exchange information on new entrants to the grandfathered IP regime and to exchange information on taxpayers benefitting from the third category of IP assets as soon as possible. This recommendation remains unchanged since the 2017 and 2018 peer review reports.
Ukraine	
	No recommendations are made.
United Kingdom	
	No recommendations are made.
United States	
The United States experienced some delays in exchanging information on one future ruling.	No recommendation is made because the United States completed the exchange on the delayed future ruling quickly after the issues were identified and resolved, and this is not a recurring issue.

Uruguay	
	No recommendations are made.
Vietnam	
Viet Nam is currently putting in place a process for completion of templates and exchange of information on rulings.	Viet Nam is recommended to develop a process to complete the templates on relevant rulings and to ensure that the exchanges of information on rulings occur in accordance with the form and timelines under the transparency framework. This recommendation remains unchanged since the 2017 and 2018 peer review reports.

Introduction

Overview of the peer review on the exchange of information on tax rulings

The Action 5 Report (OECD, 2015[1]) is one of the four BEPS minimum standards. It involves two distinct aspects: a review of certain preferential tax regimes and substantial activities in no or only nominal tax jurisdictions to ensure they are not harmful, and the transparency framework. Each of the four BEPS minimum standards is subject to peer review in order to ensure timely and accurate implementation and thus safeguard the level playing field. All members of the Inclusive Framework on BEPS commit to implementing the Action 5 minimum standard and to participating in the peer review, on an equal footing. The peer review of the Action 5 minimum standard is undertaken by the FHTP and approved by the Inclusive Framework on BEPS.

The purpose of a peer review is to ensure the effective and consistent implementation of an agreed standard and to recognise progress made by jurisdictions in this regard. The peer review evaluates the implementation of the standard against an agreed set of criteria. These criteria are set out in terms of reference, which include each of the elements that a jurisdiction needs to demonstrate it has fulfilled in order to show effective implementation of the standard.[3]

The peer review has been conducted in accordance with the agreed methodology. The methodology sets out the process for undertaking the peer review, including the process for collecting the relevant data, the preparation and approval of annual reports, the outputs of the review and the follow up process.

The terms of reference and agreed methodology do not alter the Action 5 minimum standard. Any terms used in the terms of reference or methodology take their meaning from the language and context of the Action 5 Report (OECD, 2015[1]) and the references therein. Any terms in this report which are not included in the glossary take their meaning from the language and context of the Action 5 Report (OECD, 2015[1]).

Outline of the key aspects assessed in the annual report

This annual report contains the findings of the fourth annual peer review of jurisdictions' compliance with the transparency framework. It assesses the implementation of the transparency framework for the period 1 January 2019 - 31 December 2019.

The reports on each reviewed jurisdiction cover each of the aspects of the terms of reference. These capture the key elements of the transparency framework which are briefly described below. Where recommendations from prior years' peer review reports were not addressed, the report specifically notes this. Jurisdictions are urged to address these recommendations that have remained in place for more than one review.

A. The information gathering process

This involves assessing the processes in place in each of the jurisdictions for identifying past and future rulings that fall within the scope of the transparency framework, and for each of these rulings, identifying the jurisdictions with which the information should be exchanged. With respect to past rulings which do not contain information to identify those jurisdictions for which the tax rulings would be relevant, the jurisdiction issuing the ruling should apply the "best efforts approach" to try to identify this information. The review of the information gathering process also covers any supervision mechanism that the jurisdiction has in place to ensure that all relevant information is captured adequately.

B. The exchange of information

The exchange of information requires the legal and administrative framework to be in place to allow spontaneous exchange of information on the relevant tax rulings and subsequent exchange of the relevant rulings where a valid exchange of information request is received. Information on past rulings was to be spontaneously exchanged pursuant to the relevant deadline outlined in each jurisdiction's report.[4] Information on future rulings is to be spontaneously exchanged as soon as possible and no later than three months after the date on which the ruling becomes available to the Competent Authority for exchange of information. The exchange of information should occur in the agreed standardised form, either using the template contained in Annex C of the Action 5 Report (OECD, 2015[1]), or the OECD XML Schema. Adequate completion of the summary section in the Annex C template or the OECD XML Schema should be ensured through adherence to the instruction sheet to the summary section or the internal FHTP suggested guidance, or an alternate process that allows the summary section to contain sufficient detail for the receiving jurisdiction's tax administration to appropriately assess the potential base erosion and profit shifting risks posed by the ruling where applicable.

The peer review includes reviewing (i) that there is a sufficient domestic and international legal framework for the exchange information related to rulings; (ii) that the summary templates for information on rulings being exchanged are complete and in the appropriate form; and (iii) that the systems are in place to ensure that information on rulings is transmitted to the jurisdiction's Competent Authority for exchange of information without undue delay and exchanged with relevant jurisdictions in accordance with the appropriate timelines.

With respect to the international exchange of information, the terms of reference required jurisdictions to exchange information with Inclusive Framework members being reviewed for the same year, to the extent that an exchange of information agreement was in force for such exchanges and subject to the recipient jurisdiction demonstrating that it would keep the information received confidential.[5]

C. Statistics

Each jurisdiction is required to report statistics on the exchange of information under the transparency framework including (i) the total number of spontaneous exchanges sent, (ii) the number of spontaneous exchanges under each category of ruling and (iii) a list of jurisdictions with which the information was exchanged for each type of ruling.

D. Exchange of information on IP regimes

The review of the transparency framework also includes a review of the spontaneous exchanges of information which are required to occur in respect of certain features of IP regimes, as set out in the Action 5 "nexus approach." This includes, irrespective of whether a tax ruling is provided, identifying and exchanging information on taxpayers which benefit from the third category of IP assets (as defined in paragraph 37 of the Action 5 Report), and taxpayers making use of the option to treat the nexus ratio as a rebuttable presumption (as defined in paragraphs 67-69 of the Action 5 Report). This aspect of the review is only relevant for those jurisdictions which offer IP regimes, and the minimum standard does not require any jurisdiction to introduce such a regime.

Spontaneous exchange of information is also required with respect to new entrants benefiting from grandfathered IP regimes (regardless of whether a ruling is provided). This applies with respect to IP regimes that were not compliant with the nexus approach, and where jurisdictions have taken steps to abolish the regime, or amend it, as part of the FHTP's regime review process. In some cases, when introducing those legislative changes, jurisdictions have chosen to provide grandfathering to existing taxpayers to provide time to transition to the new rules. Additional spontaneous exchange of information on the taxpayers benefiting from this grandfathering is required where taxpayers or new IP assets were transferred into a non-nexus IP regime in the period between the announcement of forthcoming changes and those changes taking place. The timelines for which these enhanced transparency vary according to the time at which the FHTP reviewed the regime, and are set out in Annex A of the 2017 Progress Report on Preferential Regimes (OECD, 2017b[2]).

Response to the report

In addition, jurisdictions had the option to include a response to the report and update on recent developments which occurred after the 2019 year in review. Where included, this reflects the individual jurisdiction's views, and not those of the FHTP or the OECD Secretariat.

References

OECD (2015), *Countering Harmful Tax Practices More Effectively, Taking into Account Transparency and Substance, Action 5 - 2015 Final Report*, OECD/G20 Base Erosion and Profit Shifting Project, OECD Publishing, Paris, https://dx.doi.org/10.1787/9789264241190-en. [1]

OECD (ed.) (2017b), *Harmful Tax Practices - 2017 Progress Report on Preferential Regimes*, OECD Publishing, Paris, http://dx.doi.org/10.1787/9789264283954-en. [2]

Notes

[1] The Action 5 Report, *Countering Harmful Tax Practices More Effectively, Taking Into Account Transparency and Substance* (OECD, 2015) also provides that additional types of rulings could be added to the scope of the transparency framework in the future, where the FHTP and the Inclusive Framework agree that such a ruling could lead to BEPS concerns in the absence of spontaneous information exchange.

[2] The relevant jurisdictions that do not issue rulings in scope of the transparency framework are: Belize, Bulgaria, Burkina Faso, Cameroon, Cook Islands, Cote d'Ivoire, Democratic Republic of Congo, Djibouti, Dominica, Greenland, Haiti, Liberia, Macau, Maldives, Monaco, Mongolia, Montserrat, Nigeria, North Macedonia, Oman, Pakistan, Papua New Guinea, Paraguay, Saint Vincent and the Grenadines, Saudi Arabia, Serbia, Sierra Leone, Tunisia, Trinidad & Tobago, Zambia.

[3] Terms of Reference and Methodology for the review available at www.oecd.org/tax/beps/beps-action-5-harmful-tax-practices-peer-review-transparency-framework.pdf (OECD, 2017).

[4] The Action 5 Report (OECD, 2015) acknowledged that some jurisdictions may need to put in place the domestic or international legal framework in order to comply with the obligations under Action 5. In such cases the timelines for exchange of information on rulings are subject to a jurisdiction's legal framework.

[5] Where a ruling related only to tax years which were not covered by the relevant exchange of information agreement, no exchange of information would be required to occur in respect of that ruling. No negative inference is drawn in the peer review where an exchange was not permitted to occur because of the absence of, or the tax years covered by, an exchange of information agreement, although Inclusive Framework members are encouraged to expand their exchange of information agreements where relevant.

Country profiles

Andorra

Andorra has met all aspects of the terms of reference (OECD, 2017[3]) (ToR) for the calendar year 2019 (year in review), except for identifying potential exchange jurisdictions for future rulings (ToR I.4.2.1) and for ensuring that the information is completed in the required form (II.5.4) and exchanges are performed in accordance with the timelines (ToR II.5.5 and II.5.6). Andorra receives two recommendations on these points for the year in review.

In the prior year report, as well as in the 2017 peer review, Andorra had received the same two recommendations. As they have not been addressed, the recommendations remain in place but for section B, in the year in review, the recommendation is targeted to specific aspects of the ToR that still need to be implemented.

Andorra can legally issue five types of rulings within the scope of the transparency framework.

In practice, Andorra issued no rulings within the scope of the transparency framework.[1]

Rulings issued in the form of written inquiries (binding consultations) are published online in anonymised form. Rulings issued in the form of special agreements are published in the Andorran official gazette.[2]

As no exchanges were required to take place no peer input was received in respect of the exchanges of information on rulings received from Andorra.

A. The information gathering process

1. Andorra can legally issue the following five types of rulings within the scope of the transparency framework: (i) preferential regimes;[3] (ii) cross-border unilateral APAs and any other cross-border unilateral tax rulings (such as an advance tax ruling) covering transfer pricing or the application of transfer pricing principles; (iii) rulings providing for unilateral downward adjustments; (iv) permanent establishment rulings; and (v) related party conduit rulings.

Past rulings (ToR I.4.1.1, I.4.1.2, I.4.2.1, I.4.2.2)

2. For Andorra, past rulings are any tax rulings within scope that are issued either (i) on or after 1 January 2015 but before 1 April 2017; and (ii) on or after 1 January 2012 but before 1 January 2015, provided they were still in effect as at 1 January 2015.

3. In the prior year's peer review report, it was determined that Andorra's undertakings to identify past rulings and all potential exchange jurisdictions were sufficient to meet the minimum standard. Andorra's implementation in this regard remains unchanged, and therefore continues to meet the minimum standard.

Future rulings (ToR I.4.1.1, I.4.1.2, I.4.2.1)

4. For Andorra, future rulings are any tax rulings within scope that are issued on or after 1 April 2017.

5. In the prior years' peer review reports, it was determined future rulings were able to be identified, but that the information on potential exchange jurisdictions was not always being collected, and instead this was being performed by the application of the "best efforts approach." The prior years' reports noted that Andorra intended to amend the application process to require the taxpayer to identify all relevant jurisdictions when requesting the ruling. However, this amendment did not take place during the year in review. Andorra is therefore recommended to continue its efforts to ensure that all potential exchange jurisdictions are identified swiftly for all future rulings.

Review and supervision (ToR I.4.3)

6. In the prior years' peer review reports, it was determined that Andorra's review and supervision mechanism was sufficient to meet the minimum standard. Andorra's implementation in this regard remains unchanged, and therefore continues to meet the minimum standard.

Conclusion on section A

7. Andorra has met all of the ToR for the information gathering process except for identifying all potential exchange jurisdictions for future rulings (ToR I.4.2.1). Andorra is recommended to ensure that all potential exchange jurisdictions are identified swiftly for all future rulings.

B. The exchange of information

Legal basis for spontaneous exchange of information (ToR II.5.1, II.5.2)

8. Andorra has the necessary domestic legal basis to exchange information spontaneously. Andorra notes that there are no legal or practical impediments that prevent the spontaneous exchange of information on rulings as contemplated in the Action 5 minimum standard.

9. Andorra has international agreements permitting spontaneous exchange of information, including being a party to the (i) *Multilateral Convention on Mutual Administrative Assistance in Tax Matters: Amended by the 2010 Protocol* (OECD/Council of Europe, 2011[4]) ("the Convention") and (ii) bilateral agreements in force with 28 jurisdictions.[4]

Completion and exchange of templates (ToR II.5.3, II.5.4, II.5.5, II.5.6, II.5.7)

10. In the prior years' peer review reports, it was determined that Andorra's process for the completion and exchange of templates met all the ToR, except for undertaking spontaneous exchange of information on tax rulings within scope of the transparency framework (ToR II.5). Therefore, Andorra was recommended to complete the templates for all relevant rulings and to ensure that the exchanges of information on rulings occur as soon as possible.

11. During the year in review, Andorra concluded that all previously issued rulings related to preferential regimes were related to wholly domestic taxpayers without any related parties in a foreign jurisdiction, , and therefore, no exchange of information needed to take place. However, in the event that a relevant ruling is issued in future, Andorra will need to have the processes in place to complete the templates and conduct the exchanges in accordance with the transparency framework.

12. In the prior year's peer review report it was noted that Andorra intends to require taxpayers to provide all relevant information needed to complete the template contained in Annex C of the BEPS Action 5 Report (OECD, 2015[1]). This obligation was being considered for inclusion in an amendment to the relevant regulations in 2019. Andorra also intends to prepare an internal note to ensure that information on rulings is made available to the Competent Authority responsible for exchange of information without undue delay.

13. As these issues have not been addressed, the recommendation from the prior year remains in place. In particular, Andorra is recommended to ensure that the information on future rulings is completed in the form of the template contained in Annex C of the Action 5 Report (OECD, 2015[1]) (ToR II.5.4), to put in place appropriate systems to ensure that information on rulings is transmitted to the competent authority responsible for international exchange of information without undue delay (ToR II.5.5) and to ensure that the information to be exchanged is transmitted to the relevant jurisdictions in accordance with the agreed timelines (ToR II.5.6).

14. As there were no exchanges for the year in review, no data on the timeliness of exchanges can be reported.

Conclusion on section B

15. Andorra has met all of the ToR for the exchange of information process except for ensuring that the information is completed in the required form (II.5.4) and having a process in place to ensure any exchanges will be performed in accordance with the timelines (ToR II.5.5 and II.5.6). Andorra is recommended to continue its efforts to put in place the necessary process to complete the information in the form of Annex C of the Action 5 Report (OECD, 2015[1]), to ensure that information is submitted to the Competent Authority without undue delay and exchanges are performed in accordance with the timelines. These recommendations remain unchanged since the 2017 and 2018 peer review reports.

C. Statistics (ToR IV)

16. As no rulings were issued, no statistics can be reported.

D. Matters related to intellectual property regimes (ToR I.4.1.3)

17. Andorra offers an intellectual property regime (IP regime)[5] that is not subject to the transparency requirements under the Action 5 Report (OECD, 2015[1]), because:

- ***New entrants benefitting from the grandfathered IP regime***: no enhanced transparency requirements apply, as follows. The regime has been amended by implementing the nexus approach. The previous regime has been closed-off, and although grandfathering was provided, it only applies to entrants that benefited from the regime prior to the relevant date from which enhanced transparency obligations would apply.
- ***Third category of IP assets***: not applicable as the regime does not allow the third category of IP assets to qualify for the benefits.
- ***Taxpayers making the use of the option to treat the nexus ratio as a rebuttable presumption***: not applicable the regime does not allow the nexus ratio to be treated as a rebuttable presumption.

Summary of recommendations on implementation of the transparency framework

Aspect of implementation of the transparency framework that should be improved	Recommendation for improvement
Andorra experienced difficulties in identifying all potential exchange jurisdictions for future rulings.	Andorra is recommended to continue its efforts to ensure that all potential exchange jurisdictions are identified swiftly for all future rulings. This recommendation remains unchanged since the 2017 and 2018 peer review reports.
Andorra is still developing a process to ensure that the information is completed in the required form and exchanges are performed in accordance with the timelines.	Andorra is recommended to continue its efforts to put in place the necessary process to complete the information in the form of Annex C of the BEPS Action 5 Report, to ensure that information is submitted to the Competent Authority without undue delay and exchanges are performed in accordance with the timelines. These recommendations remain unchanged since the 2017 and 2018 peer review reports but they are now targeted to specific aspects of the ToR that still need to be put in place.

References

OECD (2017), *BEPS Action 5 on Harmful Tax Practices - Terms of Reference and Methodology for the Conduct of the Peer Reviews of the Action 5 Transparency Framework*, OECD Publishing, Paris, http://www.oecd.org/tax/beps/beps-action-5-harmful-tax-practices-peer-review-transparency-framework.pdf. [3]

OECD (2015), *Countering Harmful Tax Practices More Effectively, Taking into Account Transparency and Substance, Action 5 - 2015 Final Report*, OECD/G20 Base Erosion and Profit Shifting Project, OECD Publishing, Paris, https://dx.doi.org/10.1787/9789264241190-en. [1]

OECD/Council of Europe (2011), *The Multilateral Convention on Mutual Administrative Assistance in Tax Matters: Amended by the 2010 Protocol*, OECD Publishing, Paris, https://dx.doi.org/10.1787/9789264115606-en. [4]

Notes

[1] In the previous years' peer review reports, it was noted that Andorra had issued 169 past and 58 future rulings. All those rulings were related to preferential regimes, but all taxpayers were domestic taxpayers (not part of a multinational group) and therefore no exchanges on these rulings were required for the Action 5 transparency framework.

[2] Available at https://www.impostos.ad/comunicats-tecnics-i-consultes-vinculants.

[3] These regimes are: 1) Holding company regime and 2) Special regime for exploitation of certain intangibles.

[4] Parties to the Convention are available here: www.oecd.org/tax/exchange-of-tax-information/convention-on-mutual-administrative-assistance-in-tax-matters.htm. Andorra also has bilateral agreements with Argentina, Australia, Austria, Belgium, Cyprus, Czech Republic, Denmark, Faroe Islands, Finland, France, Germany, Greenland, Iceland, Italy, Korea, Liechtenstein, Luxembourg, Malta, Monaco, Netherlands,

[5] Special regime for exploitation of certain intangibles.

Angola

Angola has met all aspects of the terms of reference (OECD, 2017[3]) (ToR) for the calendar year 2019 (year in review), except for identifying all past and future rulings and all potential exchange jurisdictions with a review and supervision mechanism (ToR I.4) and exchanging information on the tax rulings in a timely manner (ToR II.5). Angola receives two recommendations on this point for the year in review.

In the prior year report, as well as in the 2017 peer review, Angola had received the same two recommendations. As they have not been addressed, the recommendations remain in place.

Angola can legally issue five types of rulings within the scope of the transparency framework.

In practice, Angola issued rulings within the scope of the transparency framework as follows:

- No past rulings;
- For the period 1 April 2017 - 31 December 2017: one future ruling;
- For the calendar year 2018: no future rulings, and
- For the calendar year in review: no future rulings

As no exchanges took place, no peer input was received in respect of the exchanges of information on rulings received from Angola.

A. The information gathering process

18. Angola can legally issue the following five types of rulings within the scope of the transparency framework: (i) preferential regimes; (ii) cross-border unilateral APAs and any other cross-border unilateral tax rulings (such as an advance tax ruling) covering transfer pricing or the application of transfer pricing principles; (iii) rulings providing for unilateral downward adjustments; (iv) permanent establishment rulings; and (v) related party conduit rulings.

Past rulings (ToR I.4.1.1, I.4.1.2, I.4.2.1, I.4.2.2)

19. For Angola, past rulings are any tax rulings within scope that are issued either (i) on or after 1 January 2015 but before 1 April 2017; and (ii) on or after 1 January 2012 but before 1 January 2015, provided they were still in effect as at 1 January 2015.

20. In the prior years' peer review reports, it was determined that Angola has not recorded the information on the tax rulings issued with the necessary level of detail to meet the standard of the transparency framework and that the necessary information on past rulings is unlikely to be found on the available records. Angola noted that it would seek to apply the best efforts approach once all past rulings have been identified. Therefore, Angola was recommended to finalise its information gathering process for identifying all past rulings and potential exchange jurisdictions.

21. During the year in review, no additional implementation steps were taken.

Future rulings (ToR I.4.1.1, I.4.1.2, I.4.2.1)

22. For Angola, future rulings are any tax rulings within scope that are issued on or after 1 April 2017.

23. In the prior years' peer review reports, it was determined that Angola was following guidelines covering which rulings would fall in the scope of the transparency framework and what information should be kept in order to meet the level of detail required by the transparency framework. Angola noted that it is developing a new system to record and track all future rulings in order to be able to conduct an effective analysis of future rulings issued.

24. During the year in review, no additional implementation steps were taken.

Review and supervision (ToR I.4.3)

25. In the prior years' peer review reports, it was determined that Angola did not yet have a review and supervision mechanism for past rulings under the transparency framework. Angola started to implement a review and supervision mechanism for future rulings by requiring that the information on tax rulings be recorded in hard copy and electronically in spreadsheets with the name, date and topic of the information requested or issue being complained or appealed. However, during the year in review, no additional implementation steps were taken.

Conclusion on section A

26. Angola is recommended to finalise its information gathering process for identifying all past and future rulings and all potential exchange jurisdictions, with a review and supervision mechanism, as soon as possible (ToR I.4).

B. The exchange of information

Legal basis for spontaneous exchange of information (ToR II.5.1, II.5.2)

27. Angola is currently in the process of putting in place the necessary domestic legal basis to exchange information spontaneously. Angola has already reviewed and approved its general tax code, which includes a clause that allows the Angolan Revenue Administration to gather information from taxpayers and exchange with other jurisdictions. Angola has a bilateral agreement in force with one jurisdiction.[1] Angola is not a Party to *Multilateral Convention on Mutual Administrative Assistance in Tax Matters: Amended by the 2010 Protocol* (OECD/Council of Europe, 2011[4]) ("the Convention"). Angola is encouraged to continue its efforts to expand its international exchange of information instruments to be able to exchange rulings. It is however noted that jurisdictions are assessed on their compliance with the transparency framework in respect of the exchange of information network in effect for the year of the particular annual review.

Completion and exchange of templates (ToR II.5.3, II.5.4, II.5.5, II.5.6, II.5.7)

28. In the prior years' peer review reports, it was determined that Angola is still developing a process to complete the templates on relevant rulings, to make them available to the Competent Authority for exchange of information and to exchange them with relevant jurisdictions. Angola explained that an information exchange unit had been recently created to assume the role of the Competent Authority and legislation and procedures for the functioning of the unit are being developed.

29. During the year in review, Angola was negotiating to obtain an electronic tool for the exchange of information.

30. As Angola did not have the necessary legal basis to conduct exchanges, no data on the timeliness of exchanges can be reported.

Conclusion on section B

31. Angola is recommended to continue to put in place a domestic legal framework allowing spontaneous exchange of information on rulings and to continue its efforts to complete the templates for all relevant rulings and to ensure that the exchanges of information on rulings occur as soon as possible (ToR II.5).

C. Statistics (ToR IV)

32. As no rulings were issued, no statistics can be reported.

D. Matters related to intellectual property regimes (ToR I.4.1.3)

33. Angola does not offer an intellectual property regime for which transparency requirements under the Action 5 Report (OECD, 2015[1]) were imposed.

34.

Summary of recommendations on implementation of the transparency framework

Aspect of implementation of the transparency framework that should be improved	Recommendation for improvement
Angola has not yet finalised the steps to have in place its necessary information and gathering process.	Angola is recommended to finalise its information gathering process for identifying all past and future rulings and all potential exchange jurisdictions, with a review and supervision mechanism, as soon as possible. This recommendation remains unchanged since the 2017 and 2018 peer review reports.
Angola has not yet finalised the steps to have effective compulsory spontaneous exchange of information on the tax rulings within the scope of the transparency framework.	Angola is recommended to continue to put in place a domestic legal framework allowing spontaneous exchange of information on rulings and to continue its efforts to complete the templates for all relevant rulings and to ensure that the exchanges of information on rulings occur as soon as possible. This recommendation remains unchanged since the 2017 and 2018 peer review reports.

References

OECD (2017), *BEPS Action 5 on Harmful Tax Practices - Terms of Reference and Methodology for the Conduct of the Peer Reviews of the Action 5 Transparency Framework*, OECD Publishing, Paris, http://www.oecd.org/tax/beps/beps-action-5-harmful-tax-practices-peer-review-transparency-framework.pdf. [3]

OECD (2015), *Countering Harmful Tax Practices More Effectively, Taking into Account Transparency and Substance, Action 5 - 2015 Final Report*, OECD/G20 Base Erosion and Profit Shifting Project, OECD Publishing, Paris, https://dx.doi.org/10.1787/9789264241190-en. [1]

OECD/Council of Europe (2011), *The Multilateral Convention on Mutual Administrative Assistance in Tax Matters: Amended by the 2010 Protocol*, OECD Publishing, Paris, https://dx.doi.org/10.1787/9789264115606-en. [4]

Notes

[1] Angola has a bilateral agreement with Portugal.

Antigua and Barbuda

Antigua and Barbuda has met all aspects of the terms of reference (OECD, 2017[3]) (ToR) for the calendar year 2019 (year in review) that can be met in the absence of rulings being issued and no recommendations are made. This is Antigua and Barbuda's first review of implementation of the transparency framework.

Antigua and Barbuda can legally issue five types of rulings within the scope of the transparency framework. In practice, Antigua and Barbuda has issued no rulings within the scope of the transparency framework.

These rulings are required to be published in an anonymised form on the Inland Revenue Department website.

As no exchanges were required to take place, no peer input was received in respect of the exchanges of information on rulings received from Antigua and Barbuda.

A. The information gathering process

35. Antigua and Barbuda can legally issue the following five types of rulings within the scope of the transparency framework: (i) preferential regimes;[1] (ii) cross-border unilateral APAs and any other cross-border unilateral tax rulings (such as an advance tax ruling) covering transfer pricing or the application of transfer pricing principles; (iii) rulings providing for unilateral downward adjustments; (iv) permanent establishment rulings; and (v) related party conduit rulings.

Past rulings (ToR I.4.1.1, I.4.1.2, I.4.2.1, I.4.2.2)

36. For Antigua and Barbuda, past rulings are any tax rulings issued prior to 1 March 2019. However, there is no obligation for Antigua and Barbuda to conduct spontaneous exchange information on past rulings.

Future rulings (ToR I.4.1.1, I.4.1.2, I.4.2.1)

37. For Antigua and Barbuda, future rulings are any tax rulings within scope that are issued on or after 1 March 2019.

38. In Antigua and Barbuda, the Commissioner of the Inland Revenue Department (IRD), after consultation with the IRD's Legal Counsel and in co-operation with the Exchange of Information (EOI) unit within the IRD and with final consultation with the Attorney General's office, can issue advance rulings setting out the IRD's position regarding the application of tax provisions to a specific transaction proposed by the taxpayer. If a ruling were issued, it would be published (in anonymised form) on the IRD website.

39. The EOI Unit, in consultation with the Legal Counsel who forms part of the EOI Unit, is responsible for identifying all the rulings issued in order to establish whether they are in scope of the transparency framework. Given the expectation of small volumes of rulings in the jurisdiction, Antigua and Barbuda will identify relevant rulings for future exchanges based on the information on the IRD's website. If needed, Antigua and Barbuda will consider introducing an internal electronic repository of rulings issued.

40. Although Antigua and Barbuda has not issued any future rulings, Antigua and Barbuda has indicated that potential exchange jurisdictions could be identified through a manual review of the rulings. The taxpayer's application is initially reviewed by the Legal Counsel within the EOI Unit. During this process, the Legal Counsel may request additional information or clarification to the taxpayer in relation to the ruling application. The Attorney General's office would then conduct an independent review of the ruling application before making a decision to grant the ruling. This process assists in ensuring the relevant information is obtained in the course of issuing the ruling. If this information on potential exchange jurisdiction was not contained in the ruling, the IRD would consult with the audit department as well as available public sources.

41. Antigua and Barbuda intends to enact regulations, based on the Tax Administration and Procedures Act (TAPA), to formally provide that the necessary information to meet the requirements of the transparency framework would be obtained in all cases.

42. To date no rulings within the scope of the transparency framework have been issued as no applications have been submitted by taxpayers requiring the issuance of such rulings. As such, there was no need to identify potential exchange jurisdictions.

Review and supervision (ToR I.4.3)

43. The accuracy of the information gathering process and the identification of rulings in scope of the transparency framework is supervised by the Legal Counsel within the EOI Unit and the Attorney General's office. The EOI Unit within IRD is the Competent Authority in Antigua and Barbuda.

44. In particular, Antigua and Barbuda's review and supervision system relies upon a number of steps commencing with the preparation and filing by the taxpayer of an application for an advance tax ruling, and concluding with the issuance by the IRD of that ruling in writing. Because in Antigua and Barbuda the same offices are in charge both of the issuance and the exchange of relevant rulings, the steps bringing to the issuance of rulings will ensure that all the rulings in scope of the transparency framework will be correctly and immediately identified and all information needed for the exchanges will be adequately captured.

Conclusion on section A

45. Antigua and Barbuda has met all of the ToR for the information gathering process that can be met in the absence of rulings being issued and no recommendations are made.

B. The exchange of information

Legal basis for spontaneous exchange of information (ToR II.5.1, II.5.2)

46. Antigua and Barbuda has the necessary domestic legal basis to exchange information spontaneously. Antigua and Barbuda notes that there are no legal or practical impediments that prevent the spontaneous exchange of information on rulings as contemplated in the Action 5 minimum standard.

47. Antigua and Barbuda has international agreements permitting spontaneous exchange of information, including being a party to the (i) *Multilateral Convention on Mutual Administrative Assistance in Tax Matters: Amended by the 2010 Protocol* (OECD/Council of Europe, 2011[4]) ("the Convention"), (ii) bilateral agreements in force with 13 jurisdictions and tax information exchange agreements in force with 69 jurisdictions.[2]

Completion and exchange of templates (ToR II.5.3, II.5.4, II.5.5, II.5.6, II.5.7)

48. Although Antigua and Barbuda has not issued any future rulings, Antigua and Barbuda has indicated that the Commissioner of the IRD, in conjunction with the IRD's Legal Counsel and the EOI unit, and in consultation with the Attorney General's office, is responsible for completing the template. In practice, the same office in charge of the rulings' issuance will be responsible for completion and exchange of templates. Antigua and Barbuda intends to complete the templates in the form of Annex C of the BEPS Action 5 Report (OECD, 2015[1]), to complete the summary section of the template in line with the internal FHTP suggested guidance and to transmit the templates according to the established timelines. Antigua and Barbuda indicated that the Legal Counsel will review manually the templates and cross-check the information against the actual ruling to ensure their completeness and accuracy. Thereafter, the Attorney General office will review the templates before submission to the Competent Authority for exchanges with relevant jurisdictions. The EOI Unit within IRD is the Competent Authority in Antigua and Barbuda, therefore all tax rulings, once issued, would be readily available to the Competent Authority (and in any case within three months from their issuance) for exchanges with relevant jurisdictions, to be concluded within three months after the tax ruling becomes available to the EOI Unit.

49. As Antigua and Barbuda did not issue any rulings in scope of the transparency framework in the relevant period, during the year in review, no exchanges were required to take place and no data on the timeliness of exchanges is reported.

Conclusion on section B

50. Antigua and Barbuda has the necessary legal basis to undertake spontaneous exchange of information. Antigua and Barbuda has met all of the ToR for the exchange of information process that can be met in the absence of rulings being issued in practice and no recommendations are made.

C. Statistics (ToR IV)

51. As no rulings were issued, no statistics can be reported.

D. Matters related to intellectual property regimes (ToR I.4.1.3)

52. Antigua and Barbuda does not offer an intellectual property regime for which transparency requirements under the Action 5 Report (OECD, 2015[1]) were imposed.

Summary of recommendations on implementation of the transparency framework

Aspect of implementation of the transparency framework that should be improved	Recommendation for improvement
	No recommendations are made.

References

OECD (2017), *BEPS Action 5 on Harmful Tax Practices - Terms of Reference and Methodology for the Conduct of the Peer Reviews of the Action 5 Transparency Framework*, OECD Publishing, Paris, http://www.oecd.org/tax/beps/beps-action-5-harmful-tax-practices-peer-review-transparency-framework.pdf. [3]

OECD (2015), *Countering Harmful Tax Practices More Effectively, Taking into Account Transparency and Substance, Action 5 - 2015 Final Report*, OECD/G20 Base Erosion and Profit Shifting Project, OECD Publishing, Paris, https://dx.doi.org/10.1787/9789264241190-en. [1]

OECD/Council of Europe (2011), *The Multilateral Convention on Mutual Administrative Assistance in Tax Matters: Amended by the 2010 Protocol*, OECD Publishing, Paris, https://dx.doi.org/10.1787/9789264115606-en. [4]

Notes

[1] With respect to the following preferential regimes: 1) International business companies and 2) International banking.

[2] Parties to the Convention are available here: www.oecd.org/tax/exchange-of-tax-information/convention-on-mutual-administrative-assistance-in-tax-matters.htm. Antigua and Barbuda also has bilateral agreements with the CARICOM jurisdictions, Switzerland, United Kingdom and United Arab Emirates. The TIEAs with Albania, Andorra, Anguilla, Aruba, Argentina, Austria, Australia, Bahrain, Bahamas, Belgium, Belize, Bermuda, Brazil, British Virgin Islands, Bulgaria, Canada, Chile, Cayman Islands, Colombia, China (People's Republic of), Cook Islands, Costa Rica, Croatia, Curaçao, Cyprus, Czech Republic, Dominica, Denmark, Finland, France, Germany, Gibraltar, Greece, Grenada, Hong Kong (China), Iceland, India, Indonesia, Ireland, Israel, Italy, Japan, Jersey, Korea, Luxembourg, Mexico, Montserrat, Netherlands, Norway, New Zealand, Panama, Poland, Portugal, Russia, Romania, Saint Kitts and Nevis, Saint Lucia, Saint Vincent and the Grenadines, Saudi Arabia, Singapore, Sint Maarten, South Africa, Spain, Sweden, Switzerland, Trinidad and Tobago, Turks and Caicos, United Kingdom and United Arab Emirates also permit for the spontaneous exchange of information.

Argentina

Argentina has met all aspects of the terms of reference (OECD, 2017[3]) (ToR) for the calendar year 2019 (year in review) and no recommendations are made.

Argentina can legally issue five types of rulings within the scope of the transparency framework.

In practice, Argentina issued rulings within the scope of the transparency framework as follows:

- Two past rulings;
- For the period 1 April 2016 - 31 December 2016: no future rulings;
- For the calendar year 2017: one future ruling,
- For the calendar year 2018: no future rulings, and
- For the year in review: one future ruling.

Peer input was received from one jurisdiction in respect of the exchanges of information on rulings received from Argentina. The input was positive, noting that information was complete, in a correct format and received in a timely manner.

A. The information gathering process

53. Argentina can legally issue the following five types of rulings within the scope of the transparency framework: (i) preferential regimes;[1] (ii) cross-border unilateral APAs and any other cross-border unilateral tax rulings (such as an advance tax ruling) covering transfer pricing or the application of transfer pricing principles; (iii) rulings providing for unilateral downward adjustments; (iv) permanent establishment rulings; and (v) related party conduit rulings.

54. For Argentina, past rulings are any tax rulings within scope that are issued either: (i) on or after 1 January 2014 but before 1 April 2016; or (ii) on or after 1 January 2010 but before 1 January 2014, provided they were still in effect as at 1 January 2014. Future rulings are any tax rulings within scope that are issued on or after 1 April 2016.

55. In the prior years' peer review reports, it was determined that Argentina's undertakings to identify past and future rulings and all potential exchange jurisdictions were sufficient to meet the minimum standard. In addition, it was determined that Argentina's review and supervision mechanism was sufficient to meet the minimum standard. With respect to past rulings, Argentina's implementation remains unchanged, and therefore continues to meet the minimum standard.

56. During the year in review, the future ruling that had been issued was identified as a ruling in scope of the transparency framework four months after issuance. In order to ensure that the identification of future ruling is made in a more timely manner, Argentina issued new internal procedures. These procedures note that when a ruling application is finalised by the competent department within the tax administration, and the tax administration has identified that the ruling falls in scope of the Action 5 transparency, the department must then submit to the Institutional Relations Directorate (formerly International Affairs Directorate) within the tax administration i) a copy of the ruling issued, ii) the report underlying to the ruling), iii) the summary to be published in anonymised form[2], iv) a copy of the report notifying the taxpayer ("consultant") that the ruling was issued, and v) the information provided by the taxpayer. The submission must take place within ten working days after the issuance of the ruling has been finalised. The Institutional Relations Directorate is then responsible for as second check on identifying whether the ruling is in scope of the Action 5 transparency framework.

57. Because Argentina has taken action in the year in review to ensure this problem does not occur in the future by issuing internal processes, no recommendation is made given it was a non-recurring issue that was swiftly remedied.

58. In addition, Argentina issued new regulations to formalise the process for issuing future binding consultations (tax rulings) during the year in review.[3] When the taxpayer submits an application for a ruling in scope of the Action 5 transparency framework, it now has to provide additional information on its identity (including company or business name, tax identification number and jurisdiction of fiscal residence, etc.) and the relevant information on potential exchange jurisdictions. If the information provided is insufficient, the tax administration can request the taxpayer to provide additional information. With the new enhanced process for issuing binding consultations in Argentina, it is not necessary for Argentina anymore to draw on information from internal taxpayer files in order to identify potential exchange jurisdictions. Argentina's implementation continues to meet the minimum standard.

59. Argentina has met all of the ToR for the information gathering process and no recommendations are made.

B. The exchange of information

60. In the prior years' peer review reports, it was determined that Argentina's process for the completion and exchange of templates were sufficient to meet the minimum standard. With respect to past

rulings, no further action was required. Argentina's implementation in this regard remains unchanged and therefore continues to meet the minimum standard.

61. Argentina has international agreements permitting spontaneous exchange of information, including being a party to the (i) *Multilateral Convention on Mutual Administrative Assistance in Tax Matters: Amended by the 2010 Protocol* (OECD/Council of Europe, 2011[4]) ("the Convention") and ii) bilateral agreements in force with 24 jurisdictions.[4]

62. For the year in review, the timeliness of exchanges is as follows:

Future rulings in the scope of the transparency framework	Number of exchanges transmitted within three months of the information becoming available to the competent authority or immediately after legal impediments have been lifted	Delayed exchanges		
		Number of exchanges transmitted later than three months of the information on rulings becoming available to the competent authority	Reasons for the delays	Any other comments
	0	2	See below	See below
Total	0	2		

Follow up requests received for exchange of the ruling	Number	Average time to provide response	Number of requests not answered
	0	0	0

63. It is noted that Argentina experienced a delay with respect to two exchanges, which was due to the delay in the identification of the ruling within the tax administration (as described above). The exchange was completed within the year in review and within one month after it became available to the Competent Authority. To avoid any further delays, in the year in review Argentina has issued new internal procedures (as described above). These procedures also clarify that the Institutional Relations Directorate is responsible for completing the template in the form of Annex C of the 2015 Action 5 report (OECD, 2015[1]) which will then be sent to the Directorate for International Taxation (which is the Competent Authority) for the exchange within the timelines required by the transparency framework.

64. Argentina has the necessary legal basis for spontaneous exchange of information, a process for completing the templates in a timely way and has completed all exchanges. Argentina has met all of the ToR for the exchange of information process and no recommendations are made.

C. Statistics (ToR IV)

65. The statistics for the year in review are as follows:

Category of ruling	Number of exchanges	Jurisdictions exchanged with
Ruling related to a preferential regime	0	N/A
Cross-border unilateral advance pricing agreements (APAs) and any other cross-border unilateral tax rulings (such as an advance tax ruling) covering transfer pricing or the application of transfer pricing principles	0	N/A
Cross-border rulings providing for a unilateral downward adjustment to the taxpayer's taxable profits that is not directly reflected in the taxpayer's financial / commercial accounts	0	N/A

Permanent establishment rulings	*De minimis* rule applies	N/A
Related party conduit rulings	0	N/A
De minimis rule	2	*De minimis* rule applies
Total	2	

D. Matters related to intellectual property regimes (ToR I.4.1.3)

66. Argentina does not offer an intellectual property regime for which transparency requirements under the Action 5 Report (OECD, 2015[1]) were imposed.

Summary of recommendations on implementation of the transparency framework

Aspect of implementation of the transparency framework that should be improved	Recommendation for improvement
Argentina experienced some delays in exchanging information on one future ruling.	No recommendation is made because Argentina completed exchanges on the delayed future ruling quickly after the issues were identified and resolved, and this is not a recurring issue.

References

OECD (2017), *BEPS Action 5 on Harmful Tax Practices - Terms of Reference and Methodology for the Conduct of the Peer Reviews of the Action 5 Transparency Framework*, OECD Publishing, Paris, http://www.oecd.org/tax/beps/beps-action-5-harmful-tax-practices-peer-review-transparency-framework.pdf. [3]

OECD (2015), *Countering Harmful Tax Practices More Effectively, Taking into Account Transparency and Substance, Action 5 - 2015 Final Report*, OECD/G20 Base Erosion and Profit Shifting Project, OECD Publishing, Paris, https://dx.doi.org/10.1787/9789264241190-en. [1]

OECD/Council of Europe (2011), *The Multilateral Convention on Mutual Administrative Assistance in Tax Matters: Amended by the 2010 Protocol*, OECD Publishing, Paris, https://dx.doi.org/10.1787/9789264115606-en. [4]

Notes

[1] Promotional regime for software industry.

[2] Available at http://biblioteca.afip.gob.ar/search/query/BoletinesDGI.aspx and http://biblioteca.afip.gob.ar/estaticos/consultasVinculantes/index.aspx.

[3] AFIP General Resolution 4497/2019, published in the Official Gazette on 30 May 2019, replacing AFIP General Resolution 1948/2005.

[4] Parties to the Convention are available here: www.oecd.org/tax/exchange-of-tax-information/convention-on-mutual-administrative-assistance-in-tax-matters.htm. Argentina also has bilateral agreements with Aruba, Australia, Azerbaijan, Belgium, Bolivia, Brazil, Canada, Chile, Denmark, Ecuador, Finland, France, Italy, Mexico, Netherlands, Norway, Peru, Russia, Spain, Sweden, United Arab Emirates, United States, United Kingdom and Venezuela.

Armenia

Armenia is taking steps to implement the legal basis for the transparency framework and to commence administrative preparations in line with the terms of reference (OECD, 2017[3]) (ToR) to ensure that it finalises its information gathering process (ToR I.4) and information on rulings will be identified and exchanged in a timely manner (ToR II.5). Armenia receives two recommendations on these points for the year in review.

This is Armenia's first review of implementation of the transparency framework.

Armenia can legally issue one type of ruling within the scope of the transparency framework.

Armenia is currently in the process of identifying the number of future rulings within the scope of the transparency framework that have been issued for the year in review.

As no exchanges took place, no peer input was received in respect of the exchanges of information on rulings received from Armenia.

A. The information gathering process

67. Armenia can legally issue the following type of ruling within the scope of the transparency framework: permanent establishment rulings. Rulings (or "Notice" in the Armenian Tax Code) are issued by the International Cooperation Department (ICD) and the Administration Methodology and Procedures Department (AMPD) within the State Revenue Committee (SRC). The rulings issuance process is centralised at the level of AMPD. AMPD can issue rulings after prior consultation with ICD.

Past rulings (ToR I.4.1.1, I.4.1.2, I.4.2.1, I.4.2.2)

68. For Armenia, past rulings are any tax rulings issued prior to 1 September 2019. However, there is no obligation for Armenia to conduct spontaneous exchange information on past rulings.

Future rulings (ToR I.4.1.1, I.4.1.2, I.4.2.1)

69. For Armenia, future rulings are any tax rulings within scope that are issued on or after 1 September 2019.

70. Armenia indicates that there are not yet processes in place to ensure the implementation of the obligations relating to the transparency framework such as the record keeping of rulings. Armenia is currently in the process of identifying the number of future permanent establishment rulings that have been issued during the year in review. It is noted that Armenia intends to implement processes to make sure the necessary information to meet the requirements of the transparency framework is required in all cases. In particular, the information gathering process will be centralised at the level of the ICD. Steps will be taken to ensure efficient communication with AMPD and to obtain information on the relevant exchange jurisdictions by taxpayers requesting a ruling. This will be assessed in the next year's peer review.

Review and supervision (ToR I.4.3)

71. Armenia did not yet have a review and supervision mechanism under the transparency framework for the year in review. Armenia is discussing the implementation of a revision and supervision mechanism within ICD for ensuring implementation of the transparency framework. This will be assessed in the next year's peer review.

Conclusion on section A

72. Armenia is recommended to finalise its information gathering process for identifying all future rulings and potential exchange jurisdictions, with a review and supervision mechanism, as soon as possible (ToR I.4).

B. The exchange of information

Legal basis for spontaneous exchange of information (ToR II.5.1, II.5.2)

73. Armenia has the necessary domestic legal basis to exchange information spontaneously. Armenia notes that there are no legal or practical impediments that prevent the spontaneous exchange of information on rulings as contemplated in the Action 5 minimum standard.

74. Armenia has international agreements permitting spontaneous exchange of information, including being a party to the (i) *Multilateral Convention on Mutual Administrative Assistance in Tax Matters: Amended by the 2010 Protocol* (OECD/Council of Europe, 2011[4]) ("the Convention") *and* (ii) bilateral

agreements in force with 48 jurisdictions. Armenia ratified the Convention on 6 February 2020. The Convention entered into force on 1 June 2020 and will have effect for administrative assistance related to taxable periods beginning on or after 1 January 2021.[1]

Completion and exchange of templates (ToR II.5.3, II.5.4, II.5.5, II.5.6, II.5.7)

75. Armenia is still developing a process to complete the templates on relevant rulings, to make them available to the Competent Authority for exchange of information, and to exchange them with relevant jurisdictions. The Competent Authority in Armenia is within ICD. Steps will be taken to ensure templates on relevant rulings are duly completed, made available to ICD without undue delay and exchanged with relevant jurisdictions according to the required timelines. This will be assessed in the next year's peer review.

76. As no exchanges took place in the year of review, no data on the timeliness of exchanges can be reported.

Conclusion on section B

77. Armenia is recommended to develop a process to complete the templates on relevant rulings and to ensure that the exchanges of information on rulings occur in accordance with the form and timelines under the transparency framework going forward (ToR II.5).

C. Statistics (ToR IV)

78. As there was no information on rulings exchanged by Armenia for the year in review, no statistics can be reported.

D. Matters related to intellectual property regimes (ToR I.4.1.3)

79. Armenia does not offer an intellectual property regime for which transparency requirements under the Action 5 Report (OECD, 2015[1]) were imposed.

Summary of recommendations on implementation of the transparency framework

Aspect of implementation of the transparency framework that should be improved	Recommendation for improvement
Armenia is in the process to put in place an information gathering process and a review and supervision mechanism.	Armenia is recommended to finalise its information gathering process for identifying all future rulings and potential exchange jurisdictions, with a review and supervision mechanism, as soon as possible.
Armenia does not have a process to complete the templates on relevant rulings, to make them available to the Competent Authority for exchange of information, and to exchange them with relevant jurisdictions.	Armenia is recommended to develop a process to complete the templates on relevant rulings and to ensure that the exchanges of information on rulings occur in accordance with the form and timelines under the transparency framework.

References

OECD (2017), *BEPS Action 5 on Harmful Tax Practices - Terms of Reference and Methodology for the Conduct of the Peer Reviews of the Action 5 Transparency Framework*, OECD Publishing, Paris, http://www.oecd.org/tax/beps/beps-action-5-harmful-tax-practices-peer-review-transparency-framework.pdf. [3]

OECD (2015), *Countering Harmful Tax Practices More Effectively, Taking into Account Transparency and Substance, Action 5 - 2015 Final Report*, OECD/G20 Base Erosion and Profit Shifting Project, OECD Publishing, Paris, https://dx.doi.org/10.1787/9789264241190-en. [1]

OECD/Council of Europe (2011), *The Multilateral Convention on Mutual Administrative Assistance in Tax Matters: Amended by the 2010 Protocol*, OECD Publishing, Paris, https://dx.doi.org/10.1787/9789264115606-en. [4]

Notes

[1] Parties to the Convention are available here: www.oecd.org/tax/exchange-of-tax-information/convention-on-mutual-administrative-assistance-in-tax-matters.htm. Armenia also has bilateral agreements with Austria, Belarus, Belgium, Bulgaria, Canada, China (People's Republic of), Croatia, Cyprus, Czech Republic, Denmark, Estonia, Finland, France, Georgia, Germany, Greece, Hungary, India, Indonesia, Iran, Ireland, Israel, Italy, Kazakhstan, Kuwait, Latvia, Lebanon, Lithuania, Luxembourg, Moldova, Netherlands, Poland, Qatar, Romania, Russia, Serbia, Slovak Republic, Slovenia, Spain, Sweden, Switzerland, Syrian Arab Republic, Thailand, Tajikistan, Turkmenistan, Ukraine, United Arab Emirates and United Kingdom.

Aruba

Aruba has met all aspects of the terms of reference (OECD, 2017[3]) (ToR) for the calendar year 2019 (year in review) and no recommendations are made.

Aruba can legally issue five types of rulings within the scope of the transparency framework. In practice, Aruba has not issued any rulings within the scope of the transparency framework.

As no exchanges were required to take place, no peer input was received in respect of the exchanges of information on rulings received from Aruba.

A. The information gathering process

80. Aruba can legally issue the following five types of rulings within the scope of the transparency framework: (i) preferential regimes;[1] (ii) cross-border unilateral APAs and any other cross-border unilateral tax rulings (such as an advance tax ruling) covering transfer pricing or the application of transfer pricing principles; (iii) rulings providing for unilateral downward adjustments; (iv) permanent establishment rulings; and (v) related party conduit rulings.

81. For Aruba, past rulings are any tax rulings issued prior to 1 September 2018. However, there is no obligation for Aruba to conduct spontaneous exchange information on past rulings. Future rulings are any tax rulings within scope that are issued on or after 1 September 2018.

82. In the prior year peer review report, it was determined that Aruba's undertakings to identify future rulings and all potential exchange jurisdictions were sufficient to meet the minimum standard. In addition, it was determined that Aruba's review and supervision mechanism was sufficient to meet the minimum standard. Aruba's implementation remains unchanged, and therefore continues to meet the minimum standard.

83. Aruba has met all of the ToR for the information gathering process and no recommendations are made.

B. The exchange of information

84. In the prior years' peer review reports, it was determined that Aruba's process for the completion and exchange of templates were sufficient to meet the minimum standard. Aruba's implementation in this regard remains unchanged and therefore continues to meet the minimum standard.

85. Aruba has international agreements permitting spontaneous exchange of information, including being a party to the (i) *Multilateral Convention on Mutual Administrative Assistance in Tax Matters: Amended by the 2010 Protocol* (OECD/Council of Europe, 2011[4]) ("the Convention") and (ii) bilateral agreements in force with 25 jurisdictions.[2]

86. During the year in review, no exchanges were required to take place and no data on the timeliness of exchanges is reported. Aruba has the necessary legal basis for spontaneous exchange of information, a process for completing the templates in a timely way and has completed all exchanges. Aruba has met all of the ToR for the exchange of information process and no recommendations are made.

C. Statistics (ToR IV)

87. As no rulings were issued, no statistics can be reported.

D. Matters related to intellectual property regimes (ToR I.4.1.3)

88. Aruba offers an intellectual property regime (IP regime)[3] that is not currently subject to the transparency requirements under the Action 5 Report (OECD, 2015[1]), because:

- ***New entrants benefitting from the grandfathered IP regime***: not applicable for the year in review, as Aruba was in the process of eliminating/amending the regime and had not taken a decision on whether it will provide grandfathering to existing taxpayers.
- ***Third category of IP assets***: not applicable as the regime was in the process of being amended/eliminated.

- ***Taxpayers making the use of the option to treat the nexus ratio as a rebuttable presumption***: not applicable as the regime was in the process of being amended/eliminated.

Summary of recommendations on implementation of the transparency framework

Aspect of implementation of the transparency framework that should be improved	Recommendation for improvement
	No recommendations are made.

References

OECD (2017), *BEPS Action 5 on Harmful Tax Practices - Terms of Reference and Methodology for the Conduct of the Peer Reviews of the Action 5 Transparency Framework*, OECD Publishing, Paris, http://www.oecd.org/tax/beps/beps-action-5-harmful-tax-practices-peer-review-transparency-framework.pdf. [3]

OECD (2015), *Countering Harmful Tax Practices More Effectively, Taking into Account Transparency and Substance, Action 5 - 2015 Final Report*, OECD/G20 Base Erosion and Profit Shifting Project, OECD Publishing, Paris, https://dx.doi.org/10.1787/9789264241190-en. [1]

OECD/Council of Europe (2011), *The Multilateral Convention on Mutual Administrative Assistance in Tax Matters: Amended by the 2010 Protocol*, OECD Publishing, Paris, https://dx.doi.org/10.1787/9789264115606-en. [4]

Notes

[1] 1) Exempt companies, 2) Investment promotion, 3) Free zone, 4) Transparency regime and 5) Shipping regime.

[2] Parties to the Convention are available here: www.oecd.org/tax/exchange-of-tax-information/convention-on-mutual-administrative-assistance-in-tax-matters.htm. Aruba also has double tax agreements with Antigua and Barbuda, Argentina, Australia, Bahamas, Bermuda, British Virgin Islands, Canada, Cayman Islands, Czech Republic, Denmark, Faroe Islands, Finland, France, Greenland, Iceland, Mexico, Netherlands, Norway, Saint Kitts and Nevis, Saint Lucia, Saint Vincent and the Grenadines, Spain, Sweden, United Kingdom and United States.

[3] Exempt company.

Australia

Australia has met all aspects of the terms of reference (OECD, 2017[3]) (ToR) for the calendar year 2019 (year in review) and no recommendations are made.

Australia can legally issue four types of rulings within the scope of the transparency framework.

In practice, Australia issued rulings within the scope of the transparency framework as follows:

- 202 past rulings;
- For the period 1 April 2016 - 31 December 2016: 15 future rulings;
- For the calendar year 2017: 13 future rulings,
- For the calendar year 2018: 10 future rulings, and
- For the year in review: 15 future rulings.

Peer input was received from one jurisdiction in respect of the exchanges of information on rulings received from Australia. The input was positive, noting that information was complete, in a correct format and received in a timely manner.

A. The information gathering process

89. Australia can legally issue the following four types of rulings within the scope of the transparency framework: (i) preferential regimes;[1] (ii) cross-border unilateral APAs and any other cross-border unilateral tax rulings (such as an advance tax ruling) covering transfer pricing or the application of transfer pricing principles; (iii) permanent establishment rulings; and (iv) related party conduit rulings.

90. For Australia, past rulings are any tax rulings within scope that are issued either: (i) on or after 1 January 2014 but before 1 April 2016; or (ii) on or after 1 January 2010 but before 1 January 2014, provided they were still in effect as at 1 January 2014. Future rulings are any tax rulings within scope that are issued on or after 1 April 2016.

91. In the prior years' peer review reports, it was determined that Australia's undertakings to identify past and future rulings and all potential exchange jurisdictions were sufficient to meet the minimum standard. In addition, it was determined that Australia's review and supervision mechanism was sufficient to meet the minimum standard. Australia's implementation remains unchanged, and therefore continues to meet the minimum standard.

92. Australia has met all of the ToR for the information gathering process and no recommendations are made.

B. The exchange of information

93. In the prior years' peer review reports, it was determined that Australia's process for the completion and exchange of templates were sufficient to meet the minimum standard. With respect to past rulings, a small amount of further exchanges were made due to new exchange relationships being available during the year in review and also due to delayed confirmation from recipient jurisdictions regarding the system and format in which to receive exchanges]. Australia's implementation in this regard remains unchanged and therefore continues to meet the minimum standard.

94. Australia has international agreements permitting spontaneous exchange of information, including being a party to the (i) *Multilateral Convention on Mutual Administrative Assistance in Tax Matters: Amended by the 2010 Protocol* (OECD/Council of Europe, 2011[4]) ("the Convention") and (ii) bilateral agreements in force with 45 jurisdictions.[2]

95. For the year in review, the timeliness of exchanges is as follows:

Past rulings in the scope of the transparency framework	Number of exchanges transmitted by 31 December 2019	Delayed exchanges		
		Number of exchanges not transmitted by 31 December 2019	Reasons for the delays	Any other comments
	9	0	N/A	The exchanges include two delayed exchanges from the prior year report, and seven further exchanges due to new exchange relationships.
Future rulings in the scope of the transparency framework	Number of exchanges transmitted within three months of the information becoming available to the competent authority or immediately after legal	Delayed exchanges		
		Number of exchanges transmitted later than three months of the information on rulings becoming available to	Reasons for the delays	Any other comments

	impediments have been lifted	the competent authority		
	67	0	N/A	N/A
Total	76	0		

Follow up requests received for exchange of the ruling	Number	Average time to provide response	Number of requests not answered
	0	N/A	N/A

96. Australia has the necessary legal basis for spontaneous exchange of information, a process for completing the templates in a timely way and has completed all exchanges. Australia has met all of the ToR for the exchange of information process and no recommendations are made.

C. Statistics (ToR IV)

97. The statistics for the year in review are as follows:

Category of ruling	Number of exchanges	Jurisdictions exchanged with
Ruling related to a preferential regime	2	*De minimis* rule applies
Cross-border unilateral advance pricing agreements (APAs) and any other cross-border unilateral tax rulings (such as an advance tax ruling) covering transfer pricing or the application of transfer pricing principles	68	Austria, Brazil, Bulgaria, Canada, Chile, China, Colombia, Czech Republic, Finland, France, Germany, Ghana, Hong Kong (China), India, Indonesia, Ireland, Italy, Japan, Korea, Luxembourg, Malaysia, Mexico, Netherlands, New Zealand, Peru, Philippines, Poland, Singapore, South Africa, Spain, Sweden, Switzerland, Chinese Taipei, Thailand, United Kingdom, United States
Permanent establishment rulings	6	Belgium, Hong Kong (China), Japan, New Zealand, Singapore
Related party conduit rulings	0	N/A
Total	76	

D. Matters related to intellectual property regimes (ToR I.4.1.3)

98. Australia does not offer an intellectual property regime for which transparency requirements under the Action 5 Report (OECD, 2015[1]) were imposed.

Summary of recommendations on implementation of the transparency framework

Aspect of implementation of the transparency framework that should be improved	Recommendation for improvement
	No recommendations are made.

References

OECD (2017), *BEPS Action 5 on Harmful Tax Practices - Terms of Reference and Methodology for the Conduct of the Peer Reviews of the Action 5 Transparency Framework*, OECD Publishing, Paris, http://www.oecd.org/tax/beps/beps-action-5-harmful-tax-practices-peer-review-transparency-framework.pdf. [3]

OECD (2015), *Countering Harmful Tax Practices More Effectively, Taking into Account Transparency and Substance, Action 5 - 2015 Final Report*, OECD/G20 Base Erosion and Profit Shifting Project, OECD Publishing, Paris, https://dx.doi.org/10.1787/9789264241190-en. [1]

OECD/Council of Europe (2011), *The Multilateral Convention on Mutual Administrative Assistance in Tax Matters: Amended by the 2010 Protocol*, OECD Publishing, Paris, https://dx.doi.org/10.1787/9789264115606-en. [4]

Notes

[1] With respect to the following preferential regimes: 1) Offshore banking unit regime and 2) Conduit foreign income regime.

[2] Parties to the Convention are available here: www.oecd.org/tax/exchange-of-tax-information/convention-on-mutual-administrative-assistance-in-tax-matters.htm. Australia also has bilateral agreements with Argentina, Austria, Belgium, Canada, Chile, China (People's Republic of), Czech Republic, Denmark, Fiji, Finland, France, Germany, Hungary, India, Indonesia, Ireland, Israel, Italy, Japan, Kiribati, Korea, Malaysia, Malta, Mexico, Netherlands, New Zealand, Norway, Papua New Guinea, Philippines, Poland, Romania, Russia, Singapore, Slovak Republic, South Africa, Spain, Sri Lanka, Sweden, Switzerland, Chinese Taipei, Thailand, Turkey, United Kingdom, United States and Viet Nam.

Austria

Austria has met all aspects of the terms of reference (OECD, 2017[3]) (ToR) for the calendar year 2019 (year in review) and no recommendations are made.

Austria can legally issue one type of ruling within the scope of the transparency framework.

In practice, Austria issued rulings within the scope of the transparency framework as follows:

- 59 past rulings;
- For the period 1 April 2016 - 31 December 2016: 13 future rulings;
- For the calendar year 2017: 10 future rulings,
- For the calendar year 2018: nine future rulings, and
- For the year in review: 14 future rulings.

No peer input was received in respect of the exchanges of information on rulings received from Austria.

A. The information gathering process

99. Austria can legally issue one type of ruling within the scope of the transparency framework: cross-border unilateral APAs and any other cross-border unilateral tax rulings (such as an advance tax ruling) covering transfer pricing or the application of transfer pricing principles.

100. For Austria, past rulings are any tax rulings within scope that are issued either: (i) on or after 1 January 2014 but before 1 April 2016; or (ii) on or after 1 January 2010 but before 1 January 2014, provided they were still in effect as at 1 January 2014. Future rulings are any tax rulings within scope that are issued on or after 1 April 2016.

101. In the prior years' peer review reports, it was determined that Austria's undertakings to identify past and future rulings and all potential exchange jurisdictions were sufficient to meet the minimum standard. In addition, it was determined that Austria's review and supervision mechanism was sufficient to meet the minimum standard. Austria's implementation remains unchanged, and therefore continues to meet the minimum standard.

102. Austria has met all of the ToR for the information gathering process and no recommendations are made.

B. The exchange of information

103. In the prior years' peer review reports, it was determined that Austria's process for the completion and exchange of templates were sufficient to meet the minimum standard. With respect to past rulings, no further action was required. Austria's implementation in this regard remains unchanged and therefore continues to meet the minimum standard.

104. Austria has international agreements permitting spontaneous exchange of information, including being a party to the (i) *Multilateral Convention on Mutual Administrative Assistance in Tax Matters: Amended by the 2010 Protocol* (OECD/Council of Europe, 2011[4]) ("the Convention"), (ii) the Directive 2011/16/EU with all other European Union Member States and (iii) bilateral agreements in force with 77 jurisdictions.[1]

105. For the year in review, the timeliness of exchanges is as follows:

Future rulings in the scope of the transparency framework	Number of exchanges transmitted within three months of the information becoming available to the competent authority or immediately after legal impediments have been lifted	Delayed exchanges		
		Number of exchanges transmitted later than three months of the information on rulings becoming available to the competent authority	Reasons for the delays	Any other comments
	58	0	N/A	N/A

Follow up requests received for exchange of the ruling	Number	Average time to provide response	Number of requests not answered
	1	55 days	0

106. Austria has the necessary legal basis for spontaneous exchange of information, a process for completing the templates in a timely way and has completed all exchanges. Austria has met all of the ToR for the exchange of information process and no recommendations are made.

C. Statistics (ToR IV)

107. The statistics for the year in review are as follows:

Category of ruling	Number of exchanges	Jurisdictions exchanged with
Cross-border unilateral advance pricing agreements (APAs) and any other cross-border unilateral tax rulings (such as an advance tax ruling) covering transfer pricing or the application of transfer pricing principles	58	Brazil, Croatia, Czech Republic, Germany, Hungary, Italy, Korea, Liechtenstein, Lithuania, Luxembourg, Netherlands, Romania, Russia, Serbia, Slovak Republic, Slovenia, South Africa, Spain, Switzerland, Ukraine, United Kingdom, United States

D. Matters related to intellectual property regimes (ToR I.4.1.3)

108. Austria does not offer an intellectual property regime for which transparency requirements under the Action 5 Report (OECD, 2015[1]) were imposed.

Summary of recommendations on implementation of the transparency framework

Aspect of implementation of the transparency framework that should be improved	Recommendation for improvement
	No recommendations are made.

References

OECD (2017), *BEPS Action 5 on Harmful Tax Practices - Terms of Reference and Methodology for the Conduct of the Peer Reviews of the Action 5 Transparency Framework*, OECD Publishing, Paris, http://www.oecd.org/tax/beps/beps-action-5-harmful-tax-practices-peer-review-transparency-framework.pdf. [3]

OECD (2015), *Countering Harmful Tax Practices More Effectively, Taking into Account Transparency and Substance, Action 5 - 2015 Final Report*, OECD/G20 Base Erosion and Profit Shifting Project, OECD Publishing, Paris, https://dx.doi.org/10.1787/9789264241190-en. [1]

OECD/Council of Europe (2011), *The Multilateral Convention on Mutual Administrative Assistance in Tax Matters: Amended by the 2010 Protocol*, OECD Publishing, Paris, https://dx.doi.org/10.1787/9789264115606-en. [4]

Notes

[1] Parties to the Convention are available here: www.oecd.org/tax/exchange-of-tax-information/convention-on-mutual-administrative-assistance-in-tax-matters.htm. Austria also has bilateral agreements in force with Algeria, Armenia, Bahamas, Bahrain, Belarus, Bosnia and Herzegovina, Brunei Darussalam, Burkina Faso, Dominican Republic, Egypt, El Salvador, Gabon, Guatemala, Hong Kong (China), Jamaica, Kenya, Kuwait, Montenegro, North Macedonia, Morocco, Peru, Philippines, Qatar, Serbia, Chinese Taipei, Tajikistan, Thailand, Turkey, Turkmenistan, United Arab Emirates, United States, Venezuela and Viet Nam.

Barbados

Barbados has met all aspects of the terms of reference (OECD, 2017[3]) (ToR) for the calendar year 2019 (year in review) except for identifying and exchanging information on all new entrants to the grandfathered IP regime (ToR I.4.1.3). Barbados receives one recommendation on this point for the year in review.

In the prior year report, as well as in the 2017 peer review, Barbados had received two recommendations. One of these recommendations has been addressed and is now removed. The second recommendation has not been addressed and remains in place.

Barbados can legally issue five types of rulings within the scope of the transparency framework.

In practice, Barbados issued rulings within the scope of the transparency framework as follows:

- Two past rulings;
- For the period 1 September 2017 - 31 December 2017: no future rulings;
- For the calendar year 2018: one future ruling, and
- For the year in review: no future rulings.

As no exchanges were required to take place, no peer input was received in respect of the exchanges of information on rulings received from Barbados.

A. The information gathering process

109. Barbados can legally issue the following five types of rulings within the scope of the transparency framework: (i) preferential regimes;[1] (ii) cross-border unilateral APAs and any other cross-border unilateral tax rulings (such as an advance tax ruling) covering transfer pricing or the application of transfer pricing principles; (iii) rulings providing for unilateral downward adjustments; (iv) permanent establishment rulings; and (v) related party conduit rulings.

110. For Barbados, past rulings are any tax rulings within scope that are issued either: (i) on or after 1 January 2015 but before 1 September 2017; or (ii) on or after 1 January 2012 but before 1 January 2015, provided they were still in effect as at 1 January 2015. Future rulings are any tax rulings within scope that are issued on or after 1 September 2017.

111. In the prior years' peer review reports, it was determined that Barbados's undertakings to identify past and future rulings and all potential exchange jurisdictions were sufficient to meet the minimum standard. In addition, it was determined that Barbados's review and supervision mechanism was sufficient to meet the minimum standard. Barbados's implementation remains unchanged, and therefore continues to meet the minimum standard.

112. Barbados has met all of the ToR for the information gathering process and no recommendations are made.

B. The exchange of information

Legal basis for spontaneous exchange of information (ToR II.5.1, II.5.2)

113. Barbados has the necessary domestic legal basis to exchange information spontaneously. Barbados notes that there are no legal or practical impediments that prevent the spontaneous exchange of information on rulings as contemplated in the Action 5 minimum standard.

114. Barbados has international agreements permitting spontaneous exchange of information, including being a party to the (i) *Multilateral Convention on Mutual Administrative Assistance in Tax Matters: Amended by the 2010 Protocol* (OECD/Council of Europe, 2011[4]) ("the Convention") and (ii) bilateral agreements in force with 40 jurisdictions.[2]

Completion and exchange of templates (ToR II.5.3, II.5.4, II.5.5, II.5.6, II.5.7)

115. In the prior years' peer review reports, it was determined that Barbados' process for the completion and exchange of templates was sufficient to meet the minimum standard except for the timely exchange of information on rulings (ToR II.5).

116. During the year in review, Barbados developed and implemented a framework that allows the exchange of information to occur in a timely manner. Once a ruling is determined to be within any of the five transparency framework categories, a template in the form of Annex C is completed, a cover letter is attached and the rulings are sent by express mail. An email is then sent to the Competent Authority notifying them that the ruling has been mailed and requesting confirmation of receipt. There are no outstanding rulings to be exchanged, and therefore, the recommendation is now removed.

117. For the year in review, the timeliness of exchanges is as follows:

Past rulings in the scope of the transparency framework	Number of exchanges transmitted by 31 December 2019	Delayed exchanges		
		Number of exchanges not transmitted by 31 December 2019	Reasons for the delays	Any other comments
	2	0	N/A	These exchanges on past rulings are delayed exchanges from the previous year peer review report.
Future rulings in the scope of the transparency framework	Number of exchanges transmitted within three months of the information becoming available to the competent authority or immediately after legal impediments have been lifted	Delayed exchanges		
		Number of exchanges transmitted later than three months of the information on rulings becoming available to the competent authority	Reasons for the delays	Any other comments
	1	0	N/A	This exchange on future rulings is a delayed exchange from the previous year peer review report.
Total	3	0		

Conclusion on section B

118. Barbados has the necessary legal basis for spontaneous exchange of information, a process for completing the templates in a timely way and has completed all exchanges. Barbados has met all of the ToR for the exchange of information process and no recommendations are made.

C. Statistics (ToR IV)

119. The statistics for the year in review are as follows:

Category of ruling	Number of exchanges	Jurisdictions exchanged with
Ruling related to a preferential regime	N/A	N/A
Cross-border unilateral advance pricing agreements (APAs) and any other cross-border unilateral tax rulings (such as an advance tax ruling) covering transfer pricing or the application of transfer pricing principles	N/A	N/A
Cross-border rulings providing for a unilateral downward adjustment to the taxpayer's taxable profits that is not directly reflected in the taxpayer's financial / commercial accounts	N/A	N/A
Permanent establishment rulings	N/A	N/A
Related party conduit rulings	N/A	N/A
De minimis rule	3	N/A

IP regimes: total exchanges on taxpayers benefitting from the third category of IP assets, new entrants benefitting from grandfathered IP regimes; and taxpayers making use of the option to treat the nexus ratio as a rebuttable presumption	N/A	N/A
Total	3	

D. Matters related to intellectual property regimes (ToR I.4.1.3)

120. Barbados offered two intellectual property regimes (IP regime)[3] that were abolished as of 1 July 2018 and are subject to transparency requirements under the Action 5 Report (OECD, 2015[1]). It states that the identification of the benefitting taxpayers will occur as follows:

- ***New entrants benefitting from the grandfathered IP regime***: Transparency obligations apply for the two regimes, because grandfathering is provided to entrants that entered the regime after the relevant date from which enhanced transparency obligations apply. Barbados is currently working on a process by which it can identify and exchange information on these new entrants. Barbados is therefore recommended to identify and exchange information on all new entrants to the grandfathered IP regime as soon as possible (ToR I.4.1.3).
- ***Third category of IP assets***: not applicable as the IP regimes has been abolished.
- ***Taxpayers making use of the option to treat the nexus ratio as a rebuttable presumption***: not applicable as the IP regimes has been abolished.

Summary of recommendations on implementation of the transparency framework

Aspect of implementation of the transparency framework that should be improved	Recommendation for improvement
Barbados did not identify or exchange information on new entrants to the grandfathered IP regime.	Barbados is recommended to identify and exchange information on all new entrants to the grandfathered IP regime as soon as possible. This recommendation remains unchanged since the 2017 and 2018 peer review reports.

References

OECD (2017), *BEPS Action 5 on Harmful Tax Practices - Terms of Reference and Methodology for the Conduct of the Peer Reviews of the Action 5 Transparency Framework*, OECD Publishing, Paris, http://www.oecd.org/tax/beps/beps-action-5-harmful-tax-practices-peer-review-transparency-framework.pdf. [3]

OECD (2015), *Countering Harmful Tax Practices More Effectively, Taking into Account Transparency and Substance, Action 5 - 2015 Final Report*, OECD/G20 Base Erosion and Profit Shifting Project, OECD Publishing, Paris, https://dx.doi.org/10.1787/9789264241190-en. [1]

OECD/Council of Europe (2011), *The Multilateral Convention on Mutual Administrative Assistance in Tax Matters: Amended by the 2010 Protocol*, OECD Publishing, Paris, https://dx.doi.org/10.1787/9789264115606-en. [4]

Notes

[1] Credit for foreign currency earnings.

[2] Parties to the Convention are available here: www.oecd.org/tax/exchange-of-tax-information/convention-on-mutual-administrative-assistance-in-tax-matters.htm. Barbados also has bilateral agreements with Antigua and Barbuda, Austria, Bahrain, Belize, Botswana, Canada, China (People's Republic of), Cyprus, Cuba, Czech Republic, Dominica, Finland, Grenada, Guyana, Iceland, Italy, Jamaica, Luxembourg, Malta, Mauritius, Mexico, Netherlands, Norway, Panama, Portugal, Saint Kitts and Nevis, Saint Lucia, Saint Vincent and the Grenadines, San Marino, Seychelles, Singapore, Spain, Sweden, Switzerland, Trinidad & Tobago, Qatar, United Arab Emirates, United Kingdom, United States and Venezuela.

[3] 1) International business companies and 2) International societies with restricted liability.

Belgium

Belgium has met all aspects of the terms of reference (OECD, 2017[3]) (ToR) for the calendar year 2019 (year in review) and no recommendations are made.

Belgium can legally issue four types of rulings within the scope of the transparency framework.

In practice, Belgium issued rulings within the scope of the transparency framework as follows:

- 586 past rulings;
- For the period 1 April 2016 - 31 December 2016: 57 future rulings;
- For the calendar year 2017: 107 future rulings,
- For the calendar year 2018: 103 future rulings, and
- For the year in review: 73 future rulings.

Peer input was received from two jurisdictions in respect of the exchanges of information on rulings received from Belgium. The input was positive, noting that information was complete, in a correct format and almost all received in a timely manner.

A. The information gathering process

121. Belgium can legally issue four types of rulings within the scope of the transparency framework: (i) preferential regimes;[1] (ii) cross-border unilateral advance pricing agreements (APAs) and any other cross-border unilateral tax rulings (such as an advance tax ruling) covering transfer pricing or the application of transfer pricing principles; (iii) rulings providing for unilateral downward adjustments; and (iv) permanent establishment rulings.

122. For Belgium, past rulings are any tax rulings within scope that are issued either: (i) on or after 1 January 2014 but before 1 April 2016; or (ii) on or after 1 January 2010 but before 1 January 2014, provided they were still in effect as at 1 January 2014. Future rulings are any tax rulings within scope that are issued on or after 1 April 2016.

123. In the prior years' peer review reports, it was determined that Belgium's undertakings to identify past and future rulings and all potential exchange jurisdictions were sufficient to meet the minimum standard. In addition, it was determined that Belgium's review and supervision mechanism was sufficient to meet the minimum standard. Belgium's implementation remains unchanged, and therefore continues to meet the minimum standard.

124. Belgium has met all of the ToR for the information gathering process and no recommendations are made.

B. The exchange of information

125. In the prior years' peer review reports, it was determined that Belgium's process for the completion and exchange of templates were sufficient to meet the minimum standard. With respect to past rulings, no further action was required. Belgium's implementation in this regard remains unchanged and therefore continues to meet the minimum standard.

126. Belgium has international agreements permitting spontaneous exchange of information, including being a party to the (i) *Multilateral Convention on Mutual Administrative Assistance in Tax Matters: Amended by the 2010 Protocol* (OECD/Council of Europe, 2011[4]) ("the Convention"), (ii) the Directive 2011/16/EU with all other European Union Member States and (iii) bilateral agreements in force with 77 jurisdictions.[2]

127. For the year in review, the timeliness of exchanges is as follows:

Future rulings in the scope of the transparency framework	Number of exchanges transmitted within three months of the information becoming available to the competent authority or immediately after legal impediments have been lifted	Delayed exchanges		
		Number of exchanges transmitted later than three months of the information on rulings becoming available to the competent authority	Reasons for the delays	Any other comments
	216	0	N/A	N/A

Follow up requests received for exchange of the ruling	Number	Average time to provide response	Number of requests not answered
	0	N/A	N/A

128. Belgium has the necessary legal basis for spontaneous exchange of information, a process for completing the templates in a timely way and has completed all exchanges. Belgium has met all of the ToR for the exchange of information process and no recommendations are made.

C. Statistics (ToR IV)

129. The statistics for the year in review are as follows:

Category of ruling	Number of exchanges	Jurisdictions exchanged with
Ruling related to a preferential regime	15	Brazil, Denmark, France, Ireland, Japan, Luxembourg, Netherlands, United Kingdom, United States
Cross-border unilateral advance pricing agreements (APAs) and any other cross-border unilateral tax rulings (such as an advance tax ruling) covering transfer pricing or the application of transfer pricing principles	193	Argentina, Australia, Austria, Brazil, Bulgaria, Canada, Chile, China (People's Republic of), Colombia, Czech Republic, France, Gabon, Germany, Indonesia, Ireland, India, Isle of Man, Italy, Japan, Jersey, Kazakhstan, Korea, Luxembourg, Malaysia, Mexico, Netherlands, Norway, Poland, Portugal, Romania, Russia, Saudi Arabia, Singapore, South Africa, Spain, Switzerland, Tunisia, Turkey, United Kingdom, United States
Cross-border rulings providing for a unilateral downward adjustment to the taxpayer's taxable profits that is not directly reflected in the taxpayer's financial / commercial accounts	0	N/A
Permanent establishment rulings	22	Czech Republic, France, Germany, Indonesia, Ireland, Luxembourg, Netherlands, Portugal, Spain, Singapore, South Africa, United Kingdom, United States
IP regimes: total exchanges on taxpayers benefitting from the third category of IP assets, new entrants benefitting from grandfathered IP regimes; and taxpayers making use of the option to treat the nexus ratio as a rebuttable presumption	83	Australia, Austria, Bulgaria, China (People's Republic of), France, Germany, Hungary, India, Ireland, Israel, Italy, Japan, Lithuania, Mexico, Malaysia, Mauritius, Netherlands, Nigeria, Norway, Poland, Romania, Russia, Spain, Sweden, Switzerland, Thailand, Turkey, Ukraine, United Kingdom, United States
Total	313[3]	

D. Matters related to intellectual property regimes (ToR I.4.1.3)

130. Belgium offers an intellectual property regime (IP regime)[4] that is subject to the transparency requirements under the Action 5 Report (OECD, 2015[1]). It states that the identification of the benefitting taxpayers will occur as follows:

- ***New entrants benefitting from the grandfathered IP regime***: In the prior year peer review report, it was determined that Belgium's process for identifying and exchanging information on new entrants to the grandfathered IP regime were sufficient to meet the minimum standard. Belgium's implementation in this regard remains unchanged and therefore continues to meet the minimum standard.
- ***Third category of IP assets***: not applicable as the regime does not allow the third category of IP assets to qualify for the benefits.
- ***Taxpayers making use of the option to treat the nexus ratio as a rebuttable presumption***: Belgium confirms that no taxpayer elected to treat the nexus approach as a rebuttable presumption.

Summary of recommendations on implementation of the transparency framework

Aspect of implementation of the transparency framework that should be improved	Recommendation for improvement
	No recommendations are made.

References

OECD (2017), *BEPS Action 5 on Harmful Tax Practices - Terms of Reference and Methodology for the Conduct of the Peer Reviews of the Action 5 Transparency Framework*, OECD Publishing, Paris, http://www.oecd.org/tax/beps/beps-action-5-harmful-tax-practices-peer-review-transparency-framework.pdf. [3]

OECD (2015), *Countering Harmful Tax Practices More Effectively, Taking into Account Transparency and Substance, Action 5 - 2015 Final Report*, OECD/G20 Base Erosion and Profit Shifting Project, OECD Publishing, Paris, https://dx.doi.org/10.1787/9789264241190-en. [1]

OECD/Council of Europe (2011), *The Multilateral Convention on Mutual Administrative Assistance in Tax Matters: Amended by the 2010 Protocol*, OECD Publishing, Paris, https://dx.doi.org/10.1787/9789264115606-en. [4]

Notes

[1] With respect to the following preferential regimes: 1) Patent income deduction, 2) tax shelter regime for maritime exploitation and 3) excess profits.

[2] Parties to the Convention are available here: www.oecd.org/tax/exchange-of-tax-information/convention-on-mutual-administrative-assistance-in-tax-matters.htm. Belgium also has bilateral agreements in force with Albania, Algeria, Andorra, Antigua and Barbuda, Argentina, Armenia, Australia, Azerbaijan, Bahrain, Bangladesh, Belarus, Brazil, Belize, Bosnia and Herzegovina, Canada, Chile, China (People's Republic of), Côte d'Ivoire, Democratic Republic of the Congo, Ecuador, Egypt, Gabon, Georgia, Ghana, Hong Kong (China), Iceland, India, Indonesia, Israel, Japan, Kazakhstan, Korea, Kosovo, Kyrgyzstan, Kuwait, Malaysia, Mauritius, Mexico, Moldova, Mongolia, Montenegro, Morocco, New Zealand, Nigeria, North Macedonia, Norway, Pakistan, Philippines, Russia, Rwanda, San Marino, Senegal, Serbia, Seychelles, Singapore, South Africa, Sri Lanka, Switzerland, Tajikistan, Chinese Taipei, Thailand, Tunisia, Turkey, Turkmenistan, Ukraine, United Arab Emirates, United States, Uruguay, Uzbekistan, Venezuela and Viet Nam.

[3] There were 299 unique exchanges. The total of number of exchanges given in this table, 313, is higher due to the fact that some exchanges relate to rulings that fall under more than one category.

[4] Innovation income deduction.

Benin

Benin has met all aspects of the terms of reference (OECD, 2017[3]) (ToR) for the calendar year 2019 (year in review), except for the information gathering process (ToR I.4) and exchange of information (ToR II.5). Benin receives two recommendations on this point for the year in review.

In the prior year report, Benin had received the same two recommendations. As they have not been addressed, the recommendations remain in place.

Benin can legally issue one type of rulings within the scope of the transparency framework.

In practice, Benin has not issued any rulings within the scope of the transparency framework.

As no exchanges were required to take place, no peer input was received in respect of the exchanges of information on rulings received from Benin.

A. The information gathering process

131. Benin can legally issue the following type of ruling within the scope of the transparency framework: permanent establishment rulings.

Past rulings (ToR I.4.1.1, I.4.1.2, I.4.2.1, I.4.2.2)

132. For Benin, past rulings are any tax rulings within scope that are issued either (i) on or after 1 January 2015 but before 1 April 2017; and (ii) on or after 1 January 2012 but before 1 January 2015, provided they were still in effect as at 1 January 2015.

133. In Benin, rulings are issued by the directorate of Legislation and Litigation, within the Tax Administration. This unit is responsible for storing and reviewing such rulings and has reviewed its files, being able to confirm that no past rulings have been issued. Benin indicated no past rulings in scope of the transparency framework have been issued. As such there was no need to identify potential exchange jurisdictions.

Future rulings (ToR I.4.1.1, I.4.1.2, I.4.2.1)

134. For Benin, future rulings are any tax rulings within scope that are issued on or after 1 April 2017.

135. In the prior year peer review report, Benin indicated that there were no processes in place for the record keeping of rulings for the purposes of the transparency framework. It was also noted that Benin intended to implement guidelines and practices to make sure the necessary information to meet the requirements of the transparency framework is required in all cases. Benin was recommended to finalise its information gathering process as soon as possible.

136. During the year in review, as it has not been addressed, the recommendation remains in place.

Review and supervision (ToR I.4.3)

137. In the prior year peer review report, it was determined that Benin did not yet have a review and supervision mechanism under the transparency framework. As Benin is still in the process of considering the implementation of a revision and supervision mechanism for ensuring implementation of the transparency framework for the year in review, the recommendation remains in place.

Conclusion on section A

138. Benin is recommended to finalise its information gathering process, with a review and supervision mechanism as soon as possible (ToR I.4).

B. The exchange of information

Legal basis for spontaneous exchange of information (ToR II.5.1, II.5.2)

139. Benin is still in the process of putting in place the necessary domestic legal basis to exchange information spontaneously.

140. Benin signed the *Multilateral Convention on Mutual Administrative Assistance in Tax Matters: Amended by the 2010 Protocol* (OECD/Council of Europe, 2011[4]) ("the Convention") in November 2019. Benin is encouraged to continue its efforts to ratify the Convention and expand its international exchange of information instruments to be able to exchange information on rulings. It is noted, however, that

jurisdictions are assessed on their compliance with the transparency framework in respect of the exchange of information network in effect for the year of the particular annual review.

Completion and exchange of templates (ToR II.5.3, II.5.4, II.5.5, II.5.6, II.5.7)

141. Benin is still developing a process to complete the templates on relevant rulings, to make them available to the Competent Authority for exchange of information, and to exchange them with relevant jurisdictions.

142. As no exchanges were required to take place no data on the timeliness of exchanges can be reported.

Conclusion on section B

143. Benin is recommended to put in place a domestic legal framework allowing spontaneous exchange of information on rulings and to continue its efforts to complete the templates for all relevant rulings and to ensure that the exchanges of information on rulings occur as soon as possible (ToR II.5).

C. Statistics (ToR IV)

144. As no rulings were issued, no statistics can be reported.

D. Matters related to intellectual property regimes (ToR I.4.1.3)

145. Benin does not offer an intellectual property regime for which transparency requirements under the Action 5 Report (OECD, 2015[1]) were imposed.

Summary of recommendations on implementation of the transparency framework

Aspect of implementation of the transparency framework that should be improved	Recommendation for improvement
Benin has not yet finalised the steps to have in place its necessary information and gathering process.	Benin is recommended to finalise its information gathering process, with a review and supervision mechanism, as soon as possible. This recommendation remains unchanged since the prior year peer review report.
Benin has not yet finalised the steps to have effective compulsory spontaneous exchange of information on the tax rulings within the scope of the transparency framework.	Benin is recommended to continue to put in place a domestic legal framework allowing spontaneous exchange of information on rulings and to continue its efforts to complete the templates for all relevant rulings and to ensure that the exchanges of information on rulings occur as soon as possible. This recommendation remains unchanged since the prior year peer review report.

References

OECD (2017), *BEPS Action 5 on Harmful Tax Practices - Terms of Reference and Methodology for the Conduct of the Peer Reviews of the Action 5 Transparency Framework*, OECD Publishing, Paris, http://www.oecd.org/tax/beps/beps-action-5-harmful-tax-practices-peer-review-transparency-framework.pdf. [3]

OECD (2015), *Countering Harmful Tax Practices More Effectively, Taking into Account Transparency and Substance, Action 5 - 2015 Final Report*, OECD/G20 Base Erosion and Profit Shifting Project, OECD Publishing, Paris, https://dx.doi.org/10.1787/9789264241190-en. [1]

OECD/Council of Europe (2011), *The Multilateral Convention on Mutual Administrative Assistance in Tax Matters: Amended by the 2010 Protocol*, OECD Publishing, Paris, https://dx.doi.org/10.1787/9789264115606-en. [4]

Botswana

Botswana is taking steps to implement the legal basis for the transparency framework and to commence administrative preparations to ensure that it finalises its information gathering process (ToR I.4) and that information on rulings will be identified and exchanged in a timely manner (ToR II.5). Botswana receives two recommendations on these points for the year in review.

In the prior year report, Botswana had received the same two recommendations. As they have not been addressed, the recommendations remain in place.

Botswana can legally issue three types of rulings within the scope of the transparency framework.

In practice, Botswana issued rulings within the scope of the transparency framework as follows:

- 10 past rulings;
- For the period 1 April 2018 - 31 December 2018: one future ruling; and
- For the year in review: three future rulings.

As no exchanges took place, no peer input was received in respect of the exchanges of information on rulings received from Botswana.

A. The information gathering process

146. Botswana can legally issue the following three types of rulings within the scope of the transparency framework: (i) preferential regimes;[1] (ii) cross-border unilateral APAs and any other cross-border unilateral tax rulings (such as an advance tax ruling) covering transfer pricing or the application of transfer pricing principles; and (iii) permanent establishment rulings.

Past rulings (ToR I.4.1.1, I.4.1.2, I.4.2.1, I.4.2.2)

147. For Botswana, past rulings are any tax rulings within scope that are issued either (i) on or after 1 January 2016 but before 1 April 2018; and (ii) on or after 1 January 2014 but before 1 January 2016, provided still in effect as at 1 January 2016.

148. In the prior year peer review report, it was noted that Botswana does not have a process in place for identifying the potential exchange jurisdictions for APAs and permanent establishment rulings and did not yet apply the best efforts approach. Therefore, Botswana was recommended to apply the best efforts approach to identify all potential exchange jurisdictions for APA and PE rulings, as soon as possible.

149. During the year in review, no additional work was undertaken and therefore, the prior year recommendation remains.

Future rulings (ToR I.4.1.1, I.4.1.2, I.4.2.1)

150. For Botswana, future rulings are any tax rulings within scope that are issued on or after 1 April 2018.

151. In the prior year peer review report, it was determined that Botswana's undertakings to identify future rulings and all potential exchange jurisdictions was sufficient to meet the minimum standard. Botswana's implementation in this regard remains unchanged, and therefore continues to meet the minimum standard.

Review and supervision (ToR I.4.3)

152. In the prior year peer review report, it was noted that Botswana did not yet have a review and supervision mechanism for past or future rulings under the transparency framework for the year in review. Therefore, Botswana was recommended to put in place a review and supervision mechanism, as soon as possible.

153. During the year in review, no additional work was undertaken and therefore, the prior year recommendation remains.

Conclusion on section A

154. Botswana is recommended to apply the best efforts approach to identify all potential exchange jurisdictions for APA and PE rulings and to put in place a review and supervision mechanism, as soon as possible (ToR I.4).

B. The exchange of information

Legal basis for spontaneous exchange of information (ToR II.5.1, II.5.2)

155. Botswana does not have the necessary domestic legal basis to exchange information spontaneously. Botswana can only exchange information on request. Botswana is undergoing a comprehensive reform of its tax laws. Botswana notes that it has commenced a review of the exchange of information legislative framework with the support of the African Tax Administration Forum (ATAF) with a view to correcting identified shortcomings in this area by December 2020.

156. Botswana has international agreements permitting spontaneous exchange of information, including bilateral agreements in force with 24 jurisdictions.[2] Botswana is encouraged to continue its efforts to expand its international exchange of information instruments to be able to exchange rulings. It is noted, however, that jurisdictions are assessed on their compliance with the transparency framework in respect of the exchange of information network in effect for the year of the particular annual review.

Completion and exchange of templates (ToR II.5.3, II.5.4, II.5.5, II.5.6, II.5.7)

157. Botswana is currently developing a process to complete the templates on relevant rulings, to make them available to the Competent Authority for exchange of information, and to exchange them with relevant jurisdictions.

158. As no exchanges took place for the year in review, no data on the timeliness of exchanges can be reported.

Conclusion on section B

159. Botswana is recommended to continue to put in place a domestic legal framework allowing spontaneous exchange of information on rulings and to ensure the timely exchange of information on rulings in the form required by the transparency framework (ToR II.5).

C. Statistics (ToR IV)

160. As there was no information on rulings exchanged by Botswana for the year in review, no statistics can be reported.

D. Matters related to intellectual property regimes (ToR I.4.1.3)

161. Botswana offered an intellectual property regime (IP regime)[3] that was abolished as of 1 January 2019 and that is not subject to the transparency requirements under the Action 5 Report (OECD, 2015[1]) because:

- ***New entrants benefitting from the grandfathered IP regime***: as there were no taxpayers benefitting from the IP regime and no grandfathering provisions have been provided, no enhanced transparency requirements apply.
- ***Third category of IP assets***: not applicable as the IP regime has been abolished.
- ***Taxpayers making use of the option to treat the nexus ratio as a rebuttable presumption***: not applicable as the IP regime has been abolished.

Summary of recommendations on implementation of the transparency framework

Aspect of implementation of the transparency framework that should be improved	Recommendation for improvement
Botswana has not yet finalised the steps to have in place it necessary information gathering process.	Botswana is recommended to apply the best efforts approach to identify all potential exchange jurisdictions for APA and PE rulings and to put in place a review and supervision mechanism, as soon as possible. This recommendation remains unchanged since the prior year peer review report.
Botswana does not yet have the necessary legal framework in place for exchanging information on rulings and a process in place to ensure the timely exchange of information on rulings in the form required by the transparency framework.	Botswana is recommended to continue to put in place a domestic legal framework allowing spontaneous exchange of information on rulings and to ensure the timely exchange of information on rulings in the form required by the transparency framework. This recommendation remains unchanged since the prior year peer review report.

Jurisdiction's response and recent developments

162. Botswana notes that it has engaged with ATAF in developing a framework for the exchange of information on tax rulings under the Action 5 transparency framework, including on the identification on potential exchange jurisdictions, Botswana's review and supervision mechanism and the completion and exchange of templates. In addition, Botswana is reforming its tax laws including on the spontaneous exchange of information. It is envisaged that this framework will be in place by mid-2021.

References

OECD (2015), *Countering Harmful Tax Practices More Effectively, Taking into Account Transparency and Substance, Action 5 - 2015 Final Report*, OECD/G20 Base Erosion and Profit Shifting Project, OECD Publishing, Paris, https://dx.doi.org/10.1787/9789264241190-en. [1]

Notes

[1] With respect to the following preferential regime: International financial services company.

[2] Botswana has bilateral agreements with Barbados, China (People's Republic of), Denmark, Eswatini, Faroe Islands, Finland, France, Greenland, Iceland, India, Ireland, Isle of Man, Malta, Mauritius, Mozambique, Namibia, Norway, Russia, Seychelles, South Africa, Sweden, United Kingdom, Zambia and Zimbabwe.

[3] International financial services company.

Brazil

Brazil has met all aspects of the terms of reference (OECD, 2017[3]) (ToR) for the calendar year 2019 (year in review) and no recommendations are made.

Brazil can legally issue two types of rulings within the scope of the transparency framework.

In practice, Brazil issued rulings within the scope of the transparency framework as follows:

- 10 past rulings;
- For the period 1 April 2016 - 31 December 2016: no future rulings;
- For the calendar year 2017: no future rulings,
- For the calendar year 2018: six future rulings, and
- For the year in review: no future rulings.

These rulings are published on the Receita Federal do Brazil's website in a redacted form.[1]

As no exchanges were required to take place, no peer input was received in respect of the exchanges of information on rulings received from Brazil.

A. The information gathering process

163. Brazil can legally issue the following two types of rulings within the scope of the transparency framework: (i) preferential regimes[2] and (ii) cross-border unilateral APAs and any other cross-border unilateral tax rulings (such as an advance tax ruling) covering transfer pricing or the application of transfer pricing principles.

164. For Brazil, past rulings are any tax rulings within scope that are issued either: (i) on or after 1 January 2014 but before 1 April 2016; or (ii) on or after 1 January 2010 but before 1 January 2014, provided they were still in effect as at 1 January 2014. Future rulings are any tax rulings within scope that are issued on or after 1 April 2016.

165. In the prior years' peer review reports, it was determined that Brazil's undertakings to identify past and future rulings and all potential exchange jurisdictions were sufficient to meet the minimum standard. In addition, it was determined that Brazil's review and supervision mechanism was sufficient to meet the minimum standard. Brazil's implementation remains unchanged, and therefore continues to meet the minimum standard.

166. Brazil has met all of the ToR for the information gathering process and no recommendations are made.

B. The exchange of information

167. In the prior years' peer review reports, it was determined that Brazil's process for the completion and exchange of templates were sufficient to meet the minimum standard. With respect to past rulings, no further action was required from Brazil. Brazil's implementation in this regard remains unchanged and therefore continues to meet the minimum standard.

168. Brazil has international agreements permitting spontaneous exchange of information, including being a party to the (i) *Multilateral Convention on Mutual Administrative Assistance in Tax Matters: Amended by the 2010 Protocol* (OECD/Council of Europe, 2011[4]) ("the Convention") and (ii) bilateral agreements in force with 33 jurisdictions.[3]

169. As Brazil was not required to exchange any information on rulings for the year in review and no data on the timeliness of exchanges can be reported.

170. Brazil has the necessary legal basis for spontaneous exchange of information, a process for completing the templates in a timely way and has completed all exchanges. Brazil has met all of the ToR for the exchange of information process and no recommendations are made.

C. Statistics (ToR IV)

171. As no rulings were issued, no statistics can be reported.

D. Matters related to intellectual property regimes (ToR I.4.1.3)

172. Brazil does not offer an intellectual property regime for which transparency requirements under the Action 5 Report (OECD, 2015[1]) were imposed.

Summary of recommendations on implementation of the transparency framework

Aspect of implementation of the transparency framework that should be improved	Recommendation for improvement
	No recommendations are made.

References

OECD (2017), *BEPS Action 5 on Harmful Tax Practices - Terms of Reference and Methodology for the Conduct of the Peer Reviews of the Action 5 Transparency Framework*, OECD Publishing, Paris, http://www.oecd.org/tax/beps/beps-action-5-harmful-tax-practices-peer-review-transparency-framework.pdf. [3]

OECD (2015), *Countering Harmful Tax Practices More Effectively, Taking into Account Transparency and Substance, Action 5 - 2015 Final Report*, OECD/G20 Base Erosion and Profit Shifting Project, OECD Publishing, Paris, https://dx.doi.org/10.1787/9789264241190-en. [1]

OECD/Council of Europe (2011), *The Multilateral Convention on Mutual Administrative Assistance in Tax Matters: Amended by the 2010 Protocol*, OECD Publishing, Paris, https://dx.doi.org/10.1787/9789264115606-en. [4]

Notes

1 Available at: https://idg.receita.fazenda.gov.br/acesso-rapido/legislacao

2 With respect to the following preferential regime: PADIS – Semiconductors Industry.

3 Parties to the Convention are available here: www.oecd.org/tax/exchange-of-tax-information/convention-on-mutual-administrative-assistance-in-tax-matters.htm. Brazil also has bilateral agreements with Argentina, Austria, Belgium, Canada, Chile, China (People's Republic of), Czech Republic, Denmark, Equator, Finland, France, Hungary, India, Israel, Italy, Japan, Korea, Luxembourg, Mexico, Norway, Netherlands, Peru, Portugal, Philippines, Slovak Republic, Russia, South Africa, Spain, Sweden, Trinidad and Tobago, Turkey, Ukraine and Venezuela.

Brunei Darussalam

Brunei Darussalam has met all aspects of the terms of reference (OECD, 2017[3]) (ToR) for the calendar year 2019 (year in review) that can be met in the absence of rulings being issued in practice.

Brunei Darussalam can legally issue five types of rulings within the scope of the transparency framework.

In practice, Brunei Darussalam has not issued any rulings within the scope of the transparency framework.

As no exchanges were required to take place, no peer input was received in respect of the exchanges of information on rulings received from Brunei Darussalam.

A. The information gathering process

173. Brunei Darussalam can legally issue the following five types of rulings within the scope of the transparency framework: (i) preferential regimes;[1] (ii) cross-border unilateral APAs and any other cross-border unilateral tax rulings (such as an advance tax ruling) covering transfer pricing or the application of transfer pricing principles; (iii) rulings providing for unilateral downward adjustments; (iv) permanent establishment rulings; and (v) related party conduit rulings.

174. For Brunei Darussalam, past rulings are any tax rulings within scope that are issued either: (i) on or after 1 January 2015 but before 1 April 2017; or (ii) on or after 1 January 2012 but before 1 January 2015, provided they were still in effect as at 1 January 2015. Future rulings are any tax rulings within scope that are issued on or after 1 April 2017.

175. In the prior years' peer review reports, it was determined that Brunei Darussalam's undertakings to identify past and future rulings and all potential exchange jurisdictions were sufficient to meet the minimum standard. In addition, it was determined that Brunei Darussalam's review and supervision mechanism was sufficient to meet the minimum standard. Brunei Darussalam's implementation remains unchanged, and therefore continues to meet the minimum standard.

176. Brunei Darussalam has met all of the ToR for the information gathering process and no recommendations are made.

B. The exchange of information

177. In the prior years' peer review reports, it was determined that Brunei Darussalam's process for the completion and exchange of templates were sufficient to meet the minimum standard. With respect to past rulings, no further action was required. Brunei Darussalam's implementation in this regard remains unchanged and therefore continues to meet the minimum standard.

178. Brunei Darussalam has international agreements permitting spontaneous exchange of information, including being a party to the (i) *Multilateral Convention on Mutual Administrative Assistance in Tax Matters: Amended by the 2010 Protocol* (OECD/Council of Europe, 2011[4]) ("the Convention") and (ii) bilateral agreements in force with 17 jurisdictions.[2]

179. As Brunei Darussalam did not issue any future rulings in scope of the transparency framework in the relevant period, Brunei Darussalam was not required to exchange any information on rulings in the year in review and no data on the timeliness of exchanges can be reported.

180. Brunei Darussalam has the necessary legal basis for spontaneous exchange of information. Brunei Darussalam has met all of the ToR for the exchange of information process that can be met in the absence of rulings being issued and exchanged in practice and no recommendations are made.

C. Statistics (ToR IV)

181. As no rulings were issued, no statistics can be reported.

D. Matters related to intellectual property regimes (ToR I.4.1.3)

182. Brunei Darussalam does not offer an intellectual property regime for which transparency requirements under the Action 5 Report (OECD, 2015[1]) were imposed.

Summary of recommendations on implementation of the transparency framework

Aspect of implementation of the transparency framework that should be improved	Recommendation for improvement
	No recommendations are made.

References

OECD (2017), *BEPS Action 5 on Harmful Tax Practices - Terms of Reference and Methodology for the Conduct of the Peer Reviews of the Action 5 Transparency Framework*, OECD Publishing, Paris, http://www.oecd.org/tax/beps/beps-action-5-harmful-tax-practices-peer-review-transparency-framework.pdf. [3]

OECD (2015), *Countering Harmful Tax Practices More Effectively, Taking into Account Transparency and Substance, Action 5 - 2015 Final Report*, OECD/G20 Base Erosion and Profit Shifting Project, OECD Publishing, Paris, https://dx.doi.org/10.1787/9789264241190-en. [1]

OECD/Council of Europe (2011), *The Multilateral Convention on Mutual Administrative Assistance in Tax Matters: Amended by the 2010 Protocol*, OECD Publishing, Paris, https://dx.doi.org/10.1787/9789264115606-en. [4]

Notes

[1] Investment incentive order.

[2] Parties to the Convention are available here: www.oecd.org/tax/exchange-of-tax-information/convention-on-mutual-administrative-assistance-in-tax-matters.htm. Brunei Darussalam also has bilateral agreements with Bahrain, Cambodia, China (People's Republic of), Indonesia, Japan, Kuwait, Lao People's Democratic Republic, Luxembourg, Malaysia, Oman, Pakistan, Qatar, Singapore, Korea, United Arab Emirates, United Kingdom and Viet Nam.

Cabo Verde

Cabo Verde has met all aspects of the terms of reference (OECD, 2017[3]) (ToR) for the calendar year 2019 (year in review), except for exchanging information on the tax rulings in a timely manner (ToR II.5). Cabo Verde receives one recommendation on this point for the year in review.

This is Cabo Verde's first review of implementation of the transparency framework.

Cabo Verde can legally issue one type of ruling within the scope of the transparency framework.

In practice, Cabo Verde issued no rulings within the scope of the transparency framework.

As no exchanges were required to take place, no peer input was received in respect of the exchanges of information on rulings received from Cabo Verde.

A. The information gathering process

183. Cabo Verde can legally issue the following one type of rulings within the scope of the transparency framework: permanent establishment (PE) rulings. Rulings are issued by the National Director of the Revenue Authority.

Past rulings (ToR I.4.1.1, I.4.1.2, I.4.2.1, I.4.2.2)

184. For Cabo Verde, past rulings are any tax rulings issued prior to 1 March 2019. However, there is no obligation for Cabo Verde to conduct spontaneous exchange of information on past rulings.

Future rulings (ToR I.4.1.1, I.4.1.2, I.4.2.1)

185. For Cabo Verde, future rulings are any tax rulings within scope that are issued on or after 1 March 2019.

186. The National Director's office is the office responsible for the issuance of rulings and identification of whether any rulings issued fall into scope of the transparency framework. All requests are recorded in a dedicated register. A team appointed by the National Director of the Revenue Authority conducted a manual review of all files pertaining to tax rulings to identify potential future rulings in scope. Each physical file was manually read and reviewed to determine whether it fell into scope of the transparency framework rulings categories.

187. Although Cabo Verde has not issued any future rulings, Cabo Verde has indicated that all potential exchange jurisdictions could be identified through the review carried out by the National Director's office of all available information included in the taxpayer's file and by analysing information from the annual corporate income tax return.

188. To date no rulings within the scope of the transparency framework have been issued. As such, there was no need to identify potential exchange jurisdictions.

Review and supervision (ToR I.4.3)

189. The National Director's office is always able to collect information relating to the tax rulings that are in the scope of the transparency framework and to the relevant exchange jurisdictions. Tax officers in the National Director's office review the accuracy of this information. However, Cabo Verde indicated its intention to formalise this process by developing guidance covering the information gathering process as well as the implementation of a revision and supervision mechanism for future rulings, including appropriate training for the relevant tax officers.

Conclusion on section A

190. Cabo Verde has met the ToR for the information gathering process and no recommendations are made.

Legal basis for spontaneous exchange of information (ToR II.5.1, II.5.2)

191. Cabo Verde has the necessary domestic legal basis to exchange information spontaneously. Cabo Verde notes that there are no legal or practical impediments that prevent the spontaneous exchange of information on rulings as contemplated in the Action 5 minimum standard.

192. Cabo Verde has international agreements permitting spontaneous exchange of information, including being a party to the (i) *Multilateral Convention on Mutual Administrative Assistance in Tax*

Matters: Amended by the 2010 Protocol (OECD/Council of Europe, 2011[4]) ("the Convention") *and* ii) bilateral agreements in force with two jurisdictions. Cabo Verde signed the Convention on 26 November 2019 and ratified on 6 January 2020. The Convention entered into force on 1 May 2020. Since the Convention will have effect for administrative assistance related to taxable periods beginning on or after 1 January 2020, no exchanges could occur under the Convention for the year in review.[1]

Completion and exchange of templates (ToR II.5.3, II.5.4, II.5.5, II.5.6, II.5.7)

193. Cabo Verde is still developing a process to complete the templates on relevant rulings in the agreed form, to make them available to the Competent Authority for exchange of information without undue delay, and to exchange them with relevant jurisdictions in accordance with the agreed timelines.

194. As Cabo Verde did not issue any rulings in scope of the transparency framework during the year in year in review, no exchanges were required to take place and no data on the timeliness of exchanges is reported.

Conclusion on section B

195. Cabo Verde has the necessary legal basis to undertake spontaneous exchange of information. Cabo Verde does not have a process to complete the templates on relevant rulings and to make them available to the Competent Authority for exchange of information.

196. Cabo Verde is recommended to develop a process to complete the templates on relevant rulings and to ensure that the exchanges of information on rulings occur in accordance with the form and timelines under the transparency framework going forward (ToR II.5).

C. Statistics (ToR IV)

197. As no rulings were issued, no statistics can be reported.

D. Matters related to intellectual property regimes (ToR I.4.1.3)

198. Cabo Verde does not offer an intellectual property regime for which transparency requirements under the Action 5 Report (OECD, 2015[1]) were imposed.

Summary of recommendations on implementation of the transparency framework

Aspect of implementation of the transparency framework that should be improved	Recommendation for improvement
Cabo Verde does not have a process to complete the templates on relevant rulings and to make them available to the Competent Authority for exchange of information.	Cabo Verde is recommended to develop a process to complete the templates on relevant rulings and to ensure that the exchanges of information on rulings occur in accordance with the form and timelines under the transparency framework going forward.

References

OECD (2017), *BEPS Action 5 on Harmful Tax Practices - Terms of Reference and Methodology for the Conduct of the Peer Reviews of the Action 5 Transparency Framework*, OECD Publishing, Paris, http://www.oecd.org/tax/beps/beps-action-5-harmful-tax-practices-peer-review-transparency-framework.pdf. [3]

OECD (2015), *Countering Harmful Tax Practices More Effectively, Taking into Account Transparency and Substance, Action 5 - 2015 Final Report*, OECD/G20 Base Erosion and Profit Shifting Project, OECD Publishing, Paris, https://dx.doi.org/10.1787/9789264241190-en. [1]

OECD/Council of Europe (2011), *The Multilateral Convention on Mutual Administrative Assistance in Tax Matters: Amended by the 2010 Protocol*, OECD Publishing, Paris, https://dx.doi.org/10.1787/9789264115606-en. [4]

Notes

[1] Parties to the Convention are available here: www.oecd.org/tax/exchange-of-tax-information/convention-on-mutual-administrative-assistance-in-tax-matters.htm. Cabo Verde also has bilateral agreements with Macau (China) and Portugal.

Canada

Canada has met all aspects of the terms of reference (OECD, 2017[3]) (ToR) for the calendar year 2019 (year in review) and no recommendations are made.

Canada can legally issue four types of rulings within the scope of the transparency framework.

In practice, Canada issued rulings within the scope of the transparency framework as follows:

- 12 past rulings;
- For the period 1 April 2016 - 31 December 2016: two future rulings;
- For the calendar year 2017: two future rulings,
- For the calendar year 2018: one future ruling, and
- For the year in review: one future ruling.

Peer input was received from one jurisdiction in respect of the exchanges of information on rulings received from Canada. The input was positive, noting that information was complete, in a correct format and received in a timely manner.

A. The information gathering process

199. Canada can legally issue four types of rulings within the scope of the transparency framework: (i) preferential regimes;[1] (ii) cross-border unilateral APAs and any other cross-border unilateral tax rulings (such as an advance tax ruling) covering transfer pricing or the application of transfer pricing principles; (iii) permanent establishment rulings; and (iv) related party conduit rulings.

200. For Canada, past rulings are any tax rulings within scope that are issued either: (i) on or after 1 January 2014 but before 1 April 2016; or (ii) on or after 1 January 2010 but before 1 January 2014, provided they were still in effect as at 1 January 2014. Future rulings are any tax rulings within scope that are issued on or after 1 April 2016.

201. In the prior years' peer review reports, it was determined that Canada's undertakings to identify past and future rulings and all potential exchange jurisdictions were sufficient to meet the minimum standard. In addition, it was determined that Canada's review and supervision mechanism was sufficient to meet the minimum standard. Canada's implementation remains unchanged, and therefore continues to meet the minimum standard.

202. Canada has met all of the ToR for the information gathering process and no recommendations are made.

B. The exchange of information

203. In the prior years' peer review reports, it was determined that Canada's process for the completion and exchange of templates were sufficient to meet the minimum standard. With respect to past rulings, no further action was required. Canada's implementation in this regard remains unchanged and therefore continues to meet the minimum standard.

204. Canada has international agreements permitting spontaneous exchange of information, including being a party to the (i) *Multilateral Convention on Mutual Administrative Assistance in Tax Matters: Amended by the 2010 Protocol* (OECD/Council of Europe, 2011[4]) ("the Convention") and (ii) bilateral agreements in force with 95 jurisdictions permitting spontaneous exchange of information.[2]

205. For the year in review, the timeliness of exchanges is as follows:

Future rulings in the scope of the transparency framework	Number of exchanges transmitted within three months of the information becoming available to the competent authority or immediately after legal impediments have been lifted	Delayed exchanges		
		Number of exchanges transmitted later than three months of the information on rulings becoming available to the competent authority	Reasons for the delays	Any other comments
	3	0	N/A	N/A

Follow up requests received for exchange of the ruling	Number	Average time to provide response	Number of requests not answered
	0	N/A	N/A

206. Canada has the necessary legal basis for spontaneous exchange of information, a process for completing the templates in a timely way and has completed all exchanges. Canada has met all of the ToR for the exchange of information process and no recommendations are made.

C. Statistics (ToR IV)

207. The statistics for the year in review are as follows:

Category of ruling	Number of exchanges	Jurisdictions exchanged with
Ruling related to a preferential regime	0	N/A
Cross-border unilateral advance pricing agreements (APAs) and any other cross-border unilateral tax rulings (such as an advance tax ruling) covering transfer pricing or the application of transfer pricing principles	*De minimis* rule applies	N/A
Permanent establishment rulings	0	N/A
Related party conduit rulings	0	N/A
De minimis rule	3	N/A
Total	3	

D. Matters related to intellectual property regimes (ToR I.4.1.3)

208. Canada does not offer an intellectual property regime for which transparency requirements under the Action 5 Report (OECD, 2015[1]) were imposed.

Summary of recommendations on implementation of the transparency framework

Aspect of implementation of the transparency framework that should be improved	Recommendation for improvement
	No recommendations are made.

References

OECD (2017), *BEPS Action 5 on Harmful Tax Practices - Terms of Reference and Methodology for the Conduct of the Peer Reviews of the Action 5 Transparency Framework*, OECD Publishing, Paris, http://www.oecd.org/tax/beps/beps-action-5-harmful-tax-practices-peer-review-transparency-framework.pdf. [3]

OECD (2015), *Countering Harmful Tax Practices More Effectively, Taking into Account Transparency and Substance, Action 5 - 2015 Final Report*, OECD/G20 Base Erosion and Profit Shifting Project, OECD Publishing, Paris, https://dx.doi.org/10.1787/9789264241190-en. [1]

OECD/Council of Europe (2011), *The Multilateral Convention on Mutual Administrative Assistance in Tax Matters: Amended by the 2010 Protocol*, OECD Publishing, Paris, https://dx.doi.org/10.1787/9789264115606-en. [4]

Notes

[1] With respect to the following preferential regimes: 1) Life insurance business and 2) International shipping.

[2] Parties to the Convention are available here: www.oecd.org/tax/exchange-of-tax-information/convention-on-mutual-administrative-assistance-in-tax-matters.htm. Canada also has bilateral agreements in force with Algeria, Argentina, Armenia, Australia, Austria, Azerbaijan, Bangladesh, Barbados, Belgium, Brazil, Bulgaria, Cameroon, Chile, China (People's Republic of), Colombia, Cote d'Ivoire, Croatia, Cyprus, Czech Republic, Denmark, Dominican Republic, Ecuador, Egypt, Estonia, Finland, France, Gabon, Germany, Greece, Guyana, Hong Kong (China), Hungary, Iceland, India, Indonesia, Ireland, Israel, Italy, Jamaica, Japan, Jordan, Kazakhstan, Kenya, Korea, Kuwait, Kyrgyzstan, Latvia, Lithuania, Luxembourg, Malaysia, Malta, Mexico, Moldova, Mongolia, Morocco, Netherlands, New Zealand, Nigeria, Norway, Oman, Pakistan, Papua New Guinea, Peru, Philippines, Poland, Portugal, Romania, Russia, Senegal, Serbia, Singapore, Slovak Republic, Slovenia, South Africa, Spain, Sri Lanka, Sweden, Switzerland, Chinese Taipei, Tanzania, Thailand, Trinidad & Tobago, Tunisia, Turkey, Ukraine, United Arab Emirates, United Kingdom, United States, Uzbekistan, Venezuela, Viet Nam, Zambia and Zimbabwe. The Tax Information Exchange Agreement with Aruba also permits spontaneous exchange of information.

Chile

Chile has met all aspects of the terms of reference (OECD, 2017[3]) (ToR) for the calendar year 2019 (year in review) and no recommendations are made.

Chile can legally issue two types of rulings within the scope of the transparency framework.

In practice, Chile issued rulings within the scope of the transparency framework as follows:

- In the prior years: no rulings, and
- For the year in review: two future rulings.

As the two rulings were only issued in December 2019, no exchanges were required to take place during the year in review, no peer input was received in respect of the exchanges of information on rulings received from Chile.

A. The information gathering process

209. Chile can legally issue the following two types of rulings within the scope of the transparency framework: (i) cross-border unilateral APAs and any other cross-border unilateral tax rulings (such as an advance tax ruling) covering transfer pricing or the application of transfer pricing principles and (ii) related party conduit rulings.

210. For Chile, past rulings are any tax rulings within scope that are issued either: (i) on or after 1 January 2014 but before 1 April 2016; or (ii) on or after 1 January 2010 but before 1 January 2014, provided they were still in effect as at 1 January 2014. Future rulings are any tax rulings within scope that are issued on or after 1 April 2016.

211. In the prior years' peer review reports, it was determined that Chile's undertakings to identify past and future rulings and all potential exchange jurisdictions were sufficient to meet the minimum standard, noting however that they had not yet issued rulings in scope of the standard. In addition, it was determined that Chile's review and supervision mechanism was sufficient to meet the minimum standard. During the year in review, Chile issued relevant rulings and put its process into practice for the first time, and Chile indicates it has worked well and without difficulty.

212. Chile has met all of the ToR for the information gathering process and no recommendations are made.

B. The exchange of information

213. In the prior years' peer review reports, it was determined that Chile's process for the completion and exchange of templates that would be applicable if rulings were issued in practice were sufficient to meet the minimum standard. With respect to past rulings, no further action was required from Chile. Chile's implementation in this regard remains unchanged and therefore continues to meet the minimum standard.

214. Chile has international agreements permitting spontaneous exchange of information, including being a party to the (i) *Multilateral Convention on Mutual Administrative Assistance in Tax Matters: Amended by the 2010 Protocol* (OECD/Council of Europe, 2011[4]) ("the Convention") and (ii) bilateral agreements in force with 33 jurisdictions.[1]

215. As Chile issued two future rulings in December 2019, no exchanges were required to take place during the year in review, no data on timeliness of exchanges can be reported. Chile notes that it has exchanged information on one ruling with the relevant jurisdictions by March 2020, and in respect of the other, clarification is being sought by Chile as to whether there is a legal basis to complete the exchange with the relevant jurisdiction.

216. Chile has the necessary legal basis for spontaneous exchange of information, and a process for completing the templates in a timely way. Chile has met all of the ToR in the absence of rulings being required to be exchanged for the year in review and no recommendations are made.

C. Statistics (ToR IV)

217. As there was no information on rulings exchanged by Chile for the year in review, no statistics can be reported.

D. Matters related to intellectual property regimes (ToR I.4.1.3)

218. Chile does not offer an intellectual property regime for which transparency requirements under the Action 5 Report (OECD, 2015[1]) were imposed.

Summary of recommendations on implementation of the transparency framework

Aspect of implementation of the transparency framework that should be improved	Recommendation for improvement
	No recommendations are made.

References

OECD (2017), *BEPS Action 5 on Harmful Tax Practices - Terms of Reference and Methodology for the Conduct of the Peer Reviews of the Action 5 Transparency Framework*, OECD Publishing, Paris, http://www.oecd.org/tax/beps/beps-action-5-harmful-tax-practices-peer-review-transparency-framework.pdf. [3]

OECD (2015), *Countering Harmful Tax Practices More Effectively, Taking into Account Transparency and Substance, Action 5 - 2015 Final Report*, OECD/G20 Base Erosion and Profit Shifting Project, OECD Publishing, Paris, https://dx.doi.org/10.1787/9789264241190-en. [1]

OECD/Council of Europe (2011), *The Multilateral Convention on Mutual Administrative Assistance in Tax Matters: Amended by the 2010 Protocol*, OECD Publishing, Paris, https://dx.doi.org/10.1787/9789264115606-en. [4]

Notes

[1] Parties to the Convention are available here: www.oecd.org/tax/exchange-of-tax-information/convention-on-mutual-administrative-assistance-in-tax-matters.htm. Chile also has bilateral agreements with Argentina, Australia, Austria, Belgium, Brazil, Canada, China (People's Republic of), Colombia, Croatia, Czech Republic, Denmark, Ecuador, France, Ireland, Italy, Japan, Korea, Malaysia, Mexico, Norway, New Zealand, Paraguay, Peru, Poland, Portugal, Russia, Spain, South Africa, Sweden, Switzerland, Thailand, United Kingdom and Uruguay.

China (People's Republic of)

China has met all aspects of the terms of reference (OECD, 2017[3]) (ToR) for the calendar year 2019 (year in review) and no recommendations are made.

China can legally issue one type of ruling within the scope of the transparency framework.

In practice, China issued rulings within the scope of the transparency framework as follows:

- 11 past rulings;
- For the period 1 April 2016 - 31 December 2016: six future rulings;
- For the calendar year 2017: three future rulings,
- For the calendar year 2018: two future rulings, and
- For the year in review: four future rulings.

Peer input was received from one jurisdiction in respect of the exchanges of information on rulings received from China. The input was positive, noting that information was complete, in a correct format and received in a timely manner.

A. The information gathering process

219. China can legally issue one type of ruling within the scope of the transparency framework: cross-border unilateral APAs and any other cross-border unilateral tax rulings (such as an advance tax ruling) covering transfer pricing or the application of transfer pricing principles.

220. There was previously a legal barrier to the exchange of information on rulings in China, which did not allow the exchange of past rulings. The legal framework in China was subsequently amended to allow exchanges on future rulings. Future rulings are any tax rulings within scope that are issued on or after 1 April 2016.

221. In the prior years' peer review reports, it was determined that China's undertakings to identify past and future rulings and all potential exchange jurisdictions were sufficient to meet the minimum standard. In addition, it was determined that China's review and supervision mechanism was sufficient to meet the minimum standard. China's implementation remains unchanged, and therefore continues to meet the minimum standard.

222. China has met all of the ToR for the information gathering process and no recommendations are made.

B. The exchange of information

223. In the prior years' peer review reports, it was determined that China's process for the completion and exchange of templates were sufficient to meet the minimum standard. China's implementation in this regard remains unchanged and therefore continues to meet the minimum standard.

224. China has international agreements permitting spontaneous exchange of information, including being a party to the (i) *Multilateral Convention on Mutual Administrative Assistance in Tax Matters: Amended by the 2010 Protocol* (OECD/Council of Europe, 2011[4]) ("the Convention") and (ii) bilateral agreements in force with 100 jurisdictions.[1]

225. For the year in review, the timeliness of exchanges is as follows:

Future rulings in the scope of the transparency framework	Number of exchanges transmitted within three months of the information becoming available to the competent authority or immediately after legal impediments have been lifted	Delayed exchanges		
		Number of exchanges transmitted later than three months of the information on rulings becoming available to the competent authority	Reasons for the delays	Any other comments
	4	0	N/A	N/A
Total	4	0		

Follow up requests received for exchange of the ruling	Number	Average time to provide response	Number of requests not answered
	0	N/A	N/A

226. China has the necessary legal basis for spontaneous exchange of information, a process for completing the templates in a timely way and has completed all exchanges. China has met all of the ToR for the exchange of information process and no recommendations are made.

C. Statistics (ToR IV)

227. The statistics for the year in review are as follows:

Category of ruling	Number of exchanges	Jurisdictions exchanged with
Cross-border unilateral advance pricing agreements (APAs) and any other cross-border unilateral tax rulings (such as an advance tax ruling) covering transfer pricing or the application of transfer pricing principles	*De minimis rule* applies	N/A
De minimis rule	4	N/A
Total	4	

D. Matters related to intellectual property regimes (ToR I.4.1.3)

228. In the prior years' peer review reports, it was determined that the transparency requirements were not relevant for China's intellectual property regime (Reduced rate for high & new tech enterprises).

Summary of recommendations on implementation of the transparency framework

Aspect of implementation of the transparency framework that should be improved	Recommendation for improvement
	No recommendations are made.

References

OECD (2017), *BEPS Action 5 on Harmful Tax Practices - Terms of Reference and Methodology for the Conduct of the Peer Reviews of the Action 5 Transparency Framework*, OECD Publishing, Paris, http://www.oecd.org/tax/beps/beps-action-5-harmful-tax-practices-peer-review-transparency-framework.pdf. [3]

OECD/Council of Europe (2011), *The Multilateral Convention on Mutual Administrative Assistance in Tax Matters: Amended by the 2010 Protocol*, OECD Publishing, Paris, https://dx.doi.org/10.1787/9789264115606-en. [4]

Notes

[1] Parties to the Convention are available here: www.oecd.org/tax/exchange-of-tax-information/convention-on-mutual-administrative-assistance-in-tax-matters.htm. China also has bilateral agreements in force with Albania, Algeria, Armenia, Australia, Austria, Azerbaijan, Bahrain, Bangladesh, Barbados, Belarus, Belgium, Bosnia and Herzegovina, Brazil, Brunei Darussalam, Bulgaria, Cambodia, Canada, Chile, Croatia, Cuba, Cyprus, Czech Republic, Denmark, Ecuador, Egypt, Estonia, Ethiopia, Finland, France, Georgia, Germany, Greece, Hungary, Iceland, India, Indonesia, Iran, Ireland, Israel, Italy, Jamaica, Japan, Kazakhstan, Korea, Kuwait, Kyrgyzstan, Lao People's Democratic Republic, Latvia, Lithuania, Luxembourg, Malaysia, Malta, Mauritius, Mexico, Moldova, Mongolia, Montenegro, Morocco, Nepal, Netherlands, New Zealand, Nigeria, North Macedonia, Norway, Oman, Pakistan, Papua New Guinea, Philippines, Poland, Portugal, Qatar, Romania, Russia, Saudi Arabia, Serbia, Seychelles, Singapore, Slovenia, South Africa, Spain, Sri Lanka, Sudan, Sweden, Switzerland, Syria, Tajikistan, Thailand, Trinidad and Tobago, Tunisia, Turkey, Turkmenistan, Ukraine, United Arab Emirates, United Kingdom, United States, Uzbekistan, Venezuela, Viet Nam, Zambia and Zimbabwe.

Colombia

Colombia has met all aspects of the terms of reference (OECD, 2017[3]) (ToR) for the calendar year 2019 (year in review) and no recommendations are made.

Colombia can legally issue one type of ruling within the scope of the transparency framework.

In practice, Colombia issued rulings within the scope of the transparency framework as follows:

- One past ruling;
- For the period 1 April 2016 - 31 December 2016: no future rulings;
- For the calendar year 2017: no future rulings;
- For the calendar year 2018: no future rulings, and
- For the year in review: no future rulings.

As no exchanges were required to take place, no peer input was received in respect of the exchanges of information on rulings received from Colombia.

A. The information gathering process

229. Colombia can legally issue one type of rulings within the scope of the transparency framework: cross-border unilateral advance pricing agreements (APAs) and any other cross-border unilateral tax rulings (such as an advance tax ruling) covering transfer pricing or the application of transfer pricing principles.

230. For Colombia, past rulings are any tax rulings within scope that are issued either: (i) on or after 1 January 2014 but before 1 April 2016; or (ii) on or after 1 January 2010 but before 1 January 2014, provided they were still in effect as at 1 January 2014. Future rulings are any tax rulings within scope that are issued on or after 1 April 2016.

231. In the prior years' peer review reports, it was determined that Colombia's undertakings to identify past and future rulings and all potential exchange jurisdictions were sufficient to meet the minimum standard. In addition, it was determined that Colombia's review and supervision mechanism was sufficient to meet the minimum standard. Colombia's implementation remains unchanged, and therefore continues to meet the minimum standard.

232. Colombia has met all of the ToR for the information gathering process and no recommendations are made.

B. The exchange of information

233. In the prior year' peer review report, it was determined that Colombia's process for the completion and exchange of templates was sufficient to meet the minimum standard. With respect to past rulings, no further action was required. Colombia's implementation remains unchanged and therefore continues to meet the minimum standard.

234. Colombia has international agreements permitting spontaneous exchange of information, including being a party to the (i) *Multilateral Convention on Mutual Administrative Assistance in Tax Matters: Amended by the 2010 Protocol* (OECD/Council of Europe, 2011[4]) ("the Convention"), (ii) bilateral agreements in force with 10 jurisdictions, (iii) multilateral tax agreements in force with three jurisdictions and (iv) tax information exchange agreements with one jurisdiction.[1]

235. As Colombia was not required to exchange any information on rulings for the year in review, no data on the timeliness of exchanges can be reported.

236. Colombia has the necessary legal basis for spontaneous exchange of information, a process for completing the templates in a timely way and has completed all exchanges. Colombia has met all of the ToR for the exchange of information process and no recommendations are made.

C. Statistics (ToR IV)

237. As no rulings are issued, no statistics can be reported.

D. Matters related to intellectual property regimes (ToR I.4.1.3)

238. Colombia does not offer an intellectual property regime for which transparency requirements under the Action 5 Report (OECD, 2015[1]) were imposed.

Summary of recommendations on implementation of the transparency framework

Aspect of implementation of the transparency framework that should be improved	Recommendation for improvement
	No recommendations are made.

References

OECD (2017), *BEPS Action 5 on Harmful Tax Practices - Terms of Reference and Methodology for the Conduct of the Peer Reviews of the Action 5 Transparency Framework*, OECD Publishing, Paris, http://www.oecd.org/tax/beps/beps-action-5-harmful-tax-practices-peer-review-transparency-framework.pdf. [3]

OECD (2015), *Countering Harmful Tax Practices More Effectively, Taking into Account Transparency and Substance, Action 5 - 2015 Final Report*, OECD/G20 Base Erosion and Profit Shifting Project, OECD Publishing, Paris, https://dx.doi.org/10.1787/9789264241190-en. [1]

OECD/Council of Europe (2011), *The Multilateral Convention on Mutual Administrative Assistance in Tax Matters: Amended by the 2010 Protocol*, OECD Publishing, Paris, https://dx.doi.org/10.1787/9789264115606-en. [4]

Notes

[1] Parties to the Convention are available here: www.oecd.org/tax/exchange-of-tax-information/convention-on-mutual-administrative-assistance-in-tax-matters.htm. Colombia also has bilateral agreements with Canada, Chile, Czech Republic, India, Korea, Mexico, Portugal, Spain, Switzerland and United Kingdom; multilateral tax agreements in force with Bolivia, Ecuador and Peru; and a tax information exchange agreement with the United States.

Congo

Congo did not provide a completed peer review questionnaire to the Secretariat. It is not known whether Congo has met all aspects of the terms of reference (OECD, 2017[3]) (ToR) for the calendar year 2019 (year in review). Congo receives two recommendations covering the information gathering process (ToR I.4) and exchange of information (ToR II.5) for the year in review.

In the prior year report, as well as in the 2017 peer review, Congo had received the same two recommendations. As it is not known whether they have been addressed, the recommendations remain in place.

Congo can legally issue two types of rulings within the scope of the transparency framework.

In practice, Congo did not issue any type of rulings within the scope of the transparency framework in previous years. For the year in review, it is not known whether Congo issued any type of rulings within the scope of the transparency framework.

No peer input was received in respect of the exchanges of information on rulings received from Congo.

A. The information gathering process

239. Congo can legally issue the following two types of rulings within the scope of the transparency framework: i) cross-border unilateral advance pricing agreements (APAs) and any other cross-border unilateral tax rulings (such as an advance tax ruling) covering transfer pricing or the application of transfer pricing principles and ii) permanent establishment rulings.

Past rulings (ToR I.4.1.1, I.4.1.2, I.4.2.1, I.4.2.2)

240. For Congo, past rulings are any tax rulings within scope that are issued either (i) on or after 1 January 2015 but before 1 April 2017; and (ii) on or after 1 January 2012 but before 1 January 2015, provided they were still in effect as at 1 January 2015.

241. In the prior year peer review report, it was noted that in Congo, rulings are issued by the directorate of Legislation, within the Tax Administration. This unit is responsible for storing and reviewing such rulings and has reviewed its files, being able to confirm that no past rulings have been issued. Congo indicated no past rulings in scope of the transparency framework have been issued. As such there was no need to identify potential exchange jurisdictions.

Future rulings (ToR I.4.1.1, I.4.1.2, I.4.2.1)

242. For Congo, future rulings are any tax rulings within scope that are issued on or after 1 April 2017.

243. In the prior year peer review report, Congo indicated that there were no processes in place for the record keeping of rulings for the purposes of the transparency framework. It was noted that Congo intended to implement guidelines and practices to make sure the necessary information to meet the requirements of the transparency framework is required in all cases. Congo was recommended to finalise its information gathering process as soon as possible.

244. During the year in review, as it is not known whether Congo has finalised its information gathering process, the recommendation remains in place.

Review and supervision (ToR I.4.3)

245. In the prior year peer review report, it was determined that Congo did not yet have a review and supervision mechanism under the transparency framework. Congo was in the process of considering the implementation of a revision and supervision mechanism for ensuring implementation of the transparency framework. As it is not known whether Congo has put in place a review and supervision mechanism under the transparency framework for the year in review, the recommendation remains in place.

Conclusion on section A

246. Congo is recommended to finalise its information gathering process, with a review and supervision mechanism, as soon as possible (ToR I.4).

B. The exchange of information

Legal basis for spontaneous exchange of information (ToR II.5.1, II.5.2)

247. In the prior year peer review report, Congo was currently in the process of putting in place the necessary domestic legal basis to exchange information spontaneously. It is not known whether Congo

has already put in place the necessary domestic legal basis to exchange information spontaneously for the year in review.

248. Congo is not a party of the *Multilateral Convention on Mutual Administrative Assistance in Tax Matters: Amended by the 2010 Protocol* (OECD/Council of Europe, 2011[4]) ("the Convention"). Congo has bilateral agreements in force with 3 jurisdictions.[12] Congo is encouraged to continue its efforts to expand its international exchange of information instruments to be able to exchange information on rulings. It is noted, however, that jurisdictions are assessed on their compliance with the transparency framework in respect of the exchange of information network in effect for the year of the particular annual review.

Completion and exchange of templates (ToR II.5.3, II.5.4, II.5.5, II.5.6, II.5.7)

249. In the prior year peer review report, it was noted that Congo was still developing a process to complete the templates on relevant rulings, to make them available to the Competent Authority for exchange of information, and to exchange them with relevant jurisdictions. As it is not known whether exchanges took place in the year of review, no data on the timeliness of exchanges can be reported.

Conclusion on section B

250. Congo is recommended to put in place a domestic legal framework allowing spontaneous exchange of information on rulings and to continue its efforts to complete the templates for all relevant rulings and to ensure that the exchanges of information on rulings occur as soon as possible (ToR II.5).

C. Statistics (ToR IV)

251. As the Secretariat is not aware whether information on rulings was exchanged by Congo for the year in review, no statistics can be reported.

D. Matters related to intellectual property regimes (ToR I.4.1.3)

252. Congo does not offer an intellectual property regime for which transparency requirements under the Action 5 Report (OECD, 2015[1]) were imposed.

Summary of recommendations on implementation of the transparency framework

Aspect of implementation of the transparency framework that should be improved	Recommendation for improvement
It is not known whether Congo has finalised the steps to have in place its necessary information and gathering process.	Congo is recommended to finalise its information gathering process, with a review and supervision mechanism, as soon as possible. This recommendation remains unchanged since the 2017 and 2018 peer review reports
It is not known whether Congo has finalised the steps to have effective compulsory spontaneous exchange of information on the tax rulings within the scope of the transparency framework.	Congo is recommended to continue to put in place a domestic legal framework allowing spontaneous exchange of information on rulings and to continue its efforts to complete the templates for all relevant rulings and to ensure that the exchanges of information on rulings occur as soon as possible. This recommendation remains unchanged since the 2017 and 2018 peer review reports.

References

OECD (2017), *BEPS Action 5 on Harmful Tax Practices - Terms of Reference and Methodology for the Conduct of the Peer Reviews of the Action 5 Transparency Framework*, OECD Publishing, Paris, http://www.oecd.org/tax/beps/beps-action-5-harmful-tax-practices-peer-review-transparency-framework.pdf. [3]

OECD (2015), *Countering Harmful Tax Practices More Effectively, Taking into Account Transparency and Substance, Action 5 - 2015 Final Report*, OECD/G20 Base Erosion and Profit Shifting Project, OECD Publishing, Paris, https://dx.doi.org/10.1787/9789264241190-en. [1]

OECD/Council of Europe (2011), *The Multilateral Convention on Mutual Administrative Assistance in Tax Matters: Amended by the 2010 Protocol*, OECD Publishing, Paris, https://dx.doi.org/10.1787/9789264115606-en. [4]

Notes

[1] Congo has bilateral agreements with France, Italy and Mauritius.

Costa Rica

Costa Rica has met all aspects of the terms of reference (OECD, 2017[3]) (ToR) for the calendar year 2019 (year in review), and no recommendations are made.

In the prior year report, as well as in the 2017 peer review, Costa Rica had received three recommendations. Costa Rica has resolved these issues and therefore none of the prior year recommendations remain.

Costa Rica can legally issue two types of rulings within the scope of the transparency framework.

In practice, Costa Rica issued rulings within the scope of the transparency framework as follows:

- Six past rulings;
- For the period 1 April 2017 - 31 December 2017: three future rulings;
- For the calendar year 2018: four future rulings, and
- For the year in review: no future rulings.

No peer input was received in respect of the exchanges of information on rulings received from Costa Rica.

A. The information gathering process

253. Costa Rica can legally issue the following two types of rulings within the scope of the transparency framework: (i) cross-border unilateral APAs and any other cross-border unilateral tax rulings (such as an advance tax ruling) covering transfer pricing or the application of transfer pricing principles and (ii) permanent establishment (PE) rulings. To date, Costa Rica has issued only PE rulings given the resolution that establishes the requirements related to the issuance of APAs rulings has not been published yet and no APAs can be issued until then. As such, this report assesses the implementation with respect to PE rulings.

Past rulings (ToR I.4.1.1, I.4.1.2, I.4.2.1, I.4.2.2)

254. For Costa Rica, past rulings are any tax rulings within scope that are issued either: (i) on or after 1 January 2015 but before 1 April 2017; or (ii) on or after 1 January 2012 but before 1 January 2015, provided they were still in effect as at 1 January 2015.

255. In the prior year peer review report, it was determined that Costa Rica's undertakings to identify past rulings and all potential exchange jurisdictions were sufficient to meet the minimum standard. Costa Rica's implementation in this regard remains unchanged, and therefore continues to meet the minimum standard.

Future rulings (ToR I.4.1.1, I.4.1.2, I.4.2.1)

256. For Costa Rica, future rulings are any tax rulings within scope that are issued on or after 1 April 2017.

257. In the prior year peer review report, it was determined that Costa Rica's implementation of a new system to identify future rulings and all potential exchange jurisdictions was sufficient to meet the minimum standard.

258. In the previous years, information on potential exchange jurisdictions was obtained through publicly available sources (given that usually taxpayers requiring PE rulings are PEs of companies listed on the stock exchange and subject to a regulatory framework which includes disclosing their head office details), information in possession of the local tax administrations and follow-up requests to the taxpayer. In November 2019, Costa Rica made legislative amendments to the general resolution for PE rulings (Resolution DGT-R-64-2019) to require taxpayers to provide information on all relevant exchange jurisdictions at the time of ruling application. In particular, when a new PE ruling request is submitted to the tax administration, the taxpayer is required to provide information on the jurisdiction of residence of the immediate parent company and ultimate parent company as well as a copy of the tax return of the parent company. The information gathering process has now been formalised as part of the application process for future rulings and if the taxpayer does not provide all the requested information, the ruling will not be issued. Whilst Costa Rica's actions already meet the minimum standard under the transparency framework, it is noted that Costa Rica is continuing to develop a shareholder register that will further enhance Costa Rica's information gathering abilities for the standard.

259. In addition, in November 2019, the General Director of Tax Administration issued new internal guidance for future rulings, Directive DGT-D-10-2019 called "*Procedure for handling requests related to the special calculation of taxable liquid income to companies dedicated to international transport*" (which in practice is the industry for which PE rulings are granted). This guidance aims at operationalising the internal information gathering process and establishes, among other things, a detailed procedure that tax officials must follow when issuing PE rulings, specifies the responsible tax officials for each procedure and the requisite actions to be undertaken throughout the entire PE ruling issuance process.

260. In addition, the International Taxation Directorate developed an electronic database (Share Point) to automate the information gathering process. This allows for the registration and monitoring of PE ruling requests, from the submission of the taxpayer's request until the exchange with relevant jurisdictions.

261. Costa Rica's implementation has therefore been further formalised and strengthened, and continues to meet the minimum standard.

Review and supervision (ToR I.4.3)

262. In the prior year peer review report, additional rulings were found that had not previously been identified and it was determined that Costa Rica's had met the ToR for the information gathering process, except for having in place a review and supervision mechanism to ensure that all relevant information is captured adequately. Therefore, Costa Rica was recommended to strengthen its review and supervision mechanism to ensure that the information gathering process is working effectively.

263. During the year in review, Costa Rica identified all (a total of six) past rulings not previously reported, as well three future rulings issued in 2017 and four future rulings issued in 2018 not previously identified. Furthermore, Costa Rica identified all potential exchange jurisdictions for these rulings, and completed the additional exchanges in June 2019. Costa Rica reviewed manually all past and future rulings issued by the Transfer Pricing Unit, the unit in charge of processing permanent establishment tax ruling requests, to ensure that all rulings in scope have been identified and information promptly exchanged. The Transfer Pricing Unit carried out an initial manual check of all rulings issued and two additional cross-check verifications were performed at different stages to ensure completeness of the identification of all past and future rulings in scope of the transparency framework.

264. Costa Rica issued internal guidance (Directive DGT-D-10-2019) which also establishes the responsible tax officials in charge of the review and supervision mechanism. Before issuing a PE ruling, three levels of reviews and approvals are requested from the Deputy Director of the Transfer Pricing Unit, the Director of International Taxation Directorate, and the chief of the local tax administration or the Director of the Large Business Directorate. All PE ruling requests are registered and monitored through the Share Point database. These new review and supervision mechanism procedures ensure that all relevant information is captured adequately, and therefore the recommendation is now removed.

Conclusion on section A

265. Costa Rica has met all of the ToR for the information gathering process and no recommendations are made.

B. The exchange of information

Legal basis for spontaneous exchange of information (ToR II.5.1, II.5.2)

266. Costa Rica has the necessary domestic legal basis to exchange information spontaneously. Costa Rica notes that there are no legal or practical impediments that prevent the spontaneous exchange of information on rulings as contemplated in the Action 5 minimum standard.

267. Costa Rica has international agreements permitting spontaneous exchange of information, including being a party to the (i) *Multilateral Convention on Mutual Administrative Assistance in Tax Matters: Amended by the 2010 Protocol* (OECD/Council of Europe, 2011[4]) ("the Convention"), (ii) bilateral agreements in force with three jurisdictions, and iii) tax information exchange agreements in force with two jurisdictions.[1]

Completion and exchange of templates (ToR II.5.3, II.5.4, II.5.5, II.5.6, II.5.7)

268. In the prior years' peer review reports, it was determined that Costa Rica's process for the completion and exchange of templates met all the ToR, except for ensuring that information on rulings is transmitted to the Competent Authority responsible for international exchange of information without undue delay (ToR II.5.5). Therefore, Costa Rica was recommended to continue its efforts to ensure that information on rulings is transmitted to the Competent Authority without undue delay.

269. During the year in review, Costa Rica exchanged all previously identified past and future rulings, and no new future rulings were issued in 2019. The summary section of the template was completed in line with the internal FHTP suggested guidance. It included information regarding the nature of the ruling, a summary of the activity covered by the ruling, key conclusions in respect of the system for calculating the taxable income in Costa Rica and the legal basis for the issuance of such rulings. In addition, Costa Rica issued new internal guidance on PE future rulings establishing the process and the timelines for exchanges in compliance with ToR II.5.5. This guidance establishes, among others, the timelines for rulings to be provided to the Competent Authority and exchanged by the Competent Authority with the relevant exchange jurisdictions and specifies the responsible tax officials for each procedure. According to the new procedure, once a tax ruling is issued, the Transfer Pricing Unit will, within two months from its issuance, fill in the template for the exchanges and send it to the Exchange of Information (EOI) Unit. The EOI Unit will send an official note to the Competent Authority for its approval. Once the Competent Authority signed off the official note, the EOI Unit will send the template and the official note to the relevant jurisdictions within the three months' timeline. In practice, for all past and future rulings identified, the EOI Unit exchanged information on average within few days of their receipt. As such, the recommendation is now removed.

270. For the year in review, the timeliness of exchanges is as follows:

Past rulings in the scope of the transparency framework	Number of exchanges transmitted by 31 December 2019	Delayed exchanges		
		Number of exchanges not transmitted by 31 December 2019	Reasons for the delays	Any other comments
	6	0	N/A	N/A
Future rulings in the scope of the transparency framework	Number of exchanges transmitted within three months of the information becoming available to the competent authority or immediately after legal impediments have been lifted	Delayed exchanges		
		Number of exchanges transmitted later than three months of the information on rulings becoming available to the competent authority	N/A	N/A
	7	0	N/A	N/A
Total	13	0		

Follow up requests received for exchange of the ruling	Number	Average time to provide response	Number of requests not answered
	0	N/A	N/A

Conclusion on section B

271. Costa Rica has the necessary legal basis for spontaneous exchange of information, a process for completing the templates in a timely way and has completed all exchanges. Costa Rica has met all of the ToR for the exchange of information process and no recommendations are made.

C. Statistics (ToR IV)

272. The statistics for the year in review are as follows:

Category of ruling	Number of exchanges	Jurisdictions exchanged with
Cross-border unilateral advance pricing agreements (APAs) and any other cross-border unilateral tax rulings (such as an advance tax ruling) covering transfer pricing or the application of transfer pricing principles	N/A	N/A
Permanent establishment rulings	13	China (People's Republic of), Colombia, France, Germany, Panama, Peru, Singapore, United States
Total	13	

D. Matters related to intellectual property regimes (ToR I.4.1.3)

273. Costa Rica does not offer an intellectual property regime for which transparency requirements under the Action 5 Report (OECD, 2015[1]) were imposed.

Summary of recommendations on implementation of the transparency framework

Aspect of implementation of the transparency framework that should be improved	Recommendation for improvement
	No recommendations are made.

References

OECD (2017), *BEPS Action 5 on Harmful Tax Practices - Terms of Reference and Methodology for the Conduct of the Peer Reviews of the Action 5 Transparency Framework*, OECD Publishing, Paris, http://www.oecd.org/tax/beps/beps-action-5-harmful-tax-practices-peer-review-transparency-framework.pdf. [3]

OECD (2015), *Countering Harmful Tax Practices More Effectively, Taking into Account Transparency and Substance, Action 5 - 2015 Final Report*, OECD/G20 Base Erosion and Profit Shifting Project, OECD Publishing, Paris, https://dx.doi.org/10.1787/9789264241190-en. [1]

OECD/Council of Europe (2011), *The Multilateral Convention on Mutual Administrative Assistance in Tax Matters: Amended by the 2010 Protocol*, OECD Publishing, Paris, https://dx.doi.org/10.1787/9789264115606-en. [4]

Notes

[1] Parties to the Convention are available here: www.oecd.org/tax/exchange-of-tax-information/convention-on-mutual-administrative-assistance-in-tax-matters.htm. Costa Rica also has double tax agreements with Germany, Mexico, and Spain and tax information exchange agreements with Argentina and the United States.

Croatia

Croatia has met all aspects of the terms of reference (OECD, 2017[3]) (ToR) for the calendar year 2019 (year in review) and no recommendations are made.

Croatia can legally issue four types of rulings within the scope of the transparency framework.

In practice, Croatia issued rulings within the scope of the transparency framework as follows:

- No past rulings;
- For the period 1 April 2017 - 31 December 2017: no future rulings;
- For the calendar year 2018: one future ruling, and
- For the year in review: no future rulings.

No peer input was received in respect of the exchanges of information on rulings received from Croatia.

A. The information gathering process

274. Croatia can legally issue the following four types of rulings within the scope of the transparency framework: (i) cross-border unilateral APAs and any other cross-border unilateral tax rulings (such as an advance tax ruling) covering transfer pricing or the application of transfer pricing principles; (ii) rulings providing for unilateral downward adjustments; (iii) permanent establishment rulings; and (iv) related party conduit rulings.

275. For Croatia, past rulings are any tax rulings within scope that are issued either: (i) on or after 1 January 2015 but before 1 April 2017; or (ii) on or after 1 January 2012 but before 1 January 2015, provided they were still in effect as at 1 January 2014. Future rulings are any tax rulings within scope that are issued on or after 1 April 2017.

276. In the prior years' peer review reports, it was determined that Croatia's undertakings to identify past and future rulings and all potential exchange jurisdictions were sufficient to meet the minimum standard. In addition, it was determined that Croatia's review and supervision mechanism was sufficient to meet the minimum standard. Croatia's implementation remains unchanged, and therefore continues to meet the minimum standard.

277. Croatia has met all of the ToR for the information gathering process and no recommendations are made.

B. The exchange of information

278. In the prior years' peer review reports, it was determined that Croatia's process for the completion and exchange of templates were sufficient to meet the minimum standard. With respect to past rulings, no further action was required. Croatia's implementation in this regard remains unchanged and therefore continues to meet the minimum standard.

279. Croatia has international agreements permitting spontaneous exchange of information, including being a party to the (i) *Multilateral Convention on Mutual Administrative Assistance in Tax Matters: Amended by the 2010 Protocol* (OECD/Council of Europe, 2011[4]) ("the Convention"), (ii) the Directive 2011/16/EU with all other European Union Member States and (iii) bilateral agreements in force with 66 jurisdictions.[1]

280. For the year in review, the timeliness of exchanges is as follows:

Future rulings in the scope of the transparency framework	Number of exchanges transmitted within three months of the information becoming available to the competent authority or immediately after legal impediments have been lifted	Delayed exchanges		
		Number of exchanges transmitted later than three months of the information on rulings becoming available to the competent authority	Reasons for the delays	Any other comments
	0	1	Application of the EU DAC3 timelines.	Relating to a ruling issued in 2018 that was exchanged in April 2019.

Follow up requests received for exchange of the ruling	Number	Average time to provide response	Number of requests not answered
	0	N/A	N/A

281. Croatia has the necessary legal basis for spontaneous exchange of information, a process for completing the templates in a timely way and has completed all exchanges. Croatia has met all of the ToR for the exchange of information process and no recommendations are made.

C. Statistics (ToR IV)

282. The statistics for the year in review are as follows:

Category of ruling	Number of exchanges	Jurisdictions exchanged with
Cross-border unilateral advance pricing agreements (APAs) and any other cross-border unilateral tax rulings (such as an advance tax ruling) covering transfer pricing or the application of transfer pricing principles	*De minimis* rule applies	N/A
Cross-border rulings giving a unilateral downward adjustment to the taxpayer's taxable profits in the country giving the ruling	0	N/A
Permanent establishment rulings	0	N/A
Related party conduit rulings	0	N/A
De minimis rule	1	N/A
Total	1	

D. Matters related to intellectual property regimes (ToR I.4.1.3)

283. Croatia does not offer an intellectual property regime for which transparency requirements under the Action 5 Report (OECD, 2015[1]) were imposed.

Summary of recommendations on implementation of the transparency framework

Aspect of implementation of the transparency framework that should be improved	Recommendation for improvement
	No recommendations are made.

References

OECD (2017), *BEPS Action 5 on Harmful Tax Practices - Terms of Reference and Methodology for the Conduct of the Peer Reviews of the Action 5 Transparency Framework*, OECD Publishing, Paris, http://www.oecd.org/tax/beps/beps-action-5-harmful-tax-practices-peer-review-transparency-framework.pdf. [3]

OECD (2015), *Countering Harmful Tax Practices More Effectively, Taking into Account Transparency and Substance, Action 5 - 2015 Final Report*, OECD/G20 Base Erosion and Profit Shifting Project, OECD Publishing, Paris, https://dx.doi.org/10.1787/9789264241190-en. [1]

OECD/Council of Europe (2011), *The Multilateral Convention on Mutual Administrative Assistance in Tax Matters: Amended by the 2010 Protocol*, OECD Publishing, Paris, https://dx.doi.org/10.1787/9789264115606-en. [4]

Notes

[1] Parties to the Convention are available here: www.oecd.org/tax/exchange-of-tax-information/convention-on-mutual-administrative-assistance-in-tax-matters.htm. Croatia also has bilateral agreements with Albania, Armenia, Austria, Azerbaijan, Belarus, Belgium, Bosnia and Herzegovina, Bulgaria, Canada, Chile, China (People's Republic of), Czech Republic, Denmark, Estonia, Finland, France, Georgia, Germany, Greece, Hungary, Iceland, India, Indonesia, Iran, Ireland, Israel, Italy, Japan, Jordan, Kazakhstan, Korea, Kosovo, Kuwait, Latvia, Lithuania, Luxembourg, Malaysia, Malta, Mauritius, Morocco, Moldova, Montenegro, Netherlands, North Macedonia, Norway, Oman, Poland, Portugal, Qatar, Romania, Russia, San Marino, Serbia, Slovak Republic, Slovenia, South Africa, Spain, Syrian Arab Republic, Sweden, Switzerland, Turkey, Turkmenistan, Ukraine, United Arab Emirates, United Kingdom and Viet Nam.

Curaçao

Curaçao has met all aspects of the terms of reference (OECD, 2017[3]) (ToR) for the calendar year 2019 (year in review) except for identifying tax rulings that are in the scope of the transparency framework and which category of rulings they fall under (ToR I.4.1.2) and completing exchanges of information on rulings in accordance with the timelines (ToR II.5.5 and II.5.6). Curaçao receives two recommendations on these points for the year in review.

In the prior year report, as well as in the 2017 peer review, Curaçao received the same two recommendations. As they have not been addressed, the recommendations remain in place.

Curaçao can legally issue five types of rulings within the scope of the transparency framework.

In practice, Curaçao issued rulings that are potentially within the scope of the transparency framework as follows:

- 3,621 past rulings;
- For the period 1 April 2017 - 31 December 2017: 320 future rulings;
- For the calendar year 2018: 48 future rulings, and
- For the year in review: 40 future rulings.[1]

Peer input was received from three jurisdictions in respect of the exchanges of information on rulings received from Curaçao. The input was generally positive, noting that information was complete and in a correct format. However, one peer noted that information was not received in a timely manner, which is explained in the report.

A. The information gathering process

284. Curaçao can legally issue the following five types of rulings within the scope of the transparency framework: (i) preferential regimes;[2] (ii) cross-border unilateral APAs and any other cross-border unilateral tax rulings (such as an advance tax ruling) covering transfer pricing or the application of transfer pricing principles; (iii) rulings providing for unilateral downward adjustments; (iv) permanent establishment rulings; and (v) related party conduit rulings.

Past rulings (ToR I.4.1.1, I.4.1.2, I.4.2.1, I.4.2.2)

285. For Curaçao, past rulings are any tax rulings within scope that are issued either (i) on or after 1 January 2015 but before 1 April 2017; and (ii) on or after 1 January 2012 but before 1 January 2015, provided they were still in effect as at 1 January 2015.

286. In the prior years' peer review reports, it was determined that Curaçao's undertakings to identify past rulings and all potential exchange jurisdictions have met all the ToR, except for completing the process of reviewing the templates to confirm that all past rulings identified are cross-border rulings and therefore within the scope of the transparency framework, and to identify which category of rulings they fall under (ToR I.4.1.2). Therefore, Curaçao was recommended to continue its work to complete its information gathering process on past rulings as soon as possible.

287. During the year in review, Curaçao continued its work to accurately identify and categorise past rulings. This process is still ongoing given the large number of rulings, many of which fall into more than one category. As Curaçao completes the identification and categorisation process, they are also identifying the potential exchange jurisdictions. Curaçao anticipates that this process will be completed by the end of March 2021. Therefore, the prior year recommendation remains.

Future rulings (ToR I.4.1.1, I.4.1.2, I.4.2.1)

288. For Curaçao, future rulings are any tax rulings within scope that are issued on or after 1 April 2017.

289. In the prior years' peer review reports, it was determined that Curaçao's undertakings to identify future rulings and all potential exchange jurisdictions have met all the ToR, except for completing the process of reviewing the templates to confirm that all future rulings identified are cross border rulings and therefore within the scope of the transparency framework, and to identify which category each ruling falls into (ToR I.4.1.2). Therefore, Curaçao was recommended to continue its work to complete its information-gathering process on future rulings as soon as possible.

290. During the year in review, Curaçao continued its work on reviewing future rulings in order to identify all rulings in scope and assess the definitive number of rulings per category. As Curaçao completes the identification and categorisation process, they are also identifying the potential exchange jurisdictions. This process is still ongoing with respect to future rulings issued before July 2018, when a new procedure requiring future rulings and potential exchange jurisdictions to be immediately identified at the point of issue was put in place. This process will be completed by the end of March 2021. Therefore, the prior year recommendation remains.

291. Curaçao is also working on the development of an electronic online system to digitalise the ruling request process. This new electronic procedure is intended to further increase the speed and accuracy of the information gathering process and the exchanges performed and will be reviewed in the subsequent peer reviews as soon as the online system is in operation. Curaçao noted that this electronic system is expected to be in place in 2022.

Review and supervision (ToR I.4.3)

292. In the prior years' peer review reports, it was determined that Curaçao's review and supervision mechanism was sufficient to meet the minimum standard. Curaçao's implementation in this regard remains unchanged, and therefore continues to meet the minimum standard.

Conclusion on section A

293. Curaçao has met all of the ToR for the information gathering process except for identifying tax rulings that are in the scope of the transparency framework and which category of rulings they fall under (ToR I.4.1.2). Curaçao is recommended to finalise its information gathering process for identifying all past and future rulings in scope of the transparency framework as soon as possible.

B. The exchange of information

Legal basis for spontaneous exchange of information (ToR II.5.1, II.5.2)

294. Curaçao has the necessary domestic legal basis to exchange information spontaneously. Curaçao notes that there are no legal or practical impediments that prevent the spontaneous exchange of information on rulings as contemplated in the Action 5 minimum standard.

295. Curaçao has international agreements permitting spontaneous exchange of information, including being a party to the (i) *Multilateral Convention on Mutual Administrative Assistance in Tax Matters: Amended by the 2010 Protocol* (OECD/Council of Europe, 2011[4]) ("the Convention"), and (ii) bilateral agreements in force with two jurisdictions.[3]

Completion and exchange of templates (ToR II.5.3, II.5.4, II.5.5, II.5.6, II.5.7)

296. In the prior years' peer review reports, it was determined that Curaçao's process for the completion and exchange of templates met all the ToR, except for the timely exchange of information on past and future rulings (ToR II.5.5 and II.5.6). Therefore, Curaçao was recommended to continue its work to continue its efforts to ensure all information on past and future rulings is exchanged as soon as possible.

297. During the year in review, Curaçao continued its work on exchanging information on past and future rulings as soon as they were identified. The summary section of the template was completed by providing a summary of the content of the ruling and of the applicable tax regime, in line with the internal FHTP suggested guidance. Curaçao was able to complete a further 207 exchanges in 2019, but still needs to identify which of the approximately 3 500 rulings issued from previous years, meet the conditions to be exchanged. This process is expected to be completed by the end of March 2021. Therefore, the prior year recommendation remains.

298. For the year in review, the timeliness of exchanges is as follows:

Past rulings in the scope of the transparency framework	Number of exchanges transmitted by 31 December 2019	Delayed exchanges		
		Number of exchanges not transmitted by 31 December 2019	Reasons for the delays	Any other comments
	73	See preceding paragraph	Curaçao has a large number of rulings. Curaçao is currently identifying the rulings to be able to exchange information on all	N/A

			the cross border rulings.	
Future rulings in the scope of the transparency framework	Number of exchanges transmitted within three months of the information becoming available to the competent authority or immediately after legal impediments have been lifted	Delayed exchanges		
		Number of exchanges transmitted later than three months of the information on rulings becoming available to the competent authority	Reasons for the delays	Any other comments
	134	See preceding paragraph	Curaçao is currently identifying the rulings to be able to exchange information on all the cross border rulings.	N/A
Total	207	See preceding paragraph		

Follow up requests received for exchange of the ruling	Number	Average time to provide response	Number of requests not answered
	0	N/A	N/A

299. During the year in review, 73 exchanges were performed with regard to 58 past rulings and 134 exchanges were performed with regard to 94 future rulings issued respectively in the year 2017 (18), 2018 (36) and 2019 (40). Nearly all exchanges were completed after the three-month timeframe required from when the information became available to the Competent Authority.

Conclusion on section B

300. Curaçao has met all of the ToR for the information gathering process except for completing exchanges of information on rulings in accordance with the timelines (ToR II.5.5 and II.5.6) and Curaçao is recommended to continue its efforts to ensure that all information on past and future rulings is exchanged as soon as possible.

C. Statistics (ToR IV)

301. The statistics for the year in review are as follows:[4]

Category of ruling	Number of exchanges	Jurisdictions exchanged with
Ruling related to a preferential regime	197	Argentina, Aruba, Barbados, Belize, Brazil, Canada, Chile, China (People's Republic of), Colombia, Cyprus, Czech Republic, Finland, France, Hungary, Ireland, Israel, Jersey, Liechtenstein, Luxembourg, Malta, Netherlands, New Zealand, Panama, Poland, Romania, Russia, Saudi Arabia, Slovak Republic, South Africa, Spain, Sweden, Switzerland, Turkey, United Kingdom, United States
Cross-border unilateral advance pricing agreements (APAs) and any other cross-border unilateral tax rulings (such as an advance tax ruling) covering transfer pricing or the application of	*De minimis rule* applies	N/A

transfer pricing principles		
Cross-border rulings providing for a unilateral downward adjustment to the taxpayer's taxable profits that is not directly reflected in the taxpayer's financial / commercial accounts	*De minimis rule* applies	N/A
Permanent establishment rulings	0	N/A
Related party conduit rulings	8	Aruba, Netherlands, Saint Kitts and Nevis, Switzerland, United Kingdom
De minimis rule	2	
IP regimes: total exchanges on taxpayers benefitting from the third category of IP assets, new entrants benefitting from grandfathered IP regimes; and taxpayers making use of the option to treat the nexus ratio as a rebuttable presumption	0	N/A
Total	207	

D. Matters related to intellectual property regimes (ToR I.4.1.3)

302. Curaçao offered an intellectual property regime (IP regime)[5] that was abolished from 30 June 2018 and not subject to the transparency requirements under the Action 5 Report (OECD, 2015[1]), because:

- ***New entrants benefitting from the grandfathered IP regime:*** the IP regimes has been abolished without grandfathering for taxpayers entering after the relevant date from which enhanced transparency obligations apply. As such, no enhanced transparency requirements apply.
- ***Third category of IP assets***: not applicable as the IP regime has been abolished.
- ***Taxpayers making use of the option to treat the nexus ratio as a rebuttable presumption***: not applicable as the IP regime has been abolished.

303. In addition, Curaçao offered two IP regimes[6] that are subject to the transparency requirements under the Action 5 Report (OECD, 2015[1]). It states that the identification of the benefitting taxpayers will occur as follows:

- ***New entrants benefitting from the grandfathered IP regime***: no enhanced transparency requirements apply, because: 1) the Curaçao investment company regime has been amended as of 1 July 2018 without grandfathering for taxpayers after the relevant date from which enhanced transparency obligations apply and 2) the Innovation box is a new IP regime rather than a grandfathered regime.
- ***Third category of IP assets***: the regimes allow the third category of IP assets to qualify for the benefits. Therefore, enhanced transparency requirements apply. In order for a taxpayer to benefit from the IP regime, a specific ruling is required. When requesting the ruling, the taxpayer has to explicitly mention the type of IP assets. As such, the identification of taxpayers benefitting from the third category of IP assets occurs, when they apply for the IP regime and the process for identifying and exchanging information is as described above for future rulings. For the year in review, no taxpayers have applied to benefit from the third category of IP assets under both regimes, and therefore no information on these taxpayers needed to be exchanged.
- ***Taxpayers making use of the option to treat the nexus ratio as a rebuttable presumption***: not applicable as the regimes do not allow the nexus ratio to be treated as a rebuttable presumption.

Summary of recommendations on implementation of the transparency framework

Aspect of implementation of the transparency framework that should be improved	Recommendation for improvement
The information gathering process is still underway in Curaçao with respect to past and future rulings in scope of the transparency framework and the classification of these rulings under each category.	Curaçao is recommended to finalise its information gathering process for identifying all past and future rulings in scope of the transparency framework as soon as possible. This recommendation remains unchanged since the 2017 and 2018 peer review reports.
Curaçao experienced delays in exchanging information on past and future rulings.	Curaçao is recommended to continue its efforts to ensure that all information on past and future rulings is exchanged as soon as possible. This recommendation remains unchanged since the 2017 and 2018 peer review reports.

References

OECD (2017), *BEPS Action 5 on Harmful Tax Practices - Terms of Reference and Methodology for the Conduct of the Peer Reviews of the Action 5 Transparency Framework*, OECD Publishing, Paris, http://www.oecd.org/tax/beps/beps-action-5-harmful-tax-practices-peer-review-transparency-framework.pdf. [3]

OECD (2015), *Countering Harmful Tax Practices More Effectively, Taking into Account Transparency and Substance, Action 5 - 2015 Final Report*, OECD/G20 Base Erosion and Profit Shifting Project, OECD Publishing, Paris, https://dx.doi.org/10.1787/9789264241190-en. [1]

OECD/Council of Europe (2011), *The Multilateral Convention on Mutual Administrative Assistance in Tax Matters: Amended by the 2010 Protocol*, OECD Publishing, Paris, https://dx.doi.org/10.1787/9789264115606-en. [4]

Notes

[1] In addition to the rulings in the scope of the transparency framework Curaçao identified 11 past and future rulings relating to "other types of rulings". These "other types of rulings" related to: (i) rulings issued to determine taxpayers' tax residence; (ii) rulings to confirm the application of tax treaty provisions; and (iii) rulings to confirm the application of the profit tax ordinance legislation. Although these rulings are not within the scope of the transparency framework and no exchange was required under the terms of reference of the peer review, Curaçao exchanged these rulings with the relevant IF members using the transparency framework. These rulings were previously categorised under a different category, which accounts for the variation in the report on the number of rulings issued as compared to last year.

[2] With respect to the following preferential regimes: 1) Export facility; 2) Tax exempt entity; 3) Free zone; and 4) Offshore regime. The offshore regime has been abolished in 2001 and is grandfathered for fiscal years preceding 30 June 2019.

[3] Parties to the Convention are available here: www.oecd.org/tax/exchange-of-tax-information/convention-on-mutual-administrative-assistance-in-tax-matters.htm. Curaçao also has bilateral agreements with Netherlands and Norway.

[4] Curaçao issues dual category which have as main element a preferential regime but can also contain one of the other four categories mentioned above. In terms of counting, these dual category ruling have been included into the "preferential regime" category. Only when a ruling relates exclusively to one of the categories mentioned above, it is counted in that category.

[5] This regime is the Export facility.

[6] These regimes are: 1) Curaçao investment company (formerly Tax exempt entity) and 2) Innovation box.

Czech Republic

The Czech Republic has met all aspects of the terms of reference (OECD, 2017[3]) (ToR) for the calendar year 2019 (year in review), and no recommendations are made.

In the prior year report, as well as in the 2016 and 2017 peer reviews, the Czech Republic had received one recommendation. The Czech Republic has resolved this issue and therefore the prior years' recommendation is now removed.

The Czech Republic can legally issue two types of rulings within the scope of the transparency framework.

In practice, the Czech Republic issued rulings within the scope of the transparency framework as follows:

- 48 past rulings;
- For the period 1 April 2016 - 31 December 2016: five future rulings;
- For the calendar year 2017: 11 future rulings,
- For the calendar year 2018: seven future rulings, and
- For the year in review: 19 future rulings.

Peer input was received from one jurisdiction in respect of the exchanges of information on rulings received from the Czech Republic. The input was generally positive, noting that information was complete, in a correct format and received in a timely manner.

A. The information gathering process

304. The Czech Republic can legally issue the following two types of rulings within the scope of the transparency framework: (i) cross-border unilateral APAs and any other cross-border unilateral tax rulings (such as an advance tax ruling) covering transfer pricing or the application of transfer pricing principles and (ii) permanent establishment rulings

305. For the Czech Republic, past rulings are any tax rulings within scope that are issued either: (i) on or after 1 January 2014 but before 1 April 2016; or (ii) on or after 1 January 2010 but before 1 January 2014, provided they were still in effect as at 1 January 2014. Future rulings are any tax rulings within scope that are issued on or after 1 April 2016.

306. In the prior years' peer review reports, it was determined that the Czech Republic's undertakings to identify past and future rulings and all potential exchange jurisdictions were sufficient to meet the minimum standard. In addition, it was determined that the Czech Republic's review and supervision mechanism was sufficient to meet the minimum standard. The Czech Republic's implementation remains unchanged, and therefore continues to meet the minimum standard.

307. The Czech Republic has met all of the ToR for the information gathering process and no recommendations are made.

B. The exchange of information

Legal basis for spontaneous exchange of information (ToR II.5.1, II.5.2)

308. The Czech Republic has the necessary domestic legal basis to exchange information spontaneously. The Czech Republic notes that there are no legal or practical impediments that prevent the spontaneous exchange of information on rulings as contemplated in the Action 5 minimum standard.

309. The Czech Republic has international agreements permitting spontaneous exchange of information, including being a party to the (i) *Multilateral Convention on Mutual Administrative Assistance in Tax Matters: Amended by the 2010 Protocol* (OECD/Council of Europe, 2011[4]) ("the Convention"), (ii) the Directive 2011/16/EU with all other European Union Member States and (iii) bilateral agreements in force with 89 jurisdictions.[1]

Completion and exchange of templates (ToR II.5.3, II.5.4, II.5.5, II.5.6, II.5.7)

310. In the prior years' peer review reports, it was determined that the Czech Republic's process for the completion and exchange of templates met all the ToR, except for ensuring that information to be exchanged is transmitted to the relevant jurisdictions in accordance with the agreed timelines (ToR II.5.6). With respect to past rulings, no further action was required. The Czech Republic applies the timelines set out in the EU Directive 2011/16/EU, i.e. the exchanges of information on future rulings are carried out within three months after the end of the calendar half-year in which these rulings were issued, regardless of whether the exchange is transmitted to EU Member States or other jurisdictions. As such, the Czech Republic experienced delays in the exchange of information on future rulings due to the application of the EU timelines. Therefore, the Czech Republic was recommended to ensure that all information on future rulings is exchanged as soon as possible.

311. Although no changes were made to the legislative framework for exchanges on tax rulings, the Czech Republic undertook its best efforts to meet the FHTP timelines (and to therefore exchange faster than the domestic legislation and EU Directive would require). Exchanges performed in 2019 were performed within the requested timelines. For the sake of completeness, on average, the 19 rulings issued

in 2019 were made available to the Competent Authority within 32 days from the date of their issuance (with 66 days as the longest period spent between the date of issuance and the date of submission to the Competent Authority) and were exchanged with relevant exchange jurisdictions within 72 days. Only in two circumstances, exchanges were performed after about four months after the tax ruling became available to the competent authority. However, this relates to exchanges performed in 2020 with regard to two rulings issued respectively in August and December 2019, and therefore this will be assessed in the next year's peer review.

312. For the year in review, the timeliness of exchanges is as follows:

Future rulings in the scope of the transparency framework	Number of exchanges transmitted within three months of the information becoming available to the competent authority or immediately after legal impediments have been lifted	Delayed exchanges		
		Number of exchanges transmitted later than three months of the information on rulings becoming available to the competent authority	Reasons for the delays	Any other comments
	58	0	N/A	N/A

Follow up requests received for exchange of the ruling	Number	Average time to provide response	Number of requests not answered
	2	1 to 3 months	0

Conclusion on section B

313. The Czech Republic has the necessary legal basis for spontaneous exchange of information and a process for completing the templates in a timely way. Despite the fact that the Czech Republic's exchange on tax rulings regulatory framework is based on EU timelines, during the year in review the Czech Republic has enhanced its internal procedures to expedite the exchange of information on tax rulings in practice, in a timely manner that is consistent with the FHTP transparency framework standard. Therefore, the previous years' recommendation is now removed.

C. Statistics (ToR IV)

314. The statistics for the year in review are as follows:

Category of ruling	Number of exchanges	Jurisdictions exchanged with
Cross-border unilateral advance pricing agreements (APAs) and any other cross-border unilateral tax rulings (such as an advance tax ruling) covering transfer pricing or the application of transfer pricing principles	56	Austria, Bulgaria, Croatia, Denmark, Finland, France, Germany, Greece, Hungary, Italy, Korea, Netherlands, Norway, Poland, Romania, Russia, Slovak Republic, Slovenia, Spain, Sweden, Switzerland, United Kingdom, Viet Nam
Permanent establishment rulings	*De minimis rule* applies	N/A
De minimis rule	2	
Total	58	

D. Matters related to intellectual property regimes (ToR I.4.1.3)

315. Czech Republic does not offer an intellectual property regime for which transparency requirements under the Action 5 Report (OECD, 2015[1]) were imposed.

Summary of recommendations on implementation of the transparency framework

Aspect of implementation of the transparency framework that should be improved	Recommendation for improvement
	No recommendations are made.

References

OECD (2017), *BEPS Action 5 on Harmful Tax Practices - Terms of Reference and Methodology for the Conduct of the Peer Reviews of the Action 5 Transparency Framework*, OECD Publishing, Paris, http://www.oecd.org/tax/beps/beps-action-5-harmful-tax-practices-peer-review-transparency-framework.pdf. [3]

OECD (2015), *Countering Harmful Tax Practices More Effectively, Taking into Account Transparency and Substance, Action 5 - 2015 Final Report*, OECD/G20 Base Erosion and Profit Shifting Project, OECD Publishing, Paris, https://dx.doi.org/10.1787/9789264241190-en. [1]

OECD/Council of Europe (2011), *The Multilateral Convention on Mutual Administrative Assistance in Tax Matters: Amended by the 2010 Protocol*, OECD Publishing, Paris, https://dx.doi.org/10.1787/9789264115606-en. [4]

Notes

[1] Parties to the Convention are available here: www.oecd.org/tax/exchange-of-tax-information/convention-on-mutual-administrative-assistance-in-tax-matters.htm. The Czech Republic also has bilateral agreements with Albania, Azerbaijan, Armenia, Australia, Austria, Bahrain, Barbados, Belarus, Belgium, Bosnia and Herzegovina, Brazil, Bulgaria, Canada, Chile, China (People's Republic of), Colombia, Croatia, Cyprus, Democratic People's Republic of Korea, Denmark, Egypt, Estonia, Ethiopia, Finland, France, Georgia, Germany, Greece, Hong Kong (China), Hungary, Iceland, India, Indonesia, Iran, Ireland, Israel, Italy, Japan, Jordan, Kazakhstan, Korea, Kuwait, Latvia, Lebanon, Liechtenstein, Lithuania, Luxembourg, Malaysia, Malta, Mexico, Moldovia, Mongolia, Montenegro, Morocco, Netherlands, New Zealand, Nigeria, North Macedonia, Norway, Pakistan, Panama, Philippines, Poland, Portugal, Romania, Russia, Saudi Arabia, Serbia, Singapore, Slovak Republic, Slovenia, South Africa, Spain, Sri Lanka, Sweden, Switzerland, Syria, Tajikistan, Thailand, Tunisia, Turkey, Turkmenistan, Ukraine, United Arab Emirates, United Kingdom, United States, Uzbekistan, Venezuela and Viet Nam.

Denmark

Denmark has met all aspects of the terms of reference (OECD, 2017[3]) (ToR) for the calendar year 2019 (year in review) and no recommendations are made.

Denmark can legally issue five types of rulings within the scope of the transparency framework.

In practice, Denmark issued rulings within the scope of the transparency framework as follows:

- 43 past rulings;
- For the period 1 April 2016 - 31 December 2016: seven future rulings;
- For the calendar year 2017: 17 future rulings;
- For the calendar year 2018: 13 future rulings; and
- For the year in review: 14 future rulings.

These rulings are published in anonymised form on the tax administration's website when they are deemed of general public interest.[1]

No peer input was received in respect of the exchanges of information on rulings received from Denmark.

A. The information gathering process

316. Denmark can legally issue the following five types of rulings within the scope of the transparency framework: (i) preferential regimes;[2] (ii) cross border unilateral APAs and any other cross-border unilateral tax rulings (such as an advance tax ruling) covering transfer pricing or the application of transfer pricing principles; (iii) rulings providing for unilateral downward adjustments; (iv) permanent establishment rulings; and (v) related party conduit rulings.

317. For Denmark, past rulings are any tax rulings within scope that are issued either: (i) on or after 1 January 2014 but before 1 April 2016; or (ii) on or after 1 January 2010 but before 1 January 2014, provided they were still in effect as at 1 January 2014. Future rulings are any tax rulings within scope that are issued on or after 1 April 2016.

318. In the prior years' peer review reports, it was determined that Denmark's undertakings to identify past and future rulings and all potential exchange jurisdictions were sufficient to meet the minimum standard. In addition, it was determined that Denmark's review and supervision mechanism was sufficient to meet the minimum standard. Denmark's implementation remains unchanged, and therefore continues to meet the minimum standard.

319. Denmark has met all of the ToR for the information gathering process and no recommendations are made.

B. The exchange of information

320. In the prior years' peer review reports, it was determined that Denmark's process for the completion and exchange of templates were sufficient to meet the minimum standard. With respect to past rulings, no further action was required from Denmark. Denmark's implementation in this regard remains unchanged and therefore continues to meet the minimum standard.

321. Denmark has international agreements permitting spontaneous exchange of information, including being a party to the (i) *Multilateral Convention on Mutual Administrative Assistance in Tax Matters: Amended by the 2010 Protocol* (OECD/Council of Europe, 2011[4]) ("the Convention"), (ii) the Directive 2011/16/EU with all other European Union Member States and (iii) bilateral agreements in force with 71 jurisdictions.[3]

322. For the year in review, the timeliness of exchanges is as follows:

Future rulings in the scope of the transparency framework	Number of exchanges transmitted within three months of the information becoming available to the competent authority or immediately after legal impediments have been lifted	Delayed exchanges		
		Number of exchanges transmitted later than three months of the information on rulings becoming available to the competent authority	Reasons for the delays	Any other comments
	14	0	N/A	N/A

Follow up requests received for exchange of the ruling	Number	Average time to provide response	Number of requests not answered
	0	N/A	N/A

323. Denmark has the necessary legal basis for spontaneous exchange of information, a process for completing the templates in a timely way and has completed all exchanges. Denmark has met all of the ToR for the exchange of information process and no recommendations are made.

C. Statistics (ToR IV)

324. The statistics for the year in review are as follows:

Category of ruling	Number of exchanges	Jurisdictions exchanged with
Ruling related to a preferential regime	0	N/A
Cross-border unilateral advance pricing agreements (APAs) and any other cross-border unilateral tax rulings (such as an advance tax ruling) covering transfer pricing or the application of transfer pricing principles	0	N/A
Cross-border rulings providing for a unilateral downward adjustment to the taxpayer's taxable profits that is not directly reflected in the taxpayer's financial / commercial accounts	0	N/A
Permanent establishment rulings	12	Australia, Germany, Malaysia, Norway, Spain, Sweden, United Kingdom
Related party conduit rulings	*De minimis rule* applies	N/A
De minimis rule applies	2	
Total	14	

D. Matters related to intellectual property regimes (ToR I.4.1.3)

325. Denmark does not offer an intellectual property regime for which transparency requirements under the Action 5 Report (OECD, 2015[1]) were imposed.

Summary of recommendations on implementation of the transparency framework

Aspect of implementation of the transparency framework that should be improved	Recommendation for improvement
	No recommendations are made.

References

OECD (2017), *BEPS Action 5 on Harmful Tax Practices - Terms of Reference and Methodology for the Conduct of the Peer Reviews of the Action 5 Transparency Framework*, OECD Publishing, Paris, http://www.oecd.org/tax/beps/beps-action-5-harmful-tax-practices-peer-review-transparency-framework.pdf. [3]

OECD (2015), *Countering Harmful Tax Practices More Effectively, Taking into Account Transparency and Substance, Action 5 - 2015 Final Report*, OECD/G20 Base Erosion and Profit Shifting Project, OECD Publishing, Paris, https://dx.doi.org/10.1787/9789264241190-en. [1]

OECD/Council of Europe (2011), *The Multilateral Convention on Mutual Administrative Assistance in Tax Matters: Amended by the 2010 Protocol*, OECD Publishing, Paris, https://dx.doi.org/10.1787/9789264115606-en. [4]

Notes

[1] Available at www.skat.dk/skat.aspx?oid=80859&ik_navn=transport.

[2] With respect to the following preferential regime: tonnage tax.

[3] Parties to the Convention are available here: www.oecd.org/tax/exchange-of-tax-information/convention-on-mutual-administrative-assistance-in-tax-matters.htm. Denmark also has bilateral agreements with Argentina, Aruba, Australia, Austria, Azerbaijan, Bangladesh, Belarus, Belgium, Brazil, British Virgin Islands, Bulgaria, Canada, Chile, China (People's Republic of), Croatia, Cyprus, Czech Republic, Egypt, Estonia, Georgia, Germany, Ghana, Greece, Hungary, India, Indonesia, Ireland, Israel, Italy, Jamaica, Japan, Kenya, Korea, Kuwait, Latvia, Lithuania, Luxembourg, Malaysia, Malta, Mexico, Montenegro, Morocco, Netherlands, New Zealand, Pakistan, Philippines, Poland, Portugal, North Macedonia, Romania, Russia, Serbia, Singapore, Slovak Republic, Slovenia, South Africa, Sri Lanka, Switzerland, Chinese Taipei, Tanzania, Thailand, Trinidad and Tobago, Tunisia, Turkey, Uganda, Ukraine, United Kingdom, United States, Venezuela, Viet Nam and Zambia.

Dominican Republic

The Dominican Republic has met all aspects of the terms of reference (OECD, 2017[3]) (ToR) for the calendar year 2019 (year in review), except for the timely exchange of information on rulings (ToR II.5). The Dominican Republic receives one recommendation on this point for the year in review.

This is the Dominican Republic's first review of implementation of the transparency framework.

The Dominican Republic can legally issue five types of rulings within the scope of the transparency framework.

In practice, the Dominican Republic issued rulings within the scope of the transparency framework as follows:

- For the year in review: 23 future rulings.[1]

As no exchanges took place, no peer input was received in respect of the exchanges of information on rulings received from the Dominican Republic.

A. The information gathering process

326. The Dominican Republic can legally issue the following five types of rulings within the scope of the transparency framework: (i) preferential regimes;[2] (ii) cross-border unilateral APAs and any other cross-border unilateral tax rulings (such as an advance tax ruling) covering transfer pricing or the application of transfer pricing principles; (iii) rulings providing for unilateral downward adjustments; (iv) permanent establishment rulings; and (v) related party conduit rulings. Rulings are issued by the International Tax Agreements Unit within the tax administration.

Past rulings (ToR I.4.1.1, I.4.1.2, I.4.2.1, I.4.2.2)

327. For the Dominican Republic, past rulings are any tax rulings issued prior to 1 March 2019. However, there is no obligation for Dominican Republic to conduct spontaneous exchange information on past rulings.

Future rulings (ToR I.4.1.1, I.4.1.2, I.4.2.1)

328. For the Dominican Republic, future rulings are any tax rulings within scope that are issued on or after 1 March 2019.

329. In December 2019, the Dominican Republic created the International Taxation Department, and created a process for the information gathering for the transparency framework. The International Taxation Department within the Dominican Republic's Tax Administration consists of three units: the International Tax Agreements Unit, the Exchange of Information Unit, and the Tax Treaty Administration Unit, but only the former two are part of the ruling process. The Exchange of Information Unit was part of the International Cooperation Department and it maintained all of its existing functions when it became part of the International Taxation Department. The International Tax Agreements Unit is a newly created unit, but its functions (including the negotiation and issuance of rulings) were formerly performed by the Transfer Pricing Department.

330. The International Tax Agreements Unit is responsible for the issuance of rulings. When a ruling is issued, a physical version is stored in an archive in the unit responsible for the taxpayer's file and an electronic copy is saved on the Tax Administration's online server. In addition, the relevant officer updates a spreadsheet list which is saved in the International Taxation Department's folder in the online server, and which is accessible to all officers within the unit and is consulted at regular intervals to assess whether rulings are in scope of the transparency framework.

331. When the taxpayer requests a ruling, the responsible officer follows up by requesting information on the identity and residence of the relevant related parties, the immediate parent entity and the ultimate parent entity. In order to check whether this information is accurate, the responsible officer performs reviews based on internal available information such as the taxpayer's general data, related parties and other relevant data, which is stored in Tax Administration's "master records". In addition, the officer reviews the taxpayer's income tax returns, VAT returns and annexes, and other information such as transfer pricing documentation. This information is then stored in the above mentioned spreadsheet list, which allows the tax administration to identify the potential exchange jurisdictions.

Review and supervision (ToR I.4.3)

332. Each officer within the International Taxation Department has been trained on the correct identification of rulings in scope of the transparency framework. The Tax Administration is in the process of formalising the corresponding guidance, in accordance with the standard, that will contain the protocol the staff must follow to obtain the relevant information.

333. After the ruling and potential exchange jurisdictions have been identified by the responsible officer, a second level of review to ensure all rulings are properly identified is undertaken by the Head of the International Tax Agreements Unit and the Head of the International Taxation Department.

Conclusion on section A

334. The Dominican Republic has met all of the ToR for the information gathering process and no recommendations are made.

B. The exchange of information

Legal basis for spontaneous exchange of information (ToR II.5.1, II.5.2)

335. The Dominican Republic has the necessary domestic legal basis to exchange information spontaneously. Dominican Republic notes that there are no legal or practical impediments that prevent the spontaneous exchange of information on rulings as contemplated in the Action 5 minimum standard.

336. The Dominican Republic has international agreements permitting spontaneous exchange of information, including being a party to the (i) *Multilateral Convention on Mutual Administrative Assistance in Tax Matters: Amended by the 2010 Protocol* (OECD/Council of Europe, 2011[4]) ("the Convention") and (ii) bilateral agreements in force with three jurisdictions.[3] The Convention entered into force on 1 December 2019 and is in effect from 1 January 2020.

Completion and exchange of templates (ToR II.5.3, II.5.4, II.5.5, II.5.6, II.5.7)

337. The process to complete and exchange the templates was also put in place in December 2019, with the creation of the International Taxation Department. The International Tax Agreements Unit is also responsible for completing the templates, in line with Annex C of the BEPS Action 5 report (OECD, 2015[1]) and within the timelines under the transparency framework. The summary section of the template has to be completed in line with the internal FHTP suggested guidance. Manual reviews are undertaken to verify whether the templates are correctly completed.

338. Once the template is completed, it is then shared with the Head of the Exchange of Information Unit and the Head of the International Taxation Department (who is the Competent Authority), in order to verify the accuracy of the information to be exchanged. When the template is approved, the Exchange of Information Unit proceeds to the exchange. The exchanges of information are required to take place on a quarterly basis. The timeliness of the exchange of information is supervised by the Head of the International Taxation Department.

339. The Dominican Republic confirms that the above described procedure is well understood by all relevant staff, but will be further formalised in the future.

340. For the year in review, the timeliness of exchanges is as follows:

Future rulings in the scope of the transparency framework	Number of exchanges transmitted within three months of the information becoming available to the competent authority or immediately after legal impediments have been lifted	Delayed exchanges		
		Number of exchanges transmitted later than three months of the information on rulings becoming available to the competent authority	Reasons for the delays	Any other comments
	0	12	See below.	N/A

Follow up requests received for exchange of the ruling	Number	Average time to provide response	Number of requests not answered
	N/A	N/A	N/A

341. The 12 exchanges relate to jurisdictions with which the Dominican Republic had an exchange of information agreement in force for 2019. Additional exchanges of rulings issued in the year in review were not permitted to take place, because there was no legal basis to do so with the relevant exchange jurisdictions.

342. No exchanges have been undertaken during the year of review, as the International Taxation Department was created in December 2019. It is noted that 11 of the 12 exchanges relate to rulings that were issued by the Transfer Pricing Department (before December 2019). The first exchanges of information were scheduled for March 2020, but the Dominican Republic indicated that delays have occurred and the exchanges will take place later in 2020.

Conclusion on section B

343. The Dominican Republic is recommended to ensure that the exchanges of information on rulings occur as soon as possible (ToR II.5).

C. Statistics (ToR IV)

344. As there was no information on rulings exchanged by the Dominican Republic for the year in review, no statistics can be reported.

D. Matters related to intellectual property regimes (ToR I.4.1.3)

345. The Dominican Republic does not offer an intellectual property regime for which transparency requirements under the Action 5 Report (OECD, 2015[1]) were imposed.

Summary of recommendations on implementation of the transparency framework

Aspect of implementation of the transparency framework that should be improved	**Recommendation for improvement**
The Dominican Republic is still in the process of ensuring the timely exchange of information on rulings.	The Dominican Republic is recommended to ensure that the exchanges of information on rulings occur as soon as possible.

References

OECD (2017), *BEPS Action 5 on Harmful Tax Practices - Terms of Reference and Methodology for the Conduct of the Peer Reviews of the Action 5 Transparency Framework*, OECD Publishing, Paris, http://www.oecd.org/tax/beps/beps-action-5-harmful-tax-practices-peer-review-transparency-framework.pdf. [3]

OECD (2015), *Countering Harmful Tax Practices More Effectively, Taking into Account Transparency and Substance, Action 5 - 2015 Final Report*, OECD/G20 Base Erosion and Profit Shifting Project, OECD Publishing, Paris, https://dx.doi.org/10.1787/9789264241190-en. [1]

OECD/Council of Europe (2011), *The Multilateral Convention on Mutual Administrative Assistance in Tax Matters: Amended by the 2010 Protocol*, OECD Publishing, Paris, https://dx.doi.org/10.1787/9789264115606-en. [4]

Notes

[1] This includes 21 extensions of existing APAs.

[2] These regimes are: i) Border development, ii) Free trade zones and iii) Logistics centres. It should be noted that FHTP has not yet concluded if these regimes are in scope. If the FHTP decides that these regimes are out of scope for the FHTP, then exchange of information on rulings with respect to these regimes would no longer be required under the Action 5 transparency framework. However, until then, the Dominican Republic has committed to do the spontaneous exchange of information on rulings related to these regimes.

[3] Parties to the Convention are available here: www.oecd.org/tax/exchange-of-tax-information/convention-on-mutual-administrative-assistance-in-tax-matters.htm. The Dominican Republic also has bilateral agreements with Canada, Spain and United States.

Egypt

Egypt is taking steps to implement the legal basis for exchange of information under the transparency framework, and has commenced administrative preparations to ensure that information on rulings will be exchanged. Egypt has met all aspects of the terms of reference (OECD, 2017[3]) (ToR) for the calendar year 2019 (year in review), except for identifying all potential exchange jurisdictions for both past and future rulings (ToR I.4.2.1 and ToR I.4.2.2), having in place a review and supervision mechanism (ToR I.4.3) and having in place a process to ensure the timely exchange of information on rulings in the form required by the transparency framework (ToR II.5). Egypt receives two recommendations on these points for the year in review.

In the prior year report, Egypt had received two recommendations. As they have not been addressed, the recommendations remains in place but for section A, in the year in review, the recommendation is targeted to specific aspects of the ToR that still need to be implemented.

Egypt can legally issue three types of rulings within the scope of the transparency framework.

In practice, Egypt issued rulings within the scope of the transparency framework as follows:

- 31 past rulings;
- For the period 1 April 2018 - 31 December 2018: three future rulings;
- For the year in review: 11 future rulings.

As no exchanges took place, no peer input was received in respect of the exchanges of information on rulings received from Egypt.

A. The information gathering process

346. Egypt can legally issue the following three types of rulings within the scope of the transparency framework: (i) cross-border unilateral APAs and any other cross-border unilateral tax rulings (such as an advance tax ruling) covering transfer pricing or the application of transfer pricing principles; (ii) permanent establishment rulings; and (iii) related party conduit rulings.

Past rulings (ToR I.4.1.1, I.4.1.2, I.4.2.1, I.4.2.2)

347. For Egypt, past rulings are any tax rulings within scope that are issued either (i) on or after 1 January 2016 but before 1 April 2018; and (ii) on or after 1 January 2014 but before 1 January 2016, provided still in effect as at 1 January 2016.

348. The issued past rulings relate to permanent establishment rulings and related party conduit rulings. The following departments within the Egyptian tax administration (ETA) are responsible for issuing these rulings: the tax refund department and the researching department (both part of the international tax treaties department), and the advanced rulings office. Rulings are stored in the department archives and in an electronic database and could therefore be identified.

349. Egypt has not yet identified the potential exchange jurisdictions for all past rulings. Therefore, Egypt is recommended to apply the "best efforts approach" to identify potential exchange jurisdictions for all past rulings.

Future rulings (ToR I.4.1.1, I.4.1.2, I.4.2.1)

350. For Egypt, future rulings are any tax rulings within scope that are issued on or after 1 April 2018.

351. APAs are issued by the transfer pricing team within the (ETA). When an APA is issued, it is stored in the department archive and in an electronic database. To date, the ETA has not yet issued any APAs.

352. The Egyptian transfer pricing guidelines note that when a taxpayer requests an APA, it has to provide information including on the global organisation structure of the MNE group and the related parties that were relevant to the transaction subject to the APA, including their countries of residence. The ETA can also request additional information from the taxpayer.

353. The responsible departments for permanent establishment rulings and related party conduit rulings are described in the previous section. Egypt is currently in the process of implementing legislation to require the taxpayer to provide information on the jurisdictions of the related parties, immediate parent and ultimate parent entity. Until this has been done, the officials within the ETA have the power to request this information from taxpayers. However, in practice, no potential exchange jurisdictions have yet been identified. Therefore, Egypt is recommended to ensure that all potential exchange jurisdictions are identified swiftly for all future rulings other than APAs.

Review and supervision (ToR I.4.3)

354. Egypt does not yet have in place a review and supervision mechanism for the identification of rulings and potential exchange jurisdictions.

355. Egypt notes that it is envisaged that supervision on the identification of rulings and potential exchange jurisdictions will take place by the managers of the relevant departments. Egypt also intends to issue internal guidance for staff on the identification process.

Conclusion on section A

356. Egypt has met the ToR for the information gathering process except for identifying all potential exchange jurisdictions for past and future rulings (ToR I.4.2.1 and ToR I.4.2.2) and having in place a review and supervision mechanism (ToR I.4.3). Egypt is recommended to continue its efforts to identify all potential exchange jurisdictions for both past and future rulings and to implement a review and supervision mechanism, as soon as possible.

B. The exchange of information

Legal basis for spontaneous exchange of information (ToR II.5.1, II.5.2)

357. Egypt has the necessary domestic legal basis to exchange information spontaneously. Egypt notes that there are no legal or practical impediments that prevent the spontaneous exchange of information on rulings as contemplated in the Action 5 minimum standard.

358. Egypt has international agreements permitting spontaneous exchange of information, including double tax agreements in force with 55 jurisdictions.[1]

Completion and exchange of templates (ToR II.5.3, II.5.4, II.5.5, II.5.6, II.5.7)

359. Egypt does not have a process for the completion and exchange of templates. Egypt confirmed that it is currently developing a process to complete the templates on relevant rulings, to make them available to the Competent Authority for exchange of information and to exchange them with relevant jurisdictions.

360. During the year in review, no exchanges took place and therefore no data on the timeliness of exchanges is reported.

Conclusion on section B

361. Egypt has the necessary domestic legal basis to exchange information in connection with the transparency framework. Egypt is recommended to develop a process to complete the templates on relevant rulings and to ensure that the exchanges of information on rulings occur in accordance with the form and timelines under the transparency framework (ToR II.5).

C. Statistics (ToR IV)

362. As there was no information on rulings exchanged by Egypt for the year in review, no statistics can be reported.

D. Matters related to intellectual property regimes (ToR I.4.1.3)

363. Egypt does not offer an intellectual property regime for which transparency requirements under the Action 5 Report (OECD, 2015[1]) were imposed.

Summary of recommendations on implementation of the transparency framework

Aspect of implementation of the transparency framework that should be improved	Recommendation for improvement
Egypt has not yet identified all potential exchange jurisdictions for both past and future rulings and does not have a review and supervision mechanism in place to ensure that all relevant information on the identification of rulings and potential exchange jurisdictions is captured adequately.	Egypt is recommended to continue its efforts to identify all potential exchange jurisdictions for both past and future rulings and to implement a review and supervision mechanism, as soon as possible. This recommendation remains unchanged since the prior year peer review report.
Egypt does not have in place a process to ensure the timely exchange of information on rulings in the form required by the transparency framework.	Egypt is recommended to develop a process to complete the templates on relevant rulings and to ensure that the exchanges of information on rulings occur in accordance with the form and timelines under the transparency framework. This recommendation remains unchanged since the prior year peer review report.

References

OECD (2017), *BEPS Action 5 on Harmful Tax Practices - Terms of Reference and Methodology for the Conduct of the Peer Reviews of the Action 5 Transparency Framework*, OECD Publishing, Paris, http://www.oecd.org/tax/beps/beps-action-5-harmful-tax-practices-peer-review-transparency-framework.pdf. [3]

OECD (2015), *Countering Harmful Tax Practices More Effectively, Taking into Account Transparency and Substance, Action 5 - 2015 Final Report*, OECD/G20 Base Erosion and Profit Shifting Project, OECD Publishing, Paris, https://dx.doi.org/10.1787/9789264241190-en. [1]

Notes

[1] Albania, Algeria, Austria, Bahrain, Belarus, Belgium, Bulgaria, Canada, China (People's Republic of), Cyprus, Czech Republic, Denmark, Ethiopia, Finland, France, Georgia, Germany, Greece, Hungary, India, Indonesia, Iraq, Ireland, Italy, Japan, Jordan, Korea, Kuwait, Lebanon, Libya, Malaysia, Malta, Mauritius, Morocco, Netherlands, Norway, Pakistan, Poland, Romania, Russia, Saudi Arabia, Serbia, Singapore, Spain, South Africa, Sudan, Sweden, Syria, Tunisia, Turkey, Ukraine, United Arab Emirates, United Kingdom, United States and Yemen.

Estonia

Estonia has met all aspects of the terms of reference (OECD, 2017[3]) (ToR) for the calendar year 2019 (year in review) and no recommendations are made.

Estonia can legally issue two types of rulings within the scope of the transparency framework.

In practice, Estonia issued rulings within the scope of the transparency framework as follows:

- 20 past rulings;
- For the period 1 April 2016 - 31 December 2016: eight future rulings;
- For the calendar year 2017: 11 future rulings;
- For the calendar year 2018: nine future rulings, and
- For the year in review: nine future rulings.

Peer input was received from one jurisdiction in respect of the exchanges of information on rulings received from Estonia. The input was positive, noting that information was complete, in a correct format and almost all received in a timely manner.

A. The information gathering process

364. Estonia can legally issue the following two types of rulings within the scope of the transparency framework: (i) permanent establishment rulings and (ii) related party conduit rulings.

365. For Estonia, past rulings are any tax rulings within scope that are issued either: (i) on or after 1 January 2014 but before 1 April 2016; or (ii) on or after 1 January 2010 but before 1 January 2014, provided they were still in effect as at 1 January 2014. Future rulings are any tax rulings within scope that are issued on or after 1 April 2016.

366. In the prior years' peer review reports, it was determined that Estonia's undertakings to identify past and future rulings and all potential exchange jurisdictions were sufficient to meet the minimum standard. In addition, it was determined that Estonia's review and supervision mechanism was sufficient to meet the minimum standard. Estonia's implementation remains unchanged, and therefore continues to meet the minimum standard.

367. Estonia has met all of the ToR for the information gathering process and no recommendations are made.

B. The exchange of information

368. In the prior years' peer review reports, it was determined that Estonia's process for the completion and exchange of templates were sufficient to meet the minimum standard. With respect to past rulings, no further action was required from Estonia. Estonia's implementation in this regard remains unchanged and therefore continues to meet the minimum standard.

369. Estonia has international agreements permitting spontaneous exchange of information, including being a party to the (i) *Multilateral Convention on Mutual Administrative Assistance in Tax Matters: Amended by the 2010 Protocol* (OECD/Council of Europe, 2011[4]) ("the Convention"), (ii) the Directive 2011/16/EU with all other European Union Member States and (iii) bilateral agreements in force with 59 jurisdictions.[1]

370. For the year in review, the timeliness of exchanges is as follows:

Future rulings in the scope of the transparency framework	Number of exchanges transmitted within three months of the information becoming available to the competent authority or immediately after legal impediments have been lifted	Delayed exchanges		
		Number of exchanges transmitted later than three months of the information on rulings becoming available to the competent authority	Reasons for the delays	Any other comments
	12	0	N/A	N/A

Follow up requests received for exchange of the ruling	Number	Average time to provide response	Number of requests not answered
	0	N/A	N/A

371. Estonia has the necessary legal basis for spontaneous exchange of information, a process for completing the templates in a timely way and has completed all exchanges. Estonia has met all of the ToR for the exchange of information process and no recommendations are made.

C. Statistics (ToR IV)

372. The statistics for the year in review are as follows:

Category of ruling	Number of exchanges	Jurisdictions exchanged with
Permanent establishment rulings	*De minimis rule* applies	N/A
Related party conduit rulings	8	Finland, Luxembourg, Netherlands, Sweden, Switzerland
De minimis rule applies	4	
Total	12	

D. Matters related to intellectual property regimes (ToR I.4.1.3)

373. Estonia does not offer an intellectual property regime for which transparency requirements under the Action 5 Report (OECD, 2015[1]) were imposed.

Summary of recommendations on implementation of the transparency framework

Aspect of implementation of the transparency framework that should be improved	Recommendation for improvement
	No recommendations are made.

References

OECD (2017), *BEPS Action 5 on Harmful Tax Practices - Terms of Reference and Methodology for the Conduct of the Peer Reviews of the Action 5 Transparency Framework*, OECD Publishing, Paris, http://www.oecd.org/tax/beps/beps-action-5-harmful-tax-practices-peer-review-transparency-framework.pdf. [3]

OECD (2015), *Countering Harmful Tax Practices More Effectively, Taking into Account Transparency and Substance, Action 5 - 2015 Final Report*, OECD/G20 Base Erosion and Profit Shifting Project, OECD Publishing, Paris, https://dx.doi.org/10.1787/9789264241190-en. [1]

OECD/Council of Europe (2011), *The Multilateral Convention on Mutual Administrative Assistance in Tax Matters: Amended by the 2010 Protocol*, OECD Publishing, Paris, https://dx.doi.org/10.1787/9789264115606-en. [4]

A. The information gathering process

374. The Faroe Islands can legally issue the following three types of rulings within the scope of the transparency framework: (i) cross-border unilateral APAs and any other cross-border unilateral tax rulings (such as an advance tax ruling) covering transfer pricing or the application of transfer pricing principles; (ii) rulings providing for unilateral downward adjustments; and (iii) related party conduit rulings. Rulings are issued by the Faroe Islands' tax administration.

Past rulings (ToR I.4.1.1, I.4.1.2, I.4.2.1, I.4.2.2)

375. For the Faroe Islands, past rulings are any tax rulings issued prior to 1 September 2019. However, there is no obligation for the Faroe Islands to conduct spontaneous exchange information on past rulings.

Future rulings (ToR I.4.1.1, I.4.1.2, I.4.2.1)

376. For the Faroe Islands, future rulings are any tax rulings within scope that are issued on or after 1 September 2019.

377. No rulings were issued by the Faroe Islands during the future rulings period in the year of review. However, the Faroe Islands indicates that there are no processes in place for the record keeping of rulings for the purposes of the transparency framework. It is noted that the Faroe Islands intends to implement guidelines and practices to make sure the necessary information to meet the requirements of the transparency framework is required in all cases.

Review and supervision (ToR I.4.3)

378. The Faroe Islands did not yet have a review and supervision mechanism under the transparency framework for the year in review. The Faroe Islands is discussing the implementation of a revision and supervision mechanism for ensuring implementation of the transparency framework.

Conclusion on section A

379. The Faroe Islands is recommended to ensure that it has put in place an effective information gathering process to identify all relevant future rulings and all potential exchange jurisdictions and to implement a review and supervision mechanism, as soon as possible (ToR I.4).

B. The exchange of information

Legal basis for spontaneous exchange of information (ToR II.5.1, II.5.2)

380. The Faroe Islands has the necessary domestic legal basis to exchange information spontaneously. The Faroe Islands notes that there are no legal or practical impediments that prevent the spontaneous exchange of information on rulings as contemplated in the Action 5 minimum standard.

381. The Faroe Islands has international agreements permitting spontaneous exchange of information, including being a party to the (i) *Multilateral Convention on Mutual Administrative Assistance in Tax Matters: Amended by the 2010 Protocol* (OECD/Council of Europe, 2011[4]) ("the Convention"), (ii) the Nordic Convention on Assistance in Tax Matters and (iii) bilateral agreements in force with four jurisdictions.[1]

Completion and exchange of templates (ToR II.5.3, II.5.4, II.5.5, II.5.6, II.5.7)

382. The Faroe Islands is still developing a process to complete the templates on relevant rulings, to make them available to the Competent Authority for exchange of information, and to exchange them with relevant jurisdictions.

383. As no exchanges were required to take place in the year of review, no data on the timeliness of exchanges can be reported.

Conclusion on section B

384. The Faroe Islands is recommended to develop a process to complete the templates for all relevant rulings and to ensure that the exchanges of information on rulings occur in accordance with the form and timelines under the transparency framework going forward (ToR II.5).

C. Statistics (ToR IV)

385. As there was no information on rulings exchanged by the Faroe Islands for the year in review, no statistics can be reported.

D. Matters related to intellectual property regimes (ToR I.4.1.3)

386. The Faroe Islands does not offer an intellectual property regime for which transparency requirements under the Action 5 Report (OECD, 2015[1]) were imposed.

Summary of recommendations on implementation of the transparency framework

Aspect of implementation of the transparency framework that should be improved	Recommendation for improvement
The Faroe Islands does not yet have its necessary information and gathering process in place.	The Faroe Islands is recommended to ensure that it has put in place an effective information gathering process to identify all relevant past and future rulings and all potential exchange jurisdictions and to implement a review and supervision mechanism, as soon as possible.
The Faroe Islands does not have a process to complete the templates on relevant rulings, to make them available to the Competent Authority for exchange of information, and to exchange them with relevant jurisdictions.	The Faroe Islands is recommended to develop a process to complete the templates for all relevant rulings and to ensure that the exchanges of information on rulings occur in accordance with the form and timelines under the transparency framework going forward.

References

OECD (2017), *BEPS Action 5 on Harmful Tax Practices - Terms of Reference and Methodology for the Conduct of the Peer Reviews of the Action 5 Transparency Framework*, OECD Publishing, Paris, http://www.oecd.org/tax/beps/beps-action-5-harmful-tax-practices-peer-review-transparency-framework.pdf. [3]

OECD (2015), *Countering Harmful Tax Practices More Effectively, Taking into Account Transparency and Substance, Action 5 - 2015 Final Report*, OECD/G20 Base Erosion and Profit Shifting Project, OECD Publishing, Paris, https://dx.doi.org/10.1787/9789264241190-en. [1]

OECD/Council of Europe (2011), *The Multilateral Convention on Mutual Administrative Assistance in Tax Matters: Amended by the 2010 Protocol*, OECD Publishing, Paris, https://dx.doi.org/10.1787/9789264115606-en. [4]

Notes

[1] Parties to the Convention are available here: www.oecd.org/tax/exchange-of-tax-information/convention-on-mutual-administrative-assistance-in-tax-matters.htm. Parties to the Nordic Convention on Assistance in Tax Matters are Denmark, Finland, Iceland, Norway and Sweden. The Faroe Islands also has bilateral agreements with Greenland, India, Switzerland and the United Kingdom. The bilateral agreements with Switzerland and India are the Danish tax treaties, which are territorial extended to include the Faroe Islands.

Finland

Finland has met all aspects of the terms of reference (OECD, 2017[3]) (ToR) for the calendar year 2019 (year in review) and no recommendations are made.

Finland can legally issue four types of rulings within the scope of the transparency framework.

In practice, Finland issued rulings within the scope of the transparency framework as follows:

- 42 past rulings;
- For the period 1 April 2016 - 31 December 2016: 13 future rulings;
- For the calendar year 2017: 19 future rulings;
- For the calendar year 2018: eight future rulings; and
- For the year in review: 32 future rulings.

Some rulings are published on the Finland Tax Administration's website, at the discretion of the Central Tax Board.[1]

No peer input was received in respect of the exchanges of information on rulings received from Finland.

A. The information gathering process

387. Finland can legally issue the following four types of rulings within the scope of the transparency framework: (i) preferential regimes;[2] (ii) cross-border unilateral APAs and any other cross-border unilateral tax rulings (such as an advance tax ruling) covering transfer pricing or the application of transfer pricing principles; (iii) permanent establishment rulings; and (iv) related party conduit rulings.

388. For Finland, past rulings are any tax rulings within scope that are issued either: (i) on or after 1 January 2014 but before 1 April 2016; or (ii) on or after 1 January 2010 but before 1 January 2014, provided they were still in effect as at 1 January 2014. Future rulings are any tax rulings within scope that are issued on or after 1 April 2016.

389. In the prior years' peer review reports, it was determined that Finland's undertakings to identify past and future rulings and all potential exchange jurisdictions were sufficient to meet the minimum standard. In addition, it was determined that Finland's review and supervision mechanism was sufficient to meet the minimum standard. Finland's implementation remains unchanged, and therefore continues to meet the minimum standard.

390. Finland has met all of the ToR for the information gathering process and no recommendations are made.

B. The exchange of information

391. In the prior years' peer review reports, it was determined that Finland's process for the completion and exchange of templates were sufficient to meet the minimum standard. With respect to past rulings, no further action was required. Finland's implementation in this regard remains unchanged and therefore continues to meet the minimum standard.

392. Finland has international agreements permitting spontaneous exchange of information, including being a party to the (i) *Multilateral Convention on Mutual Administrative Assistance in Tax Matters: Amended by the 2010 Protocol* (OECD/Council of Europe, 2011[4]) ("the Convention"), (ii) the Directive 2011/16/EU with all other European Union Member States and (iii) bilateral agreements in force with 89 jurisdictions.[3]

393. For the year in review, the timeliness of exchanges is as follows:

Future rulings in the scope of the transparency framework	Number of exchanges transmitted within three months of the information becoming available to the competent authority or immediately after legal impediments have been lifted	Delayed exchanges		
		Number of exchanges transmitted later than three months of the information on rulings becoming available to the competent authority	Reasons for the delays	Any other comments
	40	26	See below	Finland exchanged the delayed rulings in January and February 2020 as soon as the issue was identified.

Follow up requests received for exchange of the ruling	Number	Average time to provide response	Number of requests not answered
	0	N/A	N/A

394. During the year in review, Finland experienced some delays for future rulings. Finland explained it was due to technical reason that the file name generated automatically had been incorrect and the rulings were stuck in the transfer folder. Finland has resolved this technical error and conducted the outstanding exchanges in January and February 2020 as soon as they identified the issue. Finland has committed to monitor the transfer folder in the future to ensure that such delays do not occur again. As such, no recommendation is made, given that the issue was quickly identified and has been resolved, and is therefore not expected to be a recurring issue.

Conclusion on section B

395. Finland has the necessary legal basis for spontaneous exchange of information, a process for completing the templates in a timely way and has completed all exchanges. Finland has met all of the ToR for the exchanges of information process and no recommendations are made.

C. Statistics (ToR IV)

396. The statistics for the year in review are as follows:

Category of ruling	Number of exchanges	Jurisdictions exchanged with
Preferential regimes	0	N/A
Cross-border unilateral advance pricing agreements (APAs) and any other cross-border unilateral tax rulings (such as an advance tax ruling) covering transfer pricing or the application of transfer pricing principles	39	Czech Republic, Denmark, Estonia, Germany, Hungary, Latvia, Lithuania, Netherlands, Poland, Slovak Republic, Sweden, United Kingdom
Permanent establishment rulings	*De minimis rule* applies	N/A
Related party conduit rulings	0	N/A
De minimis rule applies	1	
Total	40	

D. Matters related to intellectual property regimes (ToR I.4.1.3)

397. Finland does not offer an intellectual property regime for which transparency requirements under the Action 5 Report (OECD, 2015[1]) were imposed.

Summary of recommendations on implementation of the transparency framework

Aspect of implementation of the transparency framework that should be improved	Recommendation for improvement
Finland experienced some delays in exchanging information on future rulings due to technical reason.	No recommendation is made because Finland completed the exchanges on the delayed future rulings quickly after the issues were identified and resolved, and this is not a recurring issue.

References

OECD (2017), *BEPS Action 5 on Harmful Tax Practices - Terms of Reference and Methodology for the Conduct of the Peer Reviews of the Action 5 Transparency Framework*, OECD Publishing, Paris, http://www.oecd.org/tax/beps/beps-action-5-harmful-tax-practices-peer-review-transparency-framework.pdf. [3]

OECD (2015), *Countering Harmful Tax Practices More Effectively, Taking into Account Transparency and Substance, Action 5 - 2015 Final Report*, OECD/G20 Base Erosion and Profit Shifting Project, OECD Publishing, Paris, https://dx.doi.org/10.1787/9789264241190-en. [1]

OECD/Council of Europe (2011), *The Multilateral Convention on Mutual Administrative Assistance in Tax Matters: Amended by the 2010 Protocol*, OECD Publishing, Paris, https://dx.doi.org/10.1787/9789264115606-en. [4]

Notes

[1] Available at: https://www.vero.fi/syventavat-vero-ohjeet/ennakkoratkaisut/.

[2] With respect to the following preferential regime: shipping regime.

[3] Parties to the Convention are available here: www.oecd.org/tax/exchange-of-tax-information/convention-on-mutual-administrative-assistance-in-tax-matters.htm. Finland also has bilateral agreements with Argentina, Armenia, Aruba, Australia, Austria, Azerbaijan, Bailiwick of Jersey, Barbados, Belarus, Belgium Bermuda, Bosnia and Herzegovina, Brazil, British Virgin Islands, Bulgaria, Canada, Cayman Islands, China (People's Republic of), Cook Islands, Croatia, Cyprus, Czech Republic, Denmark, Egypt, Estonia, Faroe Islands, France, Georgia, Germany, Greece, Guatemala, Guernsey, Hungary, India, Indonesia, Ireland, Isle of Man, Israel, Italy, Japan, Kazakhstan, Korea, Kosovo, Kyrgyzstan, Latvia, Lebanon, Lithuania, Luxembourg, Malaysia, Malta, Mexico, Moldova, Monaco, Montenegro, Morocco, Netherlands, Netherlands Antilles, New Zealand, North Macedonia, Norway, Pakistan, Panama, Philippines, Poland, Portugal, Romania, Russia, Serbia, Singapore, Slovak Republic, Slovenia, South Africa, Spain, Sri Lanka, Sweden, Switzerland, Tajikistan, Tanzania, Thailand, Turkey, Turkmenistan, Ukraine, United Arab Emirates, United Kingdom, United States, Uruguay, Uzbekistan, Viet Nam and Zambia.

France

France has met all aspects of the terms of reference (OECD, 2017[3]) (ToR) for the calendar year 2019 (year in review), except for identifying and exchanging information on new entrants to the grandfathered IP regime and or taxpayers benefitting from the third category of IP assets (ToR I.4.1.3). France receives one recommendation on this point for the year in review.

In the prior year report, as well as in the 2016, 2017 and 2018 peer reviews, France had received the same recommendation. As it has not been addressed, the recommendation remains in place.

France can legally issue three types of rulings within the scope of the transparency framework.

In practice, France issued rulings within the scope of the transparency framework as follows:

- 45 past rulings;
- For the period 1 April 2016 - 31 December 2016: four future rulings;
- For the calendar year 2017: six future rulings,
- For the calendar year 2018: six future rulings, and
- For the year in review: 16 future rulings.

No peer input was received in respect of the exchanges of information on rulings received from France.

A. The information gathering process

398. France can legally issue the following three types of rulings within the scope of the transparency framework: (i) preferential regimes;[1] (ii) cross-border unilateral APAs and any other cross-border unilateral tax rulings (such as an advance tax ruling) covering transfer pricing or the application of transfer pricing principles; and (iii) permanent establishment rulings.

399. For France, past rulings are any tax rulings within scope that are issued either: (i) on or after 1 January 2014 but before 1 April 2016; or (ii) on or after 1 January 2010 but before 1 January 2014, provided they were still in effect as at 1 January 2014. Future rulings are any tax rulings within scope that are issued on or after 1 April 2016.

400. In the prior years' peer review reports, it was determined that France's undertakings to identify past and future rulings and all potential exchange jurisdictions were sufficient to meet the minimum standard. In addition, it was determined that France's review and supervision mechanism was sufficient to meet the minimum standard. France's implementation remains unchanged, and therefore continues to meet the minimum standard.

401. France has met all of the ToR for the information gathering process and no recommendations are made.

B. The exchange of information

402. In the prior years' peer review reports, it was determined that France's process for the completion and exchange of templates were sufficient to meet the minimum standard. With respect to past rulings, no further action was required. France's implementation in this regard remains unchanged and therefore continues to meet the minimum standard.

403. France has international agreements permitting spontaneous exchange of information, including being a party to the (i) *Multilateral Convention on Mutual Administrative Assistance in Tax Matters: Amended by the 2010 Protocol* (OECD/Council of Europe, 2011[4]) ("the Convention"), (ii) the Directive 2011/16/EU with all other European Union Member States and (iii) bilateral agreements in force with 125 jurisdictions.[2]

404. For the year in review, the timeliness of exchanges is as follows:

Future rulings in the scope of the transparency framework	Number of exchanges transmitted within three months of the information becoming available to the competent authority or immediately after legal impediments have been lifted	Delayed exchanges		
		Number of exchanges transmitted later than three months of the information on rulings becoming available to the competent authority	Reasons for the delays	Any other comments
	16	0	N/A	N/A

Follow up requests received for exchange of the ruling	Number	Average time to provide response	Number of requests not answered
	0	N/A	N/A

405. France has the necessary legal basis for spontaneous exchange of information, a process for completing the templates in a timely way and has completed all exchanges. France has met all of the ToR for the exchange of information process and no recommendations are made.

C. Statistics (ToR IV)

406. The statistics for the year in review are as follows:

Category of ruling	Number of exchanges	Jurisdictions exchanged with
Ruling related to a preferential regime	*De minimis rule* applies	N/A
Cross-border unilateral advance pricing agreements (APAs) and any other cross-border unilateral tax rulings (such as an advance tax ruling) covering transfer pricing or the application of transfer pricing principles	*De minimis rule* applies	N/A
Permanent establishment rulings	9	Germany, Japan, Luxembourg, Sweden, United Kingdom, United States
De minimis rule applies	7	
IP regimes: total exchanges on taxpayers benefitting from the third category of IP assets, new entrants benefitting from grandfathered IP regimes; and taxpayers making use of the option to treat the nexus ratio as a rebuttable presumption	0	N/A
Total	16	

D. Matters related to intellectual property regimes (ToR I.4.1.3)

407. France offers an intellectual property regimes (IP regime)[3] that is subject to the transparency requirements under the Action 5 Report (OECD, 2015[1]). This regime was amended with effect from 1 January 2019 and is compliant with the nexus approach. It states that the identification of the benefitting taxpayers will occur as follows:

- ***New entrants benefitting from the grandfathered IP regime***: With respect to the previous form of the regime that existed until 31 December 2018, France should have information available and exchanged on new entrants after the relevant date from which enhanced transparency obligations apply. France has not identified information on new entrants to the previous IP regime, and as such has not exchanged information on these taxpayers. Therefore, France is recommended to identify and exchange information on all new entrants to the IP regime. This recommendation was included in the 2016, 2017 and 2018 peer review reports, and has not yet been acted upon. The recommendation is therefore retained.
- ***Third category of IP assets***: The previous form of the regime provided benefits to income from patentable inventions, which appear to be a type of the "third category of IP asset" described in paragraph 37 of the Action 5 report (OECD, 2015[1]). France has not implemented all of the requirements associated with this category of IP assets, thus the transparency requirements described in paragraph 37 would still apply to this case. France did not identify taxpayers benefiting from the third category of IP assets, and as such, has not exchanged information on these taxpayers. This recommendation was included in the 2016, 2017 and 2018 peer review reports, and has not been acted upon. The recommendation is therefore retained.

  In addition, the amended IP regime will allow benefits for the third category of IP assets.[4] Taxpayers benefiting from the regime have to provide a list of relevant assets in their tax return. Based on the tax return, France can identify the taxpayers benefiting from the third category of IP assets.
- ***Taxpayers making use of the option to treat the nexus ratio as a rebuttable presumption***: The amended IP regime allows for the option to treat the nexus ratio as a rebuttable presumption.

Taxpayers opting to do so must obtain a ruling from the tax administration, and are required to list the specific assets for which the presumption was rebutted in their tax return. France confirms that no taxpayer elected to treat the nexus approach as a rebuttable presumption.

Summary of recommendations on implementation of the transparency framework

Aspect of implementation of the transparency framework that should be improved	Recommendation for improvement
France did not identify or exchange information on new entrants to the IP regime or taxpayers benefitting from the third category of IP asset with respect to the former IP regime.	France is recommended to identify and exchange information on all new entrants to the IP regime, and to identify and exchange information on taxpayers benefitting from the third category of IP assets. This recommendation remains unchanged since the 2016, 2017 and 2018 peer review reports.

References

OECD (2017), *BEPS Action 5 on Harmful Tax Practices - Terms of Reference and Methodology for the Conduct of the Peer Reviews of the Action 5 Transparency Framework*, OECD Publishing, Paris, http://www.oecd.org/tax/beps/beps-action-5-harmful-tax-practices-peer-review-transparency-framework.pdf. [3]

OECD (2015), *Countering Harmful Tax Practices More Effectively, Taking into Account Transparency and Substance, Action 5 - 2015 Final Report*, OECD/G20 Base Erosion and Profit Shifting Project, OECD Publishing, Paris, https://dx.doi.org/10.1787/9789264241190-en. [1]

OECD/Council of Europe (2011), *The Multilateral Convention on Mutual Administrative Assistance in Tax Matters: Amended by the 2010 Protocol*, OECD Publishing, Paris, https://dx.doi.org/10.1787/9789264115606-en. [4]

Notes

[1] With respect to the following preferential regime: Shipping regime.

[2] Parties to the Convention are available here: www.oecd.org/tax/exchange-of-tax-information/convention-on-mutual-administrative-assistance-in-tax-matters.htm. France also has bilateral agreements with: Albania, Algeria, Andorra, Argentina, Armenia, Australia, Austria, Azerbaijan, Bahrain, Bangladesh, Belarus, Belgium, Benin, Bolivia, Bosnia and Herzegovina, Botswana, Brazil, Bulgaria, Burkina Faso, Cameroon, Canada, Central African Republic, Chile, China (People's Republic of), Chinese Taipei, Congo, Côte d'Ivoire, Croatia, Cyprus, Czech Republic, Ecuador, Egypt, Estonia, Ethiopia, Finland, French Polynesia, Gabon, Georgia, Germany, Ghana, Greece, Guinea, Hong Kong (China), Hungary, Iceland, India, Indonesia, Iran, Ireland, Israel, Italy, Jamaica, Japan, Jordan, Kazakhstan, Kenya, Korea, Kosovo, Kuwait, Kyrgyzstan, Latvia, Lebanon, Libya, Lithuania, Luxembourg, Madagascar, Malawi, Malaysia, Mali, Malta, Mauritania, Mauritius, Mexico, Monaco, Mongolia, Montenegro, Morocco, Namibia, Netherlands, New Caledonia, New Zealand, Niger, Nigeria, North Macedonia, Norway, Oman, Pakistan, Panama, Philippines, Poland, Portugal, Qatar, Romania, Russia, Saudi Arabia, Senegal, Serbia, Singapore, Slovak Republic, Slovenia, South Africa, Spain, Sri Lanka, Saint Martin, Saint Pierre and Miquelon, Sweden, Switzerland, Syrian Arab Republic, Thailand, Togo, Trinidad and Tobago, Tunisia, Turkey, Turkmenistan, Ukraine, United Arab Emirates, United Kingdom, United States, Uzbekistan, Venezuela, Viet Nam, Zambia and Zimbabwe.

[3] Reduced corporation tax rate on IP income, formerly known as Reduced rate for long term capital gains and profits from the licensing of IP rights.

[4] The regime provides for the third category of IP assets (article 238(I)(5) of the French General Tax Code), but will only entry into force by a decree (article 37(III)(2) of the Finance Law for 2020) that was not yet published in 2019.

Gabon

Gabon did not provide a completed peer review questionnaire to the Secretariat. It is not known whether Gabon has met all aspects of the terms of reference (OECD, 2017[3]) (ToR) for the calendar year 2019 (year in review). Gabon receives two recommendations covering the information gathering process (ToR I.4) and exchange of information (ToR II.5) for the year in review.

In the prior year report, Gabon had received the same two recommendations. As it is not known whether they have been addressed, the recommendations remain in place.

Gabon can legally issue two types of rulings within the scope of the transparency framework.

In practice, Gabon did not issue any type of rulings within the scope of the transparency framework in previous years. For the year in review, it is not known whether Gabon issued any type of rulings within the scope of the transparency framework.

No peer input was received in respect of the exchanges of information on rulings received from Gabon.

A. The information gathering process

408. Gabon can legally issue the following two types of rulings within the scope of the transparency framework: i) rulings related to a preferential regime[1] and ii) cross-border unilateral advance pricing agreements (APAs) and any other cross-border unilateral tax rulings (such as an advance tax ruling) covering transfer pricing or the application of transfer pricing principles.

Past rulings (ToR I.4.1.1, I.4.1.2, I.4.2.1, I.4.2.2)

409. For Gabon, past rulings are any tax rulings within scope that are issued either (i) on or after 1 January 2016 but before 1 April 2018; and (ii) on or after 1 January 2014 but before 1 January 2016, provided they were still in effect as at 1 January 2016.

410. In the prior year peer review report, it was noted that in Gabon, rulings are issued by the directorate of Legislation, within the Tax Administration. This unit is responsible for storing and reviewing such rulings and has reviewed its files, being able to confirm that no past rulings have been issued. Gabon indicated no past rulings in scope of the transparency framework have been issued. As such there was no need to identify potential exchange jurisdictions.

Future rulings (ToR I.4.1.1, I.4.1.2, I.4.2.1)

411. For Gabon, future rulings are any tax rulings within scope that are issued on or after 1 April 2018.

412. In the prior year peer review report, Gabon indicated that there were no processes in place for the record keeping of rulings for the purposes of the transparency framework. It was noted that Gabon intended to implement guidelines and practices to make sure the necessary information to meet the requirements of the transparency framework is required in all cases. Gabon was recommended to finalise its information gathering process as soon as possible.

413. During the year in review, as it is not known whether Gabon has finalised its information gathering process, the recommendation remains in place.

Review and supervision (ToR I.4.3)

414. In the prior year peer review report, it was determined that Gabon did not yet have a review and supervision mechanism under the transparency framework. Gabon was in the process of considering the implementation of a revision and supervision mechanism for ensuring implementation of the transparency framework. As it is not known whether Gabon has put in place a review and supervision mechanism under the transparency framework for the year in review, the recommendation remains in place.

Conclusion on section A

415. Gabon is recommended to finalise its information gathering process, with a review and supervision mechanism, as soon as possible (ToR I.4).

B. The exchange of information

Legal basis for spontaneous exchange of information (ToR II.5.1, II.5.2)

416. In the prior year peer review report, Gabon was currently in the process of putting in place the necessary domestic legal basis to exchange information spontaneously. It is not known whether Gabon

has already put in place the necessary domestic legal basis to exchange information spontaneously for the year in review.

417. Gabon has (i) signed the *Multilateral Convention on Mutual Administrative Assistance in Tax Matters: Amended by the 2010 Protocol* (OECD/Council of Europe, 2011[4]) ("the Convention") and (ii) bilateral agreements in force with 5 jurisdictions.[2] Gabon is encouraged to continue its efforts to expand its international exchange of information instruments to be able to exchange information on rulings. It is noted, however, that jurisdictions are assessed on their compliance with the transparency framework in respect of the exchange of information network in effect for the year of the particular annual review.

Completion and exchange of templates (ToR II.5.3, II.5.4, II.5.5, II.5.6, II.5.7)

418. In the prior year peer review report, it was noted that Gabon was still developing a process to complete the templates on relevant rulings, to make them available to the Competent Authority for exchange of information, and to exchange them with relevant jurisdictions. As it is not known whether exchanges took place in the year of review, no data on the timeliness of exchanges can be reported.

Conclusion on section B

419. Gabon is recommended to put in place a domestic legal framework allowing spontaneous exchange of information on rulings and to continue its efforts to complete the templates for all relevant rulings and to ensure that the exchanges of information on rulings occur as soon as possible (ToR II.5).

C. Statistics (ToR IV)

420. As the Secretariat is not aware whether information on rulings was exchanged by Gabon for the year in review, no statistics can be reported.

D. Matters related to intellectual property regimes (ToR I.4.1.3)

421. Gabon does not offer an intellectual property regime for which transparency requirements under the Action 5 Report (OECD, 2015[1]) were imposed.

Summary of recommendations on implementation of the transparency framework

Aspect of implementation of the transparency framework that should be improved	Recommendation for improvement
It is not known whether Gabon has finalised the steps to have in place its necessary information and gathering process.	Gabon is recommended to finalise its information gathering process, with a review and supervision mechanism, as soon as possible. This recommendation remains unchanged since the prior year peer review report.
It is not known whether Gabon has finalised the steps to have effective compulsory spontaneous exchange of information on the tax rulings within the scope of the transparency framework.	Gabon is recommended to continue to put in place a domestic legal framework allowing spontaneous exchange of information on rulings and to continue its efforts to complete the templates for all relevant rulings and to ensure that the exchanges of information on rulings occur as soon as possible. This recommendation remains unchanged since the prior year peer review report.

References

OECD (2017), *BEPS Action 5 on Harmful Tax Practices - Terms of Reference and Methodology for the Conduct of the Peer Reviews of the Action 5 Transparency Framework*, OECD Publishing, Paris, http://www.oecd.org/tax/beps/beps-action-5-harmful-tax-practices-peer-review-transparency-framework.pdf. [3]

OECD (2015), *Countering Harmful Tax Practices More Effectively, Taking into Account Transparency and Substance, Action 5 - 2015 Final Report*, OECD/G20 Base Erosion and Profit Shifting Project, OECD Publishing, Paris, https://dx.doi.org/10.1787/9789264241190-en. [1]

OECD/Council of Europe (2011), *The Multilateral Convention on Mutual Administrative Assistance in Tax Matters: Amended by the 2010 Protocol*, OECD Publishing, Paris, https://dx.doi.org/10.1787/9789264115606-en. [4]

Notes

[1] With respect to the following preferential regime: Special economic zone.

[2] Parties to the Convention are available here: www.oecd.org/tax/exchange-of-tax-information/convention-on-mutual-administrative-assistance-in-tax-matters.htm. Gabon also has bilateral agreements in force with Belgium, Canada, France, Korea and Morocco.

Georgia

Georgia has met all aspects of the terms of reference (OECD, 2017[3]) (ToR) for the calendar year 2019 (year in review) and no recommendations are made.

Georgia can legally issue four types of rulings within the scope of the transparency framework. In practice, Georgia has not issued any rulings within the scope of the transparency framework.

As no exchanges were required to take place, no peer input was received in respect of the exchanges of information on rulings received from Georgia.

A. The information gathering process

422. Georgia can legally issue the following four types of rulings within the scope of the transparency framework: (i) preferential regimes;[1] (ii) cross-border unilateral APAs and any other cross-border unilateral tax rulings (such as an advance tax ruling) covering transfer pricing or the application of transfer pricing principles; (iii) permanent establishment rulings; and (iv) related party conduit rulings.

423. For Georgia, past rulings are any tax rulings within scope that are issued either: (i) on or after 1 January 2016 but before 1 April 2018; or (ii) on or after 1 January 20114 but before 1 January 2016, provided they were still in effect as at 1 January 2016. Future rulings are any tax rulings within scope that are issued on or after 1 April 2018.

424. In the prior year's peer review report, it was determined that Georgia's undertakings to identify past and future rulings and all potential exchange jurisdictions were sufficient to meet the minimum standard. In addition, it was determined that Georgia's review and supervision mechanism was sufficient to meet the minimum standard. Georgia's implementation remains unchanged, and therefore continues to meet the minimum standard.

425. Georgia has met all of the ToR for the information gathering process and no recommendations are made.

B. The exchange of information

426. In the prior year's peer review report, it was determined that Georgia's process for the completion and exchange of templates were sufficient to meet the minimum standard. With respect to past rulings, no further action was required. Georgia's implementation in this regard remains unchanged and therefore continues to meet the minimum standard.

427. Georgia has international agreements permitting spontaneous exchange of information, including being a party to the (i) *Multilateral Convention on Mutual Administrative Assistance in Tax Matters: Amended by the 2010 Protocol* (OECD/Council of Europe, 2011[4]) ("the Convention") and (ii) bilateral agreements in force with 57 jurisdictions.[2]

428. As Georgia did not issue any rulings in scope of the transparency framework in the relevant period, Georgia was not required to exchange any information on rulings in the year in review and no data on the timeliness of exchanges can be reported.

429. Georgia has the necessary legal basis for spontaneous exchange of information, a process for completing the templates in a timely way and has completed all exchanges. Georgia has met all of the ToR for the exchange of information process and no recommendations are made.

C. Statistics (ToR IV)

430. As no rulings were issued, no statistics can be reported.

D. Matters related to intellectual property regimes (ToR I.4.1.3)

431. Georgia does not offer an intellectual property regime for which transparency requirements under the Action 5 Report (OECD, 2015[1]) were imposed.

Summary of recommendations on implementation of the transparency framework

Aspect of implementation of the transparency framework that should be improved	Recommendation for improvement
	No recommendations are made.

References

OECD (2017), *BEPS Action 5 on Harmful Tax Practices - Terms of Reference and Methodology for the Conduct of the Peer Reviews of the Action 5 Transparency Framework*, OECD Publishing, Paris, http://www.oecd.org/tax/beps/beps-action-5-harmful-tax-practices-peer-review-transparency-framework.pdf. [3]

OECD (2015), *Countering Harmful Tax Practices More Effectively, Taking into Account Transparency and Substance, Action 5 - 2015 Final Report*, OECD/G20 Base Erosion and Profit Shifting Project, OECD Publishing, Paris, https://dx.doi.org/10.1787/9789264241190-en. [1]

OECD/Council of Europe (2011), *The Multilateral Convention on Mutual Administrative Assistance in Tax Matters: Amended by the 2010 Protocol*, OECD Publishing, Paris, https://dx.doi.org/10.1787/9789264115606-en. [4]

Notes

[1] With respect to the following preferential regimes: 1) International financial company and 2) Virtual zone person.

[2] Parties to the Convention are available here: www.oecd.org/tax/exchange-of-tax-information/convention-on-mutual-administrative-assistance-in-tax-matters.htm. Georgia also has bilateral agreements with Armenia, Austria, Azerbaijan, Bahamas, Bahrain, Belarus, Belgium, Bulgaria, China (People's Republic of), Croatia, Cyprus, Czech Republic, Denmark, Egypt, Estonia, Finland, France, Germany, Greece, Hungary, Iceland, India, Iran, Ireland, Israel, Italy, Japan, Kazakhstan, Korea, Kuwait, Latvia, Liechtenstein, Lithuania, Luxembourg, Malta, Moldova, Netherlands, Norway, Poland, Portugal, Qatar, Romania, San Marino, Saudi Arabia, Serbia, Singapore, Slovak Republic, Slovenia, Spain, Sweden, Switzerland, Turkey, Turkmenistan, Ukraine, United Arab Emirates, United Kingdom and Uzbekistan.

Germany

Germany has met all aspects of the terms of reference (OECD, 2017[3]) (ToR) for the calendar year 2019 (year in review) and no recommendations are made.

Germany can legally issue five types of rulings within the scope of the transparency framework.

In practice, Germany issued rulings within the scope of the transparency framework as follows:

- 30 past rulings;
- For the period 1 April 2016 - 31 December 2016: seven future rulings;
- For the calendar year 2017: 10 future rulings,
- For the calendar year 2018: 10 future rulings, and
- For the year in review: eight future rulings.

No peer input was received in respect of the exchanges of information on rulings received from Germany.

A. The information gathering process

432. Germany can legally issue five types of rulings within the scope of the transparency framework: (i) preferential regimes;[1] (ii) cross-border unilateral APAs and any other cross-border unilateral tax rulings (such as an advance tax ruling) covering transfer pricing or the application of transfer pricing principles; (iii) rulings providing for unilateral downward adjustments; (iv) permanent establishment rulings; and (v) related party conduit rulings.

433. For Germany, past rulings are any tax rulings within scope that are issued either: (i) on or after 1 January 2014 but before 1 April 2016; or (ii) on or after 1 January 2010 but before 1 January 2014, provided they were still in effect as at 1 January 2014. Future rulings are any tax rulings within scope that are issued on or after 1 April 2016.

434. In the prior years' peer review reports, it was determined that Germany's undertakings to identify past and future rulings and all potential exchange jurisdictions were sufficient to meet the minimum standard. In addition, it was determined that Germany's review and supervision mechanism was sufficient to meet the minimum standard. Germany's implementation remains unchanged, and therefore continues to meet the minimum standard.

435. Germany has met all of the ToR for the information gathering process and no recommendations are made.

B. The exchange of information

436. In the prior years' peer review reports, it was determined that Germany's process for the completion and exchange of templates were sufficient to meet the minimum standard. With respect to past rulings, no further action was required. Germany's implementation in this regard remains unchanged and therefore continues to meet the minimum standard.

437. Germany has international agreements permitting spontaneous exchange of information, including being a party to the (i) *Multilateral Convention on Mutual Administrative Assistance in Tax Matters: Amended by the 2010 Protocol* (OECD/Council of Europe, 2011[4]) ("the Convention"), (ii) the Directive 2011/16/EU with all other European Union Member States and (iii) double tax agreements in force with 95 jurisdictions.[2]

438. For the year in review, the timeliness of exchanges is as follows:

Future rulings in the scope of the transparency framework	Number of exchanges transmitted within three months of the information becoming available to the competent authority or immediately after legal impediments have been lifted	Delayed exchanges		
		Number of exchanges transmitted later than three months of the information on rulings becoming available to the competent authority	Reasons for the delays	Any other comments
	8	0	N/A	N/A

Follow up requests received for exchange of the ruling	Number	Average time to provide response	Number of requests not answered
	0	N/A	N/A

439. Germany has the necessary legal basis for spontaneous exchange of information, a process for completing the templates in a timely way and has completed all exchanges. Germany has met all of the ToR for the exchange of information process and no recommendations are made.

C. Statistics (ToR IV)

440. The statistics for the year in review are as follows:

Category of ruling	Number of exchanges	Jurisdictions exchanged with
Ruling related to a preferential regime	*De minimis rule* applies	N/A
Cross-border unilateral advance pricing agreements (APAs) and any other cross-border unilateral tax rulings (such as an advance tax ruling) covering transfer pricing or the application of transfer pricing principles	0	N/A
Cross-border rulings providing for a unilateral downward adjustment to the taxpayer's taxable profits that is not directly reflected in the taxpayer's financial / commercial accounts	0	N/A
Permanent establishment rulings	7	Canada, Hong Kong (China), Switzerland, United Kingdom, United States
Related party conduit rulings	0	N/A
De minimis rule applies	1	
Total	8	

D. Matters related to intellectual property regimes (ToR I.4.1.3)

441. Germany does not offer an intellectual property regime for which transparency requirements under the Action 5 Report (OECD, 2015[1]) were imposed.

Summary of recommendations on implementation of the transparency framework

Aspect of implementation of the transparency framework that should be improved	Recommendation for improvement
	No recommendations are made.

References

OECD (2017), *BEPS Action 5 on Harmful Tax Practices - Terms of Reference and Methodology for the Conduct of the Peer Reviews of the Action 5 Transparency Framework*, OECD Publishing, Paris, http://www.oecd.org/tax/beps/beps-action-5-harmful-tax-practices-peer-review-transparency-framework.pdf. [3]

OECD (2015), *Countering Harmful Tax Practices More Effectively, Taking into Account Transparency and Substance, Action 5 - 2015 Final Report*, OECD/G20 Base Erosion and Profit Shifting Project, OECD Publishing, Paris, https://dx.doi.org/10.1787/9789264241190-en. [1]

OECD/Council of Europe (2011), *The Multilateral Convention on Mutual Administrative Assistance in Tax Matters: Amended by the 2010 Protocol*, OECD Publishing, Paris, https://dx.doi.org/10.1787/9789264115606-en. [4]

Notes

[1] With respect to the following preferential regimes: 1) Tonnage tax regime.

[2] Parties to the Convention are available here: www.oecd.org/tax/exchange-of-tax-information/convention-on-mutual-administrative-assistance-in-tax-matters.htm. Germany also has bilateral agreements in force with Albania, Algeria, Argentina, Armenia, Australia, Austria, Bangladesh, Belarus, Belgium, Bolivia, Bosnia and Herzegovina, Bulgaria, Canada, China (People's Republic of), Costa Rica, Côte d'Ivoire, Croatia, Cyprus, Czech Republic, Denmark, Ecuador, Egypt, Estonia, Finland, France, Georgia, Ghana, Greece, Hungary, Iceland, India, Indonesia, Iran, Ireland, Israel, Italy, Jamaica, Japan, Jersey, Kazakhstan, Kenia, Korea, Kosovo, Kuwait, Kyrgyzstan, Latvia, Liberia, Liechtenstein, Lithuania, Luxembourg, Malaysia, Malta, Morocco, Mauritius, Mexico, Moldavia, Mongolia, Montenegro, Namibia, Netherlands, New Zealand, North Macedonia, Norway, Pakistan, Philippines, Poland, Portugal, Romania, Russia, Serbia, Singapore, Slovak Republic, Slovenia, South Africa, Spain, Sri Lanka, Sweden, Switzerland, Syria, Tajikistan, Thailand, Trinidad and Tobago, Tunisia, Turkey, Turkmenistan, Ukraine, United Arab Emirates, United Kingdom, United States, Uruguay, Uzbekistan, Venezuela, Viet Nam, Zambia, Zimbabwe.

Greece

Greece has met all aspects of the terms of reference (OECD, 2017[3]) (ToR) for the calendar year 2019 (year in review) and no recommendations are made.

Greece can legally issue one type of rulings within the scope of the transparency framework.

In practice, Greece issued rulings within the scope of the transparency framework as follows:

- One past ruling;
- For the period 1 April 2016 - 31 December 2016: no future rulings;
- For the calendar year 2017: no future rulings;
- For the calendar year 2018: two future rulings, and
- For the year in review: no future rulings.

As no exchanges were required to take place, no peer input was received in respect of the exchanges of information on rulings received from Greece.

A. The information gathering process

442. Greece can legally issue the following type of rulings within the scope of the transparency framework: cross-border unilateral APAs and any other cross-border unilateral tax rulings (such as an advance tax ruling) covering transfer pricing or the application of transfer pricing principles.

443. For Greece, past rulings are any tax rulings within scope that are issued either: (i) on or after 1 January 2014 but before 1 April 2016; or (ii) on or after 1 January 2010 but before 1 January 2014, provided they were still in effect as at 1 January 2014. Future rulings are any tax rulings within scope that are issued on or after 1 April 2016.

444. In the prior years' peer review reports, it was determined that Greece's undertakings to identify past and future rulings and all potential exchange jurisdictions were sufficient to meet the minimum standard. In addition, it was determined that Greece's review and supervision mechanism was sufficient to meet the minimum standard. Greece's implementation remains unchanged, and therefore continues to meet the minimum standard.

445. Greece has met all of the ToR for the information gathering process and no recommendations are made.

B. The exchange of information

446. In the prior years' peer review reports, it was determined that Greece's process for the completion and exchange of templates were sufficient to meet the minimum standard. With respect to past rulings, no further action was required from Greece. Greece's implementation in this regard remains unchanged and therefore continues to meet the minimum standard.

447. Greece has international agreements permitting spontaneous exchange of information, including being a party to the (i) *Multilateral Convention on Mutual Administrative Assistance in Tax Matters: Amended by the 2010 Protocol* (OECD/Council of Europe, 2011[4]) ("the Convention"), (ii) the Directive 2011/16/EU with all other European Union Member States and (iii) bilateral agreements in force with 57 jurisdictions.[1]

448. As Greece was not required to exchange any information on rulings for the year in review, no data on the timeliness of exchanges can be reported.

449. Greece has the necessary legal basis for spontaneous exchange of information, a process for completing the templates in a timely way and has completed all exchanges. Greece has met all of the ToR for the exchange of information process and no recommendations are made.

C. Statistics (ToR IV)

450. As no rulings are issued, no statistics can be reported.

D. Matters related to intellectual property regimes (ToR I.4.1.3)

451. Greece does not offer an intellectual property regime for which transparency requirements under the Action 5 Report (OECD, 2015[11]) were imposed.

Summary of recommendations on implementation of the transparency framework

Aspect of implementation of the transparency framework that should be improved	Recommendation for improvement
	No recommendations are made.

References

OECD (2017), *BEPS Action 5 on Harmful Tax Practices - Terms of Reference and Methodology for the Conduct of the Peer Reviews of the Action 5 Transparency Framework*, OECD Publishing, Paris, http://www.oecd.org/tax/beps/beps-action-5-harmful-tax-practices-peer-review-transparency-framework.pdf. [3]

OECD (2015), *Countering Harmful Tax Practices More Effectively, Taking into Account Transparency and Substance, Action 5 - 2015 Final Report*, OECD/G20 Base Erosion and Profit Shifting Project, OECD Publishing, Paris, https://dx.doi.org/10.1787/9789264241190-en. [1]

OECD/Council of Europe (2011), *The Multilateral Convention on Mutual Administrative Assistance in Tax Matters: Amended by the 2010 Protocol*, OECD Publishing, Paris, https://dx.doi.org/10.1787/9789264115606-en. [4]

Notes

[1] Parties to the Convention are available here: www.oecd.org/tax/exchange-of-tax-information/convention-on-mutual-administrative-assistance-in-tax-matters.htm. Greece also has bilateral agreements with Albania, Armenia, Austria, Azerbaijan, Belgium, Bosnia and Herzegovina, Bulgaria, Canada, China (People's Republic of), Qatar, Croatia, Cyprus, Czech Republic, Denmark, Egypt, Estonia, Finland, France, Germany, Georgia, Hungary, Iceland, India, Ireland, Israel, Italy, Korea, Kuwait, Latvia, Lithuania, Luxembourg, Malta, Mexico, Moldova, Morocco, Netherlands, Norway, Poland, Portugal, Romania, Russian Federation, San Marino, Saudi Arabia, Serbia, Slovak Republic, Slovenia, Spain, South Africa, Sweden, Swiss Federation, Tunisia, Turkey, Ukraine, United Arab Emirates, United Kingdom, Uzbekistan and United States.

Grenada

Grenada is taking steps to implement the transparency framework and to commence administrative preparations to ensure that it establishes an information gathering process (ToR I.4) and information on rulings will be identified and exchanged in a timely manner (ToR II.5). Grenada receives two recommendations on these points for the year in review.

This is Grenada's first review of implementation of the transparency framework.

Grenada can legally issue five types of rulings within the scope of the transparency framework.

In practice, Grenada has issued no rulings within the scope of the transparency framework.

As no exchanges were required to take place, no peer input was received in respect of the exchanges of information on rulings received from Grenada.

A. The information gathering process

452. Grenada can legally issue the following five types of rulings within the scope of the transparency framework: (i) preferential regimes; (ii) cross-border unilateral APAs and any other cross-border unilateral tax rulings (such as an advance tax ruling) covering transfer pricing or the application of transfer pricing principles; (iii) rulings providing for unilateral downward adjustments; (iv) permanent establishment rulings; and (v) related party conduit rulings. The Inland Revenue Division has a structure in place where an independent tax tribunal can issue rulings in scope of the transparency framework. To date, Grenada has never issued any rulings in scope of the transparency framework.

Past rulings (ToR I.4.1.1, I.4.1.2, I.4.2.1, I.4.2.2)

453. For Grenada, past rulings are any tax rulings issued prior to 1 March 2019. However, there is no obligation under the terms of the transparency framework for Grenada to conduct spontaneous exchange information on past rulings.

Future rulings (ToR I.4.1.1, I.4.1.2, I.4.2.1)

454. For Grenada, future rulings are any tax rulings within scope that are issued on or after 1 March 2019.

455. No rulings were issued by Grenada during the period in review. Grenada indicates that there are not yet processes in place to ensure the implementation of the obligations relating to the transparency framework such as the record keeping of rulings. It is noted that Grenada intends to implement appropriate processes to ensure the necessary information to meet the requirements of the transparency framework is required in all cases.

Review and supervision (ToR I.4.3)

456. Grenada did not yet have a review and supervision mechanism under the transparency framework for the year in review. Grenada is discussing the implementation of a revision and supervision mechanism for ensuring implementation of the transparency framework.

Conclusion on section A

457. Grenada is recommended to finalise its information gathering process for identifying all future rulings and potential exchange jurisdictions, with a review and supervision mechanism, as soon as possible (ToR I.4).

B. The exchange of information

Legal basis for spontaneous exchange of information (ToR II.5.1, II.5.2)

458. Grenada has the necessary domestic legal basis to exchange information spontaneously. Grenada notes that there are no legal or practical impediments that prevent the spontaneous exchange of information on rulings as contemplated in the Action 5 minimum standard.

459. Grenada has international agreements permitting spontaneous exchange of information, including being a party to the (i) *Multilateral Convention on Mutual Administrative Assistance in Tax Matters: Amended by the 2010 Protocol* (OECD/Council of Europe, 2011[4]) ("the Convention") and (ii) bilateral agreements in force with 15 jurisdictions.[1]

Completion and exchange of templates (ToR II.5.3, II.5.4, II.5.5, II.5.6, II.5.7)

460. Grenada is still developing a process to complete the templates on relevant rulings, to make them available to the Competent Authority for exchange of information, and to exchange them with relevant jurisdictions.

461. As no exchanges were required to take place in the year of review, no data on the timeliness of exchanges can be reported.

Conclusion on section B

462. Grenada is recommended to develop a process to complete the templates on relevant rulings and to ensure that the exchanges of information on rulings occur in accordance with the form and timelines under the transparency framework (ToR II.5).

C. Statistics (ToR IV)

463. As no rulings were issued, no statistics can be reported.

D. Matters related to intellectual property regimes (ToR I.4.1.3)

464. Grenada does not offer an intellectual property regime for which transparency requirements under the Action 5 Report (OECD, 2015[1]) were imposed.

Summary of recommendations on implementation of the transparency framework

Aspect of implementation of the transparency framework that should be improved	Recommendation for improvement
Grenada has not put in place the necessary information gathering process.	Grenada is recommended to finalise its information gathering process for identifying all future rulings and potential exchange jurisdictions, with a review and supervision mechanism, as soon as possible.
Grenada does not have a process to complete the templates on relevant rulings, to make them available to the Competent Authority for exchange of information, and to exchange them with relevant jurisdictions.	Grenada is recommended to develop a process to complete the templates on relevant rulings and to ensure that the exchanges of information on rulings occur in accordance with the form and timelines under the transparency framework.

References

OECD (2015), *Countering Harmful Tax Practices More Effectively, Taking into Account Transparency and Substance, Action 5 - 2015 Final Report*, OECD/G20 Base Erosion and Profit Shifting Project, OECD Publishing, Paris, https://dx.doi.org/10.1787/9789264241190-en. [1]

OECD/Council of Europe (2011), *The Multilateral Convention on Mutual Administrative Assistance in Tax Matters: Amended by the 2010 Protocol*, OECD Publishing, Paris, https://dx.doi.org/10.1787/9789264115606-en. [4]

Notes

[1] Parties to the Convention are available here: www.oecd.org/tax/exchange-of-tax-information/convention-on-mutual-administrative-assistance-in-tax-matters.htm. Grenada also has bilateral agreements with South Africa, the United Kingdom, and jurisdictions party to the CARICOM agreement.

Guernsey

Guernsey has met all aspects of the terms of reference (OECD, 2017[3]) (ToR) for the calendar year 2019 (year in review) and no recommendations are made.

Guernsey can legally issue four types of rulings within the scope of the transparency framework.

In practice, Guernsey issued rulings within the scope of the transparency framework as follows:

- Five past rulings;
- For the period 1 April 2017 - 31 December 2017: three future rulings;
- For the calendar year 2018: two future rulings, and
- For the year in review: one future ruling.

No peer input was received in respect of the exchanges of information on rulings received from Guernsey.

A. The information gathering process

465. Guernsey can legally issue the following four types of rulings within the scope of the transparency framework: (i) cross border unilateral APAs and any other cross-border unilateral tax rulings (such as an advance tax ruling) covering transfer pricing or the application of transfer pricing principles; (ii) rulings providing for unilateral downward adjustments; (iii) permanent establishment rulings; and (iv) related party conduit rulings.

466. For Guernsey, past rulings are any tax rulings within scope that are issued either: (i) on or after 1 January 2015 but before 1 April 2017; or (ii) on or after 1 January 2012 but before 1 January 2015, provided they were still in effect as at 1 January 2015. Future rulings are any tax rulings within scope that are issued on or after 1 April 2017.

467. In the prior years' peer review reports, it was determined that Guernsey's undertakings to identify past and future rulings and all potential exchange jurisdictions were sufficient to meet the minimum standard. In addition, it was determined that Guernsey's review and supervision mechanism was sufficient to meet the minimum standard. Guernsey's implementation remains unchanged, and therefore continues to meet the minimum standard.

468. Guernsey has met all of the ToR for the information gathering process and no recommendations are made.

B. The exchange of information

469. In the prior years' peer review reports, it was determined that Guernsey's process for the completion and exchange of templates were sufficient to meet the minimum standard. With respect to past rulings, no further action was required. Guernsey's implementation in this regard remains unchanged and therefore continues to meet the minimum standard.

470. Guernsey has international agreements permitting spontaneous exchange of information, including being a party to the (i) *Multilateral Convention on Mutual Administrative Assistance in Tax Matters: Amended by the 2010 Protocol* (OECD/Council of Europe, 2011[4]) ("the Convention") and (ii) bilateral agreements in force with 18 jurisdictions.[1]

471. For the year in review, the timeliness of exchanges is as follows:

Future rulings in the scope of the transparency framework	Number of exchanges transmitted within three months of the information becoming available to the competent authority or immediately after legal impediments have been lifted	Delayed exchanges		
		Number of exchanges transmitted later than three months of the information on rulings becoming available to the competent authority	Reasons for the delays	Any other comments
	2	0	N/A	N/A
Total	2	0		

Follow up requests received for exchange of the ruling	Number	Average time to provide response	Number of requests not answered
	0	N/A	N/A

472. Guernsey has the necessary legal basis for spontaneous exchange of information, a process for completing the templates in a timely way and has completed all exchanges. Guernsey has met all of the ToR for the exchange of information process and no recommendations are made.

C. Statistics (ToR IV)

473. The statistics for the year in review are as follows:

Category of ruling	Number of exchanges	Jurisdictions exchanged with
Cross-border unilateral advance pricing agreements (APAs) and any other cross-border unilateral tax rulings (such as an advance tax ruling) covering transfer pricing or the application of transfer pricing principles	0	N/A
Cross-border rulings providing for a unilateral downward adjustment to the taxpayer's taxable profits that is not directly reflected in the taxpayer's financial / commercial accounts	*De minimis* rule applies	N/A
Permanent establishment rulings	0	N/A
Related party conduit rulings	0	N/A
De minimis rule	2	N/A
Total	2	

D. Matters related to intellectual property regimes (ToR I.4.1.3)

474. Guernsey does not offer an intellectual property regime for which transparency requirements under the Action 5 Report (OECD, 2015[1]) were imposed.

Summary of recommendations on implementation of the transparency framework

Aspect of implementation of the transparency framework that should be improved	Recommendation for improvement
	No recommendations are made.

References

OECD (2017), *BEPS Action 5 on Harmful Tax Practices - Terms of Reference and Methodology for the Conduct of the Peer Reviews of the Action 5 Transparency Framework*, OECD Publishing, Paris, http://www.oecd.org/tax/beps/beps-action-5-harmful-tax-practices-peer-review-transparency-framework.pdf. [3]

OECD (2015), *Countering Harmful Tax Practices More Effectively, Taking into Account Transparency and Substance, Action 5 - 2015 Final Report*, OECD/G20 Base Erosion and Profit Shifting Project, OECD Publishing, Paris, https://dx.doi.org/10.1787/9789264241190-en. [1]

OECD/Council of Europe (2011), *The Multilateral Convention on Mutual Administrative Assistance in Tax Matters: Amended by the 2010 Protocol*, OECD Publishing, Paris, https://dx.doi.org/10.1787/9789264115606-en. [4]

Notes

[1] Parties to the Convention are available here: www.oecd.org/tax/exchange-of-tax-information/convention-on-mutual-administrative-assistance-in-tax-matters.htm. Guernsey also has bilateral agreements the British Virgin Islands, Cayman Islands, Cyprus, Gibraltar, Hong Kong, Isle of Man, Jersey, Liechtenstein, Luxembourg, Malta, Mauritius, Monaco, Qatar, Seychelles, Singapore, Turks and Caicos Islands, United Kingdom and United States permitting spontaneous exchange of information.

Hong Kong (China)

Hong Kong (China) ("Hong Kong") has met all aspects of the terms of reference (OECD, 2017[3]) (ToR) for the calendar year 2019 (year in review) and no recommendations are made.

Hong Kong can legally issue four types of rulings within the scope of the transparency framework.

In practice, Hong Kong issued rulings within the scope of the transparency framework as follows:

- One past ruling;
- For the calendar year 2017: no future rulings,
- For the calendar year 2018: no future rulings, and
- For the year in review: two future rulings.

The Inland Revenue Department of Hong Kong may publish some advance rulings on its website in redacted form.[1]

No peer input was received in respect of the exchanges of information on rulings received from Hong Kong.

A. The information gathering process

475. Hong Kong can legally issue the following four types of rulings within the scope of the transparency framework: (i) preferential regimes;[2] (ii) cross-border unilateral APAs and any other cross-border unilateral tax rulings (such as an advance tax ruling) covering transfer pricing or the application of transfer pricing principles; (iii) permanent establishment rulings; and (iv) related party conduit rulings.

476. For Hong Kong, past rulings are any tax rulings within scope that are issued either: (i) on or after 1 January 2015 but before 1 April 2017; or (ii) on or after 1 January 2012 but before 1 January 2015, provided they were still in effect as at 1 January 2015. Future rulings are any tax rulings within scope that are issued on or after 1 April 2017.

477. In the prior years' peer review reports, it was determined that Hong Kong's undertakings to identify past and future rulings and all potential exchange jurisdictions were sufficient to meet the minimum standard. In addition, it was determined that Hong Kong's review and supervision mechanism was sufficient to meet the minimum standard. Hong Kong's implementation remains unchanged, and therefore continues to meet the minimum standard.

478. Hong Kong has met all of the ToR for the information gathering process and no recommendations are made.

B. The exchange of information

479. In the prior years' peer review reports, it was determined that Hong Kong's process for the completion and exchange of templates were sufficient to meet the minimum standard. With respect to past rulings, no further action was required. Hong Kong's implementation in this regard remains unchanged and therefore continues to meet the minimum standard.

480. Hong Kong has international agreements permitting spontaneous exchange of information, including being a party to the (i) *Multilateral Convention on Mutual Administrative Assistance in Tax Matters: Amended by the 2010 Protocol* (OECD/Council of Europe, 2011[4]) ("the Convention") and (ii) bilateral agreements in force with 35 jurisdictions.[3]

481. For the year in review, the timeliness of exchanges is as follows:

Future rulings in the scope of the transparency framework	Number of exchanges transmitted within three months of the information becoming available to the competent authority or immediately after legal impediments have been lifted	Delayed exchanges		
		Number of exchanges transmitted later than three months of the information on rulings becoming available to the competent authority	Reasons for the delays	Any other comments
	2	0	N/A	N/A

Follow up requests received for exchange of the ruling	Number	Average time to provide response	Number of requests not answered
	0	N/A	N/A

482. Hong Kong has the necessary legal basis for spontaneous exchange of information, a process for completing the templates in a timely way and has completed all exchanges. Hong Kong has met all of the ToR for the exchange of information process and no recommendations are made.

C. Statistics (ToR IV)

483. The statistics for the year in review are as follows:

Category of ruling	Number of exchanges	Jurisdictions exchanged with
Ruling related to a preferential regime	*De minimis* rule applies	N/A
Cross-border unilateral advance pricing agreements (APAs) and any other cross-border unilateral tax rulings (such as an advance tax ruling) covering transfer pricing or the application of transfer pricing principles	0	N/A
Cross-border rulings providing for a unilateral downward adjustment to the taxpayer's taxable profits that is not directly reflected in the taxpayer's financial / commercial accounts	0	N/A
Permanent establishment rulings	*De minimis* rule applies	N/A
De minimis rule	2	N/A
Total	2	

D. Matters related to intellectual property regimes (ToR I.4.1.3)

484. Hong Kong does not offer an intellectual property regime for which transparency requirements under the Action 5 Report (OECD, 2015[1]) were imposed.

Summary of recommendations on implementation of the transparency framework

Aspect of implementation of the transparency framework that should be improved	Recommendation for improvement
	No recommendations are made.

References

OECD (2017), *BEPS Action 5 on Harmful Tax Practices - Terms of Reference and Methodology for the Conduct of the Peer Reviews of the Action 5 Transparency Framework*, OECD Publishing, Paris, http://www.oecd.org/tax/beps/beps-action-5-harmful-tax-practices-peer-review-transparency-framework.pdf. [3]

OECD (2015), *Countering Harmful Tax Practices More Effectively, Taking into Account Transparency and Substance, Action 5 - 2015 Final Report*, OECD/G20 Base Erosion and Profit Shifting Project, OECD Publishing, Paris, https://dx.doi.org/10.1787/9789264241190-en. [1]

OECD/Council of Europe (2011), *The Multilateral Convention on Mutual Administrative Assistance in Tax Matters: Amended by the 2010 Protocol*, OECD Publishing, Paris, https://dx.doi.org/10.1787/9789264115606-en. [4]

Notes

[1] https://www.ird.gov.hk/eng/ppr/arc.htm.

[2] With respect to the following preferential regimes: 1) profits tax concession for corporate treasury centres; 2) profits tax concession for professional reinsurers; 3) profits tax concession for captive insurers; 4) profits tax exemptions for ship operators; and 5) profits tax concessions for aircraft lessors and aircraft leasing managers.

[3] Parties to the Convention are available here: www.oecd.org/tax/exchange-of-tax-information/convention-on-mutual-administrative-assistance-in-tax-matters.htm. Hong Kong also has bilateral agreements with Austria, Bailiwick of Guernsey, Belarus, Belgium, Cambodia, Canada, China (People's Republic of), Estonia, Finland, France, Hungary, India, Indonesia, Ireland, Italy, Japan, Jersey, Korea, Latvia, Malta, Mexico, Netherlands, New Zealand, Pakistan, Portugal, Qatar, Romania, Saudi Arabia, South Africa, Spain, Switzerland, Thailand, United Arab Emirates, United Kingdom and Viet Nam.

Hungary

Hungary has met all aspects of the terms of reference (OECD, 2017[3]) (ToR) for the calendar year 2019 (year in review), except for applying the best efforts approach to identify potential exchange jurisdictions for all past rulings (ToR I.4.2.2), the timely exchange of information on future rulings (ToR II.5.6) and identifying or exchanging information on new entrants to the grandfathered IP regime (ToR I.4.1.3). Hungary receives three recommendations on these points for the year in review.

In the prior year report, as well as in the 2016 and 2017 peer reviews, Hungary had received the same recommendations with respect to the exchange on past rulings and the grandfathered IP regime. As they have not been addressed, the recommendations remain in place. A new recommendation with respect to the exchange on future rulings has been added.

Hungary can legally issue four types of rulings within the scope of the transparency framework. In practice, Hungary issued rulings within the scope of the transparency framework as follows:

- 77 past rulings;
- For the period 1 April 2016 - 31 December 2016: four future rulings;
- For the calendar year 2017: nine future rulings,
- For the calendar year 2018: 11 future rulings, and
- For the year in review: 21 future rulings.

No peer input was received in respect of the exchanges of information on rulings received from Hungary.

A. The information gathering process

485. Hungary can legally issue the following four types of rulings within the scope of the transparency framework: (i) preferential regimes;[1] (ii) cross-border unilateral APAs and any other cross-border unilateral tax rulings (such as an advance tax ruling) covering transfer pricing or the application of transfer pricing principles; (iii) permanent establishment rulings; and (iv) related party conduit rulings.

Past rulings (ToR I.4.1.1, I.4.1.2, I.4.2.1, I.4.2.2)

486. For Hungary, past rulings are any tax rulings within scope that are issued either: (i) on or after 1 January 2014 but before 1 April 2016; or (ii) on or after 1 January 2010 but before 1 January 2014, provided they were still in effect as at 1 January 2014.

487. In the prior years' peer review reports, it was determined that Hungary had not used the best efforts approach to identify potential exchange jurisdictions, meaning that Hungary had only identified potential exchange jurisdictions for around half of the past ATRs, although it had identified most potential exchange jurisdictions for APAs but not necessarily the ultimate parent company jurisdiction. Therefore, Hungary was recommended to continue to apply the "best efforts approach" to identify potential exchange jurisdictions for all past rulings.

488. During the year in review, Hungary has not been able to take additional steps. As such, the recommendation remains.

Future rulings (ToR I.4.1.1, I.4.1.2, I.4.2.1)

489. For Hungary, future rulings are any tax rulings within scope that are issued on or after 1 April 2016.

490. In the prior year peer review report, it was determined that Hungary's undertakings to identify future rulings and all potential exchange jurisdictions was sufficient to meet the minimum standard. Hungary's implementation in this regard remains unchanged, and therefore continues to meet the minimum standard.

Review and supervision (ToR I.4.3)

491. In the prior years' peer review reports, it was determined that Hungary's review and supervision mechanism was sufficient to meet the minimum standard. Hungary's implementation in this regard remains unchanged, and therefore continues to meet the minimum standard.

Conclusion on section A

492. Hungary has met all of the ToR for the information gathering process except for applying the best efforts approach for past rulings (ToR I.4.2.2) and Hungary is recommended to continue to apply the "best efforts approach" to identify potential exchange jurisdictions for all past rulings.

B. The exchange of information

Legal basis for spontaneous exchange of information (ToR II.5.1, II.5.2)

493. Hungary has the necessary domestic legal basis to exchange information spontaneously. Hungary notes that there are no legal or practical impediments that prevent the spontaneous exchange of information on rulings as contemplated in the Action 5 minimum standard.

494. Hungary has international agreements permitting spontaneous exchange of information, including being a party to the (i) *Multilateral Convention on Mutual Administrative Assistance in Tax Matters: Amended by the 2010 Protocol* (OECD/Council of Europe, 2011[4]) ("the Convention"), (ii) the Directive 2011/16/EU with all other European Union Member States and (iii) bilateral agreements in force with 81 jurisdictions.[2]

Completion and exchange of templates (ToR II.5.3, II.5.4, II.5.5, II.5.6, II.5.7)

495. In the prior year peer review report, it was determined that Hungary's process for the completion and exchange of templates was sufficient to meet the minimum standard. Hungary's implementation in this regard remains unchanged and therefore continues to meet the minimum standard.

496. For the year in review, the timeliness of exchanges is as follows:

Future rulings in the scope of the transparency framework	Number of exchanges transmitted within three months of the information becoming available to the competent authority or immediately after legal impediments have been lifted	Delayed exchanges		
		Number of exchanges transmitted later than three months of the information on rulings becoming available to the competent authority	Reasons for the delays	Any other comments
	20	5	See below	N/A

Follow up requests received for exchange of the ruling	Number	Average time to provide response	Number of requests not answered
	2	12 days	0

497. During the year in review, Hungary experienced some delays for future rulings. Hungary explained it was due to a review at the beginning of 2020, 3 more future rulings (5 exchanges) are required to be exchanged. Hungary conducted these outstanding exchanges at the beginning of April 2020. Hungary is recommended to ensure that all information on future rulings is exchanged as soon as possible.

Conclusion on section B

498. Hungary has the necessary legal basis for spontaneous exchange of information, a process for completing the templates in a timely way and has completed all exchanges. Hungary has met all of the ToR for the exchange of information process except for the timely exchange of information on future rulings (ToR II.5.6) and Hungary is recommended to ensure that all information on future rulings is exchanged as soon as possible.

C. Statistics (ToR IV)

499. The statistics for the year in review are as follows:

Category of ruling	Number of exchanges	Jurisdictions exchanged with
Ruling related to a preferential regime	*De minimis rule* applies	N/A
Cross-border unilateral advance pricing agreements (APAs) and any other cross-border unilateral tax rulings (such as an advance tax ruling) covering transfer pricing or the application of transfer pricing principles	12	China (People's Republic of), France, Germany, Ireland, Luxembourg, Netherlands, Russia, Switzerland, United States
Permanent establishment rulings	*De minimis rule* applies	N/A

Related party conduit rulings	0	N/A
De minimis rule	8	
IP regimes: total exchanges on taxpayers benefitting from the third category of IP assets, new entrants benefitting from grandfathered IP regimes; and taxpayers making use of the option to treat the nexus ratio as a rebuttable presumption	14	Austria, Croatia, Czech Republic, France, Slovak Republic, United States
Total	34	

D. Matters related to intellectual property regimes (ToR I.4.1.3)

500. Hungary offers an intellectual property regime (IP regime)[3] that is subject to the transparency requirements under the Action 5 Report (OECD, 2015[1]). It states that the identification of the benefitting taxpayers will occur as follows:

- ***New entrants benefitting from the grandfathered IP regime***: Taxpayers that are new entrants to the IP regime can be identified in the tax return. The first tax returns containing information on new entrants have been filed after the relevant date from which enhanced transparency obligations apply. Hungary is currently trying to identify new taxpayers by analysing previous tax returns of taxpayers who have opted into the grandfathered regime and intends to exchange the information on a retroactive basis as soon as it has identified the new entrants (i.e. both new taxpayers and new IP assets). It is noted in Hungary some new entrants resulting in 14 exchanges have already been identified during tax audits for the year in review.
- ***Third category of IP assets***: not applicable as the regime does not allow the third category of IP assets to qualify for the benefits.
- ***Taxpayers making use of the option to treat the nexus ratio as a rebuttable presumption***: not applicable as the regime does not allow the nexus ratio to be treated as a rebuttable presumption.

501. Hungary is recommended to continue its efforts to identify and exchange information on all new entrants to the grandfathered IP regime as soon as possible (ToR I.4.1.3).

Summary of recommendations on implementation of the transparency framework

Aspect of implementation of the transparency framework that should be improved	Recommendation for improvement
Hungary did not yet apply the "best efforts approach" to identify potential exchange jurisdictions for all past rulings.	Hungary is recommended to continue to apply the "best efforts approach" to identify potential exchange jurisdictions for all past rulings. This recommendation remains unchanged since the 2016, 2017 and 2018 peer review reports.
Hungary experienced some delays for the exchange of future rulings.	Hungary is recommended to ensure that all information on future rulings is exchanged as soon as possible.
Hungary did not identify or exchange all information on new entrants to the grandfathered IP regime.	Hungary is recommended to continue its efforts to identify and exchange information on all new entrants to the grandfathered IP regime. This recommendation remains unchanged since the 2016, 2017 and 2018 peer review reports.

References

OECD (2017), *BEPS Action 5 on Harmful Tax Practices - Terms of Reference and Methodology for the Conduct of the Peer Reviews of the Action 5 Transparency Framework*, OECD Publishing, Paris, http://www.oecd.org/tax/beps/beps-action-5-harmful-tax-practices-peer-review-transparency-framework.pdf. [3]

OECD (2015), *Countering Harmful Tax Practices More Effectively, Taking into Account Transparency and Substance, Action 5 - 2015 Final Report*, OECD/G20 Base Erosion and Profit Shifting Project, OECD Publishing, Paris, https://dx.doi.org/10.1787/9789264241190-en. [1]

OECD/Council of Europe (2011), *The Multilateral Convention on Mutual Administrative Assistance in Tax Matters: Amended by the 2010 Protocol*, OECD Publishing, Paris, https://dx.doi.org/10.1787/9789264115606-en. [4]

Notes

[1] With respect to the following preferential regime: IP regime for royalties and capital gains.

[2] Parties to the Convention are available here: www.oecd.org/tax/exchange-of-tax-information/convention-on-mutual-administrative-assistance-in-tax-matters.htm. Hungary also has bilateral agreements with Albania, Armenia, Australia, Austria, Azerbaijan, Bahrain, Belarus, Belgium, Bosnia and Herzegovina, Brazil, Bulgaria, Canada, China (People's Republic of), Chinese Taipei, Croatia, Cyprus, Czech Republic, Denmark, Egypt, Estonia, Finland, France, Georgia, Germany, Greece, Hong Kong (China), Iceland, India, Indonesia, Iran, Ireland, Israel, Italy, Japan, Kazakhstan, Korea, Kosovo, Kuwait, Latvia, Liechtenstein, Lithuania, Luxembourg, Malaysia, Malta, Mexico, Moldova, Mongolia, Montenegro, Morocco, Netherlands, North Macedonia, Norway, Oman, Pakistan, Philippines, Poland, Portugal, Qatar, Romania, Russia, San Marino, Saudi Arabia, Serbia, Singapore, Slovak Republic, Slovenia, South Africa, Spain, Sweden, Switzerland, Thailand, Tunisia, Turkey, Turkmenistan, Ukraine, United Arab Emirates, United Kingdom, United States, Uruguay, Uzbekistan and Viet Nam.

[3] IP regime for royalties and capital gains.

Iceland

Iceland has met all aspects of the terms of reference (OECD, 2017[3]) (ToR) for the calendar year 2019 (year in review) and no recommendations are made.

Iceland can legally issue two types of rulings within the scope of the transparency framework.

In practice, Iceland issued rulings within the scope of the transparency framework as follows:

- One past ruling;
- For the period 1 April 2016- 31 December 2016: no future rulings;
- For the calendar year 2017: no future rulings,
- For the calendar year 2018: no future rulings, and
- For the year in review: no future rulings.

Rulings are published on the tax administration website in anonymised form.

As no exchanges were required to take place, no peer input was received in respect of the exchanges of information on rulings received from Iceland.

A. The information gathering process

502. Iceland can legally issue the following two types of rulings within the scope of the transparency framework: (i) permanent establishment rulings and (ii) related party conduit rulings.

503. For Iceland, past rulings are any tax rulings within scope that are issued either: (i) on or after 1 January 2014 but before 1 April 2016; or (ii) on or after 1 January 2010 but before 1 January 2014, provided they were still in effect as at 1 January 2014. Future rulings are any tax rulings within scope that are issued on or after 1 April 2016.

504. In the prior years' peer review reports, it was determined that Iceland's undertakings to identify past and future rulings and all potential exchange jurisdictions were sufficient to meet the minimum standard. In addition, it was determined that Iceland's review and supervision mechanism was sufficient to meet the minimum standard. Iceland's implementation remains unchanged, and therefore continues to meet the minimum standard.

505. Iceland has met all of the ToR for the information gathering process and no recommendations are made.

B. The exchange of information

506. In the prior years' peer review reports, it was determined that Iceland's process for the completion and exchange of templates were sufficient to meet the minimum standard. With respect to past rulings, no further action was required. Iceland's implementation in this regard remains unchanged and therefore continues to meet the minimum standard.

507. Iceland has international agreements permitting spontaneous exchange of information, including being a party to the (i) *Multilateral Convention on Mutual Administrative Assistance in Tax Matters: Amended by the 2010 Protocol* (OECD/Council of Europe, 2011[4]) ("the Convention"), (ii) the Nordic Convention with Denmark, Faroe Islands, Finland, Norway and Sweden and (iii) bilateral agreements in force with 40 jurisdictions.[1]

508. As Iceland was not required to exchange any information on rulings for the year in review and no data on the timeliness of exchanges can be reported.

509. Iceland has the necessary legal basis for spontaneous exchange of information, a process for completing the templates in a timely way and has completed all exchanges. Iceland has met all of the ToR for the exchange of information process and no recommendations are made.

C. Statistics (ToR IV)

510. As no rulings are issued, no statistics can be reported.

D. Matters related to intellectual property regimes (ToR I.4.1.3)

511. Iceland does not offer an intellectual property regime for which transparency requirements under the Action 5 Report (OECD, 2015[1]) were imposed.

Summary of recommendations on implementation of the transparency framework

Aspect of implementation of the transparency framework that should be improved	Recommendation for improvement
	No recommendations are made.

References

OECD (2017), *BEPS Action 5 on Harmful Tax Practices - Terms of Reference and Methodology for the Conduct of the Peer Reviews of the Action 5 Transparency Framework*, OECD Publishing, Paris, http://www.oecd.org/tax/beps/beps-action-5-harmful-tax-practices-peer-review-transparency-framework.pdf. [3]

OECD (2015), *Countering Harmful Tax Practices More Effectively, Taking into Account Transparency and Substance, Action 5 - 2015 Final Report*, OECD/G20 Base Erosion and Profit Shifting Project, OECD Publishing, Paris, https://dx.doi.org/10.1787/9789264241190-en. [1]

OECD/Council of Europe (2011), *The Multilateral Convention on Mutual Administrative Assistance in Tax Matters: Amended by the 2010 Protocol*, OECD Publishing, Paris, https://dx.doi.org/10.1787/9789264115606-en. [4]

Notes

[1] Parties to the Convention are available here: www.oecd.org/tax/exchange-of-tax-information/convention-on-mutual-administrative-assistance-in-tax-matters.htm. Iceland also has bilateral agreements with Albania, Austria, Barbados, Belgium, Canada, China (People's Republic of), Croatia, Cyprus, Czech Republic, Estonia, France, Georgia, Greece, Greenland, Germany, Hungary, India, Ireland, Italy, Japan, Korea, Latvia, Liechtenstein, Lithuania, Luxembourg, Malta, Mexico, Netherlands, Poland, Portugal, Romania, Russia, Slovak Republic, Slovenia, Spain, Switzerland, Ukraine, United Kingdom, United States, Viet Nam.

India

India has met all aspects of the terms of reference (OECD, 2017[3]) (ToR) for the calendar year 2019 (year in review), except for ensuring that information on future APA rulings is exchanged as soon as possible (ToR II.5.6). India receives one recommendation on this point for the year in review.

In the prior year report, as well as in the 2017 peer review, India had received the same recommendation. A number of steps were taken in the year in review to address this, although a significant number of exchanges remained delayed for the year in review. As such, the recommendation remains in place.

India can legally issue two types of rulings within the scope of the transparency framework.

In practice, India issued rulings within the scope of the transparency framework as follows:

- 69 past rulings;
- For the period 1 April 2016 - 31 December 2016: 55 future rulings;
- For the calendar year 2017: 73 future rulings,
- For the calendar year 2018: 44 future rulings, and
- For the year in review: 137 future rulings.

PE rulings are published unless it is stated to be confidential by the Authority issuing the ruling, whereas unilateral APAs are not.

Peer input was received from seven jurisdictions in respect of the exchanges of information on rulings received from India. The input generally positive, noting that information was complete, in a correct format and almost all received in a timely manner. Some peers noted that the information was received with a delay.

A. The information gathering process

512. India can legally issue the following to types of rulings within the scope of the transparency framework: (i) cross-border unilateral APAs and any other cross-border unilateral tax rulings (such as an advance tax ruling) covering transfer pricing or the application of transfer pricing principles; and (ii) permanent establishment rulings.

513. For India, past rulings are any tax rulings within scope that are issued either: (i) on or after 1 January 2014 but before 1 April 2016; or (ii) on or after 1 January 2010 but before 1 January 2014, provided they were still in effect as at 1 January 2014. Future rulings are any tax rulings within scope that are issued on or after 1 April 2016.

514. In the prior year peer review report, it was determined that India's undertakings to identify past and future rulings and all potential exchange jurisdictions were sufficient to meet the minimum standard. In addition, it was determined that India's review and supervision mechanism was sufficient to meet the minimum standard. India's implementation remains unchanged, and therefore continues to meet the minimum standard.

515. India has met all of the ToR for the information gathering process and no recommendations are made.

B. The exchange of information

Legal basis for spontaneous exchange of information (ToR II.5.1, II.5.2)

516. India has the necessary domestic legal basis to exchange information spontaneously. India notes that there are no legal or practical impediments that prevent the spontaneous exchange of information on rulings as contemplated in the Action 5 minimum standard.

517. India has international agreements permitting spontaneous exchange of information, including being a party to the (i) *Multilateral Convention on Mutual Administrative Assistance in Tax Matters: Amended by the 2010 Protocol* (OECD/Council of Europe, 2011[4]) ("the Convention"), (ii) the South Asian Association for Regional Cooperation (SAARC) Agreement and (iii) bilateral agreements in force with 100 jurisdictions.[1]

Completion and exchange of templates (ToR II.5.3, II.5.4, II.5.5, II.5.6, II.5.7)

518. In the prior years' peer review reports, it was determined that India's process for the completion and exchange of templates met all the ToR, except for ensuring that information on future APA rulings is exchanged as soon as possible (ToR II.5.6). Therefore, India was recommended to ensure the timely exchange of information on future APA rulings. With respect to past rulings, no further action was required.

519. For the year in review, the timeliness of exchanges is as follows:

Future rulings in the scope of the transparency framework	Number of exchanges transmitted within three months of the information becoming available to the competent authority or immediately after legal impediments have been lifted	Delayed exchanges		
		Number of exchanges transmitted later than three months of the information on rulings becoming available to the competent authority	Reasons for the delays	Any other comments
	150	761	See below.	N/A
Total	150	761		

Follow up requests received for exchange of the ruling	Number	Average time to provide response	Number of requests not answered
	4	120 days	0

520. During the year in review, India continued to encounter delays with respect to the exchange of information on future APAs. This was mostly due to the fact that India had to use the "best efforts approach" to identify potential exchange jurisdictions, for APAs issued before 16 June 2017. It is noted that new ruling application templates requiring this information came into effect from 16 June 2017 (for APAs). In addition, India faced difficulties in carrying out exchanges due to the increased number of issued rulings. Therefore, India is still recommended to continue to ensure the timely exchange of information on future APA rulings (ToR II.5.6).

521. India notes that during the year in review, India made an analysis of the workload management and in response to that, redistributed work in the centralised office (the competent authority) to a higher number of divisions and made changes to the workflow. In addition, India issued guidance to tax administration officers for the timely preparation and forwarding of templates to the competent authority, amended taxpayer's application forms to capture all relevant information at the application stage, created a central data warehouse to store the templates, followed up with the relevant officers in cases of delay, and created a Standard Operation Procedure to deal with procedural delays. This procedure includes periodic communication with the responsible authorities to ensure accurate and timely reporting of data to the competent authority. In addition, it includes steps on rectification of a template in case there was inaccurate information. In that case, communication takes place with the relevant officer, and the rectified template (by the competent authority) will be exchanged within the appropriate timeframe.

522. In addition, India will issue additional internal guidance for officers within the tax administration and the competent authority. India envisages that these new procedures, guidance and internal processes that have been put in place will ensure that the completion and exchange of templates will occur in an accurate and timely manner going forward, and this will be assessed in the next year's peer review process.

Conclusion on section B

523. India has met all of the ToR for the information gathering process except for ensuring that information on future APA rulings is exchanged as soon as possible (ToR II.5.6). India is recommended to continue to ensure the timely exchange of information on future APA rulings.

C. Statistics (ToR IV)

524. The statistics for the year in review are as follows:

Category of ruling	Number of exchanges	Jurisdictions exchanged with
Cross-border unilateral advance pricing agreements (APAs) and any other cross-border unilateral tax rulings (such as an advance tax ruling) covering transfer pricing or the application of transfer pricing principles	905	Argentina, Australia, Austria, Belgium, Brazil, Canada, Chile, China (People's Republic of), Colombia, Croatia, Czech Republic, Denmark, Egypt, Estonia, Finland, France, Germany, Greece, Guatemala, Bailiwick of Guernsey, Hong Kong (China), Hungary, Indonesia, Ireland, Isle of Man, Israel, Italy, Japan, Jersey, Kenya, Korea, Latvia, Lithuania, Luxembourg, Malaysia, Malta, Mauritius, Mexico, Morocco, Nepal, Netherlands, New Zealand, Nigeria, Norway, Pakistan, Panama, Poland, Portugal, Qatar,

		Romania, Russia, Saudi Arabia, Serbia, Singapore, Slovak Republic, Slovenia, South Africa, Spain, Sweden, Switzerland, Trinidad and Tobago, Turkey, Ukraine, United Kingdom, United States
Permanent establishment rulings	6	Austria, Italy, Luxembourg, United Kingdom
Total	911	

D. Matters related to intellectual property regimes (ToR I.4.1.3)

525. India offers an intellectual property regime (IP regime)[2] that is not subject to the transparency requirements under the Action 5 Report (OECD, 2015[1]), because:

- ***New entrants benefitting from the grandfathered IP regime***: the regime is a new nexus-compliant regime and therefore there is no grandfathered IP regime for which enhanced transparency requirements will apply.
- ***Third category of IP assets***: not applicable as the regime does not allow the third category of IP assets to qualify for the benefits.
- ***Taxpayers making the use of the option to treat the nexus ratio as a rebuttable presumption***: not applicable the regime does not allow the nexus ratio to be treated as a rebuttable presumption.

Summary of recommendations on implementation of the transparency framework

Aspect of implementation of the transparency framework that should be improved	Recommendation for improvement
India experienced delays in the exchange of information on future APAs.	India is recommended to continue its efforts to ensure that all information on future APAs is exchanged as soon as possible. This recommendation remains unchanged since the 2017 and 2018 peer review reports.

References

OECD (2017), *BEPS Action 5 on Harmful Tax Practices - Terms of Reference and Methodology for the Conduct of the Peer Reviews of the Action 5 Transparency Framework*, OECD Publishing, Paris, http://www.oecd.org/tax/beps/beps-action-5-harmful-tax-practices-peer-review-transparency-framework.pdf. [3]

OECD (2015), *Countering Harmful Tax Practices More Effectively, Taking into Account Transparency and Substance, Action 5 - 2015 Final Report*, OECD/G20 Base Erosion and Profit Shifting Project, OECD Publishing, Paris, https://dx.doi.org/10.1787/9789264241190-en. [1]

OECD/Council of Europe (2011), *The Multilateral Convention on Mutual Administrative Assistance in Tax Matters: Amended by the 2010 Protocol*, OECD Publishing, Paris, https://dx.doi.org/10.1787/9789264115606-en. [4]

Notes

[1] Parties to the Convention are available here: www.oecd.org/tax/exchange-of-tax-information/convention-on-mutual-administrative-assistance-in-tax-matters.htm. India also has bilateral agreements with Albania, Armenia, Australia, Austria, Azerbaijan, Bahamas, Bangladesh, Belarus, Belgium, Bhutan, Botswana, Brazil, Brunei Darussalam, Bulgaria, Canada, China (People's Republic of), Colombia, Croatia, Cyprus, Czech Republic, Denmark, Egypt, Estonia, Ethiopia, Faroe Islands, Fiji, Finland, France, Georgia, Germany, Greece, Grenada, Hungary, Iceland, Indonesia, Ireland, Israel, Italy, Japan, Jordan, Kazakhstan, Kenya, Korea, Kuwait, Kyrgyzstan, Latvia, Libya, Lithuania, Luxembourg, Malaysia, Malta, Mauritius, Mexico, Moldova, Mongolia, Morocco, Montenegro, Mozambique, Myanmar, Namibia, Nepal, Netherlands, New Zealand, North Macedonia, Norway, Oman, Philippines, Poland, Portugal, Qatar, Romania, Russia, Saudi Arabia, Serbia, Singapore, Slovak Republic, Slovenia, South Africa, Spain, Sri Lanka, Sudan, Sweden, Switzerland, Syria, Chinese Taipei, Tajikistan, Tanzania, Thailand, Trinidad and Tobago, Turkey, Turkmenistan, Uganda, Ukraine, United Arab Emirates, United Kingdom, United States, Uruguay, Uzbekistan, Vanuatu and Zambia.

The SAARC was entered into force on 19 May 2010 and provides for exchanges with Bangladesh, Bhutan, Maldives, Nepal, Pakistan and Sri Lanka.

[2] Tax on income from patent.

Indonesia

Indonesia has met all aspects of the terms of reference (OECD, 2017[3]) (ToR) for the calendar year 2019 (year in review) and no recommendations are made.

Indonesia can legally issue one type of ruling within the scope of the transparency framework.

In practice, Indonesia issued rulings within the scope of the transparency framework as follows:

- In the prior years: no rulings, and
- For the year in review: one future ruling.

No peer input was received in respect of the exchanges of information on rulings received from Indonesia.

A. The information gathering process

526. Indonesia can legally issue one type of ruling within the scope of the transparency framework: cross-border unilateral APAs and any other cross-border unilateral tax rulings (such as an advance tax ruling) covering transfer pricing or the application of transfer pricing principles.

527. For Indonesia, past rulings are any tax rulings within scope that are issued either: (i) on or after 1 January 2014 but before 1 April 2016; or (ii) on or after 1 January 2010 but before 1 January 2014, provided they were still in effect as at 1 January 2014. Future rulings are any tax rulings within scope that are issued on or after 1 April 2016.

528. In the prior years' peer review reports, it was determined that Indonesia's undertakings to identify past and future rulings and all potential exchange jurisdictions were sufficient to meet the minimum standard. In addition, it was determined that Indonesia's review and supervision mechanism was sufficient to meet the minimum standard. Indonesia's implementation remains unchanged, and therefore continues to meet the minimum standard. During the year in review, Indonesia issued relevant rulings and put its process into practice for the first time, Indonesia indicates it has worked well and without difficulty.

529. Indonesia has met all of the ToR for the information gathering process and no recommendations are made.

B. The exchange of information

530. In the prior years' peer review reports, it was determined that Indonesia's process for the completion and exchange of templates were sufficient to meet the minimum standard. Indonesia's implementation in this regard remains unchanged and therefore continues to meet the minimum standard. Furthermore, as this is the first year that Indonesia has issued relevant rulings and put its processes into practice, Indonesia affirms that its procedures were effective, resulting in exchanges being carried out in a timely manner as required under the standard. Furthermore, Indonesia confirms that the summary section of the template is completed in line with the internal FHTP suggested guidance.

531. Indonesia has international agreements permitting spontaneous exchange of information, including being a party to the (i) *Multilateral Convention on Mutual Administrative Assistance in Tax Matters: Amended by the 2010 Protocol* (OECD/Council of Europe, 2011[4]) ("the Convention") and (ii) bilateral agreements in force with 68 jurisdictions.[1]

532. For the year in review, the timeliness of exchanges is as follows:

Future rulings in the scope of the transparency framework	Number of exchanges transmitted within three months of the information becoming available to the competent authority or immediately after legal impediments have been lifted	Delayed exchanges		
		Number of exchanges transmitted later than three months of the information on rulings becoming available to the competent authority	Reasons for the delays	Any other comments
	3	0	N/A	N/A

Follow up requests received for exchange of the ruling	Number	Average time to provide response	Number of requests not answered
	0	N/A	N/A

533. Indonesia has the necessary legal basis for spontaneous exchange of information, a process for completing the templates in a timely way and has completed all exchanges. Indonesia has met all of the ToR for the exchange of information process and no recommendations are made.

C. Statistics (ToR IV)

534. The statistics for the year in review are as follows:

Category of ruling	Number of exchanges	Jurisdictions exchanged with
Cross-border unilateral APAs and any other cross-border unilateral tax rulings (such as an advance tax ruling) covering transfer pricing or the application of transfer pricing principles	*De minimis* rule applies	N/A
De minimis rule	3	N/A
Total	3	

D. Matters related to intellectual property regimes (ToR I.4.1.3)

535. Indonesia does not offer an intellectual property regime for which transparency requirements under the Action 5 Report (OECD, 2015[1]) were imposed.

Summary of recommendations on implementation of the transparency framework

Aspect of implementation of the transparency framework that should be improved	Recommendation for improvement
	No recommendations are made.

References

OECD (2017), *BEPS Action 5 on Harmful Tax Practices - Terms of Reference and Methodology for the Conduct of the Peer Reviews of the Action 5 Transparency Framework*, OECD Publishing, Paris, http://www.oecd.org/tax/beps/beps-action-5-harmful-tax-practices-peer-review-transparency-framework.pdf. [3]

OECD (2015), *Countering Harmful Tax Practices More Effectively, Taking into Account Transparency and Substance, Action 5 - 2015 Final Report*, OECD/G20 Base Erosion and Profit Shifting Project, OECD Publishing, Paris, https://dx.doi.org/10.1787/9789264241190-en. [1]

OECD/Council of Europe (2011), *The Multilateral Convention on Mutual Administrative Assistance in Tax Matters: Amended by the 2010 Protocol*, OECD Publishing, Paris, https://dx.doi.org/10.1787/9789264115606-en. [4]

Notes

[1] Parties to the Convention are available here: www.oecd.org/tax/exchange-of-tax-information/convention-on-mutual-administrative-assistance-in-tax-matters.htm. Indonesia also has bilateral agreements with Algeria, Armenia, Australia, Austria, Bangladesh, Belarus, Belgium, Brunei Darussalam, Bulgaria, Canada, China (People's Republic of), Croatia, Czech Republic, Democratic People's Republic of Korea, Denmark, Egypt, Finland, France, Germany, Hong Kong (China), Hungary, India, Iran, Italy, Japan, Jordan, Korea, Kuwait, Lao People's Democratic Republic, Luxembourg, Malaysia, Mexico, Mongolia, Morocco, Netherlands, New Zealand, Norway, Pakistan, Papua New Guinea, Philippines, Poland, Portugal, Qatar, Romania, Russia, Serbia, Seychelles, Singapore, Slovak Republic, South Africa, Spain, Sri Lanka, Sudan, Suriname, Sweden, Syria, Chinese Taipei, Tajikistan, Thailand, Tunisia, Turkey, Ukraine, United Arab Emirates, United Kingdom, United States, Uzbekistan, Venezuela, Viet Nam.

Ireland

Ireland has met all aspects of the terms of reference (OECD, 2017[3]) (ToR) for the calendar year 2019 (year in review) and no recommendations are made.

Ireland can legally issue three types of rulings within the scope of the transparency framework.

In practice, Ireland issued rulings within the scope of the transparency framework as follows:

- 29 past rulings;
- For the period 1 April 2016 - 31 December 2016: no future rulings;
- For the calendar year 2017: two future rulings,
- For the calendar year 2018: 39 future rulings, and
- For the year in review: five future rulings.

Peer input was received from three jurisdictions in respect of the exchanges of information on rulings received from Ireland. The input was positive, noting that information was complete, in a correct format and almost all received in a timely manner.

A. The information gathering process

536. Ireland can legally issue three types of rulings within the scope of the transparency framework: (i) preferential regimes;[1] (ii) cross-border unilateral APAs and any other cross-border unilateral tax rulings (such as an advance tax ruling) covering transfer pricing or the application of transfer pricing principles; and (iii) permanent establishment rulings.

537. For Ireland, past rulings are any tax rulings within scope that are issued either: (i) on or after 1 January 2014 but before 1 April 2016; or (ii) on or after 1 January 2010 but before 1 January 2014, provided they were still in effect as at 1 January 2014. Future rulings are any tax rulings within scope that are issued on or after 1 April 2016.

538. In the prior years' peer review reports, it was determined that Ireland's undertakings to identify past and future rulings and all potential exchange jurisdictions were sufficient to meet the minimum standard. In addition, it was determined that Ireland's review and supervision mechanism was sufficient to meet the minimum standard. Ireland's implementation remains unchanged, and therefore continues to meet the minimum standard.

539. Ireland has met all of the ToR for the information gathering process and no recommendations are made.

B. The exchange of information

540. In the prior years' peer review reports, it was determined that Ireland's process for the completion and exchange of templates were sufficient to meet the minimum standard. With respect to past rulings, no further action was required. Ireland's implementation in this regard remains unchanged and therefore continues to meet the minimum standard.

541. Ireland has international agreements permitting spontaneous exchange of information, including being a party to the (i) *Multilateral Convention on Mutual Administrative Assistance in Tax Matters: Amended by the 2010 Protocol* (OECD/Council of Europe, 2011[4]) ("the Convention"), (ii) the Directive 2011/16/EU with all other European Union Member States and (iii) double tax agreements in force with 73 jurisdictions, 69 of which allow for spontaneous exchange of information.[2]

542. For the year in review, the timeliness of exchanges is as follows:

Future rulings in the scope of the transparency framework	Number of exchanges transmitted within three months of the information becoming available to the competent authority or immediately after legal impediments have been lifted	Delayed exchanges		
		Number of exchanges transmitted later than three months of the information on rulings becoming available to the competent authority	Reasons for the delays	Any other comments
	5	0	N/A	N/A

Follow up requests received for exchange of the ruling	Number	Average time to provide response	Number of requests not answered
	0	N/A	N/A

543. Ireland has the necessary legal basis for spontaneous exchange of information, a process for completing the templates in a timely way and has completed all exchanges. Ireland has met all of the ToR for the exchange of information process and no recommendations are made.

C. Statistics (ToR IV)

544. The statistics for the year in review are as follows:

Category of ruling	Number of exchanges	Jurisdictions exchanged with
Ruling related to a preferential regime	*De minimis rule* applies	N/A
Cross-border unilateral advance pricing agreements (APAs) and any other cross-border unilateral tax rulings (such as an advance tax ruling) covering transfer pricing or the application of transfer pricing principles	0	N/A
Permanent establishment rulings	*De minimis rule* applies	N/A
De minimis rule	5	
IP regimes: total exchanges on taxpayers benefitting from the third category of IP assets, new entrants benefitting from grandfathered IP regimes; and taxpayers making use of the option to treat the nexus ratio as a rebuttable presumption	0	N/A
Total	5	

D. Matters related to intellectual property regimes (ToR I.4.1.3)

545. Ireland offers an intellectual property regime (IP regime)[3] that is subject to the transparency requirements under the Action 5 Report (OECD, 2015[1]). It states that the identification of the benefitting taxpayers will occur as follows:

- ***New entrants benefitting from the grandfathered IP regime***: as this is a new IP regime rather than a grandfathered IP regime, transparency on new entrants is not relevant.
- ***Third category of IP assets***: the relevant part of the annual corporation tax return has been designed to capture the data that Ireland will require for its reporting and exchange of information obligations under the framework. So far, there have been no taxpayers benefitting from the third category of IP assets.
- ***Taxpayers making use of the option to treat the nexus ratio as a rebuttable presumption***: not applicable as the regime does not allow the nexus ratio to be treated as a rebuttable presumption.

Summary of recommendations on implementation of the transparency framework

Aspect of implementation of the transparency framework that should be improved	Recommendation for improvement
	No recommendations are made.

References

OECD (2017), *BEPS Action 5 on Harmful Tax Practices - Terms of Reference and Methodology for the Conduct of the Peer Reviews of the Action 5 Transparency Framework*, OECD Publishing, Paris, http://www.oecd.org/tax/beps/beps-action-5-harmful-tax-practices-peer-review-transparency-framework.pdf. [3]

OECD (2015), *Countering Harmful Tax Practices More Effectively, Taking into Account Transparency and Substance, Action 5 - 2015 Final Report*, OECD/G20 Base Erosion and Profit Shifting Project, OECD Publishing - Paris, https://dx.doi.org/10.1787/9789264241190-en. [1]

OECD/Council of Europe (2011), *The Multilateral Convention on Mutual Administrative Assistance in Tax Matters: Amended by the 2010 Protocol*, OECD Publishing, Paris, https://dx.doi.org/10.1787/9789264115606-en. [4]

Notes

[1] With respect to the following preferential regimes: 1) Shipping regime and 2) Knowledge development box.

[2] Parties to the Convention are available here: www.oecd.org/tax/exchange-of-tax-information/convention-on-mutual-administrative-assistance-in-tax-matters.htm. Ireland also has bilateral agreements in force with Albania, Armenia, Australia, Bahrain, Belarus, Belgium, Bosnia and Herzegovina, Botswana, Bulgaria, Canada, Chile, China (People's Republic of), Croatia, Cyprus, Czech Republic, Denmark, Egypt, Estonia, Ethiopia, Finland, France, Georgia, Germany, Greece, Hungary, Iceland, India, Israel, Italy, Japan, Kazakhstan, Korea, Kuwait, Latvia, Lithuania, Luxembourg, Malaysia, Malta, Mexico, Moldova, Montenegro, Morocco, Netherlands, New Zealand, North Macedonia, Norway, Pakistan, Poland, Portugal, Qatar, Romania, Russia, Saudi Arabia, Servia, Singapore, Slovak Republic, Slovenia, South Africa, Spain, Sweden, Thailand, Turkey, United Arab Emirates, Ukraine, United Kingdom, United States, Uzbekistan, Viet Nam, and Zambia.

[3] Knowledge development box.

Isle of Man

The Isle of Man has met all aspects of the terms of reference (OECD, 2017[3]) (ToR) for the calendar year 2019 (year in review) and no recommendations are made.

The Isle of Man can legally issue two types of rulings within the scope of the transparency framework.

In practice, the Isle of Man issued rulings within the scope of the transparency framework as follows:

- Two past rulings;
- For the period 1 April 2017 - 31 December 2017: no future rulings;
- For the calendar year 2018: no future rulings, and
- For the year in review: no future rulings.

As no exchanges took place, no peer input was received in respect of the exchanges of information on rulings received from the Isle of Man.

A. The information gathering process

546. The Isle of Man can legally issue the following two types of rulings within the scope of the transparency framework: (i) rulings providing for unilateral downward adjustments and (ii) permanent establishment rulings.

547. For The Isle of Man, past rulings are any tax rulings within scope that are issued either: (i) on or after 1 January 2015 but before 1 April 2017; or (ii) on or after 1 January 2012 but before 1 January 2015, provided they were still in effect as at 1 January 2015. Future rulings are any tax rulings within scope that are issued on or after 1 April 2017.

548. In the prior years' peer review reports, it was determined that the Isle of Man's undertakings to identify past and future rulings and all potential exchange jurisdictions were sufficient to meet the minimum standard. In addition, it was determined that the Isle of Man's review and supervision mechanism was sufficient to meet the minimum standard. The Isle of Man's implementation remains unchanged, and therefore continues to meet the minimum standard.

549. The Isle of Man has met all of the ToR for the information gathering process and no recommendations are made.

B. The exchange of information

550. In the prior years' peer review reports, it was determined that The Isle of Man's process for the completion and exchange of templates were sufficient to meet the minimum standard. With respect to past rulings, no further action was required. The Isle of Man's implementation in this regard remains unchanged and therefore continues to meet the minimum standard.

551. The Isle of Man has international agreements permitting spontaneous exchange of information, including being a party to the (i) *Multilateral Convention on Mutual Administrative Assistance in Tax Matters: Amended by the 2010 Protocol* (OECD/Council of Europe, 2011[4]) ("the Convention") and (ii) bilateral agreements in force with 14 jurisdictions.[1]

552. As the Isle of Man did not issue any future rulings in scope of the transparency framework in the relevant period, the Isle of Man was not required to exchange any information on rulings in the year in review and no data on the timeliness of exchanges can be reported.

553. The Isle of Man has the necessary legal basis for spontaneous exchange of information, a process for completing the templates in a timely way and has completed all exchanges. The Isle of Man has met all of the ToR for the exchange of information process and no recommendations are made.

C. Statistics (ToR IV)

554. As no rulings are issued, no statistics can be reported.

D. Matters related to intellectual property regimes (ToR I.4.1.3)

555. The Isle of Man does not offer an intellectual property regime for which transparency requirements under the Action 5 Report (OECD, 2015[1]) were imposed.

Summary of recommendations on implementation of the transparency framework

Aspect of implementation of the transparency framework that should be improved	Recommendation for improvement
	No recommendations are made.

References

OECD (2017), *BEPS Action 5 on Harmful Tax Practices - Terms of Reference and Methodology for the Conduct of the Peer Reviews of the Action 5 Transparency Framework*, OECD Publishing, Paris, http://www.oecd.org/tax/beps/beps-action-5-harmful-tax-practices-peer-review-transparency-framework.pdf. [3]

OECD (2015), *Countering Harmful Tax Practices More Effectively, Taking into Account Transparency and Substance, Action 5 - 2015 Final Report*, OECD/G20 Base Erosion and Profit Shifting Project, OECD Publishing - Paris, https://dx.doi.org/10.1787/9789264241190-en. [1]

OECD/Council of Europe (2011), *The Multilateral Convention on Mutual Administrative Assistance in Tax Matters: Amended by the 2010 Protocol*, OECD Publishing, Paris, https://dx.doi.org/10.1787/9789264115606-en. [4]

Notes

1 Parties to the Convention are available here: www.oecd.org/tax/exchange-of-tax-information/convention-on-mutual-administrative-assistance-in-tax-matters.htm. The Isle of Man also has bilateral agreements the Bahrain, British Virgin Islands, Cayman Islands, Estonia, Guernsey, Jersey, Luxembourg, Malta, Qatar, Seychelles, Singapore, Turks and Caicos Islands, United Kingdom and United States permitting spontaneous exchange of information.

Israel

Israel has met all aspects of the terms of reference (OECD, 2017[3]) (ToR) for the calendar year 2019 (year in review), except for ensuring that each of the mandatory fields of information required in the template contained in Annex C of the BEPS Action 5 Report (OECD, 2015[1]), especially with regard to the summary section, are present in the information exchanged (ToR II.5.3) and for the timely provision of information on rulings to the Competent Authority for exchange of information (ToR II.5.5). Israel receives two recommendations on these points for the year in review.

In the prior year report, as well as in the 2016 and 2017 peer reviews, Israel had received two recommendations. During the year in review, Israel has resolved the issue regarding the delays in the exchange of information for all future rulings (ToR II.5.6) and therefore the recommendation is now removed. As the recommendation to reduce the timelines for providing the information on future rulings to the Competent Authority (ToR II.5.5) has not been addressed, the recommendation remains in place and a new recommendation is added.

Israel can legally issue five types of rulings within the scope of the transparency framework.

In practice, Israel issued rulings within the scope of the transparency framework as follows:

- 79 past rulings;
- For the period 1 April 2016 - 31 December 2016: five future rulings;
- For the calendar year 2017: three future rulings;[1]
- For the calendar year 2018: 15 future rulings; and
- For the year in review: 19 future rulings.

Some rulings are published in anonymised form.[2]

Peer input was received from three jurisdictions in respect of the exchanges of information on rulings received from Israel. The input was generally positive, noting that overall information was complete, in a correct format and almost all received in a timely manner. However, peer input indicated that information included in the summary section of Annex C of the Action 5 report (OECD, 2015[1]) was not sufficient and exchanges on rulings were received after about ten months from the date of their issuance.

A. The information gathering process

556. Israel can legally issue the following five types of rulings within the scope of the transparency framework: (i) preferential regimes;[3] (ii) cross-border unilateral APAs and any other cross-border unilateral tax rulings (such as an advance tax ruling) covering transfer pricing or the application of transfer pricing principles; (iii) rulings providing for unilateral downward adjustments; (iv) permanent establishment rulings; and (v) related party conduit rulings.

557. For Israel, past rulings are any tax rulings within scope that are issued either: (i) on or after 1 January 2014 but before 1 April 2016; or (ii) on or after 1 January 2010 but before 1 January 2014, provided they were still in effect as at 1 January 2014. Future rulings are any tax rulings within scope that are issued on or after 1 April 2016.

558. In the prior years' peer review reports, it was determined that Israel's undertakings to identify past and future rulings and all potential exchange jurisdictions were sufficient to meet the minimum standard. In addition, it was determined that Israel's review and supervision mechanism was sufficient to meet the minimum standard. Israel's implementation remains unchanged, and therefore continues to meet the minimum standard.

559. Israel has met all of the ToR for the information gathering process and no recommendations are made.

B. The exchange of information

Legal basis for spontaneous exchange of information (ToR II.5.1, II.5.2)

560. Israel has the necessary domestic legal basis to exchange information spontaneously. Israel notes that there are no legal or practical impediments that prevent the spontaneous exchange of information on rulings as contemplated in the Action 5 minimum standard.

561. Israel has international agreements permitting spontaneous exchange of information, including being a party to the (i) *Multilateral Convention on Mutual Administrative Assistance in Tax Matters: Amended by the 2010 Protocol* (OECD/Council of Europe, 2011[4]) ("the Convention"), and (ii) bilateral agreements in force with 55 jurisdictions.[4]

Completion and exchange of templates (ToR II.5.3, II.5.4, II.5.5, II.5.6, II.5.7)

562. In the prior years' peer review reports, it was determined that Israel's process for the completion and exchange of templates met all the ToR, except for the timely provision of information on rulings to the Competent Authority (ToR II.5.5) and for the timely exchange of information on future rulings (ToR II.5.6). With respect to past rulings, no further action was required. Therefore, Israel was recommended to reduce the timelines for providing the information on future rulings to the Competent Authority and to ensure that all information on future rulings is exchanged as soon as possible. With respect to past rulings, no further action was required.

563. During the year in review, in respect of the exchanges of information on rulings received from Israel, peer input indicated that the summary section of the template was not always sufficiently informative and detailed. This raised concerns regarding the existence of a process for completion of templates in accordance with the form agreed under the transparency framework. Israel took note of these remarks and intends to instruct the departments issuing rulings about the necessity to complete the summary section of the Annex C template in line with the internal FHTP suggested guidance. In particular, Israel is planning

to put procedures in place within the EOI department for double-checking and reviewing the templates and the adequacy of the summary sections before exchanges are performed with relevant jurisdictions.

564. In regard to the recommendation for submitting information to the Competent Authority, in late 2018, the internal computer system which is used by the departments to issue rulings was amended to add a feature which marks rulings as being relevant for exchange. When this is marked as such, the ruling shall be automatically transmitted and available to the Competent Authority (EOI department). This system became operational in 2019. Notwithstanding the new system, Israel still experienced some delays in submitting information to the Competent Authority and during the last quarter of 2019, Israel put in place a new procedure according to which at the end of each quarter, the departments issuing rulings are required to transfer all the rulings in scope of the transparency framework to the EOI department.

565. During the year in review, Israel completed the exchanges of information on all rulings issued in 2017 and partially completed the exchanges of information on rulings issued in 2018. However, some rulings issued in 2018 and all rulings issued in 2019 were exchanged only in 2020, because of a delay in submitting them to the EOI department, and this will be taken into account in next year's peer review. This delay was because the internal computer system and new procedure was not fully functioning until late in 2019. As the recommendation on the timely provision of information on rulings to the EOI department (ToR II.5.5) has not been addressed, it remains in place.

566. However, when the EOI department received the information, the exchanges with relevant jurisdictions were performed within the timelines. In this respect, the timely exchange of information on future rulings (ToR II.5.6) is met and recommendation is now removed. In 2019, the EOI department began to use encrypted emails for the purpose of exchanging information on tax rulings and it also agreed with two jurisdictions on a bilateral mechanism for making a direct file transfer. This method is expected to expand during 2020 and will allow Israel to further shorten the timelines for exchanges with relevant jurisdictions.

567. For the year in review, the timeliness of exchanges is as follows:

Future rulings in the scope of the transparency framework	Number of exchanges transmitted within three months of the information becoming available to the competent authority or immediately after legal impediments have been lifted	Delayed exchanges		
		Number of exchanges transmitted later than three months of the information on rulings becoming available to the competent authority	Reasons for the delays	Any other comments
	33	N/A	N/A	See below.

Follow up requests received for exchange of the ruling	Number	Average time to provide response	Number of requests not answered
	0	N/A	N/A

568. The 33 exchanges performed in 2019 refer to: i) three future rulings issued in 2017 and exchanged with four relevant jurisdictions; and ii) nine future rulings issued in 2018 and exchanged with 29 relevant jurisdictions. In 2020, an additional 38 exchanges were performed with regard to: i) six future rulings issued in 2018 and exchanged with 15 relevant jurisdictions; and ii) 19 future rulings issued in 2019 and exchanged with 23 relevant jurisdictions.

Conclusion on section B

569. Israel has the necessary legal basis for spontaneous exchange of information. Israel has met all of the ToR for the exchange of information except for ensuring that each of the mandatory fields of

information required in the template contained in Annex C of the 2015 Action 5 Report, especially with regard to the summary section, are present in the information exchanged (ToR II.5.3) and for the timely provision of information on rulings to the Competent Authority for exchange of information (ToR II.5.5).

570. Israel is recommended to develop a process to complete the templates on future rulings, and in particular the summary section, in accordance with the form agreed under the transparency framework (Tor II.5.3). As Israel continued to experience delays when forwarding information on rulings to the Competent Authority during the year of review, the recommendation from previous years is retained and Israel is recommended to continue its efforts to ensure that information is made available to the Competent Authority without undue delay (ToR II. 5.5).

C. Statistics (ToR IV)

571. The statistics for the year in review are as follows:

Category of ruling	Number of exchanges	Jurisdictions exchanged with
Ruling related to a preferential regime	33	Australia, Austria, Canada, China (People's Republic of), Cyprus, Denmark, Finland, France, Germany, Hong Kong (China), Isle of Man, Italy, Japan, Korea, Malta, New Zealand, Norway, Poland, Switzerland, United Kingdom, United States
Cross-border unilateral advance pricing agreements (APAs) and any other cross-border unilateral tax rulings (such as an advance tax ruling) covering transfer pricing or the application of transfer pricing principles	0	N/A
Cross-border rulings providing for a unilateral downward adjustment to the taxpayer's taxable profits that is not directly reflected in the taxpayer's financial / commercial accounts	0	N/A
Permanent establishment rulings	0	N/A
Related party conduit rulings	0	N/A
IP regimes: total exchanges on taxpayers benefitting from the third category of IP assets, new entrants benefitting from grandfathered IP regimes; and taxpayers making use of the option to treat the nexus ratio as a rebuttable presumption	0	N/A
Total	33	

D. Matters related to intellectual property regimes (ToR I.4.1.3)

572. Israel offers two intellectual property regimes (IP regime)[5] that are subject to the transparency requirements under the Action 5 Report (OECD, 2015[1]). It states that the identification of the benefitting taxpayers occurs as follows:

- ***New entrants benefitting from the grandfathered IP regime***: the process on the collection of information regarding new entrants in the grandfathered IP regime is described in the previous years' peer review reports, and no recommendations were made. With respect to new entrants in the grandfathered IP regime, exchanges were completed in prior years and no further action was required.

- ***Third category of IP assets***: the regimes provide benefits to the third category of IP assets. The process on the collection of information is described in the previous years' peer review reports and meets the ToR. During the year in review, the Authority for Technological Innovation (i.e. the certifying agency) approved two applications regarding IP assets included in the third category. Information in respect of the two certificates issued in 2019 will be collected in the companies' tax returns for 2019, due at the end of 2020 and exchanged shortly thereafter. Israel's implementation on this aspect remains unchanged and continues to meet the ToR.
- ***Taxpayers making use of the option to treat the nexus ratio as a rebuttable presumption***: not applicable as the regime does not allow the nexus ratio to be treated as a rebuttable presumption.

Summary of recommendations on implementation of the transparency framework

Aspect of implementation of the transparency framework that should be improved	Recommendation for improvement
During the year in review, concerns were raised regarding the existence of a process for completion of templates in accordance with the form agreed under the transparency framework.	Israel is recommended to develop a process to complete the templates on future rulings, and in particular, the summary section, in accordance with the form agreed under the transparency framework.
During the year in review, Israel continued to experience delays in the provision of rulings to the Competent Authority.	Israel is recommended to continue its efforts to ensure that information is made available to the Competent Authority without undue delay. This recommendation remains unchanged since the 2017 and 2018 peer review reports.

References

OECD (2017), *BEPS Action 5 on Harmful Tax Practices - Terms of Reference and Methodology for the Conduct of the Peer Reviews of the Action 5 Transparency Framework*, OECD Publishing, Paris, http://www.oecd.org/tax/beps/beps-action-5-harmful-tax-practices-peer-review-transparency-framework.pdf. [3]

OECD (2015), *Countering Harmful Tax Practices More Effectively, Taking into Account Transparency and Substance, Action 5 - 2015 Final Report*, OECD/G20 Base Erosion and Profit Shifting Project, OECD Publishing, Paris, https://dx.doi.org/10.1787/9789264241190-en. [1]

OECD/Council of Europe (2011), *The Multilateral Convention on Mutual Administrative Assistance in Tax Matters: Amended by the 2010 Protocol*, OECD Publishing, Paris, https://dx.doi.org/10.1787/9789264115606-en. [4]

Notes

[1] Future rulings issued in 2017 were exchanged in 2019. In verifying all information for exchanges, Israel assessed that the number of future rulings issued in 2017 and considered within the scope of the transparency framework is three instead of 16 as reported in the 2017 and 2018 peer review reports.

[2] Available at: https://taxes.gov.il/Pages/TaxationDecisions/TaxationDecisions.aspx.

[3] With respect to the following preferential regimes: Preferred company regime and Preferred technological enterprise regime.

[4] Parties to the Convention are available here: www.oecd.org/tax/exchange-of-tax-information/convention-on-mutual-administrative-assistance-in-tax-matters.htm. Israel also has bilateral agreements with Australia, Austria, Belarus, Belgium, Brazil, Bulgaria, Canada, China (People's Republic of), Chinese Taipei, Croatia, Czech Republic, Denmark, Estonia, Ethiopia, Finland, France, Georgia, Germany, Greece, Hungary, India, Ireland, Italy, Jamaica, Japan, Korea, Latvia, Lithuania, Luxembourg, Malta, Mexico, Moldova, Netherlands, Norway, Panama, Philippines, Poland, Portugal, Romania, Russia, Serbia, Singapore, Slovak Republic, Slovenia, South Africa, Spain, Sweden, Switzerland, Thailand, Turkey, Ukraine, United Kingdom, United States, Uzbekistan and Viet Nam.

[5] The Preferred company regime which is the grandfathered regime, and the Preferred technological enterprise regime which is the amended regime.

Italy

Italy has met all aspects of the terms of reference (OECD, 2017[3]) (ToR) for the calendar year 2019 (year in review), and no recommendations are made.

In the prior year report, as well as in the 2016 and 2017 peer reviews, Italy had received two recommendations. Italy has resolved these issues and therefore none of the prior year recommendations remain.

Italy can legally issue three types of rulings within the scope of the transparency framework. In practice, Italy issued rulings within the scope of the transparency framework as follows:

- 58 past rulings;
- For the period 1 April 2016 - 31 December 2016: 39 future rulings;
- For the calendar year 2017: 123 future rulings,
- For the calendar year 2018: 308 future rulings, and
- For the year in review: 206 future rulings.

Rulings other than APAs and ad hoc Patent Box may be published, in an anonymised form, as a general ruling (Resolutions)[1] when the underlying issue is new and relevant, or the response to the query may apply to groups or types of taxpayers in the same situation, providing guidance on the position of the Italian tax administration on the matters of the query. Moreover, as of September 2018 the so called "Art. 11 rulings", i.e. the replies given to a single taxpayer by the Central Directorates pursuant to Art. 11 of the Charter of Taxpayers' Rights, are published on the Revenue Agency website (either the complete text or only the basic principles, depending on the case).[2]

Peer input was received from eight jurisdictions in respect of the exchanges of information on rulings received from Italy. The input was generally positive, noting that information was complete, in a correct format and received in a timely manner. A small number of peers noted that the summaries were complete, although they expressed interest in having increased detail in the summary section, and Italy will consider this feedback.

A. The information gathering process

573. Italy can legally issue the following three types of rulings within the scope of the transparency framework: (i) preferential regimes;[3] (ii) cross-border unilateral APAs and any other cross-border unilateral tax rulings (such as an advance tax ruling) covering transfer pricing or the application of transfer pricing principles; and (iii) permanent establishment rulings.

574. For Italy, past rulings are any tax rulings within scope that are issued either: (i) on or after 1 January 2014 but before 1 April 2016; or (ii) on or after 1 January 2010 but before 1 January 2014, provided they were still in effect as at 1 January 2014. Future rulings are any tax rulings within scope that are issued on or after 1 April 2016.

575. In the prior years' peer review reports, it was determined that Italy's undertakings to identify past and future rulings and all potential exchange jurisdictions were sufficient to meet the minimum standard. In addition, it was determined that Italy's review and supervision mechanism was sufficient to meet the minimum standard. Italy's implementation remains unchanged, and therefore continues to meet the minimum standard.

576. Italy has met all of the ToR for the information gathering process and no recommendations are made.

B. The exchange of information

Legal basis for spontaneous exchange of information (ToR II.5.1, II.5.2)

577. Italy has the necessary domestic legal basis to exchange information spontaneously. Italy notes that there are no legal or practical impediments that prevent the spontaneous exchange of information on rulings as contemplated in the Action 5 minimum standard.

578. Italy has international agreements permitting spontaneous exchange of information, including being a party to the (i) *Multilateral Convention on Mutual Administrative Assistance in Tax Matters: Amended by the 2010 Protocol* (OECD/Council of Europe, 2011[4]) ("the Convention"), (ii) the Directive 2011/16/EU with all other European Union Member States and (iii) bilateral agreements in force with 99 jurisdictions.[4]

Completion and exchange of templates (ToR II.5.3, II.5.4, II.5.5, II.5.6, II.5.7)

579. In the prior years' peer review reports, it was determined that Italy's process for the completion and exchange of templates met all the ToR, except for providing the information on future rulings to the Competent Authority in a timely manner (ToR II.5.5). With respect to past rulings, no further action was required. Therefore, Italy was recommended to continue its efforts to apply reduced timelines for providing the information on future rulings to the Competent Authority.

580. During the year in review, Italy issued new internal guidelines requiring that information on rulings is made available to the Competent Authority on a quarterly basis to ensure a quarterly exchange of information with relevant jurisdictions. The new guidelines also specify that the summary section of the template has to be completed in line with the internal FHTP suggested guidance. In addition, the Revenue Agency has implemented an IT application, currently being tested, intended to allow an automatic download of the information on rulings from relevant databases and its subsequent transmission to the Competent Authority. Therefore, the recommendation is now removed.

581. For the year in review, the timeliness of exchanges is as follows:

Future rulings in the scope of the transparency framework	Number of exchanges transmitted within three months of the information becoming available to the competent authority or immediately after legal impediments have been lifted	Delayed exchanges		
		Number of exchanges transmitted later than three months of the information on rulings becoming available to the competent authority	Reasons for the delays	Any other comments
	1 456	0	N/A	N/A

Follow up requests received for exchange of the ruling	Number	Average time to provide response	Number of requests not answered
	0	N/A	N/A

582. The 1 456 exchanges performed in 2019 refer to future rulings issued in the last months of 2018 and exchanged by the end of March 2019, as well as to future rulings issued in 2019 and exchanged on a quarterly basis according to the internal guidelines. Italy also clarified that according to the current practice, most of the rulings issued in a given year are actually issued to the taxpayer in the last months of that year and, therefore, generally exchanged within the first quarter of the following year.

Conclusion on section B

583. Italy has the necessary legal basis for spontaneous exchange of information, a process for completing the templates in a timely way and has completed all exchanges. Italy has met all of the ToR for the exchange of information process and no recommendations are made.

C. Statistics (ToR IV)

584. The statistics for the year in review are as follows:

Category of ruling	Number of exchanges	Jurisdictions exchanged with
Ruling related to a preferential regime	1 341	Argentina, Aruba, Australia, Austria, Belgium, Brazil, Bulgaria, Canada, Chile, China (People's Republic of), Colombia, Costa Rica, Croatia, Czech Republic, Denmark, Egypt, Finland, France, Germany, Greece, Hong Kong (China), Hungary, India, Indonesia, Ireland, Israel, Japan, Kazakhstan, Korea, Luxembourg, Macao (China) Malaysia, Malta, Morocco, Mexico, Monaco, Netherlands, New Zealand, Nigeria, Norway, Panama, Peru, Poland, Portugal, Qatar, Romania, Russia, San Marino, Serbia, Singapore, Slovak Republic, Slovenia, South Africa, Saudi Arabia, Spain, Sweden, Switzerland, Thailand, Tunisia, Turkey, Ukraine, United Kingdom, United States, Viet Nam
Cross-border unilateral advance pricing agreements (APAs) and any other cross-border unilateral tax rulings (such as an advance tax ruling) covering transfer pricing or the application of transfer pricing principles	103	Argentina, Australia, Austria, Belgium, Brazil, Canada, China (People's Republic of), Denmark, France, Germany, Greece, Hong Kong (China), Hungary, India, Indonesia, Ireland, Japan, Kazakhstan, Korea, Liechtenstein, Luxemburg, Macao

		(China), Malaysia, Mexico, Monaco, Netherlands, Poland, Portugal, Qatar, Russia, Singapore, Slovak Republic, South Africa, Spain, Sweden, Switzerland, Ukraine, United Kingdom
Permanent establishment rulings	12	France, Germany, Ireland, Luxembourg, United Kingdom
IP regimes: total exchanges on taxpayers benefitting from the third category of IP assets, new entrants benefitting from grandfathered IP regimes; and taxpayers making use of the option to treat the nexus ratio as a rebuttable presumption	423	Argentina, Australia, Austria, Belgium, Brazil, Bulgaria, Canada, Chile, China (People's Republic of), Colombia, Croatia, Czech Republic, Egypt, Estonia, Finland, France, Germany, Greece, Guernsey, Hong Kong (China), Hungary, India, Indonesia, Ireland, Israel, Jamaica, Japan, Kazakhstan, Korea, Lebanon, Lithuania, Luxembourg, Malaysia, Mexico, Monaco, Morocco, Netherlands, New Zealand, Norway, Panama, Poland, Portugal, Russia, Saudi Arabia, Serbia, Singapore, Slovak Republic, Slovenia, South Africa, Spain, Sweden, Switzerland, Thailand, Turkey, Ukraine, United Kingdom, United States, Viet Nam
Total	1 879[5]	

D. Matters related to intellectual property regimes (ToR I.4.1.3)

585. Italy offered an intellectual property regime (IP regime)[6] that was amended with effect as of 1 January 2017 to the extent it was not nexus compliant (i.e. for benefits for trademarks) and is subject to transparency requirements under the Action 5 Report (OECD, 2015[1]). It states that the identification of the benefitting taxpayers will occur as follows:

- ***New entrants benefitting from the grandfathered IP regime***: In the prior years' peer review reports, Italy was recommended to continue its efforts to identify and exchange information on new entrants to the grandfathered IP regime. In 2018, Italy issued an Inter-Ministerial Decree to enforce this requirement. The Decree included a notification requirement in the annual tax return for every taxpayer who has benefitted as a new entrant from the grandfathered IP regime as well a filing obligation including information on the type and the number of eligible assets to which the benefit applies, the amount of the eligible income resulting from the use of the assets, and as regards benefits for trademarks, information on relevant jurisdictions where related parties are fiscally resident.

  The first tax return containing this information was filed at the end of 2018 and the information was gathered in early 2019. During the year in review, Italy has completed the exchange of information on new entrants to the grandfathered IP regime that obtained benefits with respect to trademarks. Therefore, the recommendation is now removed.
- ***Third category of IP assets***: not applicable as the regime does not allow the third category of IP assets to qualify for the benefits.
- ***Taxpayers making use of the option to treat the nexus ratio as a rebuttable presumption***: not applicable as the regime does not allow the nexus ratio to be treated as a rebuttable presumption.

Summary of recommendations on implementation of the transparency framework

Aspect of implementation of the transparency framework that should be improved	Recommendation for improvement
	No recommendations are made.

References

OECD (2017), *BEPS Action 5 on Harmful Tax Practices - Terms of Reference and Methodology for the Conduct of the Peer Reviews of the Action 5 Transparency Framework*, OECD Publishing, Paris, http://www.oecd.org/tax/beps/beps-action-5-harmful-tax-practices-peer-review-transparency-framework.pdf. [3]

OECD (2015), *Countering Harmful Tax Practices More Effectively, Taking into Account Transparency and Substance, Action 5 - 2015 Final Report*, OECD/G20 Base Erosion and Profit Shifting Project, OECD Publishing, Paris, https://dx.doi.org/10.1787/9789264241190-en. [1]

OECD/Council of Europe (2011), *The Multilateral Convention on Mutual Administrative Assistance in Tax Matters: Amended by the 2010 Protocol*, OECD Publishing, Paris, https://dx.doi.org/10.1787/9789264115606-en. [4]

Notes

[1] Available here: https://www.agenziaentrate.gov.it/portale/web/guest/normativa-e-prassi/risoluzioni.

[2] Available here: https://www.agenziaentrate.gov.it/wps/content/nsilib/nsi/normativa+e+prassi/risposte+agli+interpelli.

[3] With respect to the following preferential regimes: 1) International shipping and 2) Patent Box.

[4] Parties to the Convention are available here: www.oecd.org/tax/exchange-of-tax-information/convention-on-mutual-administrative-assistance-in-tax-matters.htm. Italy also has bilateral agreements with Albania, Algeria, Argentina, Armenia, Australia, Austria, Azerbaijan, Bangladesh, Barbados, Belarus, Belgium, Bosnia and Herzegovina, Brazil, Bulgaria, Canada, Chile, China (People's Republic of), Congo, Côte d'Ivoire, Croatia, Cyprus, Czech Republic, Denmark, Ecuador, Egypt, Estonia, Ethiopia, Finland, Former Yugoslav Republic of Macedonia, France, Georgia, Germany, Ghana, Greece, Hong Kong (China), Hungary, Iceland, India, Indonesia, Ireland, Israel, Japan, Jordan, Kazakhstan, Korea, Kuwait, Kyrgyzstan, Latvia, Lebanon, Lithuania, Luxembourg, Malaysia, Malta, Mauritius, Mexico, Moldova, Montenegro, Morocco, Mozambique, Netherlands, New Zealand, Norway, Oman, Pakistan, Philippines, Poland, Portugal, Qatar, Romania, Russia, San Marino, Saudi Arabia, Senegal, Serbia, Singapore, Slovak Republic, Slovenia, South Africa, Spain, Sri Lanka, Sweden, Switzerland, Syrian Arab Republic, Chinese Taipei, Tajikistan, Tanzania, Thailand, Trinidad and Tobago, Tunisia, Turkey, Uganda, Ukraine, United Arab Emirates, United Kingdom, United States, Uzbekistan, Venezuela, Viet Nam and Zambia.

[5] Exchanges on new entrants benefitting from the grandfathered Patent box are not performed on the basis of a ruling. Therefore, the total number of exchanges performed in 2019 is different, i.e. higher, than the total number of exchanges of tax rulings performed in 2019.

[6] Partial exemption for income/gains derived from certain IP rights.

Jamaica

Jamaica has met all aspects of the terms of reference (OECD, 2017[3]) (ToR) for the calendar year 2019 (year in review) and no recommendations are made.

Jamaica can legally issue five types of rulings within the scope of the transparency framework. In practice, Jamaica has not issued any rulings within the scope of the transparency framework.

As no exchanges were required to take place, no peer input was received in respect of the exchanges of information on rulings received from Jamaica.

A. The information gathering process

586. Jamaica can legally issue the following five types of rulings within the scope of the transparency framework: (i) preferential regimes;[1] (ii) cross-border unilateral APAs and any other cross-border unilateral tax rulings (such as an advance tax ruling) covering transfer pricing or the application of transfer pricing principles; (iii) rulings providing for unilateral downward adjustments; (iv) permanent establishment rulings; and (v) related party conduit rulings.

587. For Jamaica, past rulings are any tax rulings within scope that are issued either (i) on or after 1 January 2015 but before 1 April 2017; and (ii) on or after 1 January 2012 but before 1 January 2015, provided they were still in effect as at 1 January 2015. Future rulings are any tax rulings within scope that are issued on or after 1 April 2017.

588. In the prior year' peer review report, it was determined that Jamaica's undertakings to identify past and future rulings and all potential exchange jurisdictions were sufficient to meet the minimum standard. Jamaica is working to have in place a more formal procedure with respect to the issuance and review of rulings for the purposes of the transparency framework. In particular, Jamaica is currently developing guidelines to be published, which will specify the information that must be included in rulings applications such as organisational charts with all relevant parties' jurisdiction of relevance. In addition, it was determined that Jamaica's review and supervision mechanism was sufficient to meet the minimum standard. Jamaica's implementation in this regard remains unchanged, and therefore continues to meet the minimum standard.

589. Jamaica has met all of the ToR for the information gathering process that can be met in the absence of rulings being issued in practice and no recommendations are made.

B. The exchange of information

590. In the prior years' peer review reports, it was determined that Jamaica's process for the completion and exchange of templates were sufficient to meet the minimum standard in the absence of rulings being issued and exchanged in practice. Jamaica's implementation in this regard remains unchanged and therefore continues to meet the minimum standard.

591. Jamaica has international agreements permitting spontaneous exchange of information, including being a party to the (i) *Multilateral Convention on Mutual Administrative Assistance in Tax Matters: Amended by the 2010 Protocol* (OECD/Council of Europe, 2011[4]) ("the Convention") and (ii) bilateral agreements in force with 26 jurisdictions.[2]

592. As Jamaica did not issue any rulings in scope of the transparency framework in the relevant period, Jamaica was not required to exchange any information on rulings in the year in review and no data on the timeliness of exchanges can be reported.

593. Jamaica has the necessary legal basis for spontaneous exchange of information and a process for completing the templates in a timely way. Jamaica has met all of the ToR for the exchange of information process that can be met in the absence of rulings being issued and exchanged in practice and no recommendations are made.

C. Statistics (ToR IV)

594. As no rulings were issued, no statistics can be reported.

D. Matters related to intellectual property regimes (ToR I.4.1.3)

595. Jamaica does not offer an intellectual property regime for which transparency requirements under the Action 5 Report (OECD, 2015[1]) were imposed.

Summary of recommendations on implementation of the transparency framework

Aspect of implementation of the transparency framework that should be improved	Recommendation for improvement
	No recommendations are made.

References

OECD (2017), *BEPS Action 5 on Harmful Tax Practices - Terms of Reference and Methodology for the Conduct of the Peer Reviews of the Action 5 Transparency Framework*, OECD Publishing, Paris, http://www.oecd.org/tax/beps/beps-action-5-harmful-tax-practices-peer-review-transparency-framework.pdf. [3]

OECD (2015), *Countering Harmful Tax Practices More Effectively, Taking into Account Transparency and Substance, Action 5 - 2015 Final Report*, OECD/G20 Base Erosion and Profit Shifting Project, OECD Publishing, Paris, https://dx.doi.org/10.1787/9789264241190-en. [1]

OECD/Council of Europe (2011), *The Multilateral Convention on Mutual Administrative Assistance in Tax Matters: Amended by the 2010 Protocol*, OECD Publishing, Paris, https://dx.doi.org/10.1787/9789264115606-en. [4]

Notes

[1] With respect to the following preferential regimes: Special economic zones.

[2] Parties to the Convention are available here: www.oecd.org/tax/exchange-of-tax-information/convention-on-mutual-administrative-assistance-in-tax-matters.htm. Jamaica also has bilateral agreements with Antigua and Barbuda, Barbados, Belize, Canada, China (People's Republic of), Denmark, Dominica, Faroe Islands, Finland, France, Germany, Greenland, Grenada, Guyana, Iceland, Israel, Mexico, Norway, Saint Kitts and Nevis, Saint Lucia, Saint Vincent and the Grenadines, Spain, Sweden, Trinidad and Tobago, United Kingdom and United States.

Japan

Japan has met all aspects of the terms of reference (OECD, 2017[3]) (ToR) for the calendar year 2019 (year in review) and no recommendations are made.

Japan can legally issue three types of rulings within the scope of the transparency framework.

In practice, Japan issued rulings within the scope of the transparency framework as follows:

- 51 past rulings;
- For the period 1 April 2016 - 31 December 2016: 12 future rulings;
- For the calendar year 2017: 14 future rulings;
- For the calendar year 2018: 16 future rulings; and
- For the year in review: four future rulings.

Peer input was received from one jurisdiction in respect of the exchanges of information on rulings received from Japan. The input was positive, noting that information was complete, in a correct format and received in a timely manner.

A. The information gathering process

596. Japan can legally issue the following three types of rulings within the scope of the transparency framework: (i) cross-border unilateral APAs and any other cross-border unilateral tax rulings (such as an advance tax ruling) covering transfer pricing or the application of transfer pricing principles; (ii) permanent establishment rulings; and (iii) related party conduit rulings.

597. For Japan, past rulings are any tax rulings within scope that are issued either: (i) on or after 1 January 2014 but before 1 April 2016; or (ii) on or after 1 January 2010 but before 1 January 2014, provided they were still in effect as at 1 January 2014. Future rulings are any tax rulings within scope that are issued on or after 1 April 2016.

598. In the prior years' peer review reports, it was determined that Japan's undertakings to identify past and future rulings and all potential exchange jurisdictions were sufficient to meet the minimum standard. In addition, it was determined that Japan's review and supervision mechanism was sufficient to meet the minimum standard. Japan's implementation remains unchanged, and therefore continues to meet the minimum standard.

599. Japan has met all of the ToR for the information gathering process and no recommendations are made.

B. The exchange of information

600. In the prior years' peer review reports, it was determined that Japan's process for the completion and exchange of templates were sufficient to meet the minimum standard. With respect to past rulings, no further action was required. Japan's implementation in this regard remains unchanged and therefore continues to meet the minimum standard.

601. Japan has international agreements permitting spontaneous exchange of information, including being a party to the (i) *Multilateral Convention on Mutual Administrative Assistance in Tax Matters: Amended by the 2010 Protocol* (OECD/Council of Europe, 2011[4]) ("the Convention") and (ii) bilateral agreements in force with 73 jurisdictions.[1]

602. For the year in review, the timeliness of exchanges is as follows:

Future rulings in the scope of the transparency framework	Number of exchanges transmitted within three months of the information becoming available to the competent authority or immediately after legal impediments have been lifted	Delayed exchanges		
		Number of exchanges transmitted later than three months of the information on rulings becoming available to the competent authority	Reasons for the delays	Any other comments
	5	0	N/A	N/A

Follow up requests received for exchange of the ruling	Number	Average time to provide response	Number of requests not answered
	0	N/A	N/A

603. Japan has the necessary legal basis for spontaneous exchange of information, a process for completing the templates in a timely way and has completed all exchanges. Japan has met all of the ToR for the exchange of information process and no recommendations are made.

C. Statistics (ToR IV)

604. The statistics for the year in review are as follows:

Category of ruling	Number of exchanges	Jurisdictions exchanged with
Cross-border unilateral advance pricing agreements (APAs) and any other cross-border unilateral tax rulings (such as an advance tax ruling) covering transfer pricing or the application of transfer pricing principles	5	Hong Kong (China), Ireland, Singapore, United States
Permanent establishment rulings	0	N/A
Related party conduit rulings	0	N/A
Total	5	

D. Matters related to intellectual property regimes (ToR I.4.1.3)

605. Japan does not offer an intellectual property regime for which transparency requirements under the Action 5 Report (OECD, 2015[1]) were imposed.

Summary of recommendations on implementation of the transparency framework

Aspect of implementation of the transparency framework that should be improved	Recommendation for improvement
	No recommendations are made.

References

OECD (2017), *BEPS Action 5 on Harmful Tax Practices - Terms of Reference and Methodology for the Conduct of the Peer Reviews of the Action 5 Transparency Framework*, OECD Publishing, Paris, http://www.oecd.org/tax/beps/beps-action-5-harmful-tax-practices-peer-review-transparency-framework.pdf. [3]

OECD (2015), *Countering Harmful Tax Practices More Effectively, Taking into Account Transparency and Substance, Action 5 - 2015 Final Report*, OECD/G20 Base Erosion and Profit Shifting Project, OECD Publishing, Paris, https://dx.doi.org/10.1787/9789264241190-en. [1]

OECD/Council of Europe (2011), *The Multilateral Convention on Mutual Administrative Assistance in Tax Matters: Amended by the 2010 Protocol*, OECD Publishing, Paris, https://dx.doi.org/10.1787/9789264115606-en. [4]

Notes

[1] Parties to the Convention are available here: www.oecd.org/tax/exchange-of-tax-information/convention-on-mutual-administrative-assistance-in-tax-matters.htm. Japan also has bilateral agreements in force with Armenia, Bangladesh, Belarus, Brunei Darussalam, Croatia, Ecuador, Egypt, Fiji, Hong Kong (China), Kuwait, Kyrgyzstan, Oman, Philippines, Qatar, Sri Lanka, Chinese Taipei, Tajikistan, Thailand, Turkey, Turkmenistan, United States, Uzbekistan, Viet Nam and Zambia.

Jersey

Jersey has met all aspects of the terms of reference (OECD, 2017[3]) (ToR) for the calendar year 2019 (year in review) and no recommendations are made.

Jersey can legally issue four types of rulings within the scope of the transparency framework.

In practice, Jersey issued rulings within the scope of the transparency framework as follows:

- 16 past rulings;
- For the period 1 April 2017 - 31 December 2017: one future ruling;
- For the calendar year 2018: no future rulings, and
- For the year in review: one future ruling.

No peer input was received in respect of the exchanges of information on rulings received from Jersey.

A. The information gathering process

606. Jersey can legally issue the following four types of rulings within the scope of the transparency framework: (i) cross-border unilateral APAs and any other cross-border unilateral tax rulings (such as an advance tax ruling) covering transfer pricing or the application of transfer pricing principles; (ii) rulings providing for unilateral downward adjustments; (iii) permanent establishment rulings; and (iv) related party conduit rulings.

607. For Jersey, past rulings are any tax rulings within scope that are issued either: (i) on or after 1 January 2015 but before 1 April 2017; or (ii) on or after 1 January 2012 but before 1 January 2015, provided they were still in effect as at 1 January 2015. Future rulings are any tax rulings within scope that are issued on or after 1 April 2017.

608. In the prior years' peer review reports, it was determined that Jersey's undertakings to identify past and future rulings and all potential exchange jurisdictions were sufficient to meet the minimum standard. In addition, it was determined that Jersey's review and supervision mechanism was sufficient to meet the minimum standard. Jersey's implementation remains unchanged, and therefore continues to meet the minimum standard.

609. Jersey has met all of the ToR for the information gathering process and no recommendations are made.

B. The exchange of information

610. In the prior years' peer review reports, it was determined that Jersey's process for the completion and exchange of templates were sufficient to meet the minimum standard. With respect to past rulings, no further action was required. Jersey's implementation in this regard remains unchanged and therefore continues to meet the minimum standard.

611. Jersey has international agreements permitting spontaneous exchange of information, including being a party to the (i) *Multilateral Convention on Mutual Administrative Assistance in Tax Matters: Amended by the 2010 Protocol* (OECD/Council of Europe, 2011[4]) ("the Convention") and (ii) bilateral agreements in force with 16 jurisdictions.[1]

612. For the year in review, the timeliness of exchanges is as follows:

Future rulings in the scope of the transparency framework	Number of exchanges transmitted within three months of the information becoming available to the competent authority or immediately after legal impediments have been lifted	Delayed exchanges		
		Number of exchanges transmitted later than three months of the information on rulings becoming available to the competent authority	Reasons for the delays	Any other comments
	2	0	N/A	N/A

Follow up requests received for exchange of the ruling	Number	Average time to provide response	Number of requests not answered
	0	N/A	N/A

613. Jersey has the necessary legal basis for spontaneous exchange of information, a process for completing the templates in a timely way and has completed all exchanges. Jersey has met all of the ToR for the exchange of information process and no recommendations are made.

C. Statistics (ToR IV)

614. The statistics for the year in review are as follows:

Category of ruling	Number of exchanges	Jurisdictions exchanged with
Cross-border unilateral advance pricing agreements (APAs) and any other cross-border unilateral tax rulings (such as an advance tax ruling) covering transfer pricing or the application of transfer pricing principles	0	N/A
Cross-border rulings providing for a unilateral downward adjustment to the taxpayer's taxable profits that is not directly reflected in the taxpayer's financial / commercial accounts	0	N/A
Permanent establishment rulings	*De minimis* rule applies	N/A
Related party conduit rulings	0	N/A
De minimis rule	2	N/A
Total	2	

D. Matters related to intellectual property regimes (ToR I.4.1.3)

615. Jersey does not offer an intellectual property regime for which transparency requirements under the Action 5 Report (OECD, 2015[1]) were imposed.

Summary of recommendations on implementation of the transparency framework

Aspect of implementation of the transparency framework that should be improved	Recommendation for improvement
	No recommendations are made.

References

OECD (2017), *BEPS Action 5 on Harmful Tax Practices - Terms of Reference and Methodology for the Conduct of the Peer Reviews of the Action 5 Transparency Framework*, OECD Publishing, Paris, http://www.oecd.org/tax/beps/beps-action-5-harmful-tax-practices-peer-review-transparency-framework.pdf. [3]

OECD (2015), *Countering Harmful Tax Practices More Effectively, Taking into Account Transparency and Substance, Action 5 - 2015 Final Report*, OECD/G20 Base Erosion and Profit Shifting Project, OECD Publishing, Paris, https://dx.doi.org/10.1787/9789264241190-en. [1]

OECD/Council of Europe (2011), *The Multilateral Convention on Mutual Administrative Assistance in Tax Matters: Amended by the 2010 Protocol*, OECD Publishing, Paris, https://dx.doi.org/10.1787/9789264115606-en. [4]

Notes

[1] Parties to the Convention are available here: www.oecd.org/tax/exchange-of-tax-information/convention-on-mutual-administrative-assistance-in-tax-matters.htm. Jersey also has bilateral agreements with Cyprus, Estonia, Guernsey, Hong Kong (China), Isle of Man, Liechtenstein, Luxembourg, Malta, Mauritius, Qatar, Rwanda, Seychelles, Singapore, United Arab Emirates, United Kingdom and United States.

Jordan

Jordan has met all aspects of the terms of reference (OECD, 2017[3]) (ToR) for the calendar year 2019 (year in review), except for identifying all past and future rulings and all potential exchange jurisdictions with a review and supervision mechanism (ToR I.4), having a domestic legal basis for spontaneous exchange of information and exchanging information on the tax rulings in accordance with the form and timelines under the transparency framework (ToR II.5) and for identifying and exchanging information on all new entrants to the IP regime (ToR I.4.3). Jordan receives three recommendations on these points for the year in review.

In the prior year report, as well as in the 2017 peer review, Jordan had received one recommendation. As it has not been addressed, the recommendation remains in place. Two new recommendations have been added.

Jordan can legally issue one type of rulings within the scope of the transparency framework. In practice, Jordan issued no rulings within the scope of the transparency framework.

These rulings are published on the official gazette website in an anonymised form.

No peer input was received in respect of the exchanges of information on rulings received from Jordan.

A. The information gathering process

616. Jordan can legally issue the following one type of rulings within the scope of the transparency framework: (i) preferential regimes.[1] Rulings are issued by a committee consisting of representatives of several government agencies under the Jordan Investment Commission (JIC) which was established under the Investment Law.

617. In the prior year report, this section was not assessed as no rulings were issued. Jordan indicated that theoretically, there is no legal impediment for Jordan to issue rulings within the scope of the transparency framework, but in practice Jordan did not put in place the administrative process to issue such rulings.

618. As of 2019, a procedure to issue private rulings became effective in Jordan. Private rulings referring to a specific taxpayer are binding on the tax administration and can be issued only in the category of preferential regimes. These rulings are endorsed and ratified by the Cabinet.

Past rulings (ToR I.4.1.1, I.4.1.2, I.4.2.1, I.4.2.2)

619. For Jordan, past rulings are any tax rulings within scope that are issued either (i) on or after 1 January 2015 but before 1 April 2017; and (ii) on or after 1 January 2012 but before 1 January 2015, provided they were still in effect as at 1 January 2015. However, as Jordan put in place an administrative process to issue rulings only in 2019, therefore there are no past rulings on which Jordan would be obligated to conduct spontaneous exchange of information.

Future rulings (ToR I.4.1.1, I.4.1.2, I.4.2.1)

620. For Jordan, future rulings are any tax rulings within scope that are issued on or after 1 September 2017.

621. Jordan put in place an administrative process to issue rulings only in 2019, but no rulings have been issued during the year in review.

622. During the year in review, Jordan did not have specific mechanisms in place for identifying future rulings and potential exchange jurisdictions within the scope of the transparency framework and relied on a case-by-case approach. The Income and Sales Tax Department (ISTD) within the Ministry of Finance is currently considering the introduction of a mechanism to identify future rulings that are in the scope of the transparency framework and all jurisdictions for which the tax ruling would be relevant.

Review and supervision (ToR I.4.3)

623. Jordan did not have a review and supervision mechanism under the transparency framework for the year in review. Jordan is currently considering the implementation of review and supervision mechanisms within ISTD to ensure that all relevant information related to future rulings is captured adequately.

Conclusion on section A

624. Jordan does not have specific mechanisms in place for identifying future rulings and potential exchange jurisdictions within the scope of the transparency framework as well as for reviewing and supervising that all relevant information is captured adequately.

625. Jordan is recommended to ensure that it has put in place an effective information gathering process to identify all future rulings and potential exchange jurisdictions, with a review and supervision mechanism, as soon as possible (ToR I.4).

B. The exchange of information

Legal basis for spontaneous exchange of information (ToR II.5.1, II.5.2)

626. Jordan does not have the necessary domestic legal basis to exchange information spontaneously. ISTD is currently in the process of putting in place the necessary domestic legal basis to exchange information spontaneously. Jordan can only exchange information on request.

627. Jordan does not have currently in effect an agreement that would allow for spontaneous exchange of information under the transparency framework. Jordan is not a Party to the *Multilateral Convention on Mutual Administrative Assistance in Tax Matters: Amended by the 2010 Protocol* (OECD/Council of Europe, 2011) ("the Convention"). Jordan is encouraged to continue its efforts to expand its international exchange of information instruments to be able to exchange rulings. It is however noted that jurisdictions are assessed on their compliance with the transparency framework in respect of the exchange of information network in effect for the year of the particular annual review.

Completion and exchange of templates (ToR II.5.3, II.5.4, II.5.5, II.5.6, II.5.7)

628. During the year in review, Jordan did not put in place a process to exchange information on rulings in accordance with the form and timelines required by the transparency framework. Jordan is recommended to ensure the timely exchange of information on rulings in the form required by the transparency framework. Jordan is currently considering the implementation of a process within ISTD to ensure the timely exchange of information on future rulings.

Conclusion on section B

629. Jordan has not the necessary domestic legal basis to exchange information spontaneously and Jordan does not yet have a process to exchange information on rulings in the required format and timelines. Jordan is recommended to put in place a domestic legal framework allowing spontaneous exchange of information on the relevant tax rulings and to ensure the timely exchange of information on rulings in the form required by the transparency framework (ToR II.5).

C. Statistics (ToR IV)

630. As no rulings were issued, no statistics can be reported.

D. Matters related to intellectual property regimes (ToR I.4.1.3)

631. Jordan offers two intellectual property regimes (IP regime).[2] The assessment of transparency requirements under the Action 5 Report (OECD, 2015[1]), is as follows:

- ***New entrants benefitting from the grandfathered IP regime***: the Development zone was reported in the year 2019 as actually harmful. Jordan did not start the legislative amendments to amend the IP regime to be in line with the nexus approach on time. Therefore, in line with the FHTP timelines for IP regimes, when Jordan amends or eliminates the regime, no grandfathering should be provided to existing taxpayers. However, as the regime has not been amended and therefore continues to allow new entrants to benefit from the regime (and therefore was already concluded as "harmful"), Jordan is expected to have information available and exchanged information on new entrants after the relevant date from which enhanced transparency obligations apply (which is 16 October 2017) until the point at which the regime is amended or abolished. According to the most recent available information, Jordan has not identified information on new entrants to the harmful Development zone regime, and as such has not exchanged information on these taxpayers. Therefore, Jordan is recommended to identify and exchange information on all new entrants to the IP regime (ToR I.4.3).

In addition, the Aqaba special economic zone is under review by the FHTP. Jordan is expected to amend or abolish this regime, but, as for the Development zone, as it has not yet started legislative amendments on time, it cannot provide grandfathering for this regime. The assessment of transparency requirements will be further considered after the FHTP's review of this regime has been concluded, and this will be taken into account during the subsequent peer review.

- ***Third category of IP assets***: not applicable to these regimes.

  Taxpayers making the use of the option to treat the nexus ratio as a rebuttable presumption: not applicable to these regimes.

Summary of recommendations on implementation of the transparency framework

Aspect of implementation of the transparency framework that should be improved	Recommendation for improvement
Jordan does not have specific mechanisms in place for identifying future rulings and potential exchange jurisdictions within the scope of the transparency framework as well as for reviewing and supervising that all relevant information is captured adequately.	Jordan is recommended to ensure that it has put in place an effective information gathering process to identify all future rulings and potential exchange jurisdictions, with a review and supervision mechanism, as soon as possible.
Jordan has not the necessary domestic legal basis to exchange information spontaneously and Jordan does not yet have a process to exchange information on rulings in the required format and timelines.	Jordan is recommended to put in place a domestic legal framework allowing spontaneous exchange of information on the relevant tax rulings and to ensure the timely exchange of information on rulings in the form required by the transparency framework.
Jordan has not identified information on new entrants to the harmful Development zone regime, and as such has not exchanged information on these taxpayers.	Jordan is recommended to identify and exchange information on all new entrants to the IP regime.

References

OECD (2017), *BEPS Action 5 on Harmful Tax Practices - Terms of Reference and Methodology for the Conduct of the Peer Reviews of the Action 5 Transparency Framework*, OECD Publishing, Paris, http://www.oecd.org/tax/beps/beps-action-5-harmful-tax-practices-peer-review-transparency-framework.pdf. [3]

OECD (2015), *Countering Harmful Tax Practices More Effectively, Taking into Account Transparency and Substance, Action 5 - 2015 Final Report*, OECD/G20 Base Erosion and Profit Shifting Project, OECD Publishing, Paris, https://dx.doi.org/10.1787/9789264241190-en. [1]

Notes

[1] Development zone regime and the tax preference (i.e. 5% income tax rate on information technology services performed inside or outside the development zones) granted to the information technology sector by the Investment law and included in the Cabinet Decision no. 14883 of 2016.

[2] These regimes are the Development zone and the Aqaba special economic zone.

Kazakhstan

Kazakhstan is taking steps to implement the legal basis for the transparency framework and to commence administrative preparations in line with the terms of reference (OECD, 2017[3]) (ToR) to ensure that it finalises information gathering process (ToR I.4) and information on rulings will be identified and exchanged in a timely manner (ToR II.5). Kazakhstan receives two recommendations on these points for the year in review.

In the prior year report, Kazakhstan had received the same two recommendations. As they have not been addressed, the recommendations remain in place.

Kazakhstan can legally issue one type of ruling within the scope of the transparency framework.

In practice, Kazakhstan issued rulings within the scope of the transparency framework as follows:

- One past ruling;
- For the period 1 April 2018 - 31 December 2018: no future rulings;
- For the year in review: no future rulings.

As no exchanges took place, no peer input was received in respect of the exchanges of information on rulings received from Kazakhstan.

A. The information gathering process

632. Kazakhstan can legally issue the following type of ruling within the scope of the transparency framework: cross-border unilateral APAs and any other cross-border unilateral tax rulings (such as an advance tax ruling) covering transfer pricing or the application of transfer pricing principles.

Past rulings (ToR I.4.1.1, I.4.1.2, I.4.2.1, I.4.2.2)

633. For Kazakhstan, past rulings are any tax rulings issued either (i) on or after 1 January 2016 but before 1 April 2018; and (ii) on or after 1 January 2014 but before 1 January 2016, provided still in effect as at 1 January 2016.

634. One past ruling has been issued. It is noted that the responsible team is continuing to put in place guidelines and practices to collect and record the relevant information for the purposes of the transparency framework.

Future rulings (ToR I.4.1.1, I.4.1.2, I.4.2.1)

635. For Kazakhstan, future rulings are any tax rulings within scope that are issued on or after 1 April 2018.

636. Kazakhstan notes that that when requesting an APA, the taxpayer must identify all transactions that will be covered by the agreement and provide all necessary information about these related parties. However, it is not clear that information on the immediate parent and ultimate parent is collected. It is noted that guidelines and practices are being implemented to make sure that the relevant information is adequately processed for the purposes of the transparency framework.

Review and supervision (ToR I.4.3)

637. Kazakhstan is in the process of implementing a review and supervision mechanism. Once issued by the transfer pricing division, rulings should be reviewed by the non-residents taxation division, which will be responsible to collect the relevant information and to make sure that all relevant information is captured adequately and submitted to all relevant jurisdictions without delay.

Conclusion on section A

638. Kazakhstan is recommended to finalise its information gathering process for identifying all relevant past and future rulings and all potential exchange jurisdictions, with a review and supervision mechanism, as soon as possible (ToR I.4).

B. The exchange of information

Legal basis for spontaneous exchange of information (ToR II.5.1, II.5.2)

639. Kazakhstan does not have the necessary domestic legal basis to exchange information spontaneously. Kazakhstan is recommended to put in place a domestic legal framework allowing spontaneous exchange of information on rulings if needed (ToR II.5.1). Kazakhstan notes that the State Revenue Committee intends to draft regulations that will allow for the spontaneous exchange of information on tax rulings in future.

640. Kazakhstan has international agreements permitting spontaneous exchange of information, including being a party to the (i) *Multilateral Convention on Mutual Administrative Assistance in Tax*

Matters: Amended by the 2010 Protocol (OECD/Council of Europe, 2011[4]) ("the Convention") and (ii) bilateral agreements in force with 59 jurisdictions.[1]

Completion and exchange of templates (ToR II.5.3, II.5.4, II.5.5, II.5.6, II.5.7)

641. Kazakhstan is still developing a process to complete the templates on relevant rulings, to make them available to the Competent Authority for exchange of information, and to exchange them with relevant jurisdictions.

642. As no exchanges took place in the year of review, no data on the timeliness of exchanges can be reported.

Conclusion on section B

643. Kazakhstan is recommended to put in place a domestic legal framework allowing spontaneous exchange of information on rulings and to ensure the timely exchange of information on rulings in the form required by the transparency framework (ToR II.5).

C. Statistics (ToR IV)

644. As there was no information on rulings exchanged by Kazakhstan for the year in review, no statistics can be reported.

D. Matters related to intellectual property regimes (ToR I.4.1.3)

645. Kazakhstan does not offer an intellectual property regime for which transparency requirements under the Action 5 Report (OECD, 2015[1]) were imposed.

Summary of recommendations on implementation of the transparency framework

Aspect of implementation of the transparency framework that should be improved	Recommendation for improvement
Kazakhstan does not have in place the necessary information gathering process.	Kazakhstan is recommended to finalise its information gathering process for identifying all future rulings and potential exchange jurisdictions, with a review and supervision mechanism, as soon as possible. This recommendation remains unchanged since the prior year peer review report.
Kazakhstan does not have a domestic legal framework allowing spontaneous exchange of information on rulings and does not have in place a process for completion of templates and exchange of information on rulings.	Kazakhstan is recommended to put in place a domestic legal framework allowing spontaneous exchange of information on rulings if needed and to ensure the timely exchange of information on rulings in the form required by the transparency framework. This recommendation remains unchanged since the prior year peer review report

References

OECD (2017), *BEPS Action 5 on Harmful Tax Practices - Terms of Reference and Methodology for the Conduct of the Peer Reviews of the Action 5 Transparency Framework*, OECD Publishing, Paris, http://www.oecd.org/tax/beps/beps-action-5-harmful-tax-practices-peer-review-transparency-framework.pdf. [3]

OECD (2015), *Countering Harmful Tax Practices More Effectively, Taking into Account Transparency and Substance, Action 5 - 2015 Final Report*, OECD/G20 Base Erosion and Profit Shifting Project, OECD Publishing, Paris, https://dx.doi.org/10.1787/9789264241190-en. [1]

OECD/Council of Europe (2011), *The Multilateral Convention on Mutual Administrative Assistance in Tax Matters: Amended by the 2010 Protocol*, OECD Publishing, Paris, https://dx.doi.org/10.1787/9789264115606-en. [4]

Notes

[1] Parties to the Convention are available here: www.oecd.org/tax/exchange-of-tax-information/convention-on-mutual-administrative-assistance-in-tax-matters.htm. Kazakhstan also has bilateral agreements with Albania, Armenia, Austria, Azerbaijan, Belarus, Belgium, Bulgaria, Canada, China (People's Republic of), Croatia, Czech Republic, Denmark, Estonia, Finland, France, Georgia, Germany, Hungary, Iceland, India, Iran, Ireland, Italy, Japan, Korea, Kyrgyzstan, Latvia, Lithuania, Luxembourg, Malaysia, Moldova, Mongolia, Montenegro, Morocco, Netherlands, North Macedonia, Norway, Pakistan, Poland, Portugal, Qatar, Romania, Russian Federation, Saud Arabia, Serbia, Singapore, Slovak Republic, Slovenia, Spain, Sweden, Switzerland, Tajikistan, Turkey, Turkmenistan, Ukraine, United Arab Emirates, United Kingdom, United States and Uzbekistan.

Kenya

Kenya has met all aspects of the terms of reference (OECD, 2017[3]) (ToR) for the calendar year 2019 (year in review) and no recommendations are made.

Kenya can legally issue four types of rulings within the scope of the transparency framework.

In practice, Kenya did not issue any type of rulings within the scope of the transparency framework.

As no exchanges were required to take place, no peer input was received in respect of the exchanges of information on rulings received from Kenya.

A. The information gathering process

646. Kenya can legally issue the following four types of rulings within the scope of the transparency framework: (i) preferential regimes;[1] (ii) rulings providing for unilateral downward adjustments; (iii) permanent establishment rulings; and (iv) related party conduit rulings.

647. For Kenya, past rulings are any tax rulings within scope that are issued either: (i) on or after 1 January 2016 but before 1 April 2018; or (ii) on or after 1 January 2014 but before 1 January 2016, provided they were still in effect as at 1 January 2016. Future rulings are any tax rulings within scope that are issued on or after 1 April 2018.

648. In the prior year peer review report, it was determined that Kenya's undertakings to identify past and future rulings and all potential exchange jurisdictions were sufficient to meet the minimum standard in the absence of rulings being issued. In addition, it was determined that Kenya's review and supervision mechanism was sufficient to meet the minimum standard. Kenya's implementation remains unchanged, and therefore continues to meet the minimum standard.

649. Kenya has met all of the ToR for the information gathering process in the absence of rulings being issued and no recommendations are made.

B. The exchange of information

650. In the prior year peer review report, it was determined that Kenya's process for the completion and exchange of templates were sufficient to meet the minimum standard in the absence of rulings being issued. With respect to past rulings, no further action was required. Kenya's implementation in this regard remains unchanged and therefore continues to meet the minimum standard.

651. Kenya (i) has signed *Multilateral Convention on Mutual Administrative Assistance in Tax Matters: Amended by the 2010 Protocol* (OECD/Council of Europe, 2011[4]) ("the Convention) which has already been ratified by the parliament and (ii) has international agreements permitting spontaneous exchange of information, including bilateral agreements in force with 15 jurisdictions.[2] Kenya is encouraged to continue its efforts to expand its international exchange of information instruments to be able to exchange rulings. It is noted, however, that jurisdictions are assessed on their compliance with the transparency framework in respect of the exchange of information network in effect for the year of the particular annual review.

652. As no rulings are issued in practice, no data on the timeliness of exchanges can be reported.

653. Kenya has the necessary legal basis for spontaneous exchange of information, a process for completing the templates in a timely way. Kenya has met all of the ToR for the exchange of information process in the absence of rulings being issued and no recommendations are made.

C. Statistics (ToR IV)

654. As no rulings were issued, no statistics can be reported.

D. Matters related to intellectual property regimes (ToR I.4.1.3)

655. Kenya does not offer an intellectual property regime for which transparency requirements under the Action 5 Report (OECD, 2015[1]) were imposed.

Summary of recommendations on implementation of the transparency framework

Aspect of implementation of the transparency framework that should be improved	Recommendation for improvement
	No recommendations are made.

References

OECD (2017), *BEPS Action 5 on Harmful Tax Practices - Terms of Reference and Methodology for the Conduct of the Peer Reviews of the Action 5 Transparency Framework*, OECD Publishing, Paris, http://www.oecd.org/tax/beps/beps-action-5-harmful-tax-practices-peer-review-transparency-framework.pdf. [3]

OECD (2015), *Countering Harmful Tax Practices More Effectively, Taking into Account Transparency and Substance, Action 5 - 2015 Final Report*, OECD/G20 Base Erosion and Profit Shifting Project, OECD Publishing, Paris, https://dx.doi.org/10.1787/9789264241190-en. [1]

OECD/Council of Europe (2011), *The Multilateral Convention on Mutual Administrative Assistance in Tax Matters: Amended by the 2010 Protocol*, OECD Publishing, Paris, https://dx.doi.org/10.1787/9789264115606-en. [4]

Notes

[1] With respect to the following preferential regimes: 1) Export processing zone and 2) Special economic zone.

[2] Parties to the Convention are available here: www.oecd.org/tax/exchange-of-tax-information/convention-on-mutual-administrative-assistance-in-tax-matters.htm. Kenya also has bilateral agreements with Canada, Denmark, France, Germany, India, Iran, Korea, Norway, Qatar, Seychelles, South Africa, Sweden, United Arab Emirates, United Kingdom and Zambia.

Korea

Korea has met all aspects of the terms of reference (OECD, 2017[3]) (ToR) for the calendar year 2019 (year in review) and no recommendations are made.

Korea can legally issue one type of rulings within the scope of the transparency framework.

In practice, Korea issued rulings within the scope of the transparency framework as follows:

- 45 past rulings;
- For the period 1 April 2016 - 31 December 2016: one future ruling;
- For the calendar year 2017: four future rulings,
- For the calendar year 2018: five future rulings, and
- For the year in review: five future rulings.

Peer input was received from two jurisdictions in respect of the exchanges of information on rulings received from Korea. The input was positive, noting that information was complete, in a correct format and received in a timely manner.

A. The information gathering process

656. Korea can legally issue the following type of ruling within the scope of the transparency framework: cross-border unilateral APAs and any other cross-border unilateral tax rulings (such as an advance tax ruling) covering transfer pricing or the application of transfer pricing principles.

657. For Korea, past rulings are any tax rulings within scope that are issued either: (i) on or after 1 January 2014 but before 1 April 2016; or (ii) on or after 1 January 2010 but before 1 January 2014, provided they were still in effect as at 1 January 2014. Future rulings are any tax rulings within scope that are issued on or after 1 April 2016.

658. In the prior years' peer review reports, it was determined that Korea's undertakings to identify past and future rulings and all potential exchange jurisdictions were sufficient to meet the minimum standard. In addition, it was determined that Korea's review and supervision mechanism was sufficient to meet the minimum standard. Korea's implementation remains unchanged, and therefore continues to meet the minimum standard.

659. Korea has met all of the ToR for the information gathering process and no recommendations are made.

B. The exchange of information

660. In the prior years' peer review reports, it was determined that Korea's process for the completion and exchange of templates were sufficient to meet the minimum standard. With respect to past rulings, no further action was required.

661. The National Tax Service (NTS) completes the templates according to Annex C of the BEPS Action 5 report (OECD, 2015[1]) and converts them into PDF to send through electronic mail. The NTS is planning to move to exchange in the XML format. As such, it has been testing the OECD Common Transmission System to exchange rulings, and confirmed that the XML files have no functional problems with several partner jurisdictions. The NTS is still developing additional in-house interfaces to ensure stable exchanges of information. This is currently under review by the NTS, and in the interim will continue exchanges in PDF format via electronic mail.

662. Korea has international agreements permitting spontaneous exchange of information, including being a party to the (i) *Multilateral Convention on Mutual Administrative Assistance in Tax Matters: Amended by the 2010 Protocol* (OECD/Council of Europe, 2011[4]) ("the Convention") and (ii) bilateral agreements in force with 93 jurisdictions.[1]

663. For the year in review, the timeliness of exchanges is as follows:

Future rulings in the scope of the transparency framework	Number of exchanges transmitted within three months of the information becoming available to the competent authority or immediately after legal impediments have been lifted	Delayed exchanges		
		Number of exchanges transmitted later than three months of the information on rulings becoming available to the competent authority	Reasons for the delays	Any other comments
	5	0	N/A	N/A

Follow up requests received for exchange of the ruling	Number	Average time to provide response	Number of requests not answered
	0	N/A	N/A

664. Korea has the necessary legal basis for spontaneous exchange of information, a process for completing the templates in a timely way and has completed all exchanges. Korea has met all of the ToR for the exchange of information process and no recommendations are made.

C. Statistics (ToR IV)

665. The statistics for the year in review are as follows:

Category of ruling	Number of exchanges	Jurisdictions exchanged with
Cross-border unilateral advance pricing agreements (APAs) and any other cross border unilateral tax rulings (such as an advance tax ruling) covering transfer pricing or the application of transfer pricing principles	5	Hong Kong (China), Singapore, United States
IP regimes: total exchanges on taxpayers benefitting from the third category of IP assets, new entrants benefitting from grandfathered IP regimes; and taxpayers making use of the option to treat the nexus ratio as a rebuttable presumption	0	N/A
Total	5	

D. Matters related to intellectual property regimes (ToR I.4.1.3)

666. Korea offers an intellectual property regime (IP regime)[2] that is subject to the transparency requirements under the Action 5 Report (OECD, 2015[1]). It states that the identification of the benefitting taxpayers will occur as follows:

- ***New entrants benefitting from the grandfathered IP regime***: as this is a new IP regime rather than a grandfathered IP regime, transparency on new entrants is not relevant.
- ***Third category of IP assets***: the regime provides benefits to the third category of IP assets. The process on the collection of information is described in the previous year peer review report and meets the ToR. In practice, no taxpayers have applied for the corporate income tax benefits for the third category of IP assets, and as such no exchanges were required to take place.
- ***Taxpayers making use of the option to treat the nexus ratio as a rebuttable presumption***: not applicable as the regime does not allow the nexus ratio to be treated as a rebuttable presumption.

Summary of recommendations on implementation of the transparency framework

Aspect of implementation of the transparency framework that should be improved	Recommendation for improvement
	No recommendations are made.

References

OECD (2017), *BEPS Action 5 on Harmful Tax Practices - Terms of Reference and Methodology for the Conduct of the Peer Reviews of the Action 5 Transparency Framework*, OECD Publishing, Paris, http://www.oecd.org/tax/beps/beps-action-5-harmful-tax-practices-peer-review-transparency-framework.pdf. [3]

OECD (2015), *Countering Harmful Tax Practices More Effectively, Taking into Account Transparency and Substance, Action 5 - 2015 Final Report*, OECD/G20 Base Erosion and Profit Shifting Project, OECD Publishing, Paris, https://dx.doi.org/10.1787/9789264241190-en. [1]

OECD/Council of Europe (2011), *The Multilateral Convention on Mutual Administrative Assistance in Tax Matters: Amended by the 2010 Protocol*, OECD Publishing, Paris, https://dx.doi.org/10.1787/9789264115606-en. [4]

Notes

[1] Parties to the Convention are available here: www.oecd.org/tax/exchange-of-tax-information/convention-on-mutual-administrative-assistance-in-tax-matters.htm. Korea also has bilateral agreements with Albania, Algeria, Australia, Austria, Azerbaijan, Bahrain, Bangladesh, Belarus, Belgium, Brazil, Brunei Darussalam, Bulgaria, Canada, Chile, China (People's Republic of), Colombia, Croatia, Czech Republic, Denmark, Ecuador, Egypt, Estonia, Ethiopia, Fiji, Finland, France, Gabon, Georgia, Germany, Greece, Hong Kong (China), Hungary, Iceland, India, Indonesia, Iran, Ireland, Israel, Italy, Japan, Jordan, Kazakhstan, Kenya, Kuwait, Kyrgyzstan, Laos, Latvia, Lithuania, Luxembourg, Malaysia, Malta, Mexico, Mongolia, Morocco, Myanmar, Nepal, Netherlands, New Zealand, Norway, Oman, Pakistan, Panama, Papua New Guinea, Peru, Philippines, Poland, Portugal, Qatar, Romania, Russia, Saudi Arabia, Serbia, Singapore, Slovak Republic, Slovenia, South Africa, Spain, Sri Lanka, Sweden, Switzerland, Tajikistan, Thailand, Tunisia, Turkey, Turkmenistan, Ukraine, United Arab Emirates, United Kingdom, United States, Uruguay, Uzbekistan, Venezuela and Viet Nam.

[2] Special taxation for transfer, acquisition, etc. of technology.

Latvia

Latvia has met all aspects of the terms of reference (OECD, 2017[3]) (ToR) for the calendar year 2019 (year in review) and no recommendations are made.

Latvia can legally issue three types of rulings within the scope of the transparency framework.

In practice, Latvia issued rulings within the scope of the transparency framework as follows:

- One past ruling;
- For the period 1 April 2016 - 31 December 2016: one future ruling;
- For the calendar year 2017: two future rulings;
- For the calendar year 2018: three future rulings; and
- For the year in review: four future rulings.

Summaries of rulings are published in an anonymised way.[1]

No peer input was received in respect of the exchanges of information on rulings received from Latvia.

A. The information gathering process

667. Latvia can legally issue the following three types of rulings within the scope of the transparency framework: (i) preferential regimes;[2] (ii) cross-border unilateral APAs and any other cross-border unilateral tax rulings (such as an advance tax ruling) covering transfer pricing or the application of transfer pricing principles; and (iii) permanent establishment rulings.

668. For Latvia, past rulings are any tax rulings within scope that are issued either: (i) on or after 1 January 2014 but before 1 April 2016; or (ii) on or after 1 January 2010 but before 1 January 2014, provided they were still in effect as at 1 January 2014. Future rulings are any tax rulings within scope that are issued on or after 1 April 2016.

669. In the prior years' peer review reports, it was determined that Latvia's undertakings to identify past and future rulings and all potential exchange jurisdictions were sufficient to meet the minimum standard. In addition, it was determined that Latvia's review and supervision mechanism was sufficient to meet the minimum standard. Latvia's implementation remains unchanged, and therefore continues to meet the minimum standard.

670. Latvia has met all of the ToR for the information gathering process and no recommendations are made.

B. The exchange of information

671. In the prior year's peer review report, it was determined that Latvia's process for the completion and exchange of templates were sufficient to meet the minimum standard. With respect to past rulings, no further action was required. Latvia's implementation in this regard remains unchanged and therefore continues to meet the minimum standard.

672. Latvia has international agreements permitting spontaneous exchange of information, including being a party to the (i) *Multilateral Convention on Mutual Administrative Assistance in Tax Matters: Amended by the 2010 Protocol* (OECD/Council of Europe, 2011[4]) ("the Convention"), (ii) the Directive 2011/16/EU with all other European Union Member States and (iii) bilateral agreements in force with 62 jurisdictions.[3]

673. For the year in review, the timeliness of exchanges is as follows:

Future rulings in the scope of the transparency framework	Number of exchanges transmitted within three months of the information becoming available to the competent authority or immediately after legal impediments have been lifted	Delayed exchanges		
		Number of exchanges transmitted later than three months of the information on rulings becoming available to the competent authority	Reasons for the delays	Any other comments
	5	1	See below.	N/A

Follow up requests received for exchange of the ruling	Number	Average time to provide response	Number of requests not answered
	0	N/A	N/A

674. During the year in review, Latvia experienced one delayed exchange, due to a misinterpretation of the definition of an APA. As the APA was related to a roll-back period only, and thus did not cover any future transaction, the Latvian administration understood that information on this APA did not need to be exchanged. After this issue was internally resolved, Latvia immediately exchanged information on this

APA. It is noted that this APA had characteristics of a bilateral APA, and therefore the counterparty tax administration was already informed of the transactions covered in the APA. As this was a non-recurring issue, no recommendation is made.

675. Latvia has the necessary legal basis for spontaneous exchange of information, a process for completing the templates in a timely way and has completed all exchanges. Latvia has met all of the ToR for the exchange of information process and no recommendations are made.

C. Statistics (ToR IV)

676. The statistics for the year in review are as follows:

Category of ruling	Number of exchanges	Jurisdictions exchanged with
Ruling related to a preferential regime	0	N/A
Cross-border unilateral advance pricing agreements (APAs) and any other cross-border unilateral tax rulings (such as an advance tax ruling) covering transfer pricing or the application of transfer pricing principles	6	*De minimis* rule applies[4]
Permanent establishment rulings	0	N/A
Total	6	

D. Matters related to intellectual property regimes (ToR I.4.1.3)

677. Latvia does not offer an intellectual property regime for which transparency requirements under the Action 5 Report (OECD, 2015[1]) were imposed.

Summary of recommendations on implementation of the transparency framework

Aspect of implementation of the transparency framework that should be improved	Recommendation for improvement
	No recommendations are made.

References

OECD (2017), *BEPS Action 5 on Harmful Tax Practices - Terms of Reference and Methodology for the Conduct of the Peer Reviews of the Action 5 Transparency Framework*, OECD Publishing, Paris, http://www.oecd.org/tax/beps/beps-action-5-harmful-tax-practices-peer-review-transparency-framework.pdf. [3]

OECD (2015), *Countering Harmful Tax Practices More Effectively, Taking into Account Transparency and Substance, Action 5 - 2015 Final Report*, OECD/G20 Base Erosion and Profit Shifting Project, OECD Publishing, Paris, https://dx.doi.org/10.1787/9789264241190-en. [1]

OECD/Council of Europe (2011), *The Multilateral Convention on Mutual Administrative Assistance in Tax Matters: Amended by the 2010 Protocol*, OECD Publishing, Paris, https://dx.doi.org/10.1787/9789264115606-en. [4]

Notes

[1] Available at: www.vid.gov.lv.

[2] With respect to the following preferential regimes: 1) Shipping tax regime and 2) Special economic zones.

[3] Parties to the Convention are available here: www.oecd.org/tax/exchange-of-tax-information/convention-on-mutual-administrative-assistance-in-tax-matters.htm. Latvia also has bilateral agreements with Albania, Armenia, Austria, Azerbaijan, Belarus, Belgium, Bulgaria, Canada, China (People's Republic of), Croatia, Cyprus, Czech Republic, Denmark, Estonia, Finland, France, Georgia, Germany, Greece, Hong Kong (China), Hungary, Iceland, India, Ireland, Israel, Italy, Japan, Kazakhstan, Korea, Kuwait, Kyrgyzstan, Lithuania, Luxembourg, Malta, Mexico, Moldova, Morocco, Netherlands, North Macedonia, Norway, Poland, Portugal, Qatar, Romania, Russia, Montenegro, Serbia, Singapore, Slovenia, Slovak Republic, Spain, Sweden, Switzerland, Tajikistan, Turkey, Turkmenistan, Ukraine, United Arab Emirates, United Kingdom, United States, Uzbekistan and Viet Nam.

[4] Four issued rulings were exchanged with six jurisdictions.

Liechtenstein

Liechtenstein has met all aspects of the terms of reference (OECD, 2017[3]) (ToR) for the calendar year 2019 (year in review) and no recommendations are made.

Liechtenstein can legally issue four types of rulings within the scope of the transparency framework.

In practice, Liechtenstein issued rulings within the scope of the transparency framework as follows:

- 18 past rulings;
- For the period 1 April 2017 - 31 December 2017: six future rulings;
- For the calendar year 2018: five future rulings; and
- For the year in review: three future rulings.

Peer input was received from two jurisdictions in respect of the exchanges of information on rulings received from Liechtenstein. The input was positive, noting that information was complete, in a correct format and received in a timely manner.

A. The information gathering process

678. Liechtenstein can legally issue the following four types of rulings within the scope of the transparency framework: (i) cross-border unilateral APAs and any other cross-border unilateral tax rulings (such as an advance tax ruling) covering transfer pricing or the application of transfer pricing principles; (ii) rulings providing for unilateral downward adjustments; (iii) permanent establishment rulings; and (iv) related party conduit rulings.

679. For Liechtenstein, past rulings are any tax rulings within scope that are issued either: (i) on or after January 2015 but before 1 April 2017; or (ii) on or after 1 January 2012 but before 1 January 2015, provided they were still in effect as at 1 January 2017. Future rulings are any tax rulings within scope that are issued on or after 1 April 2017.

680. In the prior years' peer review reports, it was determined that Liechtenstein's undertakings to identify past and future rulings and all potential exchange jurisdictions were sufficient to meet the minimum standard. In addition, it was determined that Liechtenstein's review and supervision mechanism was sufficient to meet the minimum standard. Liechtenstein's implementation remains unchanged, and therefore continues to meet the minimum standard.

681. Liechtenstein has met all of the ToR for the information gathering process and no recommendations are made.

B. The exchange of information

682. In the prior years' peer review reports, it was determined that Liechtenstein's process for the completion and exchange of templates were sufficient to meet the minimum standard. With respect to past rulings, no further action was required from Liechtenstein. Liechtenstein's implementation in this regard remains unchanged and therefore continues to meet the minimum standard.

683. Liechtenstein has international agreements permitting spontaneous exchange of information, including being a party to the (i) *Multilateral Convention on Mutual Administrative Assistance in Tax Matters: Amended by the 2010 Protocol* (OECD/Council of Europe, 2011[4]) ("the Convention") and (ii) bilateral agreements in force with 14 jurisdictions.[1]

684. For the year in review, the timeliness of exchanges is as follows:

Future rulings in the scope of the transparency framework	Number of exchanges transmitted within three months of the information becoming available to the competent authority or immediately after legal impediments have been lifted	Delayed exchanges		
		Number of exchanges transmitted later than three months of the information on rulings becoming available to the competent authority	Reasons for the delays	Any other comments
	12	0	N/A	N/A

Follow up requests received for exchange of the ruling	Number	Average time to provide response	Number of requests not answered
	0	N/A	N/A

685. Liechtenstein has the necessary legal basis for spontaneous exchange of information, a process for completing the templates in a timely way and has completed all exchanges. Liechtenstein has met all of the ToR for the exchange of information process and no recommendations are made.

C. Statistics (ToR IV)

686. The statistics for the year in review are as follows:

Category of ruling	Number of exchanges	Jurisdictions exchanged with
Cross-border unilateral advance pricing agreements (APAs) and any other cross-border unilateral tax rulings (such as an advance tax ruling) covering transfer pricing or the application of transfer pricing principles	11	Australia, Austria, France, Germany, Hong Kong (China), Ireland, Isle of Man, Luxembourg, Singapore, Switzerland, United Kingdom
Cross-border rulings providing for a unilateral downward adjustment to the taxpayer's taxable profits that is not directly reflected in the taxpayer's financial / commercial accounts	0	N/A
Permanent establishment rulings	*De minimis rule* applies	N/A
Related party conduit rulings	*De minimis rule* applies	N/A
De minimis rule	4	
Total	15[2]	

D. Matters related to intellectual property regimes (ToR I.4.1.3)

687. Liechtenstein does not offer an intellectual property regime for which transparency requirements under the Action 5 Report (OECD, 2015[1]) were imposed.

Summary of recommendations on implementation of the transparency framework

Aspect of implementation of the transparency framework that should be improved	Recommendation for improvement
	No recommendations are made.

References

OECD (2017), *BEPS Action 5 on Harmful Tax Practices - Terms of Reference and Methodology for the Conduct of the Peer Reviews of the Action 5 Transparency Framework*, OECD Publishing, Paris, http://www.oecd.org/tax/beps/beps-action-5-harmful-tax-practices-peer-review-transparency-framework.pdf. [3]

OECD (2015), *Countering Harmful Tax Practices More Effectively, Taking into Account Transparency and Substance, Action 5 - 2015 Final Report*, OECD/G20 Base Erosion and Profit Shifting Project, OECD Publishing, Paris, https://dx.doi.org/10.1787/9789264241190-en. [1]

OECD/Council of Europe (2011), *The Multilateral Convention on Mutual Administrative Assistance in Tax Matters: Amended by the 2010 Protocol*, OECD Publishing, Paris, https://dx.doi.org/10.1787/9789264115606-en. [4]

Notes

[1] Parties to the Convention are available here: www.oecd.org/tax/exchange-of-tax-information/convention-on-mutual-administrative-assistance-in-tax-matters.htm. Liechtenstein also has bilateral agreements with Andorra, Austria, Czech Republic, Germany, Hungary, Iceland, Jersey, Lithuania, Luxembourg, Monaco, San Marino, Singapore, United Arab Emirates, and United Kingdom.

[2] Including two rulings that fell into more than one category and were exchanged with more than one jurisdiction under the BEPS Action 5 report (OECD, 2015[1]).

Lithuania

Lithuania has met all aspects of the terms of reference (OECD, 2017[3]) (ToR) for the calendar year 2019 (year in review) and no recommendations are made.

Lithuania can legally issue five types of rulings within the scope of the transparency framework.

In practice, Lithuania issued rulings within the scope of the transparency framework as follows:

- Five past rulings;
- For the calendar year 2017: six future rulings;
- For the calendar year 2018: five future rulings; and
- For the year in review: nine future rulings.

No peer input was received in respect of the exchanges of information on rulings received from Lithuania.

A. The information gathering process

688. Lithuania can legally issue the following five types of rulings within the scope of the transparency framework: (i) preferential regimes;[1] (ii) cross-border unilateral APAs and any other cross-border unilateral tax rulings (such as an advance tax ruling) covering transfer pricing or the application of transfer pricing principles; (iii) rulings providing for unilateral downward adjustments; (iv) permanent establishment rulings; and (v) related party conduit rulings.

689. For Lithuania, past rulings are any tax rulings within scope that are issued either: (i) on or after 1 January 2015 but before 1 April 2017; or (ii) on or after 1 January 2012 but before 1 January 2015, provided they were still in effect as at 1 January 2015. Future rulings are any tax rulings within scope that are issued on or after 1 April 2017.

690. In the prior years' peer review reports, it was determined that Lithuania's undertakings to identify past and future rulings and all potential exchange jurisdictions were sufficient to meet the minimum standard. In addition, it was determined that Lithuania's review and supervision mechanism was sufficient to meet the minimum standard. For past rulings, Lithuania's implementation remains unchanged, and therefore continues to meet the minimum standard.

691. During the year in review, Lithuania issued additional regulations to strengthen the identification process for future rulings (other than APAs). When applying for a ruling with an international element, the taxpayer now always has to provide information with respect to the immediate parent entity and the ultimate parent entity. Previously, Lithuania would obtain additional information from the taxpayer and was able to do so in all cases and without delay. Lithuania's implementation continues to meet the minimum standard.

692. Lithuania has met all of the ToR for the information gathering process and no recommendations are made.

B. The exchange of information

693. In the prior years' peer review reports, it was determined that Lithuania's process for the completion and exchange of templates were sufficient to meet the minimum standard. With respect to past rulings, no further action was required. Lithuania's implementation in this regard remains unchanged and therefore continues to meet the minimum standard.

694. Lithuania has international agreements permitting spontaneous exchange of information, including being a party to the (i) *Multilateral Convention on Mutual Administrative Assistance in Tax Matters: Amended by the 2010 Protocol* (OECD/Council of Europe, 2011[4]) ("the Convention"), (ii) the Directive 2011/16/EU with all other European Union Member States and (iii) bilateral agreements in force with 55 jurisdictions.[2]

695. For the year in review, the timeliness of exchanges is as follows:

Future rulings in the scope of the transparency framework	Number of exchanges transmitted within three months of the information becoming available to the competent authority or immediately after legal impediments have been lifted	Delayed exchanges		
		Number of exchanges transmitted later than three months of the information on rulings becoming available to the competent authority	Reasons for the delays	Any other comments
	17	0	N/A	N/A

Follow up requests received for exchange of the ruling	Number	Average time to provide response	Number of requests not answered
	0	N/A	N/A

696. Lithuania has the necessary legal basis for spontaneous exchange of information, a process for completing the templates in a timely way and has completed all exchanges. Lithuania has met all of the ToR for the exchange of information process and no recommendations are made.

C. Statistics (ToR IV)

697. The statistics for the year in review are as follows:

Category of ruling	Number of exchanges	Jurisdictions exchanged with
Ruling related to a preferential regime	9	Canada, Estonia, Finland, Germany, Latvia, Luxembourg, Netherlands, Poland, United States
Cross-border unilateral advance pricing agreements (APAs) and any other cross-border unilateral tax rulings (such as an advance tax ruling) covering transfer pricing or the application of transfer pricing principles	6	Estonia, Finland, Ireland, Latvia, Singapore, United Kingdom
Cross-border rulings providing for a unilateral downward adjustment to the taxpayer's taxable profits that is not directly reflected in the taxpayer's financial / commercial accounts	0	N/A
Permanent establishment rulings	*De minimis rule* applies	N/A
Related party conduit rulings	0	N/A
De minimis rule	2	
Total	17	

D. Matters related to intellectual property regimes (ToR I.4.1.3)

698. Lithuania offers an intellectual property regime (IP regime) which came into effect from 1 January 2018. It is noted that this regime is not subject to transparency requirements under the Action 5 report (OECD, 2015[1]), because:

- ***New entrants benefitting from the grandfathered IP regime***: as this is a new IP regime rather than a grandfathered IP regime, transparency on new entrants was not relevant.
- ***Third category of IP assets***: not applicable as the regime does not allow the third category of IP assets to qualify for the benefits.
- ***Taxpayers making use of the option to treat the nexus ratio as a rebuttable presumption***: not applicable as the regime does not allow the nexus ratio to be treated as a rebuttable presumption.

Summary of recommendations on implementation of the transparency framework

Aspect of implementation of the transparency framework that should be improved	Recommendation for improvement
	No recommendations are made.

References

OECD (2017), *BEPS Action 5 on Harmful Tax Practices - Terms of Reference and Methodology for the Conduct of the Peer Reviews of the Action 5 Transparency Framework*, OECD Publishing, Paris, http://www.oecd.org/tax/beps/beps-action-5-harmful-tax-practices-peer-review-transparency-framework.pdf. [3]

OECD (2015), *Countering Harmful Tax Practices More Effectively, Taking into Account Transparency and Substance, Action 5 - 2015 Final Report*, OECD/G20 Base Erosion and Profit Shifting Project, OECD Publishing, Paris, https://dx.doi.org/10.1787/9789264241190-en. [1]

OECD/Council of Europe (2011), *The Multilateral Convention on Mutual Administrative Assistance in Tax Matters: Amended by the 2010 Protocol*, OECD Publishing, Paris, https://dx.doi.org/10.1787/9789264115606-en. [4]

Notes

[1] With respect to the following preferential regimes: 1) Free economic zone taxation regime, 2) Tonnage tax regime and 3) IP regime.

[2] Parties to the Convention are available here: www.oecd.org/tax/exchange-of-tax-information/convention-on-mutual-administrative-assistance-in-tax-matters.htm. Lithuania also has bilateral agreements with Armenia, Austria, Azerbaijan, Belarus, Belgium, Bulgaria, Canada, China (People's Republic of), Croatia, Czech Republic, Cyprus, Denmark, Estonia, Finland, France, Georgia, Germany, Greece, Hungary, Iceland, India, Ireland, Israel, Italy, Japan, Kazakhstan, Korea, Kuwait, Kyrgyzstan, Latvia, Luxembourg, Malta, Mexico, Moldova, Netherlands, North Macedonia, Norway, Poland, Portugal, Romania, Russia, Serbia, Singapore, Slovak Republic, Slovenia, Spain, Sweden, Switzerland, Turkey, Turkmenistan, Ukraine, United Arab Emirates, United Kingdom, United States and Uzbekistan.

Luxembourg

Luxembourg has met all aspects of the terms of reference (OECD, 2017[3]) (ToR) for the calendar year 2019 (year in review) and no recommendations are made.

Luxembourg can legally issue four types of rulings within the scope of the transparency framework.

In practice, Luxembourg issued rulings within the scope of the transparency framework as follows:

- 1922 past rulings;
- For the period 1 April 2016 - 31 December 2016: 73 future rulings;
- For the calendar year 2017: 18 future rulings,
- For the calendar year 2018: nine future rulings, and
- For the year in review: three future rulings.[1]

Peer input was received from three jurisdictions in respect of the exchanges of information on rulings received from Luxembourg. The input was positive, noting that information was complete, in a correct format and received in a timely manner.

A. The information gathering process

699. Luxembourg can legally issue the following four types of rulings within the scope of the transparency framework: (i) preferential regimes;[2] (ii) cross-border unilateral APAs and any other cross-border unilateral tax rulings (such as an advance tax ruling) covering transfer pricing or the application of transfer pricing principles; (iii) rulings providing for unilateral downward adjustments; and (iv) permanent establishment rulings.

700. For Luxembourg, past rulings are any tax rulings within scope that are issued either: (i) on or after 1 January 2014 but before 1 April 2016; or (ii) on or after 1 January 2010 but before 1 January 2014, provided they were still in effect as at 1 January 2014. Future rulings are any tax rulings within scope that are issued on or after 1 April 2016.

701. In the prior years' peer review reports, it was determined that Luxembourg's undertakings to identify past and future rulings and all potential exchange jurisdictions were sufficient to meet the minimum standard. In addition, it was determined that Luxembourg's review and supervision mechanism was sufficient to meet the minimum standard. Luxembourg's implementation remains unchanged, and therefore continues to meet the minimum standard.

702. Luxembourg has met all of the ToR for the information gathering process and no recommendations are made.

B. The exchange of information

703. In the prior years' peer review reports, it was determined that Luxembourg's process for the completion and exchange of templates were sufficient to meet the minimum standard. With respect to past rulings, no further action was required. Luxembourg's implementation in this regard remains unchanged and therefore continues to meet the minimum standard.

704. Luxembourg has international agreements permitting spontaneous exchange of information, including being a party to the (i) *Multilateral Convention on Mutual Administrative Assistance in Tax Matters: Amended by the 2010 Protocol* (OECD/Council of Europe, 2011[4]) ("the Convention"), (ii) the Directive 2011/16/EU with all other European Union Member States and (iii) bilateral agreements in force with 81 jurisdictions.[3]

705. For the year in review, the timeliness of exchanges is as follows:

Future rulings in the scope of the transparency framework	Number of exchanges transmitted within three months of the information becoming available to the competent authority or immediately after legal impediments have been lifted	Delayed exchanges		
		Number of exchanges transmitted later than three months of the information on rulings becoming available to the competent authority	Reasons for the delays	Any other comments
	11[4]	0	N/A	N/A

Follow up requests received for exchange of the ruling	Number	Average time to provide response	Number of requests not answered
	45	1.5 months	0

706. Luxembourg has the necessary legal basis for spontaneous exchange of information, a process for completing the templates in a timely way and has completed all exchanges. Luxembourg has met all of the ToR for the exchange of information process and no recommendations are made.

C. Statistics (ToR IV)

707. The statistics for the year in review are as follows:

Category of ruling	Number of exchanges	Jurisdictions exchanged with
Rulings related to a preferential regime	*De minimis rule* applies	N/A[5]
Cross-border unilateral advance pricing agreements (APAs) and any other cross-border unilateral tax rulings (such as an advance tax ruling) covering transfer pricing or the application of transfer pricing principles	0	N/A
Cross-border rulings providing for a unilateral downward adjustment to the taxpayer's taxable profits that is not directly reflected in the taxpayer's financial / commercial accounts	0	N/A
Permanent establishment rulings	*De minimis rule* applies	N/A
De minimis rule	11	
IP regimes: total exchanges on taxpayers benefitting from the third category of IP assets, new entrants benefitting from grandfathered IP regimes; and taxpayers making use of the option to treat the nexus ratio as a rebuttable presumption	22	Belgium, Finland, France, Germany, Japan, Poland, Spain, Tunisia, United States
Total	33[6]	

D. Matters related to intellectual property regimes (ToR I.4.1.3)

708. Luxembourg offered an intellectual property regime (IP regime)[7] that was abolished as of 1 July 2016 and is subject to transparency requirements under the Action 5 Report (OECD, 2015[1]). It states that the identification of the benefitting taxpayers will occur as follows:

- ***New entrants benefitting from the grandfathered IP regime:*** during the previous peer review year, an IT research application was launched with the aim of identifying the taxpayers who requested the application of the IP regime in their tax return. Some taxpayers only filed their tax return for the fiscal years 2015 and 2016 by late 2017 or in 2018. Information on these remaining new entrants and new IP assets from existing taxpayers was exchanged in 2018, with a small number of additional exchanges taking place early in the year of review. Exchanges took place generally within one month of receipt of the information. This issue is now completed.
- ***Third category of IP assets***: not applicable as the IP regime has been abolished.
- ***Taxpayers making use of the option to treat the nexus ratio as a rebuttable presumption***: not applicable as the IP regime has been abolished.

709. In addition, Luxembourg offers an IP regime that not is subject to the transparency requirements under the Action 5 Report (OECD, 2015[1]), because:

- ***New entrants benefitting from the grandfathered IP regime***: as this is a new IP regime rather than a grandfathered IP regime, transparency on new entrants is not relevant.
- ***Third category of IP assets***: not applicable as the regime does not allow the third category of IP assets to qualify for the benefits.

- ***Taxpayers making use of the option to treat the nexus ratio as a rebuttable presumption***: not applicable as the regime does not allow the nexus ratio to be treated as a rebuttable presumption.

Summary of recommendations on implementation of the transparency framework

Aspect of implementation of the transparency framework that should be improved	Recommendation for improvement
	No recommendations are made.

References

OECD (2017), *BEPS Action 5 on Harmful Tax Practices - Terms of Reference and Methodology for the Conduct of the Peer Reviews of the Action 5 Transparency Framework*, OECD Publishing, Paris, http://www.oecd.org/tax/beps/beps-action-5-harmful-tax-practices-peer-review-transparency-framework.pdf. [3]

OECD (2015), *Countering Harmful Tax Practices More Effectively, Taking into Account Transparency and Substance, Action 5 - 2015 Final Report*, OECD/G20 Base Erosion and Profit Shifting Project, OECD Publishing, Paris, https://dx.doi.org/10.1787/9789264241190-en. [1]

OECD/Council of Europe (2011), *The Multilateral Convention on Mutual Administrative Assistance in Tax Matters: Amended by the 2010 Protocol*, OECD Publishing, Paris, https://dx.doi.org/10.1787/9789264115606-en. [4]

Notes

[1] In addition to the rulings in the scope of the transparency framework Luxembourg issued and exchanged 17 rulings relating to "other types of rulings". These "other types of rulings" cover an additional category of rulings that Luxembourg identified, related to intragroup financing activities which in the absence of transparency may cause BEPS concerns. These rulings are not otherwise covered by one of the five categories within the scope of the transparency framework and are therefore defined as "other type of rulings". Luxembourg exchanged these rulings with the relevant IF members using the transparency framework.

[2] With respect to the following preferential regimes: 1) Private asset management company, 2) Investment company in risk capital, 3) Provision for fluctuations in reinsurance companies, and 4) Informal capital and partial exemption for income/gains derived from certain IP rights.

[3] Parties to the Convention are available here: www.oecd.org/tax/exchange-of-tax-information/convention-on-mutual-administrative-assistance-in-tax-matters.htm. Luxembourg also has bilateral agreements with Andorra, Armenia, Austria, Azerbaijan, Bahrain, Bailiwick of Guernsey, Barbados, Belgium, Brazil, Brunei Darussalam, Bulgaria, Canada, China (People's Republic of), Croatia, Cyprus, Czech Republic, Denmark, Estonia, Finland, France, Georgia, Germany, Greece, Hungary, Iceland, India, Indonesia, Ireland, Isle of Man, Israel, Italy, Japan, Jersey, Kazakhstan, Korea, Lao People's Democratic Republic, Latvia, Liechtenstein, Lithuania, Malaysia, Malta, Mauritius, Mexico, Moldova, Monaco, Morocco, Netherlands, North Macedonia, Norway, Panama, Poland, Portugal, Qatar, Romania, Russia, San Marino, Saudi Arabia, Senegal, Serbia, Seychelles, Singapore, Slovak Republic, Slovenia, South Africa, Spain, Sri Lanka, Sweden, Switzerland, Chinese Taipei, Tajikistan, Thailand, Trinidad and Tobago, Tunisia, Turkey, Ukraine, United Arab Emirates, United Kingdom, United States, Uruguay, Uzbekistan and Viet Nam.

[4] In addition to the rulings in the scope of the transparency framework Luxembourg transmitted 28 exchanges relating to "other types of rulings" during the year in review.

[5] One issued ruling led to nine exchanges.

[6] Additional 28 exchanges of "other types of rulings" were transmitted by 31 December 2019 to the following countries: Australia, Belgium, France, Germany, Guernsey, Italy, Jersey, Mexico, Netherlands, Singapore, South Africa, Sweden, Switzerland, United Kingdom and United States.

[7] Partial exemption for income/gains derived from certain IP rights.

Malaysia

Malaysia has met all aspects of the terms of reference (OECD, 2017[3]) (ToR) for the calendar year 2019 (year in review) except for identifying all potential exchange jurisdictions for future rulings (ToR I.4.2.1), timeliness in providing information on rulings to the Competent Authority and undertaking spontaneous exchange of information on all tax rulings within the scope of the transparency framework (ToR II.5) and identifying and exchanging information on new entrants to the grandfathered IP regime (ToR I.4.1.3). Malaysia receives three recommendations on these points for the year in review.

In the prior year report, as well as in the 2017 peer review, Malaysia had received two recommendations. As they have not been addressed, the recommendations remain in place. In addition, there were new circumstances that came to light during the peer review process, and therefore one additional recommendation has been made as relevant.

Malaysia can legally issue five types of rulings within the scope of the transparency framework.

In practice, Malaysia issued rulings within the scope of the transparency framework as follows:

- 455 past rulings;[1]
- For the calendar year 2017: 23 future rulings,[2]
- For the calendar year 2018: 51 future rulings,[3] and
- For the year in review: 69 future rulings.

Peer input was received from two jurisdictions in respect of the exchanges of information on rulings received from Malaysia. The input was generally positive, noting that information was complete and in a correct format. Some peers noted that the exchange of information on rulings from Malaysia was delayed.

A. The information gathering process

710. Malaysia can legally issue the following five types of rulings within the scope of the transparency framework: (i) preferential regimes;[4] (ii) cross-border unilateral APAs and any other cross-border unilateral tax rulings (such as an advance tax ruling) covering transfer pricing or the application of transfer pricing principles; (iii) rulings providing for unilateral downward adjustments; (iv) permanent establishment rulings; and (v) related party conduit rulings.

711. For Malaysia, past rulings are any tax rulings within scope that are issued either (i) on or after 1 January 2015 but before 1 September 2017; and (ii) on or after 1 January 2012 but before 1 January 2015, provided they were still in effect as at 1 January 2015. Future rulings are any tax rulings within scope that are issued on or after 1 September 2017.

712. In the prior years' peer review reports, it was determined that Malaysia's undertakings to identify past and future rulings and all potential exchange jurisdictions were sufficient to meet the minimum standard. In addition, it was determined that Malaysia's review and supervision mechanism was sufficient to meet the minimum standard. During the year in review, it has come to light that the previous processes used by Malaysia were not sufficient to identify all potential exchange jurisdictions in a timely manner. Malaysia has recognised this issue, and is working on amending and improving its processes to more efficiently identify all potential exchange jurisdictions for future rulings. The key issue encountered were obstacles in compelling the required information for the Annex C template from taxpayers. For past rulings, Malaysia has utilised the best efforts approach, by requesting the additional information directly from taxpayers. For future rulings, Malaysia is in the process of putting in place new requirements to make it a condition that taxpayers provide the information required for the Annex C template upfront, including data on potential exchange jurisdictions, and this condition will be stated in their approval letter for a preferential regime. Malaysia is therefore recommended to continue its efforts to ensure that all potential exchange jurisdictions are identified swiftly for all future rulings.

713. Malaysia has met all of the ToR for the information gathering process except for identifying all potential exchange jurisdictions for future rulings (ToR I.4.2.1). Malaysia is recommended to ensure that all potential exchange jurisdictions are identified swiftly for all future rulings.

B. The exchange of information

Legal basis for spontaneous exchange of information (ToR II.5.1, II.5.2)

714. Malaysia has the necessary domestic legal basis to exchange information spontaneously. Malaysia notes that there are no legal or practical impediments that prevent the spontaneous exchange of information on rulings as contemplated in the Action 5 minimum standard.

715. Malaysia has international agreements permitting spontaneous exchange of information, including being a party to the (i) *Multilateral Convention on Mutual Administrative Assistance in Tax Matters: Amended by the 2010 Protocol* (OECD/Council of Europe, 2011[4]) ("the Convention") and (ii) double tax agreements in force with 71 jurisdictions.[5]

Completion and exchange of templates (ToR II.5.3, II.5.4, II.5.5, II.5.6, II.5.7)

716. In the prior year peer review report, it was determined that Malaysia's internal policies, processes and procedures for the completion and exchange of templates were sufficient to meet the minimum standard, except for the provision of information on rulings to the Competent Authority without undue delay, and the timely spontaneous exchange of information on past and future rulings (ToR II.5).

717. Malaysia's internal procedures and timelines to provide information on rulings to the Competent Authority remain unchanged, and therefore the recommendation to reduce the timelines for providing information on rulings to the Competent Authority without undue delay remains. During the year in review, Malaysia prioritised resources for the exchange of information on past rulings. Whilst 92 exchanges on past rulings were conducted during the year in review, there still remain 160 past rulings that have not been exchanged. Furthermore, Malaysia has not exchanged information on any future rulings, which includes 69 rulings issued in 2019, 53 rulings issued in 2018, and 21 rulings issued in 2017. Therefore, the recommendation to complete the templates for all relevant past and future rulings and to ensure that the exchanges of information on rulings occur as soon as possible, remains.

718. For the year in review, the timeliness of exchanges is as follows:

Past rulings in the scope of the transparency framework	Number of exchanges transmitted by 31 December 2019	Delayed exchanges		
		Number of exchanges not transmitted by 31 December 2019	Reasons for the delays	Any other comments
	92	160	N/A	There are approximately 160 past rulings yet to be exchanged. The precise number of delayed exchanges will be assessed in the next year's peer review process.
Future rulings in the scope of the transparency framework	Number of exchanges transmitted within three months of the information becoming available to the competent authority or immediately after legal impediments have been lifted	Delayed exchanges		
		Number of exchanges transmitted later than three months of the information on rulings becoming available to the competent authority	Reasons for the delays	Any other comments
	0	0	Malaysia has prioritised completing the exchanges for past rulings, and therefore, no exchanges for future rulings have been conducted thus far.	There are approximately 143 future rulings yet to be exchanged. The precise number of delayed exchanges will be assessed in the next year's peer review process.
Total	92	160		

Follow up requests received for exchange of the ruling	Number	Average time to provide response	Number of requests not answered
	0	N/A	N/A

Conclusion on section B

719. Malaysia has the necessary legal basis to undertake spontaneous exchange of information. Malaysia is recommended to continue its efforts to reduce the timelines for providing the information on rulings to the Competent Authority and to complete the templates for all relevant rulings and to ensure that the exchanges of information on rulings occur as soon as possible (ToR II.5).

C. Statistics (ToR IV)

720. The statistics for the year in review are as follows:

Category of ruling	Number of exchanges	Jurisdictions exchanged with
Ruling related to a preferential regime	92	Australia, Canada, China (People's Republic of), Denmark, Finland, France, Hong Kong (China) , India, Indonesia, Japan, Jordan, Korea, Luxembourg, Mauritius, Netherlands, New Zealand, Singapore, Switzerland, Thailand, United Kingdom, Vietnam
Cross-border unilateral advance pricing agreements (APAs) and any other cross-border unilateral tax rulings (such as an advance tax ruling) covering transfer pricing or the application of transfer pricing principles	0	N/A
Cross-border rulings providing for a unilateral downward adjustment to the taxpayer's taxable profits that is not directly reflected in the taxpayer's financial / commercial accounts	0	N/A
Permanent establishment rulings	0	N/A
Related party conduit rulings	0	N/A
IP regimes: total exchanges on taxpayers benefitting from the third category of IP assets, new entrants benefitting from grandfathered IP regimes; and taxpayers making use of the option to treat the nexus ratio as a rebuttable presumption	0	N/A
Total	92	

D. Matters related to intellectual property regimes (ToR I.4.1.3)

721. Malaysia offered three intellectual property regimes (IP regime)[6] that were abolished as of 1 July 2018 and are subject to transparency requirements under the Action 5 Report (OECD, 2015[1]). It states that the identification of the benefitting taxpayers will occur as follows:

- ***New entrants benefitting from the grandfathered IP regime***: Transparency obligations apply for the three regimes, because grandfathering is provided to entrants that entered the regime after the relevant date from which enhanced transparency obligations apply. Malaysia has not yet been able to identify these new entrants. Malaysia is therefore recommended to identify and exchange information on all new entrants to the grandfathered IP regime as soon as possible (ToR I.4.1.3).
- ***Third category of IP assets***: not applicable as the IP regimes have been abolished.
- ***Taxpayers making use of the option to treat the nexus ratio as a rebuttable presumption***: not applicable as the IP regimes have been abolished.

Summary of recommendations on implementation of the transparency framework

Aspect of implementation of the transparency framework that should be improved	Recommendation for improvement
Malaysia experienced difficulties in identifying all potential exchange jurisdictions for future rulings.	Malaysia is recommended to continue its efforts to ensure that all potential exchange jurisdictions are identified swiftly for all future rulings.
Malaysia experienced delays in the provision of rulings to the Competent Authority and did not undertake spontaneous exchange of information on all tax rulings within scope of the transparency framework during the year in review.	Malaysia is recommended to continue its efforts to reduce the timelines for providing the information on rulings to the Competent Authority and to complete the templates for all relevant rulings and to ensure that the exchanges of information on rulings occur as soon as possible. This recommendation remains unchanged since the 2017 and 2018 peer review reports.
Malaysia did not identify or exchange information on new entrants to the grandfathered IP regime.	Malaysia is recommended to identify and exchange information on all new entrants to the grandfathered IP regime as soon as possible. This recommendation remains unchanged since the 2017 and 2018 peer review reports.

References

OECD (2017), *BEPS Action 5 on Harmful Tax Practices - Terms of Reference and Methodology for the Conduct of the Peer Reviews of the Action 5 Transparency Framework*, OECD Publishing, Paris, http://www.oecd.org/tax/beps/beps-action-5-harmful-tax-practices-peer-review-transparency-framework.pdf. [3]

OECD (2015), *Countering Harmful Tax Practices More Effectively, Taking into Account Transparency and Substance, Action 5 - 2015 Final Report*, OECD/G20 Base Erosion and Profit Shifting Project, OECD Publishing, Paris, https://dx.doi.org/10.1787/9789264241190-en. [1]

OECD/Council of Europe (2011), *The Multilateral Convention on Mutual Administrative Assistance in Tax Matters: Amended by the 2010 Protocol*, OECD Publishing, Paris, https://dx.doi.org/10.1787/9789264115606-en. [4]

Notes

[1] In the previous year peer review report, it was stated that there were 428 past rulings were issued by Malaysia. However, Malaysia has reported a further 27 past rulings due to an omission of rulings from the Treasury management centre and High technology regimes.

[2] In the previous year peer review report, it was stated that 21 future rulings were issued in 2017. However, Malaysia has reported a further two future rulings for 2017 due to an omission of rulings from the High technology regime.

[3] In the previous year peer review report, it was stated that 53 future rulings were issued in 2018. However, Malaysia has now amended this number to 51 future rulings issued in 2018. This error was due to an accidental duplication of records.

[4] 1) Pioneer status – contract R&D, 2) Biotechnology industry, 3) Principal hub, 4) MSC Malaysia, 5) Green technology services and 6) Special economic regions, 7) High technology regime and 8) Treasury management centre.

[5] Parties to the Convention are available here: www.oecd.org/tax/exchange-of-tax-information/convention-on-mutual-administrative-assistance-in-tax-matters.htm. Malaysia also has bilateral agreements with Albania, Argentina, Australia, Austria, Bahrain, Bangladesh, Belgium, Bosnia and Herzegovina, Brunei, Canada, Chile, China (People's Republic of), Croatia, Czech Republic, Denmark, Egypt, Fiji, Finland, France, Germany, Hong Kong (China), Hungary, India, Indonesia, Iran, Ireland, Italy, Japan, Jordan, Kazakhstan, Korea, Kuwait, Kyrgyzstan, Laos, Lebanon, Luxembourg, Malta, Mauritius, Mongolia, Morocco, Myanmar, Namibia, The Netherlands, New Zealand, Norway, Pakistan, Papua New Guinea, Philippines, Poland, Qatar, Romania, Russia, San Marino, Saudi Arabia, Seychelles, Singapore, South Africa, Spain, Slovak Republic, Sri Lanka, Sudan, Sweden, Switzerland, Syria, Thailand, Turkey, Turkmenistan, United Arab Emirates, United Kingdom, Uzbekistan, Venezuela, Viet Nam, Zimbabwe.

[6] These regimes are: 1) Biotechnology industry, 2) MSC Malaysia and 3) Principal hub.

Malta

Malta has met all aspects of the terms of reference (OECD, 2017[3]) (ToR) for the calendar year 2019 (year in review) and no recommendations are made.

Malta can legally issue four types of rulings within the scope of the transparency framework.

In practice, Malta issued rulings within the scope of the transparency framework as follows:

- Seven past rulings;
- For the period 1 April 2017 - 31 December 2017: four future rulings;
- For the calendar year 2018: seven future rulings, and
- For the year in review: 15 future rulings.

Peer input was received from one jurisdiction in respect of the exchanges of information on rulings received from Malta. The input was positive, noting that information was complete, in a correct format and received in a timely manner.

A. The information gathering process

722. Malta can legally issue the following four types of rulings within the scope of the transparency framework: (i) cross-border unilateral APAs and any other cross-border unilateral tax rulings (such as an advance tax ruling) covering transfer pricing or the application of transfer pricing principles; (ii) rulings providing for unilateral downward adjustments; (iii) permanent establishment rulings; and (iv) related party conduit rulings.

723. For Malta, past rulings are any tax rulings within scope that are issued either: (i) on or after 1 January 2015 but before 1 April 2017; and (ii) on or after 1 January 2012 but before 1 January 2015, provided they were still in effect as at 1 January 2015. Future rulings are any tax rulings within scope that are issued on or after 1 April 2017.

724. In the prior years' peer review reports, it was determined that Malta's undertakings to identify past and future rulings and all potential exchange jurisdictions were sufficient to meet the minimum standard. In addition, it was determined that Malta's review and supervision mechanism was sufficient to meet the minimum standard. Malta's implementation remains unchanged, and therefore continues to meet the minimum standard.

725. Malta has met all of the ToR for the information gathering process and no recommendations are made.

B. The exchange of information

726. In the prior years' peer review reports, it was determined that Malta's process for the completion and exchange of templates were sufficient to meet the minimum standard. With respect to past rulings, no further action was required. Malta's implementation in this regard remains unchanged and therefore continues to meet the minimum standard.

727. Malta has international agreements permitting spontaneous exchange of information, including being a party to the (i) *Multilateral Convention on Mutual Administrative Assistance in Tax Matters: Amended by the 2010 Protocol* (OECD/Council of Europe, 2011[4]) ("the Convention") and (ii) bilateral agreements in force with 76 jurisdictions.[1]

728. For the year in review, the timeliness of exchanges is as follows:

Future rulings in the scope of the transparency framework	Number of exchanges transmitted within three months of the information becoming available to the competent authority or immediately after legal impediments have been lifted	Delayed exchanges		
		Number of exchanges transmitted later than three months of the information on rulings becoming available to the competent authority	Reasons for the delays	Any other comments
	11[2]	0	N/A	N/A

Follow up requests received for exchange of the ruling	Number	Average time to provide response	Number of requests not answered
	0	N/A	N/A

729. Malta has the necessary legal basis for spontaneous exchange of information, a process for completing the templates in a timely way and has completed all exchanges. Malta has met all of the ToR for the exchange of information process and no recommendations are made.

C. Statistics (ToR IV)

730. The statistics for the year in review are as follows:

Category of ruling	Number of exchanges	Jurisdictions exchanged with
Cross-border unilateral advance pricing agreements (APAs) and any other cross-border unilateral tax rulings (such as an advance tax ruling) covering transfer pricing or the application of transfer pricing principles	0	N/A
Cross-border rulings providing for a unilateral downward adjustment to the taxpayer's taxable profits that is not directly reflected in the taxpayer's financial / commercial accounts	0	N/A
Permanent establishment rulings	*De minimis rule* applies	N/A
Related party conduit rulings	8	Canada, Curaçao, Hungary, Netherlands, United Kingdom, United States
De minimis rule	3	
IP regimes: total exchanges on taxpayers benefitting from the third category of IP assets, new entrants benefitting from grandfathered IP regimes; and taxpayers making use of the option to treat the nexus ratio as a rebuttable presumption	0	N/A
Total	11	

D. Matters related to intellectual property regimes (ToR I.4.1.3)

731. Malta offers an intellectual property regime (IP regime)[3] that is subject to the transparency requirements under the Action 5 Report (OECD, 2015[1]). It states that the identification of the benefitting taxpayers will occur as follows:

- ***New entrants benefitting from the grandfathered IP regime***: as this is a new IP regime rather than a grandfathered IP regime, transparency on new entrants is not relevant.
- ***Third category of IP assets***: the regime provides benefits to the third category of IP assets. Malta Enterprise is the government authority that is responsible for the certification process of the third category of IP assets. Malta Enterprise provides the tax authorities with information on confirmations issued to taxpayers once these are issued, including a confirmation describing the particular qualifying IP asset and confirming that the qualifying IP asset is actually in existence. This is how the tax authorities identify the taxpayers using the third category of IP assets. In addition, from the year of assessment 2020 (i.e. the year of assessment that covers financial year 2019, and which is the first year for which the IP regime was in effect) a new attachment to the corporate tax return has been introduced. This attachment requires the taxpayer to declare the type of qualifying IP assets and provide the confirmation reference number and date issued by Malta Enterprise and declare that the company falls within the definition of a 'small entity' as defined in the legislation. This data can be extracted from the tax returns as these are filed electronically. Once the tax return for the relevant period is filed, showing the benefit claimed, such taxpayers would be requested to provide any further necessary details to enable spontaneous exchange of information under the transparency framework. Once received, this information will be sent to the Competent Authority for exchange with the jurisdictions involved. Malta confirms that for the year

in review, there were no taxpayers benefitting from the third category of IP assets. As such, no exchanges needed to take place.

- ***Taxpayers making use of the option to treat the nexus ratio as a rebuttable presumption***: not applicable as the regime does not allow the nexus ratio to be treated as a rebuttable presumption.

Summary of recommendations on implementation of the transparency framework

Aspect of implementation of the transparency framework that should be improved	Recommendation for improvement
	No recommendations are made.

References

OECD (2017), *BEPS Action 5 on Harmful Tax Practices - Terms of Reference and Methodology for the Conduct of the Peer Reviews of the Action 5 Transparency Framework*, OECD Publishing, Paris, http://www.oecd.org/tax/beps/beps-action-5-harmful-tax-practices-peer-review-transparency-framework.pdf. [3]

OECD (2015), *Countering Harmful Tax Practices More Effectively, Taking into Account Transparency and Substance, Action 5 - 2015 Final Report*, OECD/G20 Base Erosion and Profit Shifting Project, OECD Publishing, Paris, https://dx.doi.org/10.1787/9789264241190-en. [1]

OECD/Council of Europe (2011), *The Multilateral Convention on Mutual Administrative Assistance in Tax Matters: Amended by the 2010 Protocol*, OECD Publishing, Paris, https://dx.doi.org/10.1787/9789264115606-en. [4]

Notes

[1] Parties to the Convention are available here: www.oecd.org/tax/exchange-of-tax-information/convention-on-mutual-administrative-assistance-in-tax-matters.htm. Malta also has bilateral agreements with Albania, Andorra, Australia, Austria, Azerbaijan, Bahrain, Barbados, Belgium, Botswana, Bulgaria, Canada, China (People's Republic of), Croatia, Cyprus, Czech Republic, Denmark, Egypt, Estonia, Finland, France, Georgia, Germany, Greece, Guernsey, Hungary, Iceland, India, Ireland, Isle of Man, Israel, Italy, Jersey, Jordan, Korea, Kosovo, Kuwait, Latvia, Lebanon, Libya, Liechtenstein, Lithuania, Luxembourg, Malaysia, Mauritius, Mexico, Moldova, Monaco, Montenegro, Morocco, Netherlands, Norway, Pakistan, Poland, Portugal, Qatar, Romania, Russia, San Marino, Saudi Arabia, Serbia, Singapore, Slovak Republic, Slovenia, South Africa, Spain, Sweden, Switzerland, Syria, Tunisia, Turkey, Ukraine, United Arab Emirates, United Kingdom, United States, Uruguay and Viet Nam.

[2] The number of exchanged information on rulings is bigger than the number of issued rulings. This is because some rulings were issued at the end of 2019 and only exchanged in 2020.

[3] Patent box deduction rules.

Mauritius

Mauritius has met all aspects of the terms of reference (OECD, 2017[3]) (ToR) for the calendar year 2019 (year in review) and no recommendations are made.

Mauritius can legally issue three types of rulings within the scope of the transparency framework.

In practice, Mauritius issued rulings within the scope of the transparency framework as follows:

- 20 past rulings;
- For the period 1 September 2017 - 31 December 2017: no future rulings;
- For the calendar year 2018: one future ruling, and
- For the year in review: no future rulings.

Mauritius publishes taxpayer specific rulings in redacted form.[1]

No peer input was received in respect of the exchanges of information on rulings received from Mauritius.

A. The information gathering process

732. Mauritius can legally issue the following three types of rulings within the scope of the transparency framework: (i) preferential regimes;[2] (ii) cross-border unilateral APAs and any other cross-border unilateral tax rulings (such as an advance tax ruling) covering transfer pricing or the application of transfer pricing principles; and (iii) permanent establishment rulings.

733. For Mauritius, past rulings are any tax rulings within scope that are issued either: (i) on or after 1 January 2015 but before 1 September 2017; and (ii) on or after 1 January 2012 but before 1 January 2015, provided they were still in effect as at 1 January 2015. Future rulings are any tax rulings within scope that are issued on or after 1 September 2017.

734. In the prior years' peer review reports, it was determined that Mauritius' undertakings to identify past and future rulings and all potential exchange jurisdictions were sufficient to meet the minimum standard. In addition, it was determined that Mauritius' review and supervision mechanism was sufficient to meet the minimum standard. Mauritius' implementation remains unchanged, and therefore continues to meet the minimum standard.

735. Mauritius has met all of the ToR for the information gathering process and no recommendations are made.

B. The exchange of information

736. In the prior years' peer review reports, it was determined that Mauritius' process for the completion and exchange of templates were sufficient to meet the minimum standard. With respect to past rulings, no further action was required. Mauritius' implementation in this regard remains unchanged and therefore continues to meet the minimum standard.

737. Mauritius has international agreements permitting spontaneous exchange of information, including being a party to the (i) *Multilateral Convention on Mutual Administrative Assistance in Tax Matters: Amended by the 2010 Protocol* (OECD/Council of Europe, 2011[4]) ("the Convention") and (ii) bilateral agreements in force with 45 jurisdictions.[3]

738. As Mauritius did not issue any rulings in scope of the transparency framework in the relevant period, Mauritius was not required to exchange any information on rulings in the year in review and no data on the timeliness of exchanges can be reported. The table on statistics below relates to exchanges on the IP regime, which were required to be conducted notwithstanding that no ruling was issued.

739. Mauritius has the necessary legal basis for spontaneous exchange of information, a process for completing the templates in a timely way and has completed all exchanges. Mauritius has met all of the ToR for the exchange of information process and no recommendations are made.

C. Statistics (ToR IV)

740. The statistics for the year in review are as follows:

Category of ruling	Number of exchanges	Jurisdictions exchanged with
Ruling related to a preferential regime	0	N/A
Cross-border unilateral advance pricing agreements (APAs) and any other cross-border unilateral tax rulings (such as an advance tax ruling) covering transfer pricing or the application of transfer pricing principles	0	N/A

Permanent establishment rulings	0	N/A
De minimis rule	3	N/A
IP regimes: total exchanges on taxpayers benefitting from the third category of IP assets, new entrants benefitting from grandfathered IP regimes; and taxpayers making use of the option to treat the nexus ratio as a rebuttable presumption	*De minimis* rule applies	N/A
Total	3	

D. Matters related to intellectual property regimes (ToR I.4.1.3)

741. Mauritius offered two intellectual property regimes (IP regime)[4] that are abolished as of 1 July 2018 and are subject to transparency requirements under the Action 5 Report (OECD, 2015[1]). It states that the identification of the benefitting taxpayers will occur as follows:

- ***New entrants benefitting from the grandfathered IP regime***: In the prior year peer review report, it was determined that Mauritius' process for identifying and exchanging information on new entrants to the grandfathered IP regime were sufficient to meet the minimum standard. Mauritius' implementation in this regard remains unchanged and therefore continues to meet the minimum standard.
  During the year in review, Mauritius has identified one existing taxpayer that was benefitting from grandfathering with new IP assets and exchanged information on this taxpayer with three jurisdictions. Mauritius confirms that it has now completed the identification and exchange of all new entrants to the grandfathered IP regime.
- ***Third category of IP assets***: not applicable as the IP regimes have been abolished.
- ***Taxpayers making use of the option to treat the nexus ratio as a rebuttable presumption***: not applicable as the IP regimes have been abolished.

742. In addition, Mauritius offers an IP regime[5] that is subject to the transparency requirements under the Action 5 Report (OECD, 2015[1]). It states that the identification of the benefitting taxpayers will occur as follows:

- ***New entrants benefitting from the grandfathered IP regime***: as this is a new IP regime rather than a grandfathered IP regime, transparency on new entrants is not relevant.
- ***Third category of IP assets***: the regime provides benefits to the third category of IP assets. All taxpayers benefitting from the IP regime should self-identify this in the tax return, which includes a separate box for the third category of IP assets. Only taxpayers with a certificate for the third category of IP assets issued by the Mauritius Research and Innovation Council are eligible. The Research and Innovation Council is still in the process of finalising its certification application process. However, to date, no taxpayer has approached the Council for certification and as such, Mauritius confirms that no taxpayer has benefitted from the third category of IP assets. Once the certification application process is finalised, there will be a co-operation mechanism put in place with the Mauritius Revenue Authority to ensure that any taxpayer's claims to benefit from the third category of assets are verified.
- ***Taxpayers making use of the option to treat the nexus ratio as a rebuttable presumption***: not applicable as the regime does not allow the nexus ratio to be treated as a rebuttable presumption.

Summary of recommendations on implementation of the transparency framework

Aspect of implementation of the transparency framework that should be improved	Recommendation for improvement
	No recommendations are made.

References

OECD (2017), *BEPS Action 5 on Harmful Tax Practices - Terms of Reference and Methodology for the Conduct of the Peer Reviews of the Action 5 Transparency Framework*, OECD Publishing, Paris, http://www.oecd.org/tax/beps/beps-action-5-harmful-tax-practices-peer-review-transparency-framework.pdf. [3]

OECD (2015), *Countering Harmful Tax Practices More Effectively, Taking into Account Transparency and Substance, Action 5 - 2015 Final Report*, OECD/G20 Base Erosion and Profit Shifting Project, OECD Publishing, Paris, https://dx.doi.org/10.1787/9789264241190-en. [1]

OECD/Council of Europe (2011), *The Multilateral Convention on Mutual Administrative Assistance in Tax Matters: Amended by the 2010 Protocol*, OECD Publishing, Paris, https://dx.doi.org/10.1787/9789264115606-en. [4]

Notes

[1] Available at: http://www.mra.mu/index.php/media-centre/rulings/income-tax-rulings.

[2] With respect to the following preferential regimes: 1) Global business license 1, 2) Global business license 2, 3) Global headquarters administration regime, 4) Global treasury activities, 5) Captive insurances, 6) Segment B banking, 7) Investment banking, 8) Freeport zone, 9) Shipping regime, 10) Innovation box and 11) Partial exemption system.

[3] Parties to the Convention are available here: www.oecd.org/tax/exchange-of-tax-information/convention-on-mutual-administrative-assistance-in-tax-matters.htm. Mauritius also has bilateral agreements in force with Bangladesh, Barbados, Belgium, Botswana, Cabo Verde, China (People's Republic of), Congo, Croatia, Cyprus, France, Germany, Ghana, Guernsey, India, Italy, Jersey, Kuwait, Latvia, Lesotho, Luxembourg, Madagascar, Malaysia, Malta, Monaco, Mozambique, Namibia, Nepal, Oman, Pakistan, Qatar, Rwanda, Senegal, Seychelles, Singapore, South Africa, Sri Lanka, Swaziland, Sweden, Thailand, Tunisia, Uganda, United Arab Emirates, United Kingdom, Zambia and Zimbabwe. In addition, Mauritius' TIEA with the United States permits for the spontaneous exchange of information.

[4] These regimes are: 1) Global business licence 1 and 2) Global business licence 2.

[5] Innovation box.

Mexico

Mexico has met all aspects of the terms of reference (OECD, 2017[3]) (ToR) for the calendar year 2019 (year in review) and no recommendations are made.

Mexico can legally issue two types of rulings within the scope of the transparency framework.

In practice, Mexico issued rulings within the scope of the transparency framework as follows:

- 13 past rulings;
- For the period 1 April 2016 - 31 December 2016: one future ruling;
- For the calendar year 2017: 328 future rulings;
- For the calendar year 2018: 294 future rulings, and
- For the year in review: 48 future rulings.

Mexico publishes their tax rulings in redacted form.[1]

Peer input was received from one jurisdiction in respect of the exchanges of information on rulings received from Mexico. The input was positive, noting that information was complete, in a correct format and almost all received in a timely manner.

A. The information gathering process

743. Mexico can legally issue the following two types of rulings within the scope of the transparency framework: (i) cross-border unilateral advance pricing arrangements (APAs) and any other cross-border unilateral tax rulings (such as an advance tax ruling) covering transfer pricing or the application of transfer pricing principles and (ii) permanent establishment rulings.

744. For Mexico, past rulings are any tax rulings within scope that are issued either: (i) on or after 1 January 2014 but before 1 April 2016; or (ii) on or after 1 January 2010 but before 1 January 2014, provided they were still in effect as at 1 January 2014. Future rulings are any tax rulings within scope that are issued on or after 1 April 2016.

745. In the prior years' peer review reports, it was determined that Mexico's undertakings to identify past and future rulings and all potential exchange jurisdictions were sufficient to meet the minimum standard. In addition, it was determined that Mexico's review and supervision mechanism was sufficient to meet the minimum standard. Mexico's implementation remains unchanged, and therefore continues to meet the minimum standard.

746. Mexico has met all of the ToR for the information gathering process and no recommendations are made.

B. The exchange of information

Legal basis for spontaneous exchange of information (ToR II.5.1, II.5.2)

747. Mexico has the necessary domestic legal basis to exchange information spontaneously. Mexico notes that there are no legal or practical impediments that prevent the spontaneous exchange of information on rulings as contemplated in the Action 5 minimum standard.

748. Mexico has international agreements permitting spontaneous exchange of information, including being a party to the (i) *Multilateral Convention on Mutual Administrative Assistance in Tax Matters: Amended by the 2010 Protocol* (OECD/Council of Europe, 2011[4]) ("the Convention") and (ii) bilateral agreements in force with seven jurisdictions and (iii) tax information exchange agreements in force with three jurisdictions.[2]

Completion and exchange of templates (ToR II.5.3, II.5.4, II.5.5, II.5.6, II.5.7)

749. In the prior years' peer review reports, it was determined that Mexico's process for the completion and exchange of templates were sufficient to meet the minimum standard. With respect to past rulings, no further action was required from Mexico. Mexico's implementation in this regard remains unchanged and therefore continues to meet the minimum standard.

750. For the year in review, the timeliness of exchanges is as follows:

Future rulings in the scope of the transparency framework	Number of exchanges transmitted within three months of the information becoming available to the competent authority or immediately after legal impediments have been lifted	Delayed exchanges		
		Number of exchanges transmitted later than three months of the information on rulings becoming available to the competent authority	Reasons for the delays	Any other comments
	77	1	See below	Mexico has already exchanged the ruling in December 2019 as soon as the issue was identified.

Follow up requests received for exchange of the ruling	Number	Average time to provide response	Number of requests not answered
	0	N/A	N/A

751. During the year in review, Mexico experienced one delay for future rulings. Mexico explained it was due to a mistake at the time of processing information received by the competent authority, and was rectified with a one month delay in exchange. Mexico conducted the relevant delayed exchange, and improved internal processes to ensure the same issue will not occur again. Therefore, no recommendation is made given the minor and non-recurring nature of the delayed exchange.

Conclusion on section B

752. Mexico has the necessary legal basis for spontaneous exchange of information, a process for completing the templates in a timely way and has completed all exchanges. Mexico has met all of the ToR for the exchange of information process and no recommendations are made.

C. Statistics (ToR IV)

753. The statistics for the year in review are as follows:

Category of ruling	Number of exchanges	Jurisdictions exchanged with
Cross-border unilateral advance pricing agreements (APAs) and any other cross-border unilateral tax rulings (such as an advance tax ruling) covering transfer pricing or the application of transfer pricing principles	78	Canada, China (People's Republic of), France, Ireland, Korea, Luxembourg, Netherlands, Poland, Singapore, Switzerland, United States
Permanent establishment rulings	0	N/A
Total	78	

D. Matters related to intellectual property regimes (ToR I.4.1.3)

754. Mexico does not offer an intellectual property regime for which transparency requirements under the Action 5 Report (OECD, 2015[1]) were imposed.

Summary of recommendations on implementation of the transparency framework

Aspect of implementation of the transparency framework that should be improved	Recommendation for improvement
Mexico experienced one minor delay in exchanging information on future rulings.	No recommendation is made because Mexico completed the exchange on the delayed future ruling quickly after the issue was identified and resolved, and this is not a recurring issue.

References

OECD (2017), *BEPS Action 5 on Harmful Tax Practices - Terms of Reference and Methodology for the Conduct of the Peer Reviews of the Action 5 Transparency Framework*, OECD Publishing, Paris, http://www.oecd.org/tax/beps/beps-action-5-harmful-tax-practices-peer-review-transparency-framework.pdf. [3]

OECD (2015), *Countering Harmful Tax Practices More Effectively, Taking into Account Transparency and Substance, Action 5 - 2015 Final Report*, OECD/G20 Base Erosion and Profit Shifting Project, OECD Publishing, Paris, https://dx.doi.org/10.1787/9789264241190-en. [1]

OECD/Council of Europe (2011), *The Multilateral Convention on Mutual Administrative Assistance in Tax Matters: Amended by the 2010 Protocol*, OECD Publishing, Paris, https://dx.doi.org/10.1787/9789264115606-en. [4]

Notes

[1] Available at: http://www2.sat.gob.mx/sitio_internet/sitio_aplicaciones/Resoluciones_Favorables/

[2] Parties to the Convention are available here: www.oecd.org/tax/exchange-of-tax-information/convention-on-mutual-administrative-assistance-in-tax-matters.htm. Mexico also has bilateral agreements in force with Austria, Canada, Hong Kong (China), Russian Federation, South Africa, Ukraine and the United States. In addition, Mexico has tax information exchange agreements permitting spontaneous exchange of information with Aruba, Canada and the United States.

Morocco

Morocco has met all aspects of the terms of reference (OECD, 2017[3]) (ToR) for the calendar year 2019 (year in review), except for ensuring that the exchanges of information on rulings occur in accordance with the form and timelines under the transparency framework (ToR II.5). Morocco receives one recommendation on this point for the year in review. This is Morocco's first review of implementation of the transparency framework.

Morocco can legally issue one type of rulings within the scope of the transparency framework.

In practice, Morocco has issued no rulings within the scope of the transparency framework.

As no exchanges were required to take place, no peer input was received in respect of the exchanges of information on rulings received from Morocco.

A. The information gathering process

755. Morocco can legally issue the following one type of rulings within the scope of the transparency framework: cross-border unilateral APAs and any other cross-border unilateral tax rulings (such as an advance tax ruling) covering transfer pricing or the application of transfer pricing principles. Rulings are issued by the General Tax Directorate.

Past rulings (ToR I.4.1.1, I.4.1.2, I.4.2.1, I.4.2.2)

756. For Morocco, past rulings are any tax rulings issued prior to 1 September 2019. However, there is no obligation for Morocco to conduct spontaneous exchange information on past rulings.

Future rulings (ToR I.4.1.1, I.4.1.2, I.4.2.1)

757. For Morocco, future rulings are any tax rulings within scope that are issued on or after 1 September 2019.

758. No rulings were issued by Morocco during the period in review. APAs rulings are processed, negotiated, approved, signed and monitored at the level of a central unit within the Legislation, Studies and International Cooperation directorate. The unit responsible for exchanges of information also belongs to this directorate. Therefore, the process is centralised at the level of the Legislation, Studies and International Cooperation directorate that immediately identifies and processes any future rulings in scope of the transparency framework that might be issued.

759. Morocco can only issue APA rulings and the procedure relating to their issuance is available on the General Tax Directorate's website[1]. When a taxpayer applies for an APA, it has to provide information on the jurisdictions of residence of related parties with which the taxpayers enter into a transaction covered by the ruling. According to the existing procedure related to the issuance of APAs rulings, as provided for by a decree and related circular, the taxpayer shall also enclose with the APA request information on the worldwide organisational structure of all associated entities and their legal relationship (i.e. group organisation chart), the financial and tax statements of associated entities and all information and documents necessary to profiling the group and identifying all possible risks concerning the taxpayer's file, including information on the ultimate parent entity and the immediate parent entity.

760. Morocco undertakes to put in place a formal process to provide additional clarity to identify all relevant potential exchange jurisdictions relating to future APAs rulings and to ensure the implementation of the obligations relating to the transparency framework. In practice, no future rulings were issued during the year of review.

Review and supervision (ToR I.4.3)

761. The accuracy of the information gathering process and the identification of rulings in scope of the transparency framework is monitored and supervised by two units within the Legislation, Studies and International Cooperation directorate: a central unit which processes, negotiates, approves, signs and monitors information relating to future rulings in scope of the transparency framework; and a central unit responsible for exchanges of information. Because all the activities related to the issuance and the exchange of relevant rulings are centralised at the level of the Legislation, Studies and International Cooperation directorate, this will ensure that all the rulings in scope of the transparency framework will be correctly and immediately identified and all information needed for the exchanges will be adequately captured.

Conclusion on section A

762. Morocco has met all of the ToR for the information gathering process that can be met in the absence of rulings being issued and no recommendations are made.

B. The exchange of information

Legal basis for spontaneous exchange of information (ToR II.5.1, II.5.2)

763. Morocco has the necessary domestic legal basis to exchange information spontaneously. Morocco notes that there are no legal or practical impediments that prevent the spontaneous exchange of information on rulings as contemplated in the Action 5 minimum standard.

764. Morocco has international agreements permitting spontaneous exchange of information, including being a party to the (i) *Multilateral Convention on Mutual Administrative Assistance in Tax Matters: Amended by the 2010 Protocol* (OECD/Council of Europe, 2011[4]) ("the Convention") and (ii) bilateral agreements in force with 55 jurisdictions.[2]

Completion and exchange of templates (ToR II.5.3, II.5.4, II.5.5, II.5.6, II.5.7)

765. Morocco is still developing a process to complete the templates on relevant rulings, to make them available to the Competent Authority for exchange of information, and to exchange them with relevant jurisdictions, in the event rulings are issued.

766. As no exchanges were required to take place in the year of review, no data on the timeliness of exchanges can be reported.

Conclusion on section B

767. Morocco has the necessary legal basis for spontaneous exchange of information.

768. Morocco is recommended to develop a process to complete the templates on relevant rulings and to ensure that the exchanges of information on rulings occur in accordance with the form and timelines under the transparency framework going forward (ToR II.5).

C. Statistics (ToR IV)

769. As there was no information on rulings required to be exchanged by Morocco for the year in review, no statistics can be reported.

D. Matters related to intellectual property regimes (ToR I.4.1.3)

770. Morocco does not offer an intellectual property regime for which transparency requirements under the Action 5 Report (OECD, 2015[1]) were imposed.

Summary of recommendations on implementation of the transparency framework

Aspect of implementation of the transparency framework that should be improved	Recommendation for improvement
Morocco does not have a process to complete the templates on relevant rulings, to make them available to the Competent Authority for exchange of information, and to exchange them with relevant jurisdictions.	Morocco is recommended to develop a process to complete the templates on relevant rulings and to ensure that the exchanges of information on rulings occur in accordance with the form and timelines under the transparency framework.

References

OECD (2017), *BEPS Action 5 on Harmful Tax Practices - Terms of Reference and Methodology for the Conduct of the Peer Reviews of the Action 5 Transparency Framework*, OECD Publishing, Paris, http://www.oecd.org/tax/beps/beps-action-5-harmful-tax-practices-peer-review-transparency-framework.pdf. [3]

OECD (2015), *Countering Harmful Tax Practices More Effectively, Taking into Account Transparency and Substance, Action 5 - 2015 Final Report*, OECD/G20 Base Erosion and Profit Shifting Project, OECD Publishing, Paris, https://dx.doi.org/10.1787/9789264241190-en. [1]

OECD/Council of Europe (2011), *The Multilateral Convention on Mutual Administrative Assistance in Tax Matters: Amended by the 2010 Protocol*, OECD Publishing, Paris, https://dx.doi.org/10.1787/9789264115606-en. [4]

Notes

[1] Available here: https://www.tax.gov.ma/wps/portal/DGI/Documentation-fiscale/Recommandations-des-Assises.

[2] Parties to the Convention are available here: www.oecd.org/tax/exchange-of-tax-information/convention-on-mutual-administrative-assistance-in-tax-matters.htm. Morocco also has bilateral agreements with Arab Maghreb Union jurisdictions and Austria, Bahrain, Belgium, Bulgaria, Canada, China (People's Republic of), Côte d'Ivoire, Croatia, Czech Republic, Denmark, Egypt, Finland, France, Gabon, Germany, Greece, Guinea, Hungary, India, Indonesia, Ireland, Italy, Jordan, Korea, Kuwait, Latvia, Lebanon, Luxembourg, Malaysia, Mali, Malta, Netherlands, North Macedonia, Norway, Oman, Pakistan, Poland, Portugal, Qatar, Romania, Russia, Senegal, Singapore, Spain, Syrian Arab Republic, Turkey, Ukraine, United Arab Emirates, United Kingdom, United States, Viet Nam.

The Netherlands

The Netherlands has met all aspects of the terms of reference (OECD, 2017[3]) (ToR) for the calendar year 2019 (year in review) and no recommendations are made.

The Netherlands can legally issue four types of rulings within the scope of the transparency framework.

In practice, the Netherlands issued rulings within the scope of the transparency framework as follows:

- 2 206 past rulings;
- For the period 1 April 2016 - 31 December 2016: 297 future rulings;
- For the calendar year 2017: 214 future rulings,
- For the calendar year 2018: 272 future rulings, and
- For the year in review: 403 future rulings.

From 1 July, anonymised summaries are published for all rulings of an international nature.[1]

Peer input was received from six jurisdictions in respect of the exchanges of information on rulings received from the Netherlands. The input was positive, noting that information was complete, in a correct format and received in a timely manner.

A. The information gathering process

771. The Netherlands can legally issue the following four types of rulings within the scope of the transparency framework: (i) preferential regimes;[2] (ii) cross-border unilateral APAs and any other cross-border unilateral tax rulings (such as an advance tax ruling) covering transfer pricing or the application of transfer pricing principles; (iii) rulings providing for unilateral downward adjustments;[3] and (iv) permanent establishment rulings.

772. For the Netherlands, past rulings are any tax rulings within scope that are issued either: (i) on or after 1 January 2014 but before 1 April 2016; or (ii) on or after 1 January 2010 but before 1 January 2014, provided they were still in effect as at 1 January 2014. Future rulings are any tax rulings within scope that are issued on or after 1 April 2016.

773. In the prior years' peer review reports, it was determined that the Netherlands' undertakings to identify past and future rulings and all potential exchange jurisdictions were sufficient to meet the minimum standard. In addition, it was determined that the Netherlands' review and supervision mechanism was sufficient to meet the minimum standard. The Netherlands' implementation remains unchanged, and therefore continues to meet the minimum standard.

774. The Netherlands has met all of the ToR for the information gathering process and no recommendations are made.

B. The exchange of information

775. In the prior years' peer review reports, it was determined that the Netherlands' process for the completion and exchange of templates were sufficient to meet the minimum standard. The Netherlands' implementation in this regard remains unchanged and therefore continues to meet the minimum standard.

776. The Netherlands has international agreements permitting spontaneous exchange of information, including being a party to the (i) *Multilateral Convention on Mutual Administrative Assistance in Tax Matters: Amended by the 2010 Protocol* (OECD/Council of Europe, 2011[4]) ("the Convention"), (ii) the Directive 2011/16/EU with all other European Union Member States and (iii) bilateral agreements in force with 141 jurisdictions.[4]

777. For the year in review, the timeliness of exchanges is as follows:

Past rulings in the scope of the transparency framework	Number of exchanges transmitted by 31 December 2019	Delayed exchanges		
		Number of exchanges not transmitted by 31 December 2019	Reasons for the delays	Any other comments
	3	0	N/A	N/A
Future rulings in the scope of the transparency framework	Number of exchanges transmitted within three months of the information becoming available to the competent authority or immediately after legal impediments have been lifted	Delayed exchanges		
		Number of exchanges transmitted later than three months of the information on rulings becoming available to the competent authority	Reasons for the delays	Any other comments
	978	0	N/A	N/A
Total	981	0		

Follow up requests received for exchange of the ruling	Number	Average time to provide response	Number of requests not answered
	21	96 days	One request, due to ongoing investigation.

778. With respect to the three exchanges on two past rulings, it is noted that these had not been identified in 2016 or 2017, because of a human error in the manual review process. As there was no centralised process for issuing past rulings in the Netherlands, part of the issued rulings were manually identified in every local office. The rulings were identified in the year in review in the course of other work on the relevant files. This is a relatively small error in the context of the Netherlands' exchange of information on rulings, given the substantial number of rulings issued, and the exchange took place within a very short period of the issue being identified. As such, no recommendation is made. It should also be noted that the manual identification process only applied to past rulings and that for future rulings, the registration takes place in a central system and the identification process is therefore automated.

779. The Netherlands has the necessary legal basis for spontaneous exchange of information, a process for completing the templates in a timely way and has completed all exchanges. The Netherlands has met all of the ToR for the exchange of information process and no recommendations are made.

C. Statistics (ToR IV)

780. The statistics for the year in review are as follows:

Category of ruling	Number of exchanges	Jurisdictions exchanged with
Ruling related to a preferential regime	428	Argentina, Australia, Brazil, Canada, Chile, China (People's Republic of), Colombia, Curaçao, Egypt, Guatemala, Hong Kong (China), Iceland, India, Indonesia, Israel, Japan, Kazakhstan, Korea, Lebanon, Malaysia, Mexico, Morocco, New Zealand, Norway, Oman, Pakistan, Panama, Peru, Philippines, Russia, Saudi Arabia, Serbia, Singapore, South Africa, Sri Lanka, Switzerland, Chinese Taipei, Thailand, Turkey, Ukraine, United States, Uruguay, Viet Nam
Cross-border unilateral advance pricing agreements (APAs) and any other cross-border unilateral tax rulings (such as an advance tax ruling) covering transfer pricing or the application of transfer pricing principles	326	Argentina, Aruba, Australia, Azerbaijan, Barbados, Belarus, Brazil, Canada, Chile, China (People's Republic of), Colombia, Costa Rica, Curaçao, Egypt, Gibraltar, Guatemala, Hong Kong (China), India, Indonesia, Israel, Japan, Jersey, Korea, Lebanon, Malaysia, Mexico, Morocco, New Zealand, Nigeria, Norway, Oman, Pakistan, Panama, Peru, Philippines, Qatar, Russia, Saint Lucia, Saudi Arabia, Serbia, Singapore, South Africa, Sri Lanka, Suriname, Switzerland, Chinese Taipei, Thailand, Tunisia, Turkey, Ukraine, United States, Uruguay, Viet Nam
Cross-border rulings providing for a unilateral downward adjustment to the taxpayer's taxable profits that is not directly reflected in the taxpayer's financial / commercial accounts	213	Australia, Austria, Barbados, Brazil, Canada, Chile, China (People's Republic of), Curaçao, Cyprus, Finland, France, Georgia, Germany, Guernsey, Hong Kong (China),

		Hungary, Ireland, Isle of Man, Israel, Italy, Japan, Jersey, Luxembourg, Malaysia, Mexico, New Zealand, Oman, Portugal, Russia, Singapore, Spain, Sweden, Chinese Taipei, Turkey, United Kingdom, United States, Uruguay
Permanent establishment rulings	14	Brazil, Curaçao, Norway, Peru, Singapore, Switzerland, United States
IP regimes: total exchanges on taxpayers benefitting from the third category of IP assets, new entrants benefitting from grandfathered IP regimes; and taxpayers making use of the option to treat the nexus ratio as a rebuttable presumption	Included in "rulings related to a preferential regime".	N/A
Total	981	

D. Matters related to intellectual property regimes (ToR I.4.1.3)

781. The Netherlands offers an intellectual property regime (IP regime)[5] that is subject to the transparency requirements under the Action 5 Report (OECD, 2015[1]). It states that the identification of the benefitting taxpayers will occur as follows:

- ***New entrants benefitting from the grandfathered IP regime***: the application of the IP regime[6] is usually offered by way of ruling. In those cases, the Netherlands identified taxpayers entering new into the regime or bringing new assets into the regime through the rulings process.

  For those cases in which no ruling was granted but the benefit was claimed directly in the tax return, the Netherlands has undertaken the following steps:

  - It has inserted a new question in the tax return which requires taxpayers to indicate whether the IP regime is applied without a ruling.
  - Based on the filed tax returns in respect of 2017 (received by the tax administration by the end of 2019), the Netherlands identified 342 taxpayers that applied the innovation box without a ruling and which potentially could fall under the transparency framework. However, the necessary information to establish whether taxpayers are benefitting from the third category of IP assets or are grandfathered new entrants is often not present in the relevant tax return. Therefore, in February 2020, these 342 taxpayers were asked whether they are benefitting from the third category of IP assets or are grandfathered new entrants. This is a manual process after the tax return has been filed.
  - Of these 342 requests, it appeared that 148 taxpayers are either new entrants to the grandfathered regime or taxpayers benefitting from the third category of IP assets, for which information must be exchanged. These 148 taxpayers have an aggregate amount of EUR 63,3 million worth of tax benefits (decrease of the taxable base), which corresponds to approximately 1% of the total amount. The templates for this group will be exchanged with the relevant jurisdictions as soon as possible. The Netherlands is currently in the process of exchanging information on these 148 taxpayers. As of July 2020, information on 112 taxpayers has been collected and exchanged. For the remaining 36 cases, the Netherlands is still in the process of collecting the relevant information from taxpayers in order to conduct exchanges. The Netherlands confirms that all necessary exchanges will be conducted by the end of 2020.

- ***Third category of IP assets***: the regime allows the third category of IP assets to benefit from the preferential tax treatment. Most taxpayers apply for a ruling in order to obtain this benefit with regard to the IP regime,[7] and information would be exchanged using the process for future rulings.

  In order to identify those small portion of taxpayers using the third category of IP assets without having applied for a ruling, a new question was inserted in the tax return, which requires taxpayers to indicate whether the IP regime is applied without a ruling. This process is described under the previous section. For 2017, the Netherlands has identified the taxpayers using the third category of IP assets, as described above. The tax returns for 2018 and 2019 will be ultimately filed by the end of 2020 and the end of 2021, respectively. The Dutch Tax Administration will then use the same approach for the years 2018 and 2019 (i.e. performing a query on all tax returns and manually collecting additional information to complete any necessary exchanges within one year of the dates mentioned before, i.e. the end of 2020, respectively 2021).
- ***Taxpayers making use of the option to treat the nexus ratio as a rebuttable presumption***: not applicable as the regime does not allow the nexus ratio to be treated as a rebuttable presumption.

Summary of recommendations on implementation of the transparency framework

Aspect of implementation of the transparency framework that should be improved	Recommendation for improvement
	No recommendations are made.

References

OECD (2017), *BEPS Action 5 on Harmful Tax Practices - Terms of Reference and Methodology for the Conduct of the Peer Reviews of the Action 5 Transparency Framework*, OECD Publishing, Paris, http://www.oecd.org/tax/beps/beps-action-5-harmful-tax-practices-peer-review-transparency-framework.pdf. [3]

OECD (2015), *Countering Harmful Tax Practices More Effectively, Taking into Account Transparency and Substance, Action 5 - 2015 Final Report*, OECD/G20 Base Erosion and Profit Shifting Project, OECD Publishing, Paris, https://dx.doi.org/10.1787/9789264241190-en. [1]

OECD/Council of Europe (2011), *The Multilateral Convention on Mutual Administrative Assistance in Tax Matters: Amended by the 2010 Protocol*, OECD Publishing, Paris, https://dx.doi.org/10.1787/9789264115606-en. [4]

Notes

[1] This summary contains a short statement of: 1) the facts and circumstances and, when appropriate, the main conclusions from transfer pricing reports or other documents; 2) the issue on which certainty is requested based on relevant legislation and regulations; and 3) the conclusion on the basis of which the ruling was reached. If a ruling request is rejected, a summary will be published with the explanation as to why the request was rejected.

The summaries are made available on the Dutch Tax Administration's website:

- Rulings IP regime: https://www.belastingdienst.nl/wps/wcm/connect/bldcontentnl/standaard_functies/prive/contact/rechten_en_plichten_bij_de_belastingdienst/ruling/rulings-ihkv-innovatiebox
- ATRs: https://www.belastingdienst.nl/wps/wcm/connect/bldcontentnl/standaard_functies/prive/contact/rechten_en_plichten_bij_de_belastingdienst/ruling/atr
- APAs: https://www.belastingdienst.nl/wps/wcm/connect/bldcontentnl/standaard_functies/prive/contact/rechten_en_plichten_bij_de_belastingdienst/ruling/apa
- Other rulings of an international nature: https://www.belastingdienst.nl/wps/wcm/connect/bldcontentnl/standaard_functies/prive/contact/rechten_en_plichten_bij_de_belastingdienst/ruling/overige-internationale-rulings

[2] With respect to the following preferential regimes: 1) Innovation box and 2) International shipping.

[3] From 1 July 2019, a new ruling policy is in place which no longer allows rulings with regard to unilateral downward adjustments to be concluded.

[4] Parties to the Convention are available here: www.oecd.org/tax/exchange-of-tax-information/convention-on-mutual-administrative-assistance-in-tax-matters.htm. The Netherlands also has bilateral agreements with Albania, Argentina, Armenia, Australia, Austria, Azerbaijan, Bahrain, Bangladesh, Barbados, Belarus, Belgium, Bermuda, Bosnia and Herzegovina, Brazil, Bulgaria, Canada, China (People's Republic of), Croatia, Curaçao, Czech Republic, Denmark, Egypt, Estonia, Ethiopia, Finland, France, Georgia, Germany, Ghana, Greece, Hong Kong (China), Hungary, Iceland, India, Indonesia, Ireland, Israel, Italy, Japan, Jordan, Kazakhstan, Kenya, Korea, Kuwait, Latvia, Lithuania, Luxembourg, Malaysia, Malta, Mexico, Moldova, Montenegro, Morocco, New Zealand, Nigeria, North Macedonia, Norway, Oman, Pakistan, Panama, Philippines, Poland, Portugal, Qatar, Romania, Russia, Saint Martin, Saudi Arabia, Serbia, Singapore, Slovak Republic, Slovenia, South Africa, Spain, Sri Lanka, Suriname, Sweden, Switzerland, Chinese Taipei, Tajikistan, Thailand, Tunisia, Turkey, Uganda, Ukraine, United Arab Emirates, United Kingdom, United States, Uzbekistan, Venezuela, Viet Nam, Zambia and Zimbabwe.

[5] Innovation box.

[6] The non-lump-sum IP regime. In the lump-sum-regime, 25% of the profit of a taxpayer with a maximum of € 25,000 can be taxed in the IP regime. This means that the maximum IP regime deduction is € 20,000 per taxpayer in 2017.

[7] The non-lump-sum IP regime.

New Zealand

New Zealand has met all aspects of the terms of reference (OECD, 2017[3]) (ToR) for the calendar year 2019 (year in review) and no recommendations are made.

New Zealand can legally issue five types of rulings within the scope of the transparency framework, but in practice only issues three types of rulings within scope of the transparency framework.

In practice, New Zealand issued rulings within the scope of the transparency framework as follows:

- 69 past rulings;
- For the period 1 April 2016 - 31 December 2016: 14 future rulings;
- For the calendar year 2017: 15 future rulings,
- For the calendar year 2018: eight future rulings, and
- For the year in review: 21 future rulings.

Peer input was received from one jurisdiction in respect of the exchanges of information on rulings received from New Zealand. The input was positive, noting that information was complete, in a correct format and received in a timely manner.

A. The information gathering process

782. New Zealand can legally issue five types of rulings within the scope of the transparency framework, but in practice issues the three following types of rulings within the scope of the transparency framework: (i) cross-border unilateral APAs and any other cross-border unilateral tax rulings (such as an advance tax ruling) covering transfer pricing or the application of transfer pricing principles; (ii) permanent establishment rulings; and (iii) related party conduit rulings.

783. For New Zealand, past rulings are any tax rulings within scope that are issued either: (i) on or after 1 January 2014 but before 1 April 2016; or (ii) on or after 1 January 2010 but before 1 January 2014, provided they were still in effect as at 1 January 2014. Future rulings are any tax rulings within scope that are issued on or after 1 April 2016.

784. In the prior years' peer review reports, it was determined that New Zealand's undertakings to identify past and future rulings and all potential exchange jurisdictions were sufficient to meet the minimum standard. In addition, it was determined that New Zealand's review and supervision mechanism was sufficient to meet the minimum standard. New Zealand's implementation remains unchanged, and therefore continues to meet the minimum standard.

785. New Zealand has met all of the ToR for the information gathering process and no recommendations are made.

B. The exchange of information

786. In the prior years' peer review reports, it was determined that New Zealand's process for the completion and exchange of templates were sufficient to meet the minimum standard. With respect to past rulings, no further action was required. New Zealand's implementation in this regard remains unchanged and therefore continues to meet the minimum standard.

787. New Zealand has international agreements permitting spontaneous exchange of information, including being a party to the (i) *Multilateral Convention on Mutual Administrative Assistance in Tax Matters: Amended by the 2010 Protocol* (OECD/Council of Europe, 2011[4]) ("the Convention") and (ii) bilateral agreements in force with 40 jurisdictions.[1]

788. For the year in review, the timeliness of exchanges is as follows:

Future rulings in the scope of the transparency framework	Number of exchanges transmitted within three months of the information becoming available to the competent authority or immediately after legal impediments have been lifted	Delayed exchanges		
		Number of exchanges transmitted later than three months of the information on rulings becoming available to the competent authority	Reasons for the delays	Any other comments
	29	0	N/A	N/A

Follow up requests received for exchange of the ruling	Number	Average time to provide response	Number of requests not answered
	0	N/A	N/A

789. New Zealand has the necessary legal basis for spontaneous exchange of information, a process for completing the templates in a timely way and has completed all exchanges. New Zealand has met all of the ToR for the exchange of information process and no recommendations are made.

C. Statistics (ToR IV)

790. The statistics for the year in review are as follows:

Category of ruling	Number of exchanges	Jurisdictions exchanged with
Cross-border unilateral advance pricing agreements (APAs) and any other cross-border unilateral tax rulings (such as an advance tax ruling) covering transfer pricing or the application of transfer pricing principles	29	Australia, China (People's Republic of), Germany, Hong Kong (China), India, Japan, Luxembourg, Netherlands, Singapore, Sweden, Switzerland, Chinese Taipei, United Kingdom, United States
Permanent establishment rulings	0	N/A
Related party conduit rulings	0	N/A
Total	29	

D. Matters related to intellectual property regimes (ToR I.4.1.3)

791. New Zealand does not offer an intellectual property regime for which transparency requirements under the Action 5 Report (OECD, 2015[1]) were imposed.

Summary of recommendations on implementation of the transparency framework

Aspect of implementation of the transparency framework that should be improved	Recommendation for improvement
	No recommendations are made.

References

OECD (2017), *BEPS Action 5 on Harmful Tax Practices - Terms of Reference and Methodology for the Conduct of the Peer Reviews of the Action 5 Transparency Framework*, OECD Publishing, Paris, http://www.oecd.org/tax/beps/beps-action-5-harmful-tax-practices-peer-review-transparency-framework.pdf. [3]

OECD (2015), *Countering Harmful Tax Practices More Effectively, Taking into Account Transparency and Substance, Action 5 - 2015 Final Report*, OECD/G20 Base Erosion and Profit Shifting Project, OECD Publishing, Paris, https://dx.doi.org/10.1787/9789264241190-en. [1]

OECD/Council of Europe (2011), *The Multilateral Convention on Mutual Administrative Assistance in Tax Matters: Amended by the 2010 Protocol*, OECD Publishing, Paris, https://dx.doi.org/10.1787/9789264115606-en. [4]

Notes

[1] Parties to the Convention are available here: www.oecd.org/tax/exchange-of-tax-information/convention-on-mutual-administrative-assistance-in-tax-matters.htm. New Zealand also has bilateral agreements with Fiji, Papua New Guinea, Philippines, Chinese Taipei, Thailand, United States and Viet Nam.

Norway

Norway has met all aspects of the terms of reference (OECD, 2017[3]) (ToR) for the calendar year 2019 (year in review) and no recommendations are made.

Norway can legally issue three types of rulings within the scope of the transparency framework.

In practice, Norway issued rulings within the scope of the transparency framework as follows:

- One past ruling;
- For the period 1 April 2016 - 31 December 2016: no future rulings;
- For the calendar year 2017: one future ruling,
- For the calendar year 2018: no future rulings, and
- For the year in review: no future rulings.

No peer input was received in respect of the exchanges of information on rulings received from Norway.

A. The information gathering process

792. Norway can legally issue the following three types of rulings within the scope of the transparency framework: (i) preferential regimes;[1] (ii) cross-border unilateral advance pricing arrangements (APAs) covering transfer pricing or the application of transfer pricing principles in relation to realisation of natural gas for companies liable to tax under the Petroleum Tax Act; and (iii) related party conduit rulings.

793. For Norway, past rulings are any tax rulings within scope that are issued either: (i) on or after 1 January 2014 but before 1 April 2016; or (ii) on or after 1 January 2010 but before 1 January 2014, provided they were still in effect as at 1 January 2014. Future rulings are any tax rulings within scope that are issued on or after 1 April 2016.

794. In the prior years' peer review reports, it was determined that Norway's undertakings to identify past and future rulings and all potential exchange jurisdictions were sufficient to meet the minimum standard. In addition, it was determined that Norway's review and supervision mechanism was sufficient to meet the minimum standard. Norway's implementation remains unchanged, and therefore continues to meet the minimum standard.

795. Norway has met all of the ToR for the information gathering process and no recommendations are made.

B. The exchange of information

796. In the prior years' peer review reports, it was determined that Norway's process for the completion and exchange of templates were sufficient to meet the minimum standard. With respect to past rulings, no further action was required. Norway's implementation in this regard remains unchanged and therefore continues to meet the minimum standard.

797. Norway has international agreements permitting spontaneous exchange of information, including being a party to the (i) *Multilateral Convention on Mutual Administrative Assistance in Tax Matters: Amended by the 2010 Protocol* (OECD/Council of Europe, 2011[4]) ("the Convention"), (ii) the Nordic Convention on Assistance in Tax Matters and (iii) bilateral agreements in force with 84 jurisdictions.[2]

798. For the year in review, the timeliness of exchanges is as follows:

Future rulings in the scope of the transparency framework	Number of exchanges transmitted within three months of the information becoming available to the competent authority or immediately after legal impediments have been lifted	Delayed exchanges		
		Number of exchanges transmitted later than three months of the information on rulings becoming available to the competent authority	Reasons for the delays	Any other comments
	2	0	See below.	N/A

Follow up requests received for exchange of the ruling	Number	Average time to provide response	Number of requests not answered
	0	N/A	N/A

799. Norway notes that in late 2018, one future ruling was identified which was issued in February 2017. Details on the ruling, including the template for exchange, was sent to the Competent Authority in February 2019 and the ruling was exchanged in early March 2019. The ruling was identified based on a routine check by the Tax Directorate within the Central Tax Office for Large Enterprises and the Petroleum Taxation Office. Norway indicates that this was an isolated incident due to human error and that the Tax

Directorate has conducted a follow up investigation of the issue. In addition, as a precautionary measure, the Tax Directorate has reiterated its instructions to the offices and will increase the frequency of its routine checks in the future. As this was a one-time issue, and information on the ruling has already been exchanged, no recommendation is made.

800. Norway has the necessary legal basis for spontaneous exchange of information, a process for completing the templates in a timely way and has completed all exchanges. Norway has met all of the ToR for the exchange of information process and no recommendations are made.

C. Statistics (ToR IV)

801. The statistics for the year in review are as follows:

Category of ruling	Number of exchanges	Jurisdictions exchanged with
Ruling related to a preferential regime	0	N/A
Cross-border unilateral advance pricing agreements (APAs) and any other cross-border unilateral tax rulings (such as an advance tax ruling) covering transfer pricing or the application of transfer pricing principles	*De minimis* rule applies	N/A
Related party conduit rulings	0	N/A
De minimis rule	2	N/A
Total	2	

D. Matters related to intellectual property regimes (ToR I.4.1.3)

802. Norway does not offer an intellectual property regime for which transparency requirements under the Action 5 Report (OECD, 2015[1]) were imposed.

Summary of recommendations on implementation of the transparency framework

Aspect of implementation of the transparency framework that should be improved	Recommendation for improvement
Norway experienced some delays in exchanging information on one future ruling.	No recommendation is made because Norway completed exchanges on the delayed future ruling quickly after the issues were identified and resolved, and this is not a recurring issue.

References

OECD (2017), *BEPS Action 5 on Harmful Tax Practices - Terms of Reference and Methodology for the Conduct of the Peer Reviews of the Action 5 Transparency Framework*, OECD Publishing, Paris, http://www.oecd.org/tax/beps/beps-action-5-harmful-tax-practices-peer-review-transparency-framework.pdf. [3]

OECD (2015), *Countering Harmful Tax Practices More Effectively, Taking into Account Transparency and Substance, Action 5 - 2015 Final Report*, OECD/G20 Base Erosion and Profit Shifting Project, OECD Publishing, Paris, https://dx.doi.org/10.1787/9789264241190-en. [1]

OECD/Council of Europe (2011), *The Multilateral Convention on Mutual Administrative Assistance in Tax Matters: Amended by the 2010 Protocol*, OECD Publishing, Paris, https://dx.doi.org/10.1787/9789264115606-en. [4]

Notes

[1] With respect to the following regime: International shipping.

[2] Parties to the Convention are available here: www.oecd.org/tax/exchange-of-tax-information/convention-on-mutual-administrative-assistance-in-tax-matters.htm. Parties to the Nordic Convention on Assistance in Tax Matters are Denmark, Faroe Islands, Finland, Iceland and Sweden. Norway also has bilateral agreements in force with Albania, Argentina, Australia, Austria, Azerbaijan, Bangladesh, Barbados, Belgium, Benin, Bonaire, Bosnia and Herzegovina, Brazil, Bulgaria, Canada, Chile, China (People's Republic of), Croatia, Curaçao, Cyprus, Czech Republic, Egypt, Estonia, France, Gambia, Georgia, Germany, Greece, Hungary, India, Indonesia, Ireland, Israel, Italy, Ivory Coast, Jamaica, Japan, Kazakhstan, Kenya, Korea, Latvia, Lithuania, Luxembourg, Malawi, Malaysia, Malta, Mexico, Montenegro, Morocco, Nepal, Netherlands, New Zealand, North Macedonia, Pakistan, Philippines, Poland, Portugal, Qatar, Romania, Russia, Saba, Senegal, Serbia, Sierra Leone, Singapore, Saint Eustatius, Sint Maarten, Slovak Republic, Slovenia, South Africa, Spain, Sri Lanka, Switzerland, Tanzania, Thailand, Tunisia, Turkey, Uganda, Ukraine, United Kingdom, United States, Venezuela, Viet Nam, Zambia and Zimbabwe.

Panama

Panama has met all aspects of the terms of reference (OECD, 2017[3]) (ToR) for the calendar year 2019 (year in review) and no recommendations are made.

In the prior year report, Panama had received one recommendation. Panama has resolved this issue and therefore the prior year recommendation is removed.

As of 2019, Panama cannot legally issue any type of rulings within the scope of the transparency framework.

No peer input was received in respect of the exchanges of information on rulings received from Panama.

A. The information gathering process

803. As of 2019, Panama cannot legally issue any type of rulings within the scope of the transparency framework. In the prior years, Panama could legally issue one type of ruling within the scope of the transparency framework: rulings related to preferential regimes.[1] In practice, Panama issued only one past ruling within the scope of the transparency framework.

Past rulings (ToR I.4.1.1, I.4.1.2, I.4.2.1, I.4.2.2)

804. For Panama, past rulings are any tax rulings within scope that are issued either: (i) on or after 1 January 2015 but before 1 April 2017; or (ii) on or after 1 January 2012 but before 1 January 2015, provided they were still in effect as at 1 January 2015.

805. In the prior years' peer review reports, it was determined that Panama's undertakings to identify past rulings and all potential exchange jurisdictions were sufficient to meet the minimum standard. Panama's implementation in this regard remains unchanged, and therefore continues to meet the minimum standard.

Future rulings (ToR I.4.1.1, I.4.1.2, I.4.2.1)

806. For Panama, future rulings are any tax rulings within scope that are issued on or after 1 April 2017.

807. In the prior years' peer review reports, it was determined that Panama's implementation of a new system to identify future rulings and all potential exchange jurisdictions was sufficient to meet the minimum standard. As Panama can no longer issue rulings in scope of the transparency framework, this section is no longer required to be assessed.

Review and supervision (ToR I.4.3)

808. In the prior year peer review report, it was determined that Panama's review and supervision mechanism was sufficient to meet the minimum standard except for identifying certain potential exchange jurisdictions through the review and supervision mechanism (ToR I.4.3). Therefore, Panama was recommended to strengthen its review and supervision mechanism to ensure that the information gathering process is working effectively.

809. During the year in review, the Directorate of Financial and International Fiscal Strategy has developed a five-step guide to strengthen Panama's mechanism for the review and verification of rulings that had been issued prior to 2019: 1) an attorney reviewed the tax agreements to identify rulings within the scope of the transparency framework and assessed the jurisdictions for which the rulings may be relevant; 2) the information was verified by the head of legal department to validate the accuracy of the data and forwarded to the deputy director's office; 3) the deputy director validated the information received and forwarded it to the director's office; 4) the information was reviewed a fourth time by the Director and sent to the Exchange Information Department; and 5) the Exchange Information Department sends the information to the relevant jurisdictions. This five-step process ensured that all relevant information was captured adequately. The outcome of this process confirmed that no additional rulings or information on exchange jurisdictions had been missing. Therefore, the recommendation is now removed.

Conclusion on section A

810. For the year in review, Panama has met the ToR for the information gathering process and no recommendations are made.

B. The exchange of information

811. Panama has the necessary domestic legal basis to exchange information spontaneously. Panama notes that there are no legal or practical impediments that prevent the spontaneous exchange of information on rulings as contemplated in the Action 5 minimum standard.

812. Panama has international agreements permitting spontaneous exchange of information, including being a party to the (i) *Multilateral Convention on Mutual Administrative Assistance in Tax Matters: Amended by the 2010 Protocol* (OECD/Council of Europe, 2011[4]) ("the Convention") and (ii) bilateral agreements in force with 17 jurisdictions,[2] however spontaneous exchange of information under these agreements is not authorised by Panama's domestic law.

Completion and exchange of templates (ToR II.5.3, II.5.4, II.5.5, II.5.6, II.5.7)

813. In the prior year peer review report, it was determined that Panama's process for the completion and exchange of templates were sufficient to meet the minimum standard given the ability of Panama to quickly identify and resolve the issues related to some delays experienced in the process of completing and exchanging the templates and considering this was not a recurring issue. Panama's implementation in this regard remains unchanged and therefore continues to meet the minimum standard.

814. During the year in review, Panama completed and exchanged the template for the one identified past ruling due to an error in the review and supervision mechanism that occurred in 2018 with regard to the information gathering process, as well as uncertainty in determining whether the Convention allowed the spontaneous exchange of information on tax rulings, given the Convention applied for taxable periods from 1 January 2018. Panama noted that the summary section of the template was completed in line with the internal FHTP suggested guidance.

815. For the year in review, the timeliness of exchanges is as follows:

Past rulings in the scope of the transparency framework	Number of exchanges transmitted by 31 December 2019	Delayed exchanges		
		Number of exchanges not transmitted by 31 December 2019	Reasons for the delays	Any other comments
	3	0	N/A	N/A
Future rulings in the scope of the transparency framework	Number of exchanges transmitted within three months of the information becoming available to the competent authority or immediately after legal impediments have been lifted	Delayed exchanges		
		Number of exchanges transmitted later than three months of the information on rulings becoming available to the competent authority	Reasons for the delays	Any other comments
	0	0	N/A	N/A
Total	3	0		

Follow up requests received for exchange of the ruling	Number	Average time to provide response	Number of requests not answered
	0	N/A	N/A

Conclusion on section B

816. Panama has the necessary legal basis for spontaneous exchange of information, a process for completing the templates in a timely way and has completed all exchanges. Panama has met all of the

ToR for the exchange of information process and has completed the outstanding exchanges from prior years. Given that no future rulings can be issued from 2019, no recommendations would be made.

C. Statistics (ToR IV)

817. The statistics for the year in review are as follows:

Category of ruling	Number of exchanges	Jurisdictions exchanged with
Ruling related to a preferential regime	*De minimis* rule applies	N/A
De minimis rule	3	N/A
Total	3	

D. Matters related to intellectual property regimes (ToR I.4.1.3)

818. Panama offers two intellectual property regimes (IP regime)[3] that are not subject to the transparency requirements under the Action 5 Report (OECD, 2015[1]), because:

- ***New entrants benefitting from the grandfathered IP regime***: the City of knowledge technical zone regime has been amended by implementing the nexus approach from 27 December 2018. Taxpayers benefitting from the previous regime cannot benefit from grandfathering. As such, no enhanced transparency requirements apply. The general IP regime came into effect from 27 December 2018. As it is a new IP regime rather than a grandfathered IP regime, transparency on new entrants is not relevant.
- ***Third category of IP assets***: not applicable as the regimes do not allow the third category of IP assets to qualify for the benefits.
- ***Taxpayers making the use of the option to treat the nexus ratio as a rebuttable presumption***: not applicable as the regimes do not allow the nexus ratio to be treated as a rebuttable presumption.

Summary of recommendations on implementation of the transparency framework

Aspect of implementation of the transparency framework that should be improved	Recommendation for improvement
	No recommendations are made.

References

OECD (2017), *BEPS Action 5 on Harmful Tax Practices - Terms of Reference and Methodology for the Conduct of the Peer Reviews of the Action 5 Transparency Framework*, OECD Publishing, Paris, http://www.oecd.org/tax/beps/beps-action-5-harmful-tax-practices-peer-review-transparency-framework.pdf. [3]

OECD (2015), *Countering Harmful Tax Practices More Effectively, Taking into Account Transparency and Substance, Action 5 - 2015 Final Report*, OECD/G20 Base Erosion and Profit Shifting Project, OECD Publishing, Paris, https://dx.doi.org/10.1787/9789264241190-en. [1]

OECD/Council of Europe (2011), *The Multilateral Convention on Mutual Administrative Assistance in Tax Matters: Amended by the 2010 Protocol*, OECD Publishing, Paris, https://dx.doi.org/10.1787/9789264115606-en. [4]

Notes

[1] With respect to the following preferential regime: Multinational Companies Headquarters' regime (i.e. MHQ/SEM). These rulings are known as "fiscal agreements". Law 57 of 2018, entered into force on 1 January 2019, repealed the provision that included the possibility for Multinational headquarters (MHQ) Licensed Companies to obtain a fiscal agreement. Therefore as of 2019, Panama cannot legally issue any type of rulings within the scope of the transparency framework.

[2] Parties to the Convention are available here: www.oecd.org/tax/exchange-of-tax-information/convention-on-mutual-administrative-assistance-in-tax-matters.htm. Panama also has bilateral agreements with Barbados, Czech Republic, France, Ireland, Israel, Italy, Korea, Luxembourg, Mexico, Netherlands, Portugal, Qatar, Singapore, Spain, United Arab Emirates, United Kingdom and Viet Nam.

[3] 1) City of knowledge technical zone and 2) General IP regime.

Peru

Peru has met all aspects of the terms of reference (OECD, 2017[3]) (ToR) for the calendar year 2019 (year in review) and no recommendations are made.

In the prior year report, as well as in the 2017 peer review, Peru had received one recommendation. Peru has resolved this issue and therefore the prior year recommendation is removed.

Peru can legally issue one type of ruling within the scope of the transparency framework.

In practice, Peru issued no rulings within the scope of the transparency framework.

As no exchanges were required to take place, no peer input was received in respect of the exchanges of information on rulings received from Peru.

A. The information gathering process

819. Peru can legally issue the following type of ruling within the scope of the transparency framework: cross-border unilateral APAs and any other cross-border unilateral tax rulings (such as an advance tax ruling) covering transfer pricing or the application of transfer pricing principles;[1]

820. For Peru, past rulings are any tax rulings within scope that are issued either: (i) on or after 1 January 2015 but before 1 September 2017; or (ii) on or after 1 January 2012 but before 1 January 2015, provided they were still in effect as at 1 January 2015. Future rulings are any tax rulings within scope that are issued on or after 1 September 2017.

821. In the prior years' peer review reports, it was determined that Peru's undertakings to identify past and future rulings and all potential exchange jurisdictions were sufficient to meet the minimum standard. In addition, it was determined that Peru's review and supervision mechanism was sufficient to meet the minimum standard. For the purpose of formalising the process, Peru notes its intention to put in place a procedure by the end of 2021 for identifying the relevant exchange jurisdictions at the time of the taxpayer's request. Peru's implementation remains unchanged, and therefore continues to meet the minimum standard.

822. Peru has met all of the ToR for the information gathering process and no recommendations are made.

B. The exchange of information

823. In the prior years' peer review reports, it was determined that Peru's process for the completion and exchange of templates were sufficient to meet the minimum standard. With respect to past rulings, no action was required. Peru's implementation in this regard remains unchanged and therefore continues to meet the minimum standard.

824. Peru has international agreements permitting spontaneous exchange of information, including being a party to the (i) *Multilateral Convention on Mutual Administrative Assistance in Tax Matters: Amended by the 2010 Protocol* (OECD/Council of Europe, 2011[4]) ("the Convention"), (ii) bilateral agreements in force with seven jurisdictions, (iii) multilateral tax agreements in force with three jurisdictions, and iv) tax information exchange agreements in force with two jurisdictions.[2]

825. As Peru did not issue any past or future rulings in scope of the transparency framework in the relevant periods, Peru was not required to exchange any information on rulings in the year in review and no data on the timeliness of exchanges can be reported.

826. Peru has the necessary legal basis and administrative process in place for spontaneous exchange of information. For the purpose of formalising the process, Peru notes that a formal procedure for the completion and exchange of templates will be established by the end of 2021. Peru has met all of the ToR for the exchange of information process that can be met in the absence of rulings being issued and exchanged in practice and no recommendations are made.

C. Statistics (ToR IV)

827. As no rulings were issued, no statistics can be reported.

D. Matters related to intellectual property regimes (ToR I.4.1.3)

828. Peru does not offer an intellectual property regime for which transparency requirements under the Action 5 Report (OECD, 2015[1]) were imposed.

Summary of recommendations on implementation of the transparency framework

Aspect of implementation of the transparency framework that should be improved	Recommendation for improvement
	No recommendations are made.

References

OECD (2017), *BEPS Action 5 on Harmful Tax Practices - Terms of Reference and Methodology for the Conduct of the Peer Reviews of the Action 5 Transparency Framework*, OECD Publishing, Paris, http://www.oecd.org/tax/beps/beps-action-5-harmful-tax-practices-peer-review-transparency-framework.pdf. [3]

OECD (2015), *Countering Harmful Tax Practices More Effectively, Taking into Account Transparency and Substance, Action 5 - 2015 Final Report*, OECD/G20 Base Erosion and Profit Shifting Project, OECD Publishing, Paris, https://dx.doi.org/10.1787/9789264241190-en. [1]

OECD/Council of Europe (2011), *The Multilateral Convention on Mutual Administrative Assistance in Tax Matters: Amended by the 2010 Protocol*, OECD Publishing, Paris, https://dx.doi.org/10.1787/9789264115606-en. [4]

Notes

[1] Rulings other than APAs are known in Peru as "particular consultations". Particular consultations are issued in accordance with article 95-A of the Tax Code and relate to the tax regime applicable to specific facts or situations addressed by a taxpayer with a legitimate interest. Particular consultations are specific rulings on which the particular taxpayer is entitled to rely. However, Peru clarified that particular consultations cannot be issued on any of the categories of rulings in scope of the transparency framework except for transfer pricing issues that fall short of an APA.

[2] Parties to the Convention are available here: www.oecd.org/tax/exchange-of-tax-information/convention-on-mutual-administrative-assistance-in-tax-matters.htm. Peru also has bilateral agreements with Brazil, Canada, Chile, Korea, Mexico, Portugal and Switzerland; multilateral tax agreement (Decision 578 of the Andean Community Commission) with Bolivia, Colombia and Ecuador; and tax information exchange agreements in force with Ecuador and the United States.

Philippines

The Philippines is taking steps to implement the legal basis for exchange under the transparency framework, and by commencing administrative preparations to ensure that information on rulings will be exchanged once the new legal basis is in place. The Philippines has met all aspects of the terms of reference (OECD, 2017[3]) (ToR) for the calendar year 2019 (year in review), except for identifying all potential exchange jurisdictions for both past and future rulings (ToR I.4.2.1 and ToR I.4.2.2), having in place a review and supervision mechanism (ToR I.4.3) and having in place a domestic legal framework allowing spontaneous exchange of information on rulings by ensuring the timely exchange of information on rulings in the form required by the transparency framework (ToR II.5). The Philippines receives four recommendations on this point for the year in review.

In the prior year report, as well as in the 2017 peer review, the Philippines had received the same four recommendations. As they have not been addressed, the recommendations remain in place.

Philippines can legally issue one type of rulings within the scope of the transparency framework.

In practice, the Philippines issued rulings within the scope of the transparency framework as follows:

- 78 past rulings;
- For the period 1 September 2017 - 31 December 2017: four future rulings;
- For the calendar year 2018: 30 future rulings, and
- For the year in review: ten future rulings.

As no exchanges took place, no peer input was received in respect of the exchanges of information on rulings received from Philippines.

A. The information gathering process

829. The Philippines can legally issue the following type of rulings within the scope of the transparency framework: permanent establishment rulings.

Past rulings (ToR I.4.1.1, I.4.1.2, I.4.2.1, I.4.2.2)

830. For the Philippines, past rulings are any tax rulings within scope that are issued either: (i) on or after 1 January 2015 but before 1 September 2017; or (ii) on or after 1 January 2012 but before 1 January 2015, provided they were still in effect as at 1 January 2015.

831. In the prior years' peer review reports, it was determined that the Philippines' undertakings to identify past rulings met the ToR. However, the Philippines was recommended to apply the "best efforts approach" to identify potential exchange jurisdictions, in particular for the ultimate parent company, as this was the only type of information on potential exchange jurisdictions that was not provided by the taxpayer upon application.

832. During the year in review, the Philippines experienced similar problems and therefore the prior years' recommendation remains. The Philippines notes that it is currently addressing these issues, including capacity building and working in co-operation with the Department of Finance.

Future rulings (ToR I.4.1.1, I.4.1.2, I.4.2.1)

833. For the Philippines, future rulings are any tax rulings within scope that are issued on or after 1 September 2017.

834. In the prior years' peer review reports, it was determined that the Philippines' undertakings in respect of future rulings met the ToR, except for identifying all potential exchange jurisdictions (ToR I.4.2.1). As for past rulings, the only required information on potential exchange jurisdictions that was not provided by the taxpayer upon application was related to the ultimate parent company. Therefore, the Philippines was recommended to ensure that all potential exchange jurisdictions are identified swiftly for future rulings.

835. During the year in review, the Philippines experienced similar problems and therefore the prior years' recommendation remains. The Philippines notes that it is currently addressing these issues, including capacity building and working in co-operation with the Department of Finance.

Review and supervision (ToR I.4.3)

836. In the prior years' peer review reports, it was not clear whether the Philippines had a review and supervision process in place (ToR I.4.3). Therefore, the Philippines was recommended to have in place a review and supervision mechanism to ensure that all relevant information is captured adequately. The Philippines does still not have a review and supervision process in place and therefore the prior years' recommendation remains.

Conclusion on section A

837. The Philippines has met all of the ToR for the information gathering process, except for applying the "best efforts approach" for past rulings (ToR I.4.2.2), identifying all potential exchange jurisdictions for future rulings (ToR I.4.2.1) and having in place a review and supervision mechanism (ToR I.4.3). The Philippines is recommended to apply the best efforts approach for past rulings with respect to identifying the ultimate parent company, to ensure that all potential exchange jurisdictions are identified swiftly for

future rulings, and to have in place a review and supervision mechanism to ensure that all relevant information is captured adequately.

B. The exchange of information

Legal basis for spontaneous exchange of information (ToR II.5.1, II.5.2)

838. The Philippines does not have the necessary domestic legal basis to exchange information on rulings spontaneously. This is because the Philippines is legally prohibited from sharing information on, or copies of, rulings other than to the applicant taxpayer. The Philippines is currently in the process of issuing regulations to allow the Philippines to spontaneously exchange information on rulings.

839. The Philippines is a party to international agreements permitting spontaneous exchange of information, including double tax agreements with 43 jurisdictions.[1] The Philippines has signed the *Multilateral Convention on Mutual Administrative Assistance in Tax Matters: Amended by the 2010 Protocol* (OECD/Council of Europe, 2011) ("the Convention") which is currently with the Philippine Senate for concurrence. Once the Convention enters into force, the spontaneous exchange of information could also be undertaken with jurisdictions that are covered by the Convention.

Completion and exchange of templates (ToR II.5.3, II.5.4, II.5.5, II.5.6, II.5.7)

840. As the Philippines does not yet have the legal basis for exchanges, the process for the completion and exchange of templates has not been put in place. The Philippines is recommended to put in place a process for the completion and exchange of templates to ensure the exchanges can take place as soon as the legal basis is in force.

841. For the year in review, as there is no domestic legal basis for exchange, no data on the timeliness of exchanges can be reported.

Conclusion on section B

842. The Philippines is recommended to continue its efforts to put in place a domestic legal framework allowing spontaneous exchange of information on rulings and to ensure the timely exchange of information on rulings in the form required by the transparency framework (ToR II.5).

C. Statistics (ToR IV)

843. As there was no information on rulings exchanged by the Philippines for the year in review, no statistics can be reported.

D. Matters related to intellectual property regimes (ToR I.4.1.3)

844. The Philippines does not offer an intellectual property regime for which transparency requirements under the Action 5 Report (OECD, 2015[1]) were imposed.

Summary of recommendations on implementation of the transparency framework

Aspect of implementation of the transparency framework that should be improved	Recommendation for improvement
The Philippines does not currently collect information on all potential exchange jurisdictions, particularly the ultimate parent company for past rulings.	The Philippines is recommended to apply the "best efforts approach" to identify potential exchange jurisdictions for all past rulings. This recommendation remains unchanged since the 2017 and 2018 peer review reports.
The Philippines does not currently collect information on all potential exchange jurisdictions, particularly the ultimate parent company for past rulings.	The Philippines is recommended to apply the "best efforts approach" to identify potential exchange jurisdictions for all past rulings. This recommendation remains unchanged since the 2017 and 2018 peer review reports.
The Philippines does not have a review and supervision mechanism in place to ensure that all relevant information on the identification of rulings and potential exchange jurisdictions is captured adequately.	The Philippines is recommended to have in place a review and supervision mechanism to ensure that all relevant information is captured adequately. This recommendation remains unchanged since the 2017 and 2018 peer review reports.
The Philippines does not yet have the necessary domestic legal framework in place for exchanging information on rulings or a process in place to ensure the timely exchange of information on rulings in the form required by the transparency framework.	The Philippines is recommended to continue to put in place a domestic legal framework allowing spontaneous exchange of information on rulings and to ensure the timely exchange of information on rulings in the form required by the transparency framework. This recommendation remains unchanged since the 2017 and 2018 peer review reports.

References

OECD (2017), *BEPS Action 5 on Harmful Tax Practices - Terms of Reference and Methodology for the Conduct of the Peer Reviews of the Action 5 Transparency Framework*, OECD Publishing, Paris, http://www.oecd.org/tax/beps/beps-action-5-harmful-tax-practices-peer-review-transparency-framework.pdf. [3]

OECD (2015), *Countering Harmful Tax Practices More Effectively, Taking into Account Transparency and Substance, Action 5 - 2015 Final Report*, OECD/G20 Base Erosion and Profit Shifting Project, OECD Publishing, Paris, https://dx.doi.org/10.1787/9789264241190-en. [1]

Notes

[1] The Philippines has bilateral agreements in force with Australia, Austria, Bahrain, Bangladesh, Belgium, Brazil, Canada, China (People's Republic), Czech Republic, Denmark, Finland, France, Germany, Hungary, India, Indonesia, Israel, Italy, Japan, Korea, Kuwait, Malaysia, Mexico, Netherlands, New Zealand, Nigeria, Norway, Pakistan, Poland, Qatar, Romania, Russia, Singapore, Spain, Sri Lanka, Sweden, Switzerland, Thailand, Turkey, United Arab Emirates, United Kingdom, United States and Viet Nam.

Poland

Poland has met all aspects of the terms of reference (OECD, 2017[3]) (ToR) for the calendar year 2019 (year in review) and no recommendations are made.

In the prior year report, as well as in the 2016 and 2017 peer reviews, Poland had received one recommendation. Poland has resolved this issue and therefore this recommendation is removed.

Poland can legally issue four types of rulings within the scope of the transparency framework.

In practice, Poland issued rulings within the scope of the transparency framework as follows:

- 84 past rulings;
- For the period 1 April 2016 - 31 December 2016: six future rulings;
- For the calendar year 2017: 20 future rulings,
- For the calendar year 2018: 16 future rulings, and
- For the year in review: 100 future rulings.

Poland publishes their tax rulings, except for APA rulings, in redacted form on Poland's Ministry of Finance website.

Peer input was received from 2 jurisdictions in respect of the exchanges of information on rulings received from Poland. The input was positive, noting that information was complete, in a correct format and received in a timely manner.

A. The information gathering process

845. Poland can legally issue the following four types of rulings within the scope of the transparency framework: (i) cross-border unilateral APAs and any other cross-border unilateral tax rulings (such as an advance tax ruling) covering transfer pricing or the application of transfer pricing principles; (ii) rulings providing for unilateral downward adjustments; (iii) permanent establishment rulings; and (iv) related party conduit rulings.

Past rulings (ToR I.4.1.1, I.4.1.2, I.4.2.1, I.4.2.2)

846. For Poland, past rulings are any tax rulings within scope that are issued either: (i) on or after 1 January 2014 but before 1 April 2016; or (ii) on or after 1 January 2010 but before 1 January 2014, provided they were still in effect as at 1 January 2014.

847. In the prior years' peer review reports, it was determined that Poland's undertakings to identify past rulings and all potential exchange jurisdictions were sufficient to meet the minimum standard. Poland's implementation in this regard remains unchanged, and therefore continues to meet the minimum standard.

Future rulings (ToR I.4.1.1, I.4.1.2, I.4.2.1)

848. For Poland, future rulings are any tax rulings within scope that are issued on or after 1 April 2016.

849. In the prior years' peer review reports, it was determined that Poland's undertakings to identify future rulings and all potential exchange jurisdictions have met all the ToR, except for identifying all potential exchange jurisdictions for future rulings other than APAs (ToR I.4.2.1). Therefore, Poland was recommended to ensure that all potential exchange jurisdictions are identified swiftly for future rulings other than APAs.

850. During the year in review, Poland addressed the recommendation by amending its legislation to require taxpayers requesting cross-border rulings to include information related to all potentially affected jurisdictions in the ruling request form. Therefore, the recommendation is now removed.

Review and supervision (ToR I.4.3)

851. In the prior years' peer review reports, it was determined that Poland's review and supervision mechanism was sufficient to meet the minimum standard. Poland's implementation in this regard remains unchanged, and therefore continues to meet the minimum standard.

Conclusion on section A

852. Poland has met all of the ToR for the information gathering process and no recommendations are made.

B. The exchange of information

853. In the prior years' peer review reports, it was determined that Poland's process for the completion and exchange of templates were sufficient to meet the minimum standard. With respect to past rulings, no further action was required. Poland's implementation in this regard remains unchanged and therefore continues to meet the minimum standard.

854. Poland has international agreements permitting spontaneous exchange of information, including being a party to the (i) *Multilateral Convention on Mutual Administrative Assistance in Tax Matters:*

Amended by the 2010 Protocol (OECD/Council of Europe, 2011[4]) ("the Convention"), (ii) the Directive 2011/16/EU with all other European Union Member States and (iii) bilateral agreements in force with 88 jurisdictions.[1]

855. In the prior years' peer review reports, it was determined that Poland's process for the completion and exchange of templates were sufficient to meet the minimum standard. With respect to past rulings, no further action was required. Poland's implementation in this regard remains unchanged and therefore continues to meet the minimum standard.

856. For the year in review, the timeliness of exchanges is as follows:

Future rulings in the scope of the transparency framework	Number of exchanges transmitted within three months of the information becoming available to the competent authority or immediately after legal impediments have been lifted	Delayed exchanges		
		Number of exchanges transmitted later than three months of the information on rulings becoming available to the competent authority	Reasons for the delays	Any other comments
	62	0	N/A	A large proportion of rulings were issued in the latter half of the year in review, and therefore a further 76 exchanges were transmitted in January and February 2020. These exchanges were transmitted in a timely manner, and will be accounted for in the next year's peer review.

Follow up requests received for exchange of the ruling	Number	Average time to provide response	Number of requests not answered
	0	N/A	N/A

857. Poland has the necessary legal basis for spontaneous exchange of information, a process for completing the templates in a timely way and has completed all exchanges. Poland has met all of the ToR for the exchange of information process and no recommendations are made.

C. Statistics (ToR IV)

858. The statistics for the year in review are as follows:

Category of ruling	Number of exchanges	Jurisdictions exchanged with
Cross-border unilateral advance pricing agreements (APAs) and any other cross-border unilateral tax rulings (such as an advance tax ruling) covering transfer pricing or the application of transfer pricing principles	0	N/A

Cross-border rulings providing for a unilateral downward adjustment to the taxpayer's taxable profits that is not directly reflected in the taxpayer's financial / commercial accounts	21	Australia, Canada, Georgia, Israel, Korea, Norway, Russia, Serbia, Switzerland, United States
Permanent establishment rulings	0	N/A
Related party conduit rulings	41	Australia, Canada, Korea, Singapore, Switzerland, United States
Total	62	

D. Matters related to intellectual property regimes (ToR I.4.1.3)

859. Poland offers an intellectual property regime (IP regime)[2] that is not subject to the transparency requirements under the Action 5 Report (OECD, 2015[1]), because:

- ***New entrants benefitting from the grandfathered IP regime***: as this is a new IP regime rather than a grandfathered IP regime, transparency on new entrants is not relevant.
- ***Third category of IP assets***: not applicable as the regime does not allow the third category of IP assets to qualify for the benefits.
- ***Taxpayers making the use of the option to treat the nexus ratio as a rebuttable presumption***: not applicable the regime does not allow the nexus ratio to be treated as a rebuttable presumption.

Summary of recommendations on implementation of the transparency framework

Aspect of implementation of the transparency framework that should be improved	Recommendation for improvement
	No recommendations are made.

References

OECD (2017), *BEPS Action 5 on Harmful Tax Practices - Terms of Reference and Methodology for the Conduct of the Peer Reviews of the Action 5 Transparency Framework*, OECD Publishing, Paris, http://www.oecd.org/tax/beps/beps-action-5-harmful-tax-practices-peer-review-transparency-framework.pdf. [3]

OECD (2015), *Countering Harmful Tax Practices More Effectively, Taking into Account Transparency and Substance, Action 5 - 2015 Final Report*, OECD/G20 Base Erosion and Profit Shifting Project, OECD Publishing, Paris, https://dx.doi.org/10.1787/9789264241190-en. [1]

OECD/Council of Europe (2011), *The Multilateral Convention on Mutual Administrative Assistance in Tax Matters: Amended by the 2010 Protocol*, OECD Publishing, Paris, https://dx.doi.org/10.1787/9789264115606-en. [4]

Notes

[1] Parties to the Convention are available here: www.oecd.org/tax/exchange-of-tax-information/convention-on-mutual-administrative-assistance-in-tax-matters.htm. Poland also has bilateral agreements with Albania, Armenia, Australia, Austria, Azerbaijan, Bangladesh, Belarus, Belgium, Bosnia and Herzegovina, Bulgaria, Canada, Chile, China (People's Republic of), Croatia, Cyprus, Czech Republic, Denmark, Egypt, Estonia, Finland, France, Georgia, Germany, Greece, Guernsey, Hungary, Iceland, India, Indonesia, Iran, Ireland, Isle of Man, Israel, Italy, Jamaica, Japan, Jersey, Jordan, Kazakhstan, Korea, Kuwait, Kyrgyzstan, Latvia, Lebanon, Lithuania, Luxembourg, Malaysia, Malta, Mexico, Moldova, Mongolia, Montenegro, Morocco, Netherlands, New Zealand, North Macedonia, Norway, Pakistan, Peru, Philippines, Portugal, Qatar, Romania, Russia, Saudi Arabia, Serbia, Singapore, Slovak Republic, Slovenia, South Africa, Spain, Sri Lanka, Sweden, Switzerland, Syria, Chinese Taipei, Tajikistan, Thailand, Tunisia, Turkey, Ukraine, United Arab Emirates, United Kingdom, United States, Uzbekistan, Vanuatu, Viet Nam and Zimbabwe.

[2] IP box.

Portugal

Portugal has met all aspects of the terms of reference (OECD, 2017[3]) (ToR) for the calendar year 2019 (year in review) and no recommendations are made.

Portugal can legally issue two types of rulings within the scope of the transparency framework.

In practice, Portugal issued rulings within the scope of the transparency framework as follows:

- 24 past rulings;
- For the period 1 April 2016 - 31 December 2016: two future rulings;
- For the calendar year 2017: 11 future rulings,
- For the calendar year 2018: 11 future rulings, and
- For the year in review: six future rulings.

No peer input was received in respect of the exchanges of information on rulings received from Portugal.

A. The information gathering process

860. Portugal can legally issue two types of rulings within the scope of the transparency framework: (i) cross-border unilateral APAs and any other cross-border unilateral tax rulings (such as an advance tax ruling) covering transfer pricing or the application of transfer pricing principles and (ii) permanent establishment rulings.

861. For Portugal, past rulings are any tax rulings within scope that are issued either: (i) on or after 1 January 2014 but before 1 April 2016; or (ii) on or after 1 January 2010 but before 1 January 2014, provided they were still in effect as at 1 January 2014. Future rulings are any tax rulings within scope that are issued on or after 1 April 2016.

862. In the prior years' peer review reports, it was determined that Portugal's undertakings to identify past and future rulings and all potential exchange jurisdictions were sufficient to meet the minimum standard. In addition, it was determined that Portugal's review and supervision mechanism was sufficient to meet the minimum standard. Portugal's implementation remains unchanged, and therefore continues to meet the minimum standard.

863. Portugal has met all of the ToR for the information gathering process and no recommendations are made.

B. The exchange of information

864. In the prior years' peer review reports, it was determined that Portugal's process for the completion and exchange of templates were sufficient to meet the minimum standard. With respect to past rulings, no further action was required. Portugal's implementation in this regard remains unchanged and therefore continues to meet the minimum standard.

865. Portugal has international agreements permitting spontaneous exchange of information, including being a party to the (i) *Multilateral Convention on Mutual Administrative Assistance in Tax Matters: Amended by the 2010 Protocol* (OECD/Council of Europe, 2011[4]) ("the Convention"), (ii) the Directive 2011/16/EU with all other European Union Member States and (iii) double tax agreements in force with 78 jurisdictions.[1]

866. For the year in review, the timeliness of exchanges is as follows:

Future rulings in the scope of the transparency framework	Number of exchanges transmitted within three months of the information becoming available to the competent authority or immediately after legal impediments have been lifted	Delayed exchanges		
		Number of exchanges transmitted later than three months of the information on rulings becoming available to the competent authority	Reasons for the delays	Any other comments
	13	0	N/A	N/A

Follow up requests received for exchange of the ruling	Number	Average time to provide response	Number of requests not answered
	0	N/A	N/A

867. Portugal has the necessary legal basis for spontaneous exchange of information, a process for completing the templates in a timely way and has completed all exchanges. Portugal has met all of the ToR for the exchange of information process and no recommendations are made.

C. Statistics (ToR IV)

868. The statistics for the year in review are as follows:

Category of ruling	Number of exchanges	Jurisdictions exchanged with
Cross-border unilateral advance pricing agreements (APAs) and any other cross-border unilateral tax rulings (such as an advance tax ruling) covering transfer pricing or the application of transfer pricing principles	13	Belgium, France, Germany, Hong Kong (China), Netherlands, Poland, Sweden, Switzerland, United States, Viet Nam
Permanent establishment rulings	0	N/A
IP regimes: total exchanges on taxpayers benefitting from the third category of IP assets, new entrants benefitting from grandfathered IP regimes; and taxpayers making use of the option to treat the nexus ratio as a rebuttable presumption	0	N/A
Total	13	

D. Matters related to intellectual property regimes (ToR I.4.1.3)

869. Portugal offers an intellectual property regime (IP regime)[2] that is subject to the transparency requirements under the Action 5 Report (OECD, 2015[1]). It states that the identification of the benefitting taxpayers will occur as follows:

- ***New entrants benefitting from the grandfathered IP regime***: Portugal did not identify any new entrants benefitting from the grandfathered IP regime that should be subject to spontaneous exchange of information with other jurisdictions.
- ***Third category of IP assets***: not applicable as the regime does not allow the third category of IP assets to qualify for the benefits.
- ***Taxpayers making use of the option to treat the nexus ratio as a rebuttable presumption***: not applicable as the regime does not allow the nexus ratio to be treated as a rebuttable presumption.

Summary of recommendations on implementation of the transparency framework

Aspect of implementation of the transparency framework that should be improved	Recommendation for improvement
	No recommendations are made.

References

OECD (2017), *BEPS Action 5 on Harmful Tax Practices - Terms of Reference and Methodology for the Conduct of the Peer Reviews of the Action 5 Transparency Framework*, OECD Publishing, Paris, http://www.oecd.org/tax/beps/beps-action-5-harmful-tax-practices-peer-review-transparency-framework.pdf. [3]

OECD (2015), *Countering Harmful Tax Practices More Effectively, Taking into Account Transparency and Substance, Action 5 - 2015 Final Report*, OECD/G20 Base Erosion and Profit Shifting Project, OECD Publishing, Paris, https://dx.doi.org/10.1787/9789264241190-en. [1]

OECD/Council of Europe (2011), *The Multilateral Convention on Mutual Administrative Assistance in Tax Matters: Amended by the 2010 Protocol*, OECD Publishing, Paris, https://dx.doi.org/10.1787/9789264115606-en. [4]

Notes

[1] Parties to the Convention are available here: www.oecd.org/tax/exchange-of-tax-information/convention-on-mutual-administrative-assistance-in-tax-matters.htm. Portugal also has bilateral agreements in force with Algeria, Andorra, Angola, Austria, Bahrain, Barbados, Belgium, Brazil, Bulgaria, Cabo Verde, Canada, Chile, China (People's Republic of), Colombia, Côte d'Ivoire, Croatia, Cuba, Cyprus, Czech Republic, Denmark, Estonia, Ethiopia, France, Georgia, Germany, Greece, Guinea-Bissau, Hong Kong (China), Hungary, Iceland, India, Indonesia, Ireland, Israel, Italy, Japan, Korea, Kuwait, Latvia, Lithuania, Luxembourg, Macau (China), Malta, Mexico, Moldova, Montenegro, Morocco, Mozambique, Netherlands, Norway, Oman, Pakistan, Panama, Peru, Poland, Qatar, Romania, Russia, San Marino, Sao Tome and Principe, Saudi Arabia, Senegal, Singapore, Slovak Republic, Slovenia, South Africa, Spain, Sweden, Switzerland, Tunisia, Turkey, Ukraine, United Arab Emirates, United Kingdom, United States, Uruguay, Venezuela and Viet Nam.

[2] Partial exemption for income from patents and other industrial property rights.

Qatar

Qatar has met all aspects of the terms of reference (OECD, 2017[3]) (ToR) for the calendar year 2019 (year in review) and no recommendations are made.

Qatar can legally issue five types of rulings within the scope of the transparency framework.

In practice, Qatar issued rulings within the scope of the transparency framework as follows:

- For the calendar year 2018: no future rulings, and
- For the year in review: one future ruling.

As no exchanges were required to take place by the end of the year in review, no peer input was received in respect of the exchanges of information on rulings received from Qatar.

A. The information gathering process

870. Qatar can legally issue the following five types of rulings within the scope of the transparency framework: (i) preferential regimes;[1] (ii) cross-border unilateral APAs and any other cross-border unilateral tax rulings (such as an advance tax ruling) covering transfer pricing or the application of transfer pricing principles; (iii) rulings providing for unilateral downward adjustments; (iv) permanent establishment rulings; and (v) related party conduit rulings.

871. For Qatar, past rulings are any tax rulings issued prior to 1 September 2018. Future rulings are any tax rulings within scope that are issued on or after 1 September 2018.

872. In the prior year's peer review report, it was determined that Qatar's undertakings to identify future rulings and all potential exchange jurisdictions were sufficient to meet the minimum standard. In addition, it was determined that Qatar's review and supervision mechanism was sufficient to meet the minimum standard. Qatar's implementation in this regard remains unchanged, and therefore continues to meet the minimum standard.

873. Qatar has met all of the ToR for the information gathering process and no recommendations are made.

B. The exchange of information

874. In the prior years' peer review reports, it was determined that Qatar's process for the completion and exchange of templates were sufficient to meet the minimum standard. With respect to past rulings, no action was required. Qatar's implementation in this regard remains unchanged and therefore continues to meet the minimum standard.

875. Qatar has international agreements permitting spontaneous exchange of information, including being a party to the (i) *Multilateral Convention on Mutual Administrative Assistance in Tax Matters: Amended by the 2010 Protocol* (OECD/Council of Europe, 2011[4]) ("the Convention") and (ii) bilateral agreements in force with 74 jurisdictions.[2]

876. During the year in review, no exchanges were required to take place and no data on the timeliness of exchanges is reported. It is noted that one ruling was issued in the year in review, but this was only in December and therefore, the exchange took place in March 2020. This will be taken into account during next year's peer review.

877. Qatar has the necessary legal basis for spontaneous exchange of information, a process for completing the templates in a timely way and has completed all exchanges. Qatar has met all of the ToR for the exchange of information process and no recommendations are made.

C. Statistics (ToR IV)

878. As there was no information on rulings exchanged by Qatar for the year in review, no statistics can be reported.

D. Matters related to intellectual property regimes (ToR I.4.1.3)

879. Qatar offers two intellectual property regimes. However, during the year in review these regimes were under review by the FHTP and therefore no transparency requirements under the Action 5 Report (OECD, 2015[1]) were relevant.[3]

Summary of recommendations on implementation of the transparency framework

Aspect of implementation of the transparency framework that should be improved	Recommendation for improvement
	No recommendations are made.

References

OECD (2017), *BEPS Action 5 on Harmful Tax Practices - Terms of Reference and Methodology for the Conduct of the Peer Reviews of the Action 5 Transparency Framework*, OECD Publishing, Paris, http://www.oecd.org/tax/beps/beps-action-5-harmful-tax-practices-peer-review-transparency-framework.pdf. [3]

OECD (2015), *Countering Harmful Tax Practices More Effectively, Taking into Account Transparency and Substance, Action 5 - 2015 Final Report*, OECD/G20 Base Erosion and Profit Shifting Project, OECD Publishing, Paris, https://dx.doi.org/10.1787/9789264241190-en. [1]

OECD/Council of Europe (2011), *The Multilateral Convention on Mutual Administrative Assistance in Tax Matters: Amended by the 2010 Protocol*, OECD Publishing, Paris, https://dx.doi.org/10.1787/9789264115606-en. [4]

Notes

[1] Qatar financial centre (QFC).

[2] Parties to the Convention are available here: www.oecd.org/tax/exchange-of-tax-information/convention-on-mutual-administrative-assistance-in-tax-matters.htm. Qatar also has bilateral agreements with Albania, Algeria, Armenia, Austria, Azerbaijan, Barbados, Belarus, Belgium, Bermuda, Bosnia and Herzegovina, Brunei Darussalam, Bulgaria, Chad, China (People's Republic of), Croatia, Cuba, Cyprus, Ecuador, Eritrea, Ethiopia, Fiji, France, Gambia, Georgia, Greece, Guernsey, Hong Kong (China), Hungary, India, Indonesia, Iran, Ireland, Isle of Man, Italy, Japan, Jersey, Jordan, Kazakhstan, Kenya, Korea, Kyrgyzstan, Latvia, Lebanon, Luxembourg, Malaysia, Malta, Mauritania, Mauritius, Mexico, Monaco, Morocco, Nepal, Netherlands, Nigeria, North Macedonia, Norway, Pakistan, Panama, Paraguay, Philippines, Poland, Portugal, Romania, Russia, San Marino, Senegal, Serbia, Seychelles, Singapore, Slovenia, South Africa, Spain, Sri Lanka, Sudan.

[3] These regimes are: 1) Free zone at science & technology park and 2) Free zone areas.

Romania

Romania has met all aspects of the terms of reference (OECD, 2017[3]) (ToR) for the calendar year 2019 (year in review) except for the timely exchange of information on future rulings (ToR II.5.6). Romania receives one recommendation on this point for the year in review.

In the prior year report, as well as in the 2017 peer review, Romania had received the same recommendation. As it has not been addressed, the recommendation remains in place.

Romania can legally issue two types of rulings within the scope of the transparency framework.

In practice, Romania issued rulings within the scope of the transparency framework as follows:

- 16 past rulings;
- For the period 1 April 2017 - 31 December 2017: five future rulings,
- For the calendar year 2018: one future ruling,
- For the year in review: six future rulings.[1]

No peer input was received in respect of the exchanges of information on rulings received from Romania.

A. The information gathering process

880. Romania can legally issue the following two types of rulings within the scope of the transparency framework: (i) cross-border unilateral APAs and any other cross-border unilateral tax rulings (such as an advance tax ruling) covering transfer pricing or the application of transfer pricing principles and (ii) permanent establishment rulings.

881. For Romania, past rulings are any tax rulings within scope that are issued either: (i) on or after 1 January 2015 but before 1 April 2017; or (ii) on or after 1 January 2012 but before 1 January 2015, provided they were still in effect as at 1 January 2015. Future rulings are any tax rulings within scope that are issued on or after 1 April 2017.

882. In the prior years' peer review reports, it was determined that Romania's undertakings to identify past and future rulings and all potential exchange jurisdictions were sufficient to meet the minimum standard. In addition, it was determined that Romania's review and supervision mechanism was sufficient to meet the minimum standard. Romania's implementation remains unchanged, and therefore continues to meet the minimum standard.

883. Romania has met all of the ToR for the information gathering process and no recommendations are made.

B. The exchange of information

Legal basis for spontaneous exchange of information (ToR II.5.1, II.5.2)

884. Romania has the necessary domestic legal basis to exchange information spontaneously. Romania notes that there are no legal or practical impediments that prevent the spontaneous exchange of information on rulings as contemplated in the Action 5 minimum standard.

885. Romania has international agreements permitting spontaneous exchange of information, including being a party to the (i) *Multilateral Convention on Mutual Administrative Assistance in Tax Matters: Amended by the 2010 Protocol* (OECD/Council of Europe, 2011[4]) ("the Convention"); (ii) the Directive 2011/16/EU with all other European Union Member States and (iii) bilateral agreements in force with 88 jurisdictions.[2]

Completion and exchange of templates (ToR II.5.3, II.5.4, II.5.5, II.5.6, II.5.7)

886. In the prior years' peer review reports, it was determined that Romania' process for the completion and exchange of templates was sufficient to meet the minimum standard except for the timely exchange of information on rulings (ToR II.5).

887. During the year in review, Romania continued to experience delays in the exchange process for future rulings, and therefore the recommendation remains in place. However, all exchanges for past rulings have been completed during the year in review and no further action is required, and therefore, this part of the recommendation has been removed. Romania has indicated that delays in exchanges were attributable to organisational changes experienced by the tax administration during the year in review, and that these issues have now been resolved. Romania expects to carry out the outstanding exchanges for future rulings by the end of 2020, and this will be assessed in the next year's peer review process.

888. For the year in review, the timeliness of exchanges is as follows:

Past rulings in the scope of the transparency framework	Number of exchanges transmitted by 31 December 2019	Delayed exchanges		
		Number of exchanges not transmitted by 31 December 2019	Reasons for the delays	Any other comments
	19	N/A	N/A	N/A
Future rulings in the scope of the transparency framework	Number of exchanges transmitted within three months of the information becoming available to the competent authority or immediately after legal impediments have been lifted	Delayed exchanges		
		Number of exchanges transmitted later than three months of the information on rulings becoming available to the competent authority	Reasons for the delays	Any other comments
	2	6	Romania experienced delays in exchanges due to a reorganisation of the tax administration and the impact on human resources.	A further four exchanges are outstanding and to be transmitted in 2020.
Total	21	6		

Follow up requests received for exchange of the ruling	Number	Average time to provide response	Number of requests not answered
	0	N/A	N/A

Conclusion on section B

889. Romania has met all of the ToR for the exchange of information process except for the timely exchange of information on rulings. Romania is recommended to ensure that all information on future rulings is exchanged as soon as possible (ToR II.5.6).

C. Statistics (ToR IV)

890. The statistics for the year in review are as follows:

Category of ruling	Number of exchanges	Jurisdictions exchanged with
Cross-border unilateral advance pricing agreements (APAs) and any other cross-border unilateral tax rulings (such as an advance tax ruling) covering transfer pricing or the application of transfer pricing principles	24	Belgium, Bulgaria, Germany, Italy, Korea, Luxembourg, Malaysia, Netherlands, Poland, Sweden, Switzerland, United Kingdom,
Permanent establishment rulings	3	*De minimis rule applies*
Total	27	

D. Matters related to intellectual property regimes (ToR I.4.1.3)

891. Romania does not offer an intellectual property regime for which transparency requirements under the Action 5 Report (OECD, 2015[1]) were imposed.

Summary of recommendations on implementation of the transparency framework

Aspect of implementation of the transparency framework that should be improved	Recommendation for improvement
Although Romania has now completed the outstanding exchanges on past ruling and future rulings issued in 2017 and 2018, Romania experienced delays in the exchange of future rulings issued in 2019.	Romania is recommended to ensure that all information on future rulings is exchanged as soon as possible. Romania also received a recommendation on timely exchange of information on rulings in the 2017 and 2018 peer review reports.

References

OECD (2017), *BEPS Action 5 on Harmful Tax Practices - Terms of Reference and Methodology for the Conduct of the Peer Reviews of the Action 5 Transparency Framework*, OECD Publishing, Paris, http://www.oecd.org/tax/beps/beps-action-5-harmful-tax-practices-peer-review-transparency-framework.pdf. [3]

OECD (2015), *Countering Harmful Tax Practices More Effectively, Taking into Account Transparency and Substance, Action 5 - 2015 Final Report*, OECD/G20 Base Erosion and Profit Shifting Project, OECD Publishing, Paris, https://dx.doi.org/10.1787/9789264241190-en. [1]

OECD/Council of Europe (2011), *The Multilateral Convention on Mutual Administrative Assistance in Tax Matters: Amended by the 2010 Protocol*, OECD Publishing, Paris, https://dx.doi.org/10.1787/9789264115606-en. [4]

Notes

1 The number of past rulings and future rulings have been updated since the previous year peer review report. This is due to discrepancies found by Romania when reconciling the number of rulings issued, which occurred due to human error. The number of rulings presented in the report have now been corrected.

2 Parties to the Convention are available here: www.oecd.org/tax/exchange-of-tax-information/convention-on-mutual-administrative-assistance-in-tax-matters.htm. Romania also has bilateral agreements with Albania, Algeria, Armenia, Australia, Austria, Azerbaijan, Bangladesh, Belarus, Belgium, Bosnia and Herzegovina, Bulgaria, Canada, China (People's Republic of), Croatia, Cyprus, Czech Republic, Democratic People's Republic of Korea, Denmark, Ecuador, Egypt, Estonia, Ethiopia, Finland, France, Georgia, Germany, Greece, Hong Kong (China), Hungary, Iceland, India, Indonesia, Iran, Ireland, Israel, Italy, Japan, Jordan, Kazakhstan, Korea, Kuwait, Latvia, Lebanon, Lithuania, Luxembourg, Malaysia, Malta, Mexico, Moldova, Montenegro, Morocco, Namibia, Netherlands, Nigeria, North Macedonia, Norway, Pakistan, Philippines, Poland, Portugal, Qatar, Russia, San Marino, Saudi Arabia, Serbia, Montenegro, Singapore, Slovenia, Slovak Republic, South Africa, Spain, Sri Lanka, Sudan, Sweden, Switzerland, Syrian Arab Republic, Tajikistan, Thailand, Tunisia, Turkey, Turkmenistan, Ukraine, United Arab Emirates, United Kingdom, United States, Uruguay, Uzbekistan, Viet Nam and Zambia.

Russia

Russian Federation ("Russia") has met all aspects of the terms of reference (OECD, 2017[3]) (ToR) for the calendar year 2019 (year in review) and no recommendations are made.

Russia can legally issue five types of rulings within the scope of the transparency framework.

In practice, Russia issued rulings within the scope of the transparency framework as follows:

- One past ruling;
- For the period 1 April 2016 - 31 December 2016: no future rulings;
- For the calendar year 2017: no future rulings;
- For the calendar year 2018: no future rulings; and
- For the year in review: no future rulings.

As no exchanges were required to take place, no peer input was received in respect of the exchanges of information on rulings received from Russia.

A. The information gathering process

892. Russia can legally issue the following five types of rulings within the scope of the transparency framework: (i) preferential regimes;[1] (ii) cross-border unilateral APAs and any other cross-border unilateral tax rulings (such as an advance tax ruling) covering transfer pricing or the application of transfer pricing principles; (iii) rulings providing for unilateral downward adjustments; (iv) permanent establishment rulings; and (v) related party conduit rulings.

893. For Russia, past rulings are any tax rulings within scope that are issued either: (i) on or after 1 January 2014 but before 1 April 2016; or (ii) on or after 1 January 2010 but before 1 January 2014, provided they were still in effect as at 1 January 2014. Future rulings are any tax rulings within scope that are issued on or after 1 April 2016.

894. In the prior years' peer review reports, it was determined that Russia's undertakings to identify past and future rulings and all potential exchange jurisdictions were sufficient to meet the minimum standard. In addition, it was determined that Russia's review and supervision mechanism was sufficient to meet the minimum standard. Russia's implementation remains unchanged, and therefore continues to meet the minimum standard.

895. Russia has met all of the ToR for the information gathering process and no recommendations are made.

B. The exchange of information

896. In the prior years' peer review reports, it was determined that Russia's process for the completion and exchange of templates were sufficient to meet the minimum standard. With respect to past rulings, no further action was required from Russia. Russia's implementation in this regard remains unchanged and therefore continues to meet the minimum standard.

897. Russia has international agreements permitting spontaneous exchange of information, including being a party to the (i) *Multilateral Convention on Mutual Administrative Assistance in Tax Matters: Amended by the 2010 Protocol* (OECD/Council of Europe, 2011[4]) ("the Convention") and (ii) bilateral agreements in force with 84 jurisdictions.[2]

898. As Russia was not required to exchange any information on rulings for the year in review, no data on the timeliness of exchanges can be reported.

899. Russia has the necessary legal basis for spontaneous exchange of information, a process for completing the templates in a timely way and has completed all exchanges. Russia has met all of the ToR for the exchange of information process and no recommendations are made.

C. Statistics (ToR IV)

900. As no rulings were issued, no statistics can be reported.

D. Matters related to intellectual property regimes (ToR I.4.1.3)

901. Russia does not offer an intellectual property regime for which transparency requirements under the Action 5 Report (OECD, 2015[1]) were imposed.

Summary of recommendations on implementation of the transparency framework

Aspect of implementation of the transparency framework that should be improved	Recommendation for improvement
	No recommendations are made.

References

OECD (2017), *BEPS Action 5 on Harmful Tax Practices - Terms of Reference and Methodology for the Conduct of the Peer Reviews of the Action 5 Transparency Framework*, OECD Publishing, Paris, http://www.oecd.org/tax/beps/beps-action-5-harmful-tax-practices-peer-review-transparency-framework.pdf. [3]

OECD (2015), *Countering Harmful Tax Practices More Effectively, Taking into Account Transparency and Substance, Action 5 - 2015 Final Report*, OECD/G20 Base Erosion and Profit Shifting Project, OECD Publishing, Paris, https://dx.doi.org/10.1787/9789264241190-en. [1]

OECD/Council of Europe (2011), *The Multilateral Convention on Mutual Administrative Assistance in Tax Matters: Amended by the 2010 Protocol*, OECD Publishing, Paris, https://dx.doi.org/10.1787/9789264115606-en. [4]

Notes

1 With respect to the following preferential regimes: Special economic/industry zones.

2 Parties to the Convention are available here: www.oecd.org/tax/exchange-of-tax-information/convention-on-mutual-administrative-assistance-in-tax-matters.htm. Russia also has bilateral agreements with Albania, Algeria, Argentina, Armenia, Australia, Austria, Azerbaijan, Belarus, Belgium, Botswana, Bulgaria, Canada, Chile, China (People's Republic of), Croatia, Cuba, Cyprus, Czech Republic, Democratic People's Republic of Korea, Denmark, Ecuador, Egypt, Finland, France, Georgia, Germany, Greece, Hungary, Iceland, India, Indonesia, Iran, Ireland, Israel, Italy, Japan, Kazakhstan, Korea, Kuwait, Kyrgyzstan, Latvia, Lebanon, Lithuania, Luxembourg, Malaysia, Mali, Malta, Morocco, Mexico, Moldova, Mongolia, Montenegro, Namibia, Netherlands, New Zealand, Nigeria, North Macedonia, Norway, Philippines, Poland, Portugal, Qatar, Romania, Saudi Arabia, Serbia, Singapore, Slovak Republic, Slovenia, South Africa, Spain, Sri Lanka, Sweden, Syria, Tajikistan, Thailand, Turkey, Turkmenia, Ukraine, United Arab Emirates, United Kingdom, United States, Uzbekistan, Venezuela and Viet Nam.

Saint Kitts and Nevis

Saint Kitts and Nevis has met all aspects of the terms of reference (OECD, 2017[3]) (ToR) for the calendar year 2019 (year in review) and no recommendations are made.

Saint Kitts and Nevis can legally issue five types of rulings within the scope of the transparency framework but in practice has never issued any rulings.

As no exchanges were required to take place, no peer input was received in respect of the exchanges of information on rulings received from Saint Kitts and Nevis.

A. The information gathering process

902. Saint Kitts and Nevis can legally issue the following five types of rulings within the scope of the transparency framework: (i) preferential regimes;[1] (ii) cross-border unilateral APAs and any other cross-border unilateral tax rulings (such as an advance tax ruling) covering transfer pricing or the application of transfer pricing principles; (iii) rulings providing for unilateral downward adjustments; (iv) permanent establishment rulings; and (v) related party conduit rulings.

903. For Saint Kitts and Nevis, past rulings are any tax rulings within scope that are issued prior to 1 September 2018. However, there is no obligation for Saint Kitts and Nevis to conduct spontaneous exchange information on past rulings. Future rulings are any tax rulings within scope that are issued on or after 1 September 2018.

904. In the prior years' peer review reports, it was determined that Saint Kitts and Nevis's undertakings to identify rulings and all potential exchange jurisdictions were sufficient to meet the minimum standard. In addition, it was determined that Saint Kitts and Nevis's review and supervision mechanism was sufficient to meet the minimum standard. Saint Kitts and Nevis's implementation remains unchanged, and therefore continues to meet the minimum standard.

905. Saint Kitts and Nevis has met all of the ToR for the information gathering process and no recommendations are made.

B. The exchange of information

906. In the prior years' peer review reports, it was determined that Saint Kitts and Nevis' process for the completion and exchange of templates were sufficient to meet the minimum standard. Saint Kitts and Nevis' implementation in this regard remains unchanged and therefore continues to meet the minimum standard.

907. Saint Kitts and Nevis has international agreements permitting spontaneous exchange of information, including being a party to the (i) *Multilateral Convention on Mutual Administrative Assistance in Tax Matters: Amended by the 2010 Protocol* (OECD/Council of Europe, 2011[4]) ("the Convention").[2]

908. As Saint Kitts and Nevis did not issue any future rulings in scope of the transparency framework in the relevant period, Saint Kitts and Nevis was not required to exchange any information on rulings in the year in review and no data on the timeliness of exchanges can be reported.

Conclusion on section B

909. Saint Kitts and Nevis has the necessary legal basis for spontaneous exchange of information, a process for completing the templates in a timely way and has completed all exchanges. Saint Kitts and Nevis has met all of the ToR for the exchange of information process and no recommendations are made.

C. Statistics (ToR IV)

910. As no rulings were issued, no statistics can be reported.

D. Matters related to intellectual property regimes (ToR I.4.1.3)

911. Saint Kitts and Nevis offered three preferential regimes, which also provided benefits to income from intellectual property (IP regime).[3] However, for the year in review, no transparency requirements were relevant, as follows:

- ***New entrants benefitting from the grandfathered IP regime***: not applicable for the year in review, because Saint Kitts and Nevis was in the process of finalising the grandfathering rules for all three regimes. The implementation of the enhanced transparency requirements will be taken into account during the subsequent peer review.
- ***Third category of IP assets***: not applicable to these regimes, as the regimes were inoperative during the year in review.
- ***Taxpayers making use of the option to treat the nexus ratio as a rebuttable presumption***: not applicable to these regimes, as the regimes were inoperative during the year in review.

Summary of recommendations on implementation of the transparency framework

Aspect of implementation of the transparency framework that should be improved	Recommendation for improvement
	No recommendations are made.

References

OECD (2017), *BEPS Action 5 on Harmful Tax Practices - Terms of Reference and Methodology for the Conduct of the Peer Reviews of the Action 5 Transparency Framework*, OECD Publishing, Paris, http://www.oecd.org/tax/beps/beps-action-5-harmful-tax-practices-peer-review-transparency-framework.pdf. [3]

OECD (2015), *Countering Harmful Tax Practices More Effectively, Taking into Account Transparency and Substance, Action 5 - 2015 Final Report*, OECD/G20 Base Erosion and Profit Shifting Project, OECD Publishing, Paris, https://dx.doi.org/10.1787/9789264241190-en. [1]

OECD/Council of Europe (2011), *The Multilateral Convention on Mutual Administrative Assistance in Tax Matters: Amended by the 2010 Protocol*, OECD Publishing, Paris, https://dx.doi.org/10.1787/9789264115606-en. [4]

Notes

[1] 1) Nevis LLC, 2) Nevis business corporation and 3) Companies act – exempt companies.

[2] Parties to the Convention are available here: www.oecd.org/tax/exchange-of-tax-information/convention-on-mutual-administrative-assistance-in-tax-matters.htm.

[3] 1) Nevis LLC, 2) Nevis business corporation and 3) Companies act – exempt companies.

Saint Lucia

Saint Lucia is taking steps to implement the legal basis for the transparency framework and to finalise administrative preparations, in line with the terms of reference (OECD, 2017[3]) (ToR), to ensure that it finalises its information gathering process (ToR I.4), and information on rulings will be identified and exchanged in a timely manner (ToR II.5).

In the prior year report, Saint Lucia had received three recommendations. Saint Lucia has resolved one of these issues, however two recommendations have not been addressed and remain in place.

Saint Lucia can legally issue two types of rulings within the scope of the transparency framework.

In practice, Saint Lucia has not issued any rulings within the scope of the transparency framework.

As no exchanges were required to take place, no peer input was received in respect of the exchanges of information on rulings received from Saint Lucia.

A. The information gathering process

912. Saint Lucia can legally issue the following two types of rulings within the scope of the transparency framework: (i) preferential regimes[1] and (ii) permanent establishment rulings.

Past rulings (ToR I.4.1.1, I.4.1.2, I.4.2.1, I.4.2.2)

913. For Saint Lucia, past rulings are any tax rulings issued prior to 1 September 2018. However, there is no obligation for Saint Lucia to conduct spontaneous exchange information on past rulings.

Future rulings (ToR I.4.1.1, I.4.1.2, I.4.2.1)

914. For Saint Lucia, future rulings are any tax rulings within scope that are issued on or after 1 September 2018.

915. In the prior year peer review report, it was determined that Saint Lucia's had not put in place the appropriate processes for future rulings for the purposes of the transparency framework. Therefore, Saint Lucia was recommended to continue its work to make sure the necessary information gathering processes to meet the requirements of the transparency framework is put in place. During the year in review, Saint Lucia developed a new draft rulings framework that provides for identification of all taxpayer specific rulings. This framework will be implemented once the draft rulings framework has been approved. The Tax Administration Department is responsible for the vetting and authorisation of rulings to be issued in Saint Lucia. Saint Lucia is in the process of establishing a Rulings Committee, to be chaired by the Tax Administration Department's Legal Officer, which will determine whether rulings issued fall within scope of the Transparency Framework. Although Saint Lucia has not issued any future rulings, Saint Lucia indicates that their rulings framework will require that any taxpayer requesting a ruling must provide information on all potential exchange jurisdictions. Saint Lucia notes that the practical implementation of these procedures and the draft rulings framework is yet to occur. Therefore, the recommendation is retained for Saint Lucia to continue its work to make sure the necessary information gathering processes to meet the requirements of the transparency framework is put in place.

Review and supervision (ToR I.4.3)

916. In accordance with the draft rulings framework, the accuracy of the information gathering process and the identification of rulings in scope of the transparency framework is the responsibility of a dedicated team within the Rulings Committee. The Legal Officer that is both part of the Tax Administration Department that issues tax rulings and the chairperson of the Rulings Committee that oversees rulings, will identify those in scope of the transparency framework. This review and supervision mechanism is already functioning and will be ratified once the draft rulings framework is approved.

Conclusion on section A

917. Saint Lucia is recommended to finalise its information gathering process for identifying all future rulings and potential exchange jurisdictions, with a review and supervision mechanism, as soon as possible (ToR I.4).

B. The exchange of information

Legal basis for spontaneous exchange of information (ToR II.5.1, II.5.2)

918. Saint Lucia has the necessary domestic legal basis to exchange information spontaneously. Saint Lucia notes that there are no legal or practical impediments that prevent the spontaneous exchange of information on rulings as contemplated in the Action 5 minimum standard.

919. Saint Lucia has international agreements permitting spontaneous exchange of information, including being a party to the (i) *Multilateral Convention on Mutual Administrative Assistance in Tax Matters: Amended by the 2010 Protocol* (OECD/Council of Europe, 2011[4]) ("the Convention") and (ii) bilateral agreements in force with 16 jurisdictions.[2]

Completion and exchange of templates (ToR II.5.3, II.5.4, II.5.5, II.5.6, II.5.7)

920. In the prior year peer review report, it was determined that Saint Lucia had not put in place the appropriate processes for the completion and exchange of templates. Therefore, Saint Lucia was recommended to continue its work to complete its processes for the completion and exchange of templates as soon as possible.

921. During the year in review, Saint Lucia developed a draft rulings framework, whereby a Rulings Committee, assisted by the Exchange of Information Unit, would be responsible for completing the template contained in Annex C of the Action 5 Report (OECD, 2015[1]), which would include providing a summary of the ruling in line with the internal FHTP suggested guidance and the instructions in the Annex C template. The template would then be quality checked by a supervisor in the Tax Administration Department, and then provided to the Comptroller of Inland Revenue for final approval and exchange. As the Comptroller of Inland Revenue oversees the issuance of rulings by the Tax Administration Department, and is also the Competent Authority for Saint Lucia, all tax rulings would therefore be readily available to the Competent Authority. This draft rulings framework will be assessed in the next annual peer review, once the framework has been put in place.

922. As Saint Lucia did not issue any future rulings in scope of the transparency framework in the relevant period, Saint Lucia was not required to exchange any information on rulings in the year in review and no data on the timeliness of exchanges can be reported.

Conclusion on section B

923. Saint Lucia is recommended to put in place a process to complete the templates on relevant rulings and to ensure that the exchanges of information on rulings occur in accordance with the form and timelines under the transparency framework going forward (ToR II.5).

C. Statistics (ToR IV)

924. As no rulings were issued, no statistics can be reported.

D. Matters related to intellectual property regimes (ToR I.4.1.3)

925. Saint Lucia does not offer an intellectual property regime for which transparency requirements under the Action 5 Report (OECD, 2015[1]) were imposed. However, additional transparency requirements were applied with respect to new taxpayers that entered three intellectual property regimes (IP regimes)[3] offered by Saint Lucia in the period 15 November 2018 – 11 December 2018 which were eligible for

grandfathering before the regimes were abolished. As all international business companies, international trusts or international partnerships must be registered with the relevant authorities in Saint Lucia, Saint Lucia was able to identify all new taxpayers during the relevant period. Saint Lucia completed exchanges on these taxpayers during the year in review with all potential exchange jurisdictions.[4] Accordingly, the prior year recommendation is now removed.

Summary of recommendations on implementation of the transparency framework

Aspect of implementation of the transparency framework that should be improved	Recommendation for improvement
Saint Lucia has not yet finalised the steps to have in place its information gathering process.	Saint Lucia is recommended to finalise its information gathering process for identifying all future rulings and potential exchange jurisdictions, with a review and supervision mechanism, as soon as possible. This recommendation remains unchanged since the prior year peer review report.
Saint Lucia has not yet finalised a process to complete the templates on relevant rulings, to make them available to the Competent Authority for exchange of information, and to exchange them with relevant jurisdictions.	Saint Lucia is recommended to put in place a process to complete the templates on relevant rulings and to ensure that the exchanges of information on rulings occur in accordance with the form and timelines under the transparency framework. This recommendation remains unchanged since the prior year peer review report.

References

OECD (2017), *BEPS Action 5 on Harmful Tax Practices - Terms of Reference and Methodology for the Conduct of the Peer Reviews of the Action 5 Transparency Framework*, OECD Publishing, Paris, http://www.oecd.org/tax/beps/beps-action-5-harmful-tax-practices-peer-review-transparency-framework.pdf. [3]

OECD (2015), *Countering Harmful Tax Practices More Effectively, Taking into Account Transparency and Substance, Action 5 - 2015 Final Report*, OECD/G20 Base Erosion and Profit Shifting Project, OECD Publishing, Paris, https://dx.doi.org/10.1787/9789264241190-en. [1]

OECD/Council of Europe (2011), *The Multilateral Convention on Mutual Administrative Assistance in Tax Matters: Amended by the 2010 Protocol*, OECD Publishing, Paris, https://dx.doi.org/10.1787/9789264115606-en. [4]

Notes

[1] 1) International business company, 2) International trust and 3) International partnership regimes.

[2] Parties to the Convention are available here: www.oecd.org/tax/exchange-of-tax-information/convention-on-mutual-administrative-assistance-in-tax-matters.htm. Saint Lucia also has bilateral agreements with CARICOM jurisdictions and the United States.

[3] 1) International business company, 2) International trust and 3) International partnership regimes.

[4] A total of 17 exchanges were transmitted to five jurisdictions, in relation to new International business companies and International trusts that were registered during the relevant period. There were no new International partnerships registered during the relevant period.

San Marino

San Marino has met all aspects of the terms of reference (OECD, 2017[3]) (ToR) for the calendar year 2019 (year in review), and no recommendations are made.

In the prior year report, San Marino had received three recommendations. San Marino has resolved these issues and therefore none of the prior year recommendations remain.

San Marino can legally issue two types of rulings within the scope of the transparency framework.

In practice, San Marino issued rulings within the scope of the transparency framework as follows:

- One past ruling;
- For the period 1 April 2017 - 31 December 2017: no future rulings;
- For the calendar year 2018: no future rulings; and
- For the year in review: no future rulings.

As no exchanges took place, no peer input was received in respect of the exchanges of information on rulings received from San Marino.

A. The information gathering process

926. San Marino can legally issue the following two types of rulings within the scope of the transparency framework: (i) preferential regimes[1] and (ii) permanent establishment (PE) rulings. Rulings are issued by the Tax Office of San Marino.

Past rulings (ToR I.4.1.1, I.4.1.2, I.4.2.1, I.4.2.2)

927. For San Marino, past rulings are any tax rulings within scope that are issued either (i) on or after 1 January 2015 but before 1 April 2017; and (ii) on or after 1 January 2012 but before 1 January 2015, provided they were still in effect as at 1 January 2015.

928. In the prior year peer review report, this section was not assessed because of the absence of past rulings in scope. However, during the year in review, San Marino took extensive actions for mapping the issuance of rulings (called "preventive agreements") on tax matters in order to identify any agreements that could fall within the scope of the transparency framework. Previously, San Marino had not taken the view that such preventive agreements were in the scope of the standard, but this was clarified during the year in review. The Tax Office manually analysed all requests received from 2015, as well as all requests received in the previous years that were still in effect as at 1 January 2015, to identify possible preventive agreements in scope of the transparency framework. As a result, one preventive agreement issued in 2016 was identified as in scope of the transparency framework because the preventive agreement related to permanent establishment matters. Once the ruling was identified, San Marino was able to identify all the relevant exchange jurisdictions by reviewing the certificate of incorporation of the non-resident head office and by carrying out appropriate checks on the parent companies through the use of databases available to the public administration.

929. As San Marino quickly took steps to identify and remedy the issue and this is not expected to be a recurring issue, no recommendations are made.

Future rulings (ToR I.4.1.1, I.4.1.2, I.4.2.1)

930. For San Marino, future rulings are any tax rulings within scope that are issued on or after 1 April 2017.

931. In the prior year peer review report, it was determined that San Marino did not have an information gathering process to identify the rulings and all potential exchange jurisdictions (ToR I.4). Therefore, San Marino was recommended to finalise its information gathering process for identifying future rulings and potential exchange jurisdictions as soon as possible.

932. During the year in review, San Marino defined a new procedure to ensure that all relevant information related to future rulings and exchange jurisdictions is captured accurately. The new procedure was shared with the relevant offices dealing with rulings. The process was in place in 2019, and it was formalised with the issuance of an internal circular ("Internal Circular no. 1 - Process to implement the Transparency Framework, BEPS Action 5 OECD/G20") on 18 February 2020. The new procedure provides a detailed process to identify future rulings in scope and all information on potential exchange jurisdictions which must be provided by the taxpayers when requesting a ruling as a prerequisite to its issuance. As such, the recommendation is now removed.

933. In addition, during the year in review, San Marino adopted extensive actions for mapping any rulings that had been issued since 1 April 2017 and should have been identified as future rulings in order to identify any agreements that could fall within the scope of the transparency framework. No future rulings were identified.

Review and supervision (ToR I.4.3)

934. In the prior year peer review report, it was determined that San Marino did not yet have a review and supervision mechanism in place for future rulings under the transparency framework (ToR I.4). During the year in review, San Marino adopted a new procedure to ensure that all relevant information is captured accurately and a review and supervision mechanism is in place. According to the new procedure noted above, the Director of the Tax Office, together with the coordinator of the transparency framework, who is an expert in the Finance and Budget Department, supervises and reviews the process for collecting the information needed for the transparency framework. The Director assumes the role of team leader responsible for supervising and validating the data. The new procedure was defined and shared with the relevant offices dealing with rulings and transparency framework compliance. In addition, as noted above San Marino applied an enhanced quality control review, to verify that all relevant past and future rulings have been correctly identified. As such, the recommendation is now removed.

Conclusion on section A

935. San Marino has met all of the ToR for the information gathering process and no recommendations are made.

B. The exchange of information

Legal basis for spontaneous exchange of information (ToR II.5.1, II.5.2)

936. San Marino has the necessary domestic legal basis to exchange information spontaneously. San Marino notes that there are no legal or practical impediments that prevent the spontaneous exchange of information on rulings as contemplated in the Action 5 minimum standard.

937. San Marino has international agreements permitting spontaneous exchange of information, including being a party to the (i) *Multilateral Convention on Mutual Administrative Assistance in Tax Matters: Amended by the 2010 Protocol* (OECD/Council of Europe, 2011[4]) ("the Convention") and (ii) bilateral agreements in force with 23 jurisdictions.[2]

Completion and exchange of templates (ToR II.5.3, II.5.4, II.5.5, II.5.6, II.5.7)

938. In the prior year peer review report, it was determined that San Marino did not yet have in place a process for the completion and exchange of templates (ToR II.5). Therefore, San Marino was recommended to develop a process to complete the templates on relevant rulings and to ensure that the exchanges of information on rulings occur in accordance with the form and timelines under the transparency framework.

939. During the year in review, San Marino adopted a new procedure for completion of templates and exchange of information on rulings. According to the new procedure, exchanges have to be performed according to the template contained in Annex C of the BEPS Action 5 Report (OECD, 2015[1]) and the summary section has to be completed in line with the internal FHTP suggested guidance. The procedure also specified the process and timelines for making the template available to the Competent Authority responsible for international exchange of information, so-called Central Liaison Office (CLO), and for the Competent Authority to exchange with all relevant jurisdictions. According to the procedure, the Tax Office shall complete the Annex C template within 10 days after the issuance of the tax ruling. Within 30 days after issuing the ruling, the director of the Tax Office shall validate the data contained in the template and transmit it to the CLO. The CLO shall exchange the template with the Competent Authority of the relevant exchange jurisdictions within 90 days. The new procedure was defined and shared with the relevant offices

dealing with rulings and transparency framework compliance. As such, the recommendation is now removed.

940. For the year in review, the timeliness of exchanges is as follows:

Past rulings in the scope of the transparency framework	Number of exchanges transmitted by 31 December 2019	Delayed exchanges		
		Number of exchanges not transmitted by 31 December 2019	Reasons for the delays	Any other comments
	0	1	The ruling was identified in November 2019 and exchanged in February 2020.	This relates to the additional past ruling identified, noted in section A above.
Future rulings in the scope of the transparency framework	Number of exchanges transmitted within three months of the information becoming available to the competent authority or immediately after legal impediments have been lifted	Delayed exchanges		
		Number of exchanges transmitted later than three months of the information on rulings becoming available to the competent authority	Reasons for the delays	Any other comments
	0	0	N/A	N/A
Total	0	1		

Follow up requests received for exchange of the ruling	Number	Average time to provide response	Number of requests not answered
	0	N/A	N/A

Conclusion on section B

941. San Marino has the necessary legal basis for spontaneous exchange of information, a process for completing the templates in a timely way and has completed all exchanges. San Marino has met all of the ToR for the exchange of information process and no recommendations are made.

C. Statistics (ToR IV)

942. As there was no information on rulings exchanged by San Marino for the year in review, no statistics can be reported.

D. Matters related to intellectual property regimes (ToR I.4.1.3)

943. San Marino offered three intellectual property regimes (IP regime)[3] that are not subject to the transparency requirements under the Action 5 Report (OECD, 2015[1]), because:

- ***New entrants benefitting from the grandfathered IP regime***: not applicable, because 1) the IP regime and the High innovative enterprise regime[4] are new IP regimes rather than grandfathered IP regimes and transparency on new entrants is not relevant and 2) the High tech regime is an abolished regime and no entrants ever benefitted from this regime.
- ***Third category of IP assets***: not applicable as the regimes do not allow the third category of IP assets to qualify for the benefits.

- ***Taxpayers making use of the option to treat the nexus ratio as a rebuttable presumption***: not applicable as the regimes do not allow the nexus ratio to be treated as a rebuttable presumption.

944. San Marino offered one IP regime[5] that is subject to the transparency requirements under the Action 5 Report (OECD, 2015[1]). It states that the identification of the benefitting taxpayers will occur as follows:

- ***New entrants benefitting from the grandfathered IP regime:*** transparency obligations apply for the New companies regime, because grandfathering is provided to entrants that entered the regime after the relevant date from which enhanced transparency obligations apply. In the prior year report, it was determined that San Marino had not exchanged all information on new entrants (i.e. new taxpayers and new assets of existing taxpayers) benefitting from the grandfathered regime as this information was not able to be collected during the year in review. Therefore, San Marino was recommended to continue its efforts to identify and exchange information on new entrants to the grandfathered IP regime. During the year in review, San Marino put in place a process to identify new entrants in the grandfathered regime. The process involved reviewing the taxpayer's file and those of any associates, analysing the balance sheets in order to verify the existence of both existing and new IP assets as well as accessing publicly available information. The identification process informed that there were no new entrants in the relevant period that benefitted from the grandfathered regime and therefore no information needed to be exchanged. As such, the recommendation is now removed.
- ***Third category of IP assets:*** not applicable as the regime does not allow the third category of IP assets to qualify for the benefits.
- ***Taxpayers making use of the option to treat the nexus ratio as a rebuttable presumption***: not applicable as the regime does not allow the nexus ratio to be treated as a rebuttable presumption.

Summary of recommendations on implementation of the transparency framework

Aspect of implementation of the transparency framework that should be improved	Recommendation for improvement
San Marino experienced difficulties in the identification of past rulings and identified one additional past ruling that was not previously captured.	No recommendations are made because San Marino has quickly taken steps to identify and remedy the issue, completed the exchanges on the one identified past ruling quickly after the issues were identified and resolved, and this is not a recurring issue.

References

OECD (2017), *BEPS Action 5 on Harmful Tax Practices - Terms of Reference and Methodology for the Conduct of the Peer Reviews of the Action 5 Transparency Framework*, OECD Publishing, Paris, http://www.oecd.org/tax/beps/beps-action-5-harmful-tax-practices-peer-review-transparency-framework.pdf. [3]

OECD (2015), *Countering Harmful Tax Practices More Effectively, Taking into Account Transparency and Substance, Action 5 - 2015 Final Report*, OECD/G20 Base Erosion and Profit Shifting Project, OECD Publishing, Paris, https://dx.doi.org/10.1787/9789264241190-en. [1]

OECD/Council of Europe (2011), *The Multilateral Convention on Mutual Administrative Assistance in Tax Matters: Amended by the 2010 Protocol*, OECD Publishing, Paris, https://dx.doi.org/10.1787/9789264115606-en. [4]

Notes

[1] With respect to the following preferential regime: IP regime. In the prior year report, it was noted that San Marino could legally issue rulings with respect to the following preferential regimes: 1) New companies regime (New companies regime provided by art. 73, law no. 166/2013), 2) High tech regime (Regime for high-tech start-up companies under law no. 71/2013 and delegated decree no. 116/2014) and 3) IP regime. San Marino has since clarified that rulings can be issued only with respect to the IP regime.

[2] Parties to the Convention are available here: www.oecd.org/tax/exchange-of-tax-information/convention-on-mutual-administrative-assistance-in-tax-matters.htm. San Marino also has bilateral agreements with Austria, Azerbaijan, Barbados, Belgium, Croatia, Cyprus, Georgia, Greece, Hungary, Italy, Liechtenstein, Luxembourg, Malaysia, Malta, Portugal, Qatar, Romania, Saint Kitts and Nevis, Serbia, Seychelles, Singapore, United Arab Emirates and Viet Nam.

[3] 1) IP regime, 2) High tech regime (Regime for high-tech start-up companies under law no. 71/2013 and delegated decree no. 116/2014), and 3) High innovative enterprise regime (High innovative enterprise regime introduced by delegated decree no. 101/2019 of 13 June 2019).

[4] San Marino introduced this new IP regime which came into effect from June 2019 and it has not yet been reviewed by the Forum.

[5] New companies regime (New companies regime provided by art. 73, law no. 166/2013).

Senegal

Senegal has met all aspects of the terms of reference (OECD, 2017[3]) (ToR) for the calendar year 2019 (year in review) that can be met in the absence of rulings being issued.

In the prior year report, Senegal had received two recommendations. Senegal has resolved the issues relating to finalising its information gathering process, with a review and supervision mechanism, and to having in place a process to undertake spontaneous exchange of information on tax rulings. Therefore, these recommendations have now been removed.

Senegal can legally issue one type of ruling within the scope of the transparency framework.

In practice, Senegal has issued no rulings within the scope of the transparency framework.

As no rulings were issued, no exchanges were required to take place, and no peer input was received in respect of the exchanges of information on rulings received from Senegal.

A. The information gathering process

945. Senegal can legally issue the following type of ruling within the scope of the transparency framework: cross-border unilateral APAs and any other cross-border unilateral tax rulings (such as an advance tax ruling) covering transfer pricing or the application of transfer pricing principles. Rulings are issued by the Minister of Finance or the Director General of taxation. The Legislation and International Cooperation directorate, within the Tax Administration, is in charge of both drafting and identifying rulings in scope of the transparency framework.

Past rulings (ToR I.4.1.1, I.4.1.2, I.4.2.1, I.4.2.2)

946. For Senegal, past rulings are any tax rulings within scope that are issued either (i) on or after 1 January 2016 but before 1 April 2018; and (ii) on or after 1 January 2014 but before 1 January 2016, provided still in effect as at 1 January 2016.

947. In the prior year peer review report, it was determined that Senegal had not yet finalised the steps to have in place its necessary information and gathering process rulings for the purposes of the transparency framework (ToR I.4). Therefore, Senegal was recommended to finalise its information gathering process as soon as possible. During the year in review, Senegal confirmed that during the past rulings period the only decisions rendered were interpretative decisions which do not fall within the types of rulings in scope of the transparency framework. As no past rulings were issued during the past rulings period and as such there was no need to identify potential exchange jurisdictions.

Future rulings (ToR I.4.1.1, I.4.1.2, I.4.2.1)

948. For Senegal, future rulings are any tax rulings within scope that are issued on or after 1 April 2018.

949. In the prior year peer review report, it was determined that Senegal had not yet finalised the steps to have in place its necessary information and gathering process for the purposes of the transparency framework (ToR I.4). Therefore, Senegal was recommended to finalise its information gathering process as soon as possible.

950. During the year in review, Senegal clarified that the Legislation and International Cooperation directorate has been tasked with identifying and classifying information relating to future rulings in scope of the transparency framework. The process is centralised at the level of the Legislation and International Cooperation directorate that immediately identifies and processes any future rulings in scope of the transparency framework that might be issued.

951. In terms of identifying potential exchange jurisdictions, Senegal can only issue APA rulings; and the transfer pricing return to be filed every year in a standardised format together with additional documentary obligations imposed by the Tax Code, already provide information, in all cases, on the jurisdictions of residence of the ultimate parent entity, the immediate parent entity and related parties with which the taxpayers enter into a transaction covered by the ruling. Given Senegal can utilise a centralised information gathering process and has the possibility to identify all relevant jurisdictions in all cases, the recommendation is now removed. Senegal also indicated that it is currently working on developing a formal process to provide additional clarity to identify all relevant potential exchange jurisdictions. In practice, no future rulings were issued during the year of review.

Review and supervision (ToR I.4.3)

952. In the prior year peer review report, it was determined that Senegal did not yet have a review and supervision mechanism under the transparency framework sufficient to meet the minimum standard.

953. During the year in review, Senegal indicated the Legislation and International Cooperation directorate is a centralised office that drafts, identifies and classifies information relating to future rulings in scope of the transparency framework. Because all the activities related to the issuance of the rulings are centralised at the level of the Legislation and International Cooperation directorate, this will ensure that all the rulings in scope of the transparency framework will be correctly and immediately identified and all information needed for the exchanges will be adequately captured. The Legislation and International Cooperation directorate will supervise this process. Therefore the recommendation is now removed.

Conclusion on section A

954. Senegal has met all of the ToR for the information gathering process that can be met in the absence of rulings being issued and no recommendations are made.

B. The exchange of information

Legal basis for spontaneous exchange of information (ToR II.5.1, II.5.2)

955. Senegal has the necessary domestic legal basis to exchange information spontaneously. Senegal notes that there are no legal or practical impediments that prevent the spontaneous exchange of information on rulings as contemplated in the Action 5 minimum standard.

956. Senegal has international agreements permitting spontaneous exchange of information, including being a party to the (i) *Multilateral Convention on Mutual Administrative Assistance in Tax Matters: Amended by the 2010 Protocol* (OECD/Council of Europe, 2011[4]) ("the Convention") and (ii) bilateral agreements in force with 21 jurisdictions.[1]

Completion and exchange of templates (ToR II.5.3, II.5.4, II.5.5, II.5.6, II.5.7)

957. In the prior year peer review report, Senegal was recommended to develop a process to complete the templates on relevant rulings and to ensure that the exchanges of information on rulings occur in accordance with the form and timelines under the transparency framework.

958. During the year in review, Senegal indicated that the Legislation and International Cooperation directorate would be responsible for the completion of the information required in the template contained in Annex C of the Action 5 Report (OECD, 2015). The Director General of Taxes and Domains is the Competent Authority in Senegal, responsible for exchanging information on tax rulings with relevant jurisdictions.

959. According to the annual work plan, Senegal indicated that it intends to apply a quarterly deadline to monitor the implementation of the transparency framework. This pertains to deadlines for internal actions (issuance, identification, completion of the template and exchange of the information with the Competent Authority). Exchanges with relevant jurisdictions will be conducted within three months after the tax ruling becomes available to the competent authority. Senegal also indicated that training might be provided in the future to the officers involved in the transparency framework requirements, in the event that rulings are issued in practice.

960. To provide additional clarity, Senegal intends to formalise the process to complete the templates on relevant rulings, to make them available to the Competent Authority for exchange of information, and to exchange them with relevant jurisdictions.

961. During the year in review, no exchanges were required to take place and no data on the timeliness of exchanges is reported.

Conclusion on section B

962. Senegal has the necessary legal basis for spontaneous exchange of information.

963. Senegal has met all of the ToR for the exchange of information process that can be met in the absence of rulings being issued and exchanged in practice and no recommendations are made.

C. Statistics (ToR IV)

964. As no rulings were issued, no statistics can be reported.

D. Matters related to intellectual property regimes (ToR I.4.1.3)

965. Senegal does not offer an intellectual property regime for which transparency requirements under the Action 5 Report (OECD, 2015[1]) were imposed.

Summary of recommendations on implementation of the transparency framework

Aspect of implementation of the transparency framework that should be improved	Recommendation for improvement
	No recommendations are made.

References

OECD (2017), *BEPS Action 5 on Harmful Tax Practices - Terms of Reference and Methodology for the Conduct of the Peer Reviews of the Action 5 Transparency Framework*, OECD Publishing, Paris, http://www.oecd.org/tax/beps/beps-action-5-harmful-tax-practices-peer-review-transparency-framework.pdf. [3]

OECD (2015), *Countering Harmful Tax Practices More Effectively, Taking into Account Transparency and Substance, Action 5 - 2015 Final Report*, OECD/G20 Base Erosion and Profit Shifting Project, OECD Publishing, Paris, https://dx.doi.org/10.1787/9789264241190-en. [1]

OECD/Council of Europe (2011), *The Multilateral Convention on Mutual Administrative Assistance in Tax Matters: Amended by the 2010 Protocol*, OECD Publishing, Paris, https://dx.doi.org/10.1787/9789264115606-en. [4]

Notes

[1] Parties to the Convention are available here: www.oecd.org/tax/exchange-of-tax-information/convention-on-mutual-administrative-assistance-in-tax-matters.htm. Senegal also has bilateral agreements with West African Economic and Monetary Union jurisdictions, African and Malagasy Common Organisation jurisdictions and Belgium, Canada, Chinese Taipei, France, Italy, Kuwait, Lebanon, Malaysia, Mauritania, Mauritius, Morocco, Norway, Portugal, Spain, United Arab Emirates and United Kingdom.

Seychelles

Seychelles has met all aspects of the terms of reference (OECD, 2017[3]) (ToR) for the calendar year 2019 (year in review) and no recommendations are made.

Seychelles can legally issue five types of rulings within the scope of the transparency framework. In practice, Seychelles issued no rulings within the scope of the transparency framework. During the year in review, Seychelles only provided general decisions, which are not binding on the tax administration.

As no exchanges were required to take place, no peer input was received in respect of the exchanges of information on rulings received from Seychelles.

A. The information gathering process

966. Seychelles can legally issue the following five types of rulings within the scope of the transparency framework: (i) preferential regimes;[1] (ii) cross-border unilateral APAs and any other cross-border unilateral tax rulings (such as an advance tax ruling) covering transfer pricing or the application of transfer pricing principles; (iii) rulings providing for unilateral downward adjustments; (iv) permanent establishment rulings; and (v) related party conduit rulings.

967. For Seychelles, past rulings are any tax rulings within scope that are issued either: (i) on or after 1 January 2015 but before 1 April 2017; or (ii) on or after 1 January 2012 but before 1 January 2015, provided they were still in effect as at 1 January 2015. Future rulings are any tax rulings within scope that are issued on or after 1 April 2017.

968. In the prior years' peer review reports, it was determined that Seychelles' undertakings to identify past and future rulings and all potential exchange jurisdictions were sufficient to meet the minimum standard. In addition, it was determined that Seychelles' review and supervision mechanism was sufficient to meet the minimum standard. Seychelles' implementation remains unchanged, and therefore continues to meet the minimum standard. It is noted that the Seychelles Revenue Commission (SRC) is continuing to develop a new form to request a private ruling to capture all the needed information. Until that takes place, Seychelles would continue to use its information gathering powers under the Revenue Administration Act to obtain information on all potential exchange jurisdictions.

969. Seychelles has met all of the ToR for the information gathering process and no recommendations are made.

B. The exchange of information

970. In the prior years' peer review reports, it was determined that Seychelles' process for the completion and exchange of templates were sufficient to meet the minimum standard. With respect to past rulings, no action was required. Seychelles' implementation in this regard remains unchanged and therefore continues to meet the minimum standard.

971. Seychelles has international agreements permitting spontaneous exchange of information, including being a party to the (i) *Multilateral Convention on Mutual Administrative Assistance in Tax Matters: Amended by the 2010 Protocol* (OECD/Council of Europe, 2011[4]) ("the Convention") and (ii) bilateral agreements in force with 28 jurisdictions.[2]

972. As Seychelles did not issue any past or future rulings in scope of Action 5 in the relevant periods, Seychelles did not exchange any information on rulings in the year in review and no data on the timeliness of exchanges can be reported.

973. Seychelles has the necessary legal basis for spontaneous exchange of information. Seychelles has met all of the ToR for the exchange of information process and no recommendations are made.

C. Statistics (ToR IV)

974. As no rulings were issued, no statistics can be reported.

D. Matters related to intellectual property regimes (ToR I.4.1.3)

975. Seychelles offered three intellectual property regimes (IP regime)[3] that were abolished as of 1 January 2019 and not subject to the transparency requirements under the Action 5 Report (OECD, 2015[1]), because:

- ***New entrants benefitting from the grandfathered IP regime***: the IP regimes have been abolished without grandfathering for taxpayers entering after the relevant date from which enhanced transparency obligations apply. As such, no enhanced transparency requirements apply.
- ***Third category of IP assets***: not applicable as the IP regimes have been abolished.
- ***Taxpayers making use of the option to treat the nexus ratio as a rebuttable presumption***: not applicable as the IP regimes have been abolished.

Summary of recommendations on implementation of the transparency framework

Aspect of implementation of the transparency framework that should be improved	Recommendation for improvement
	No recommendations are made.

References

OECD (2017), *BEPS Action 5 on Harmful Tax Practices - Terms of Reference and Methodology for the Conduct of the Peer Reviews of the Action 5 Transparency Framework*, OECD Publishing, Paris, http://www.oecd.org/tax/beps/beps-action-5-harmful-tax-practices-peer-review-transparency-framework.pdf. [3]

OECD (2015), *Countering Harmful Tax Practices More Effectively, Taking into Account Transparency and Substance, Action 5 - 2015 Final Report*, OECD/G20 Base Erosion and Profit Shifting Project, OECD Publishing, Paris, https://dx.doi.org/10.1787/9789264241190-en. [1]

OECD/Council of Europe (2011), *The Multilateral Convention on Mutual Administrative Assistance in Tax Matters: Amended by the 2010 Protocol*, OECD Publishing, Paris, https://dx.doi.org/10.1787/9789264115606-en. [4]

Notes

[1] With respect to the following preferential regimes: 1) International business companies, 2) Companies special license, 3) International trade zone licensees, 4) Offshore banking, 5) Non domestic insurance business, 6) Fund administration business, 7) Securities business under the securities act and 8) Reinsurance business.

[2] Parties to the Convention are available here: www.oecd.org/tax/exchange-of-tax-information/convention-on-mutual-administrative-assistance-in-tax-matters.htm. Seychelles also has bilateral agreements with Bahrain, Barbados, Belgium, Bermuda, Botswana, China (People's Republic of), Cyprus, Ethiopia, Guernsey, Indonesia, Isle of Man, Jersey, Kenya, Luxembourg, Malaysia, Mauritius, Monaco, Oman,

Qatar, San Marino, Singapore, South Africa, Sri Lanka, Swaziland, Thailand, United Arab Emirates, Viet Nam and Zambia.

[3] These regimes are: 1) International business companies; 2) Companies special license; and 3) International trade zone.

Singapore

Singapore has met all aspects of the terms of reference (OECD, 2017[3]) (ToR) for the calendar year 2019 (year in review) and no recommendations are made.

Singapore can legally issue five types of rulings within the scope of the transparency framework.

In practice, Singapore issued rulings within the scope of the transparency framework as follows:

- 1 008 past rulings;
- For the calendar year 2017: 85 future rulings;
- For the calendar year 2018: 222 future rulings; and
- For the year in review: 274 future rulings.

Peer input was received from five jurisdictions in respect of the exchanges of information on rulings received from Singapore. The input was positive, noting that information was complete, in a correct format and almost all received in a timely manner.

A. The information gathering process

976. Singapore can legally issue the following five types of rulings within the scope of the transparency framework: (i) preferential regimes;[1] (II) cross-border unilateral APAs and any other cross-border unilateral tax rulings (such as an advance tax ruling) covering transfer pricing or the application of transfer pricing principles; (iii) rulings providing for unilateral downward adjustments; (iv) permanent establishment rulings; and (v) related party conduit rulings.

977. For Singapore, past rulings are any tax rulings within scope that are issued either: (i) on or after 1 January 2015 but before 1 April 2017; or (ii) on or after 1 January 2012 but before 1 January 2015, provided they were still in effect as at 1 January 2015. Future rulings are any tax rulings within scope that are issued on or after 1 April 2017.

978. In the prior years' peer review reports, it was determined that Singapore's undertakings to identify past and future rulings and all potential exchange jurisdictions were sufficient to meet the minimum standard. In addition, it was determined that Singapore's review and supervision mechanism was sufficient to meet the minimum standard. Singapore's implementation remains unchanged, and therefore continues to meet the minimum standard.

979. Singapore has met all of the ToR for the information gathering process and no recommendations are made.

B. The exchange of information

980. In the prior years' peer review reports, it was determined that Singapore's process for the completion and exchange of templates were sufficient to meet the minimum standard. With respect to past rulings, no further action was required. Singapore's implementation in this regard remains unchanged and therefore continues to meet the minimum standard.

981. Singapore has international agreements permitting spontaneous exchange of information, including being a party to the (i) *Multilateral Convention on Mutual Administrative Assistance in Tax Matters: Amended by the 2010 Protocol* (OECD/Council of Europe, 2011[4]) ("the Convention"), and (ii) bilateral agreements in force with 82 jurisdictions.[2]

982. For the year in review, the timeliness of exchanges is as follows:

Future rulings in the scope of the transparency framework	Number of exchanges transmitted within three months of the information becoming available to the competent authority or immediately after legal impediments have been lifted	Delayed exchanges		
		Number of exchanges transmitted later than three months of the information on rulings becoming available to the competent authority	Reasons for the delays	Any other comments
	986	5	A minor delay of two months was experienced for five exchanges due to human error by new staff members.	This issue has been rectified through further training of the relevant personnel, and is not expected to recur.
Total	986	5		

Follow up requests received for exchange of the ruling	Number	Average time to provide response	Number of requests not answered
	3	57 days	0

983. Singapore has the necessary legal basis for spontaneous exchange of information, a process for completing the templates in a timely way and has completed all exchanges. Singapore has met all of the ToR for the exchange of information process and no recommendations are made.

C. Statistics (ToR IV)

984. The statistics for the year in review are as follows:

Category of ruling	Number of exchanges	Jurisdictions exchanged with
Ruling/letters of awards related to a preferential regime	978	Argentina, Australia, Austria, Belgium, Brazil, Canada, Chile, China (People's Republic of), Colombia, Croatia, Czech Republic, Denmark, Estonia, Finland, France, Germany, Greece, Guernsey, Hong Kong (China), Hungary, India, Ireland, Isle of Man, Israel, Italy, Japan, Jersey, Korea, Latvia, Liechtenstein, Lithuania, Luxembourg, Malaysia, Mauritius, Mexico, Netherlands, New Zealand, Norway, Poland, Portugal, Russia, Saudi Arabia, Seychelles, Slovak Republic, South Africa, Spain, Sweden, Switzerland, Turkey, United Kingdom, Uruguay
Cross-border unilateral advance pricing agreements (APAs) and any other cross-border unilateral tax rulings (such as an advance tax ruling) covering transfer pricing or the application of transfer pricing principles	13	China (People's Republic of), India, Japan, Korea, Malaysia, Netherlands, Sweden, Switzerland, Uruguay
Cross-border rulings providing for a unilateral downward adjustment to the taxpayer's taxable profits that is not directly reflected in the taxpayer's financial / commercial accounts	0	N/A
Permanent establishment rulings	0	N/A
Related party conduit rulings	0	N/A
De minimis rule	4	N/A
IP regimes: total exchanges on taxpayers benefitting from the third category of IP assets, new entrants benefitting from grandfathered IP regimes; and taxpayers making use of the option to treat the nexus ratio as a rebuttable presumption	*De minimis* rule applies	N/A
Total	995	

D. Matters related to intellectual property regimes (ToR I.4.1.3)

985. Singapore has two preferential regimes, which also offered benefits to income from intellectual property (IP regimes).[3] The IP parts of both regimes were abolished as of 30 June 2018 and are subject

to transparency requirements under the Action 5 Report (OECD, 2015[1]). It states that the identification of the benefitting taxpayers occurred as follows:

- ***New entrants benefitting from the grandfathered IP regime***: Transparency obligations apply for the two IP regimes, because grandfathering is provided to entrants that entered the regime after the relevant date from which enhanced transparency obligations apply. New entrants include both (i) new taxpayers not previously benefitting from the regimes and (ii) new IP assets owned by taxpayers already benefitting from the regimes. Singapore's approach is described in detail in the prior year's report and which meets the ToR. Four exchanges occurred during the year in review, in addition to seven exchanges in the previous year. Singapore has now completed the identification and exchange of all new entrants to the grandfathered IP regimes.
- ***Third category of IP assets***: not applicable as the IP regimes have been abolished.
- ***Taxpayers making use of the option to treat the nexus ratio as a rebuttable presumption***: not applicable as the IP regimes have been abolished.

986. Singapore offers an IP regime[4] which came into effect from 1 July 2018. It is noted that this regime is not subject to the transparency requirements under the Action 5 Report (OECD, 2015[1]), because:

- ***New entrants benefitting from the grandfathered IP regime***: the regime is a new nexus-compliant regime and therefore there is no grandfathered IP regime for which enhanced transparency requirements will apply.
- ***Third category of IP assets***: not applicable as the regime does not allow the third category of IP assets to qualify for the benefits.
- ***Taxpayers making the use of the option to treat the nexus ratio as a rebuttable presumption***: not applicable as the regime does not allow the nexus ratio to be treated as a rebuttable presumption.

Summary of recommendations on implementation of the transparency framework

Aspect of implementation of the transparency framework that should be improved	Recommendation for improvement
	No recommendations are made.

References

OECD (2017), *BEPS Action 5 on Harmful Tax Practices - Terms of Reference and Methodology for the Conduct of the Peer Reviews of the Action 5 Transparency Framework*, OECD Publishing, Paris, http://www.oecd.org/tax/beps/beps-action-5-harmful-tax-practices-peer-review-transparency-framework.pdf. [3]

OECD (2015), *Countering Harmful Tax Practices More Effectively, Taking into Account Transparency and Substance, Action 5 - 2015 Final Report*, OECD/G20 Base Erosion and Profit Shifting Project, OECD Publishing, Paris, https://dx.doi.org/10.1787/9789264241190-en. [1]

OECD/Council of Europe (2011), *The Multilateral Convention on Mutual Administrative Assistance in Tax Matters: Amended by the 2010 Protocol*, OECD Publishing, Paris, https://dx.doi.org/10.1787/9789264115606-en. [4]

Notes

[1] 1) Development and expansion incentive - services, 2) Pioneer service company, 3) Aircraft leasing scheme, 4) Finance and treasury centre, 5) Insurance business development, 6) Financial sector incentive, 7) Global trader programme.

[2] Parties to the Convention are available here: www.oecd.org/tax/exchange-of-tax-information/convention-on-mutual-administrative-assistance-in-tax-matters.htm. Singapore also has bilateral agreements with Albania, Australia, Bahrain, Bangladesh, Barbados, Belarus, Belgium, Brunei Darussalam, Bulgaria, Cambodia, Canada, China (People's Republic of), Cyprus, Czech Republic, Denmark, Ecuador, Egypt, Estonia, Ethiopia, Fiji, Finland, France, Georgia, Germany, Ghana, Guernsey, Hungary, India, Indonesia, Ireland, Isle of Man, Israel, Italy, Japan, Jersey, Kazakhstan, Korea, Kuwait, Lao People's Democratic Republic, Latvia, Libya, Lithuania, Luxembourg, Malaysia, Malta, Mauritius, Mexico, Mongolia, Morocco, Myanmar, Netherlands, New Zealand, Nigeria, Norway, Oman, Pakistan, Papua New Guinea, Philippines, Poland, Portugal, Qatar, Romania, Russia, Rwanda, San Marino, Saudi Arabia, Seychelles, Slovak Republic, Slovenia, South Africa, Spain, Sri Lanka, Sweden, Thailand, Tunisia, Turkey, Ukraine, United Arab Emirates, United Kingdom, Uruguay, Uzbekistan and Viet Nam.

[3] 1) Pioneer service company and 2) Development and expansion incentive – services.

[4] IP development incentive.

Sint Maarten

Sint Maarten has met all aspects of the terms of reference (OECD, 2017[3]) (ToR) for the calendar year 2019 (year in review) that can be met in the absence of rulings being issued.

This is Sint Maarten's first review of implementation of the transparency framework. As Sint Maarten was affected by a natural disaster, earlier peer reviews were deferred.

Sint Maarten can legally issue five types of rulings within the scope of the transparency framework but in practice has not issued any rulings within the scope of the transparency framework.

As no rulings have been issued in practice, no exchanges of information were required to be conducted. Therefore, no peer input was received in respect of the exchanges of information on rulings received from Sint Maarten.

A. The information gathering process

987. Sint Maarten can legally issue the following five types of rulings within the scope of the transparency framework: (i) preferential regimes;[1] (ii) cross-border unilateral APAs and any other cross-border unilateral tax rulings (such as an advance tax ruling) covering transfer pricing or the application of transfer pricing principles; (iii) rulings providing for unilateral downward adjustments; (iv) permanent establishment rulings; and (v) related party conduit rulings. Rulings are issued by the tax administration upon application by the taxpayer.

Past rulings (ToR I.4.1.1, I.4.1.2, I.4.2.1, I.4.2.2)

988. For Sint Maarten, past rulings are any tax rulings within scope that are issued either: (i) on or after 1 January 2015 but before 1 September 2017; or (ii) on or after 1 January 2012 but before 1 January 2015, provided they were still in effect as at 1 January 2015.

989. In the period for past rulings, there was one tax inspector working within the Sint Maarten tax administration. Only the tax inspector is responsible for issuing rulings. During this period, no ruling requests were handled. Therefore, Sint Maarten confirms that no past rulings in scope of the transparency framework were issued.

Future rulings (ToR I.4.1.1, I.4.1.2, I.4.2.1)

990. For Sint Maarten, future rulings are any tax rulings within scope that are issued on or after 1 September 2017.

991. There are currently two tax inspectors in the Sint Maarten tax administration who are responsible for issuing rulings. If a ruling is issued, the tax inspector then determines whether it is in scope of the transparency framework. Rulings are registered in a central spreadsheet by the tax administration. If the ruling is in scope, the inspector then identifies who the immediate parent, ultimate parent and related parties with which the taxpayer entered into a transaction with are by checking the internal available information. If the information is not internally available, the inspector requests the taxpayer to provide this information, as the inspector is empowered by the domestic law to require this from the taxpayer.

992. To date, Sint Maarten has not issued any future rulings in scope of the transparency framework.

Review and supervision (ToR I.4.3)

993. As noted before, there are two tax inspectors responsible for issuing rulings. These inspectors supervise each other's work on the accuracy of the information gathering process and the identification of rulings in scope of the transparency framework.

Conclusion on section A

994. Sint Maarten has met all of the ToR for the information gathering process and no recommendations are made.

B. The exchange of information

Legal basis for spontaneous exchange of information (ToR II.5.1, II.5.2)

995. Sint Maarten has the necessary domestic legal basis to exchange information spontaneously. Sint Maarten notes that there are no legal or practical impediments that prevent the spontaneous exchange of information on rulings as contemplated in the Action 5 minimum standard.

996. Sint Maarten has international agreements permitting spontaneous exchange of information, including being a party to the (i) *Multilateral Convention on Mutual Administrative Assistance in Tax Matters: Amended by the 2010 Protocol* (OECD/Council of Europe, 2011[4]) ("the Convention") and (ii) bilateral agreements in force with three jurisdictions.[2]

Completion and exchange of templates (ToR II.5.3, II.5.4, II.5.5, II.5.6, II.5.7)

997. Sint Maarten notes that the EOI manager (field officer) is responsible for completing the template in Annex C of the BEPS Action 5 report (OECD, 2015[1]). The field officer obtains information from the tax inspector that issued the ruling, who then also reviews the template. The summary section will be competed in line with the FHTP internal guidance. Sint Maarten confirms that this process will take place within three months after the ruling is issued.

998. After that, the template will be sent to the Competent Authority who is responsible for the final review of the template and the exchanges. Sint Maarten confirms that the information on the ruling will be exchanged immediately after the template is completed, which will be within the FHTP timelines.

999. As Sint Maarten did not issue any rulings in scope of the transparency framework in the relevant period, Sint Maarten was not required to exchange any information on rulings in the year in review and no data on the timeliness of exchanges can be reported.

Conclusion on section B

1000. Sint Maarten has the necessary legal basis to undertake spontaneous exchange of information. Sint Maarten has met all of the ToR for the exchange of information process that can be met in the absence of rulings being issued and exchanged in practice and no recommendations are made.

C. Statistics (ToR IV)

1001. As no rulings were issued, no statistics can be reported.

D. Matters related to intellectual property regimes (ToR I.4.1.3)

1002. Sint Maarten does not offer an intellectual property regime for which transparency requirements under the Action 5 Report (OECD, 2015[1]) were imposed.

Summary of recommendations on implementation of the transparency framework

Aspect of implementation of the transparency framework that should be improved	Recommendation for improvement
	No recommendations are made.

References

OECD (2017), *BEPS Action 5 on Harmful Tax Practices - Terms of Reference and Methodology for the Conduct of the Peer Reviews of the Action 5 Transparency Framework*, OECD Publishing, Paris, http://www.oecd.org/tax/beps/beps-action-5-harmful-tax-practices-peer-review-transparency-framework.pdf. [3]

OECD (2015), *Countering Harmful Tax Practices More Effectively, Taking into Account Transparency and Substance, Action 5 - 2015 Final Report*, OECD/G20 Base Erosion and Profit Shifting Project, OECD Publishing, Paris, https://dx.doi.org/10.1787/9789264241190-en. [1]

OECD/Council of Europe (2011), *The Multilateral Convention on Mutual Administrative Assistance in Tax Matters: Amended by the 2010 Protocol*, OECD Publishing, Paris, https://dx.doi.org/10.1787/9789264115606-en. [4]

Notes

[1] Tax exempt company.

[2] Parties to the Convention are available here: www.oecd.org/tax/exchange-of-tax-information/convention-on-mutual-administrative-assistance-in-tax-matters.htm. Sint Maarten also has bilateral agreements with the Netherlands, Norway and the United States.

Slovak Republic

The Slovak Republic has met all aspects of the terms of reference (OECD, 2017[3]) (ToR) for the calendar year 2019 (year in review) and no recommendations are made.

The Slovak Republic can legally issue two types of rulings within the scope of the transparency framework.

In practice, the Slovak Republic issued rulings within the scope of the transparency framework as follows:

- One past ruling;
- For the period 1 April 2016 - 31 December 2016: two future rulings;
- For the calendar year 2017: five future rulings;
- For the calendar year 2018: three future rulings; and
- For the year in review: three future rulings.

No peer input was received in respect of the exchanges of information on rulings received from the Slovak Republic.

A. The information gathering process

1003. The Slovak Republic can legally issue the following two types of rulings within the scope of the transparency framework: (i) cross-border unilateral APAs and any other cross-border unilateral tax rulings (such as an advance tax ruling) covering transfer pricing or the application of transfer pricing principles and (ii) permanent establishment rulings.

1004. For the Slovak Republic, past rulings are any tax rulings within scope that are issued either: (i) on or after 1 January 2014 but before 1 April 2016; or (ii) on or after 1 January 2010 but before 1 January 2014, provided they were still in effect as at 1 January 2014. Future rulings are any tax rulings within scope that are issued on or after 1 April 2016.

1005. In the prior years' peer review reports, it was determined that the Slovak Republic's undertakings to identify past and future rulings and all potential exchange jurisdictions were sufficient to meet the minimum standard. In addition, it was determined that the Slovak Republic's review and supervision mechanism was sufficient to meet the minimum standard. The Slovak Republic's implementation remains unchanged, and therefore continues to meet the minimum standard.

1006. The Slovak Republic has met all of the ToR for the information gathering process and no recommendations are made.

B. The exchange of information

1007. In the prior years' peer review reports, it was determined that the Slovak Republic's process for the completion and exchange of templates were sufficient to meet the minimum standard. With respect to past rulings, no further action was required. The Slovak Republic's implementation in this regard remains unchanged and therefore continues to meet the minimum standard.

1008. The Slovak Republic has international agreements permitting spontaneous exchange of information, including being a party to the (i) *Multilateral Convention on Mutual Administrative Assistance in Tax Matters: Amended by the 2010 Protocol* (OECD/Council of Europe, 2011[4]) ("the Convention"), (ii) the Directive 2011/16/EU with all other European Union Member States and (iii) bilateral agreements in force with 70 jurisdictions.[1]

1009. For the year in review, the timeliness of exchanges is as follows:

Future rulings in the scope of the transparency framework	Number of exchanges transmitted within three months of the information becoming available to the competent authority or immediately after legal impediments have been lifted	Delayed exchanges		
		Number of exchanges transmitted later than three months of the information on rulings becoming available to the competent authority	Reasons for the delays	Any other comments
	3	0	N/A	N/A

Follow up requests received for exchange of the ruling	Number	Average time to provide response	Number of requests not answered
	0	N/A	N/A

1010. The Slovak Republic has the necessary legal basis for spontaneous exchange of information, a process for completing the templates in a timely way and has completed all exchanges. The Slovak Republic has met all of the ToR for the exchange of information process and no recommendations are made.

C. Statistics (ToR IV)

1011. The statistics for the year in review are as follows:

Category of ruling	Number of exchanges	Jurisdictions exchanged with
Cross-border unilateral advance pricing agreements (APAs) and any other cross-border unilateral tax rulings (such as an advance tax ruling) covering transfer pricing or the application of transfer pricing principles	*De minimis* rule applies	N/A
Permanent establishment rulings	N/A	N/A
De minimis rule	3	N/A
Total	3	

D. Matters related to intellectual property regimes (ToR I.4.1.3)

1012. The Slovak Republic offers an intellectual property regime (IP regime)[2] that is not subject to the transparency requirements under the Action 5 Report (OECD, 2015[1]), because:

- ***New entrants benefitting from the grandfathered IP regime***: the regime is a new nexus-compliant regime and therefore there is no grandfathered IP regime for which enhanced transparency requirements will apply.
- ***Third category of IP assets***: not applicable as the regimes do not allow the third category of IP assets to qualify for the benefits.
- ***Taxpayers making use of the option to treat the nexus ratio as a rebuttable presumption***: not applicable as the regimes do not allow the nexus ratio to be treated as a rebuttable presumption.

Summary of recommendations on implementation of the transparency framework

Aspect of implementation of the transparency framework that should be improved	Recommendation for improvement
	No recommendations are made.

References

OECD (2017), *BEPS Action 5 on Harmful Tax Practices - Terms of Reference and Methodology for the Conduct of the Peer Reviews of the Action 5 Transparency Framework*, OECD Publishing, Paris, http://www.oecd.org/tax/beps/beps-action-5-harmful-tax-practices-peer-review-transparency-framework.pdf. [3]

OECD (2015), *Countering Harmful Tax Practices More Effectively, Taking into Account Transparency and Substance, Action 5 - 2015 Final Report*, OECD/G20 Base Erosion and Profit Shifting Project, OECD Publishing, Paris, https://dx.doi.org/10.1787/9789264241190-en. [1]

OECD/Council of Europe (2011), *The Multilateral Convention on Mutual Administrative Assistance in Tax Matters: Amended by the 2010 Protocol*, OECD Publishing, Paris, https://dx.doi.org/10.1787/9789264115606-en. [4]

Notes

[1] Parties to the Convention are available here: www.oecd.org/tax/exchange-of-tax-information/convention-on-mutual-administrative-assistance-in-tax-matters.htm. The Slovak Republic also has bilateral agreements with Armenia, Australia, Austria, Belarus, Belgium, Bosnia and Herzegovina, Brazil, Bulgaria, Canada, China (People's Republic of), Croatia, Cyprus, Czech Republic, Denmark, Estonia, Ethiopia, Finland, France, Georgia, Germany, Greece, Hungary, Iceland, India, Indonesia, Iran, Ireland, Israel, Italy, Japan, Kazakhstan, Korea, Kuwait, Latvia, Libya, Lithuania, Luxembourg, Malaysia, Malta, Mexico, Moldova, Mongolia, Montenegro, Netherlands, Nigeria, North Macedonia, Norway, Poland, Portugal, Romania, Russia, Serbia, Singapore, Slovenia, South Africa, Spain, Sri Lanka, Sweden, Switzerland, Syrian Arab Republic, Chinese Taipei, Tunisia, Turkey, Turkmenistan, Ukraine, United Arab Emirates, United Kingdom, United States, Uzbekistan and Viet Nam.

[2] Patent box.

Slovenia

Slovenia has met all aspects of the terms of reference (OECD, 2017[3]) (ToR) for the calendar year 2019 (year in review) and no recommendations are made.

Slovenia can legally issue three types of rulings within the scope of the transparency framework.

In practice, Slovenia issued rulings within the scope of the transparency framework as follows:

- Eight past rulings;
- For the period 1 April 2016 - 31 December 2016: no future rulings;
- For the calendar year 2017: one future ruling;
- For the calendar year 2018: one future ruling; and
- For the year in review: two future rulings.

No peer input was received in respect of the exchanges of information on rulings received from Slovenia.

A. The information gathering process

1013. Slovenia can legally issue the following three types of rulings within the scope of the transparency framework: (i) cross-border unilateral APAs and any other cross-border unilateral tax rulings (such as an advance tax ruling) covering transfer pricing or the application of transfer pricing principles; (ii) permanent establishment rulings; and (iii) related party conduit rulings.

1014. For Slovenia, past rulings are any tax rulings within scope that are issued either: (i) on or after 1 January 2014 but before 1 April 2016; or (ii) on or after 1 January 2010 but before 1 January 2014, provided they were still in effect as at 1 January 2014. Future rulings are any tax rulings within scope that are issued on or after 1 April 2016.

1015. In the prior years' peer review reports, it was determined that Slovenia's undertakings to identify past and future rulings and all potential exchange jurisdictions were sufficient to meet the minimum standard. In addition, it was determined that Slovenia's review and supervision mechanism was sufficient to meet the minimum standard. Slovenia's implementation remains unchanged, and therefore continues to meet the minimum standard.

1016. Slovenia has met all of the ToR for the information gathering process and no recommendations are made.

B. The exchange of information

1017. In the prior years' peer review reports, it was determined that Slovenia's process for the completion and exchange of templates were sufficient to meet the minimum standard. With respect to past rulings, no further action was required. Slovenia's implementation in this regard remains unchanged and therefore continues to meet the minimum standard.

1018. Slovenia has international agreements permitting spontaneous exchange of information, including being a party to the (i) *Multilateral Convention on Mutual Administrative Assistance in Tax Matters: Amended by the 2010 Protocol* (OECD/Council of Europe, 2011[4]) ("the Convention"), (ii) the Directive 2011/16/EU with all other European Union Member States and (iii) bilateral agreements in force with 60 jurisdictions.[1]

1019. For the year in review, the timeliness of exchanges is as follows:

Future rulings in the scope of the transparency framework	Number of exchanges transmitted within three months of the information becoming available to the competent authority or immediately after legal impediments have been lifted	Delayed exchanges		
		Number of exchanges transmitted later than three months of the information on rulings becoming available to the competent authority	Reasons for the delays	Any other comments
	1	1	Lack of staff due to illness.	The exchange was made with a delay of 18 days, therefore no recommendation is made.

Follow up requests received for exchange of the ruling	Number	Average time to provide response	Number of requests not answered
	0	0	0

1020. Because of staff issues due to illness, one exchange was delayed with 18 days. As this was a one-time issue, and information on the ruling has already been exchanged, no recommendation is made.

1021. Slovenia has the necessary legal basis for spontaneous exchange of information, a process for completing the templates in a timely way and has completed all exchanges. Slovenia has met all of the ToR for the exchange of information process and no recommendations are made.

C. Statistics (ToR IV)

1022. The statistics for the year in review are as follows:

Category of ruling	Number of exchanges	Jurisdictions exchanged with
Cross-border unilateral advance pricing agreements (APAs) and any other cross-border unilateral tax rulings (such as an advance tax ruling) covering transfer pricing or the application of transfer pricing principles	*De minimis* rule applies	N/A
Permanent establishment rulings	0	N/A
Related party conduit rulings	0	N/A
De minimis rule	2	N/A
Total	2	

D. Matters related to intellectual property regimes (ToR I.4.1.3)

1023. Slovenia does not offer an intellectual property regime for which transparency requirements under the Action 5 Report (OECD, 2015[1]) were imposed.

Summary of recommendations on implementation of the transparency framework

Aspect of implementation of the transparency framework that should be improved	Recommendation for improvement
Slovenia experienced some delays in exchanging information on one future ruling.	No recommendation is made because Slovenia completed the exchange on the delayed future ruling quickly after the issues were identified and resolved, and this is not a recurring issue.

References

OECD (2017), *BEPS Action 5 on Harmful Tax Practices - Terms of Reference and Methodology for the Conduct of the Peer Reviews of the Action 5 Transparency Framework*, OECD Publishing, Paris, http://www.oecd.org/tax/beps/beps-action-5-harmful-tax-practices-peer-review-transparency-framework.pdf. [3]

OECD (2015), *Countering Harmful Tax Practices More Effectively, Taking into Account Transparency and Substance, Action 5 - 2015 Final Report*, OECD/G20 Base Erosion and Profit Shifting Project, OECD Publishing, Paris, https://dx.doi.org/10.1787/9789264241190-en. [1]

OECD/Council of Europe (2011), *The Multilateral Convention on Mutual Administrative Assistance in Tax Matters: Amended by the 2010 Protocol*, OECD Publishing, Paris, https://dx.doi.org/10.1787/9789264115606-en. [4]

Notes

[1] Parties to the Convention are available here: www.oecd.org/tax/exchange-of-tax-information/convention-on-mutual-administrative-assistance-in-tax-matters.htm. Slovenia also has bilateral agreements with Albania, Armenia, Austria, Azerbaijan, Belgium, Belarus, Bosnia and Herzegovina, Bulgaria, Canada, China (People's Republic of), Croatia, Cyprus, Czech Republic, Denmark, Estonia, Finland, France, Georgia, Germany, Greece, Hungary, Iceland, India, Iran, Ireland, Isle Of Man, Israel, Italy, Japan, Kazakhstan, Korea, Kosovo, Kuwait, Latvia, Lithuania, Luxembourg, Malta, Moldova, Netherlands, North Macedonia, Norway, Poland, Portugal, Qatar, Romania, Russia, Serbia, Montenegro, Singapore, Slovak Republic, Spain, Sweden, Switzerland, Thailand, Turkey, Ukraine, United Arab Emirates, United Kingdom, United States and Uzbekistan.

South Africa

South Africa has met all aspects of the terms of reference (OECD, 2017[3]) (ToR) for the calendar year 2019 (year in review) and no recommendations are made.

South Africa can legally issue one type of rulings within the scope of the transparency framework.

In practice, South Africa issued rulings within the scope of the transparency framework as follows:

- One past ruling;
- For the period 1 April 2016 - 31 December 2016: no future rulings;
- For the calendar year 2017: no future rulings;
- For the calendar year 2018: no future rulings; and
- For the year in review: no future rulings.

As no exchanges were required to take place, no peer input was received in respect of the exchanges of information on rulings received from South Africa.

A. The information gathering process

1024. South Africa can legally issue the following type of ruling within the scope of the transparency framework: preferential regimes.[1]

1025. For South Africa, past rulings are any tax rulings within scope that are issued either: (i) on or after 1 January 2014 but before 1 April 2016; or (ii) on or after 1 January 2010 but before 1 January 2014, provided they were still in effect as at 1 January 2014. Future rulings are any tax rulings within scope that are issued on or after 1 April 2016.

1026. In the prior years' peer review reports, it was determined that South Africa's undertakings to identify past and future rulings and all potential exchange jurisdictions were sufficient to meet the minimum standard. In addition, it was determined that South Africa's review and supervision mechanism was sufficient to meet the minimum standard. South Africa's implementation remains unchanged, and therefore continues to meet the minimum standard.

1027. South Africa's has met all of the ToR for the information gathering process and no recommendations are made.

B. The exchange of information

1028. In the prior years' peer review reports, it was determined that South Africa's process for the completion and exchange of templates were sufficient to meet the minimum standard. With respect to past rulings, no further action was required from South Africa. South Africa's implementation in this regard remains unchanged and therefore continues to meet the minimum standard.

1029. South Africa has international agreements permitting spontaneous exchange of information, including being a party to the (i) *Multilateral Convention on Mutual Administrative Assistance in Tax Matters: Amended by the 2010 Protocol* (OECD/Council of Europe, 2011[4]) ("the Convention") and (ii) bilateral agreements in force with 69 jurisdictions.[2]

1030. As South Africa was not required to exchange any information on rulings for the year in review and no data on the timeliness of exchanges can be reported.

1031. South Africa has the necessary legal basis for spontaneous exchange of information, a process for completing the templates in a timely way and has completed all exchanges. South Africa has met all of the ToR for the exchange of information process and no recommendations are made.

C. Statistics (ToR IV)

1032. As no rulings were issued, no statistics can be reported.

D. Matters related to intellectual property regimes (ToR I.4.1.3)

1033. South Africa does not offer an intellectual property regime for which transparency requirements under the Action 5 Report (OECD, 2015[1]) were imposed.

Summary of recommendations on implementation of the transparency framework

Aspect of implementation of the transparency framework that should be improved	Recommendation for improvement
	No recommendations are made.

References

OECD (2017), BEPS Action 5 on Harmful Tax Practices - Terms of Reference and Methodology for the Conduct of the Peer Reviews of the Action 5 Transparency Framework, OECD Publishing, Paris, http://www.oecd.org/tax/beps/beps-action-5-harmful-tax-practices-peer-review-transparency-framework.pdf. [3]

OECD (2015), *Countering Harmful Tax Practices More Effectively, Taking into Account Transparency and Substance, Action 5 - 2015 Final Report*, OECD/G20 Base Erosion and Profit Shifting Project, OECD Publishing, Paris, https://dx.doi.org/10.1787/9789264241190-en. [1]

OECD/Council of Europe (2011), The Multilateral Convention on Mutual Administrative Assistance in Tax Matters: Amended by the 2010 Protocol, OECD Publishing, Paris, https://dx.doi.org/10.1787/9789264115606-en. [4]

Notes

[1] With respect to the following preferential regimes: 1) Shipping regime and 2) Headquarters regime.

[2] Parties to the Convention are available here: www.oecd.org/tax/exchange-of-tax-information/convention-on-mutual-administrative-assistance-in-tax-matters.htm. South Africa also has bilateral agreements with Algeria, Australia, Austria, Belarus, Belgium, Botswana, Brazil, Bulgaria, Cameroon, Canada, Chile, China (People's Republic of), Croatia, Cyprus, Czech Republic, Democratic Republic of Congo, Denmark, Egypt, Ethiopia, Finland, France, Ghana, Greece, Hong Kong (China), Hungary, India, Indonesia, Iran, Ireland, Italy, Japan, Kenya, Korea, Lesotho, Luxembourg, Malaysia, Malta, Mauritius, Mexico, Mozambique, Namibia, Netherlands, New Zealand, Nigeria, Norway, Oman, Pakistan, Poland, Portugal, Qatar, Rwanda, Samoa, Saudi Arabia, Seychelles, Singapore, Slovak Republic, Spain, Swaziland, Sweden, Tanzania, Turkey, Turks and Caicos Islands, Uganda, Ukraine, United Arab Emirates, United Kingdom, United States, Uruguay and Zimbabwe.

Spain

Spain has met all aspects of the terms of reference (OECD, 2017[3]) (ToR) for the calendar year 2019 (year in review), except for collecting and exchanging information on new assets of existing taxpayers benefitting from the grandfathered IP regime (ToR I.4.1.3). Spain receives one recommendation on this point for the year in review.

In the prior year report, as well as in the 2017 peer review, Spain had received the same recommendation. As it has not been addressed, the recommendation remains in place.

Spain can legally issue three types of rulings within the scope of the transparency framework.

In practice, Spain issued rulings within the scope of the transparency framework as follows:

- 146 past rulings;
- For the period 1 April 2016 - 31 December 2016: 28 future rulings;
- For the calendar year 2017: 46 future rulings;
- For the calendar year 2018: 22 future rulings; and
- For the year in review: 19 future rulings.

Rulings excluding APAs are published in anonymised form.

Peer input was received from two jurisdictions in respect of the exchanges of information on rulings received from Spain. The input was positive, noting that information was complete, in a correct format and almost all received in a timely manner.

A. The information gathering process

1034. Spain can legally issue the following three types of rulings within the scope of the transparency framework: (i) preferential regimes;[1] (ii) cross-border unilateral APAs and any other cross-border unilateral tax rulings (such as an advance tax ruling) covering transfer pricing or the application of transfer pricing principles; and (iii) permanent establishment rulings.

1035. For Spain, past rulings are any tax rulings within scope that are issued either: (i) on or after 1 January 2014 but before 1 April 2016; or (ii) on or after 1 January 2010 but before 1 January 2014, provided they were still in effect as at 1 January 2014. Future rulings are any tax rulings within scope that are issued on or after 1 April 2016.

1036. In the prior years' peer review reports, it was determined that Spain's undertakings to identify past and future rulings and all potential exchange jurisdictions were sufficient to meet the minimum standard. In addition, it was determined that Spain's review and supervision mechanism was sufficient to meet the minimum standard. Spain's implementation remains unchanged, and therefore continues to meet the minimum standard.

1037. Spain has met all of the ToR for the information gathering process and no recommendations are made.

B. The exchange of information

1038. In the prior years' peer review reports, it was determined that Spain's process for the completion and exchange of templates were sufficient to meet the minimum standard. With respect to past rulings, no further action was required. Spain's implementation in this regard remains unchanged and therefore continues to meet the minimum standard.

1039. Spain has international agreements permitting spontaneous exchange of information, including being a party to the (i) *Multilateral Convention on Mutual Administrative Assistance in Tax Matters: Amended by the 2010 Protocol* (OECD/Council of Europe, 2011[4]) ("the Convention"), (ii) the Directive 2011/16/EU with all other European Union Member States and (iii) bilateral agreements in force with 93 jurisdictions.[2]

1040. For the year in review, the timeliness of exchanges is as follows:

Future rulings in the scope of the transparency framework	Number of exchanges transmitted within three months of the information becoming available to the competent authority or immediately after legal impediments have been lifted	Delayed exchanges		
		Number of exchanges transmitted later than three months of the information on rulings becoming available to the competent authority	Reasons for the delays	Any other comments
	173	0	N/A	N/A

Follow up requests received for exchange of the ruling	Number	Average time to provide response	Number of requests not answered
	0	N/A	N/A

1041. Spain has the necessary legal basis for spontaneous exchange of information, a process for completing the templates in a timely way and has completed all exchanges. Spain has met all of the ToR for the exchange of information process and no recommendations are made.

C. Statistics (ToR IV)

1042. The statistics for the year in review are as follows:

Category of ruling	Number of exchanges	Jurisdictions exchanged with
Ruling related to a preferential regime	0	N/A
Cross-border unilateral advance pricing agreements (APAs) and any other cross-border unilateral tax rulings (such as an advance tax ruling) covering transfer pricing or the application of transfer pricing principles	170	Argentina, Australia, Austria, Barbados, Belgium, Brazil, Bulgaria, Canada, Chile, China (People's Republic of), Colombia, Croatia, Czech Republic, Denmark, Finland, France, Germany, Greece, Hong Kong (China), Hungary, India, Indonesia, Ireland, Italy, Japan, Korea, Luxembourg, Mexico, Monaco, Netherlands, New Zealand, Norway, Poland, Portugal, Romania, Russia, Slovak Republic, Slovenia, South Africa, Sweden, Switzerland, Turkey, United Kingdom, United States, Uruguay
Permanent establishment rulings	*De minimis rule* applies	N/A
De minimis rule	3	
IP regimes: total exchanges on taxpayers benefitting from the third category of IP assets, new entrants benefitting from grandfathered IP regimes; and taxpayers making use of the option to treat the nexus ratio as a rebuttable presumption	0	N/A
Total	173	

D. Matters related to intellectual property regimes (ToR I.4.1.3)

1043. Spain offers three intellectual property regimes (IP regime)[3] that are subject to the transparency requirements under the Action 5 Report (OECD, 2015[1]). It states that the identification of the benefitting taxpayers will occur as follows:

- ***New entrants benefitting from the grandfathered IP regime***: Transparency obligations apply for the regimes, because grandfathering is provided to entrants that entered the regime after the relevant date from which enhanced transparency obligations apply. In the previous years' peer review reports, it was explained that Spain adopted a new tax form in August 2017 so that it could identify the new taxpayers for which the enhanced transparency requirements apply. However, Spain was not able to identify new IP assets entering the regime after the relevant date and benefiting from grandfathering. Spain was therefore recommended to identify and exchange relevant information on new assets of existing taxpayers benefitting from the grandfathered IP regime.

  In order to act on this recommendation, Spain tried to include a new reporting obligation in the tax form that was adopted in August 2017. However, in October 2017 the tax form was the subject of an appeal before the National Court. Spain notes that the appeal to the National Court has been resolved in June 2020 and the judicial procedure is now at the level of the Supreme Court. As such, this information has not been able to be collected for exchange. Therefore, the prior years' recommendation remains.
- ***Third category of IP assets***: not applicable as the regimes do not allow the third category of IP assets to qualify for the benefits.

- ***Taxpayers making use of the option to treat the nexus ratio as a rebuttable presumption***: not applicable as the regimes do not allow the nexus ratio to be treated as a rebuttable presumption.

Summary of recommendations on implementation of the transparency framework

Aspect of implementation of the transparency framework that should be improved	Recommendation for improvement
Spain has not exchanged information on new assets of existing taxpayers benefitting from the grandfathered regime, as this information was not available during the year in review. It is noted that Spain has already started to take steps to amend the tax form adopted in August 2017 to address this, but the tax form was appealed before the National Court and proceedings remained underway for the year in review.	Spain is recommended to continue its efforts to identify and exchange relevant information on new assets of existing taxpayers benefitting from the grandfathered IP regime. This recommendation remains unchanged since the 2017 and 2018 peer review reports.

References

OECD (2017), *BEPS Action 5 on Harmful Tax Practices - Terms of Reference and Methodology for the Conduct of the Peer Reviews of the Action 5 Transparency Framework*, OECD Publishing, Paris, http://www.oecd.org/tax/beps/beps-action-5-harmful-tax-practices-peer-review-transparency-framework.pdf. [3]

OECD (2015), *Countering Harmful Tax Practices More Effectively, Taking into Account Transparency and Substance, Action 5 - 2015 Final Report*, OECD/G20 Base Erosion and Profit Shifting Project, OECD Publishing, Paris, https://dx.doi.org/10.1787/9789264241190-en. [1]

OECD/Council of Europe (2011), *The Multilateral Convention on Mutual Administrative Assistance in Tax Matters: Amended by the 2010 Protocol*, OECD Publishing, Paris, https://dx.doi.org/10.1787/9789264115606-en. [4]

Notes

[1] With respect to the following preferential regimes: 1) Partial exemption for income from certain intangible assets and 2) Shipping regime.

[2] Parties to the Convention are available here: www.oecd.org/tax/exchange-of-tax-information/convention-on-mutual-administrative-assistance-in-tax-matters.htm. Spain also has bilateral agreements with: Albania, Algeria, Andorra, Argentina, Armenia, Australia, Austria, Barbados, Belarus, Belgium, Bolivia, Bosnia and Herzegovina, Brazil, Bulgaria, Canada, Chile, China (People's Republic of), Colombia, Costa Rica, Croatia, Cuba, Cyprus, Czech Republic, Dominican Republic, Ecuador, Egypt, El Salvador, Estonia, Finland, France, Georgia, Germany, Greece, Hong Kong (China), Hungary, Iceland, India, Indonesia, Iran, Ireland, Israel, Italy, Jamaica, Japan, Kazakhstan, Korea, Kuwait, Kyrgyzstan, Latvia, Lithuania, Luxembourg, Malaysia, Malta, Mexico, Moldova, Morocco, Netherlands, New Zealand, Nigeria, North Macedonia, Norway, Oman, Pakistan, Panama, Philippines, Poland, Portugal, Qatar, Romania, Russia, Saudi Arabia, Senegal, Serbia, Singapore, Slovak Republic, Slovenia, South Africa, Sweden, Switzerland,

Tajikistan, Thailand, Trinidad and Tobago, Tunisia, Turkey, Turkmenistan, Ukraine, United Arab Emirates, United Kingdom, United States, Uruguay, Uzbekistan, Venezuela and Viet Nam.

[3] These regimes are the partial exemptions for income from certain intangible assets for: 1) Federal regime, 2) Basque country and 3) Navarra.

Sri Lanka

Sri Lanka did not provide a completed peer review questionnaire to the Secretariat. It is not known whether Sri Lanka has implemented the transparency framework in line with the terms of reference (OECD, 2017[3]) (ToR) for the calendar year 2019 (year in review). Sri Lanka receives two recommendations covering the information gathering process (ToR I.4) andexchange of information (ToR II.5) for the year in review.

In the prior year report, as well as in the 2017 peer review, Sri Lanka received the same two recommendations. As they have not been addressed, the recommendations remain in place.

It is not known whether Sri Lanka can legally issue any types of ruling within the scope of the transparency framework, or whether in practice Sri Lanka issued any such rulings.

No peer input was received in respect of the exchanges of information on rulings received from Sri Lanka.

A. The information gathering process

1044. Sri Lanka was not yet able to complete the peer review questionnaire. It is not known whether Sri Lanka has implemented the transparency framework during the year in review..

Conclusion on section A

1045. Sri Lanka is recommended to ensure that it has put in place an effective information gathering process to identify all relevant past and future rulings and all potential exchange jurisdictions and to implement a review and supervision mechanism, as soon as possible (ToR I.4).

B. The exchange of information

Legal basis for spontaneous exchange of information (ToR II.5.1, II.5.2)

1046. It is not known whether Sri Lanka has the necessary domestic legal basis to exchange information spontaneously. Sri Lanka is recommended to put in place a domestic legal framework allowing spontaneous exchange of information on rulings if needed.

1047. Sri Lanka has international agreements permitting spontaneous exchange of information, including being a party to the (i) *Multilateral Convention on Mutual Administrative Assistance in Tax Matters: Amended by the 2010 Protocol* (OECD/Council of Europe, 2011[4]) ("the Convention") and (ii) bilateral agreements in force with 44 jurisdictions.[1]

Completion and exchange of templates (ToR II.5.3, II.5.4, II.5.5, II.5.6, II.5.7)

1048. It is not known whether Sri Lanka has put in place a process to exchange information on rulings in accordance with the form and timelines required by the transparency framework. Sri Lanka is recommended to ensure the timely exchange of information on rulings in the form required by the transparency framework.

Conclusion on section B

1049. Sri Lanka is recommended to put in place a domestic legal framework allowing spontaneous exchange of information on rulings and develop a process to complete the templates on relevant rulings and to ensure that the exchanges of information on rulings occur in accordance with the form and timelines under the transparency framework (ToR II.5).

C. Statistics (ToR IV)

1050. As there was no information on rulings exchanged by Sri Lanka for the year in review, no statistics can be reported.

D. Matters related to intellectual property regimes (ToR I.4.1.3)

1051. Sri Lanka does not offer an intellectual property regime for which transparency requirements under the Action 5 Report (OECD, 2015[1]) were imposed.

Summary of recommendations on implementation of the transparency framework

Aspect of implementation of the transparency framework that should be improved	Recommendation for improvement
Sri Lanka has not put in place the necessary information gathering process.	Sri Lanka is recommended to finalise its information gathering process for identifying all future rulings and potential exchange jurisdictions, with a review and supervision mechanism, as soon as possible. This recommendation remains unchanged since the 2017 and 2018 peer review reports.
Sri Lanka does not have a process to complete the templates on relevant rulings, to make them available to the Competent Authority for exchange of information, and to exchange them with relevant jurisdictions.	Sri Lanka is recommended to put in place a domestic legal framework allowing spontaneous exchange of information on rulings and to develop a process to complete the templates on relevant rulings and to ensure that the exchanges of information on rulings occur in accordance with the form and timelines under the transparency framework. This recommendation remains unchanged since the 2017 and 2018 peer review reports.

References

OECD (2017), *BEPS Action 5 on Harmful Tax Practices - Terms of Reference and Methodology for the Conduct of the Peer Reviews of the Action 5 Transparency Framework*, OECD Publishing, Paris, http://www.oecd.org/tax/beps/beps-action-5-harmful-tax-practices-peer-review-transparency-framework.pdf. [3]

OECD (2015), *Countering Harmful Tax Practices More Effectively, Taking into Account Transparency and Substance, Action 5 - 2015 Final Report*, OECD/G20 Base Erosion and Profit Shifting Project, OECD Publishing, Paris, https://dx.doi.org/10.1787/9789264241190-en. [1]

OECD/Council of Europe (2011), *The Multilateral Convention on Mutual Administrative Assistance in Tax Matters: Amended by the 2010 Protocol*, OECD Publishing, Paris, https://dx.doi.org/10.1787/9789264115606-en. [4]

Notes

[1] Parties to the Convention are available here: www.oecd.org/tax/exchange-of-tax-information/convention-on-mutual-administrative-assistance-in-tax-matters.htm. Sri Lanka also has bilateral agreements Sri Lanka also has bilateral agreements in force with Australia, Bangladesh, Bahrain, Belarus, Belgium, Canada, China (People's Republic of), Czech Republic, Denmark, Finland, France, Germany, Hong Kong (China), India, Indonesia, Iran, Italy, Japan, Korea, Kuwait, Luxembourg, Malaysia, Mauritius, Nepal, Netherlands, Norway, Oman, Pakistan, Palestinian Authority, Philippines, Poland, Qatar, Romania, Russia, Saudi Arabia, Seychelles, Singapore, Sweden, Switzerland, Thailand, United Arab Emirates, United Kingdom, United States, and Viet Nam.

Sweden

Sweden has met all aspects of the terms of reference (OECD, 2017[3]) (ToR) for the calendar year 2019 (year in review), except for identifying all potential exchange jurisdictions for future rulings (ToR I.4.2.1). Sweden receives one recommendation on this point for the year in review.

In the prior year report, as well as in the 2016 and 2017 peer reviews, Sweden received the same recommendation. As it has not been addressed, the recommendation remains in place.

Sweden can legally issue three types of rulings within the scope of the transparency framework.

In practice, Sweden issued rulings within the scope of the transparency framework as follows:

- 28 past rulings;
- For the period 1 April 2016 - 31 December 2016: five future rulings;
- For the calendar year 2017: three future rulings;
- For the calendar year 2018: six future rulings; and
- For the year in review: one future ruling.

Sweden publishes some of their tax rulings in redacted form on Swedish Board of Advanced Tax Rulings' website.[1]

No peer input was received in respect of the exchanges of information on rulings received from Sweden.

A. The information gathering process

1052. Sweden can legally issue the following three types of rulings within the scope of the transparency framework: (i) preferential regimes;[2] (ii) permanent establishment rulings; and (iii) related party conduit rulings.

Past rulings (ToR I.4.1.1, I.4.1.2, I.4.2.1, I.4.2.2)

1053. For Sweden, past rulings are any tax rulings within scope that are issued either: (i) on or after 1 January 2014 but before 1 April 2016; or (ii) on or after 1 January 2010 but before 1 January 2014, provided they were still in effect as at 1 January 2014.

1054. In the prior years' peer review reports, it was determined that Sweden's undertakings to identify past rulings and all potential exchange jurisdictions were sufficient to meet the minimum standard. Sweden's implementation in this regard remains unchanged, and therefore continues to meet the minimum standard.

Future rulings (ToR I.4.1.1, I.4.1.2, I.4.2.1)

1055. For Sweden, future rulings are any tax rulings within scope that are issued on or after 1 April 2016.

1056. In the prior years' peer review reports, Sweden was recommended to amend its rulings practice in order to be able to identify all potential exchange jurisdictions for future rulings.

1057. During the year in review, the Swedish Ministry of Finance has drafted new legislation in order to fulfil the Action 5 minimum standard. The proposed legislation will be presented to parliament for approval in 2020. The Swedish Tax Agency ("the STA") has also amended its ruling practice and framework. Sweden indicates that they will make the last changes to the STA framework as soon as the new legislation has been approved by parliament. In most cases, Sweden reports it is able to identify potential exchange jurisdictions. According to the new legislation and the new STA framework, the STA will be able to identify all potential exchange jurisdictions regarding future rulings. However this cannot be finalised until the legislation on tax rulings has been approved by the Swedish parliament, and therefore, the prior year recommendation remains.

Review and supervision (ToR I.4.3)

1058. In the prior years' peer review reports, it was determined that Sweden's review and supervision mechanism was sufficient to meet the minimum standard. Sweden's implementation in this regard remains unchanged, and therefore continues to meet the minimum standard.

Conclusion on section A

1059. Sweden has met all of the ToR for the information gathering except for identifying all potential exchange jurisdictions for future rulings (ToR I.4.2.1). Sweden is recommended to continue its efforts to finalise its rulings practice to require taxpayers to provide information on all potential exchange jurisdictions for future rulings as soon as possible.

B. The exchange of information

1060. In the prior years' peer review reports, it was determined that Sweden's process for the completion and exchange of templates were sufficient to meet the minimum standard. With respect to past rulings, no further action was required. Sweden's implementation in this regard remains unchanged and therefore continues to meet the minimum standard.

1061. Sweden has international agreements permitting spontaneous exchange of information, including being a party to the (i) *Multilateral Convention on Mutual Administrative Assistance in Tax Matters: Amended by the 2010 Protocol* (OECD/Council of Europe, 2011[4]) ("the Convention"), (ii) the Directive 2011/16/EU with all other European Union Member States, (iii) the Nordic Convention on Assistance in Tax Matters and (iv) bilateral agreements in force with 62 jurisdictions.[3]

1062. For the year in review, the timeliness of exchanges is as follows:

Future rulings in the scope of the transparency framework	Number of exchanges transmitted within three months of the information becoming available to the competent authority or immediately after legal impediments have been lifted	Delayed exchanges		
		Number of exchanges transmitted later than three months of the information on rulings becoming available to the competent authority	Reasons for the delays	Any other comments
	3	0	N/A	N/A

Follow up requests received for exchange of the ruling	Number	Average time to provide response	Number of requests not answered
	0	N/A	N/A

1063. Sweden has the necessary legal basis for spontaneous exchange of information, a process for completing the templates in a timely way and has completed all exchanges. Sweden has met all of the ToR for the exchange of information process and no recommendations are made.

C. Statistics (ToR IV)

1064. The statistics for the year in review are as follows:

Category of ruling	Number of exchanges	Jurisdictions exchanged with
Ruling related to a preferential regime	*De minimis* rule applies	N/A
Permanent establishment rulings	*De minimis* rule applies	N/A
Related party conduit rulings	0	N/A
De minimis rule	3	N/A
Total	3	

D. Matters related to intellectual property regimes (ToR I.4.1.3)

1065. Sweden does not offer an intellectual property regime for which transparency requirements under the Action 5 Report (OECD, 2015[1]) were imposed.

Summary of recommendations on implementation of the transparency framework

Aspect of implementation of the transparency framework that should be improved	Recommendation for improvement
Sweden experienced delays in identifying all potential exchange jurisdictions for future rulings.	Sweden is recommended to continue its efforts to finalise its rulings practice to require taxpayers to provide information on all potential exchange jurisdictions for future rulings as soon as possible. This recommendation remains unchanged since the 2016, 2017 and 2018 peer review reports.

References

OECD (2017), *BEPS Action 5 on Harmful Tax Practices - Terms of Reference and Methodology for the Conduct of the Peer Reviews of the Action 5 Transparency Framework*, OECD Publishing, Paris, http://www.oecd.org/tax/beps/beps-action-5-harmful-tax-practices-peer-review-transparency-framework.pdf. [3]

OECD (2015), *Countering Harmful Tax Practices More Effectively, Taking into Account Transparency and Substance, Action 5 - 2015 Final Report*, OECD/G20 Base Erosion and Profit Shifting Project, OECD Publishing, Paris, https://dx.doi.org/10.1787/9789264241190-en. [1]

OECD/Council of Europe (2011), *The Multilateral Convention on Mutual Administrative Assistance in Tax Matters: Amended by the 2010 Protocol*, OECD Publishing, Paris, https://dx.doi.org/10.1787/9789264115606-en. [4]

Notes

1 Available at: https://www.skatterattsnamnden.se/.

2 With respect to the following preferential regime: Tonnage tax regime.

3 Parties to the Convention are available here: www.oecd.org/tax/exchange-of-tax-information/convention-on-mutual-administrative-assistance-in-tax-matters.htm. Parties to the Nordic Convention on Assistance in Tax Matters are Denmark, Faroe Islands, Finland, Iceland, Norway and Sweden. Sweden also has bilateral agreements with Argentina, Armenia, Australia, Austria, Barbados, Belgium, Botswana, Brazil, Bulgaria, Canada, Chile, China (People's Republic of), Croatia, Czech Republic, Egypt, Estonia, France, Georgia, Germany, Greece, Hungary, India, Indonesia, Ireland, Israel, Italy, Jamaica, Japan, Kazakhstan, Kenya, Korea, Latvia, Lithuania, Luxembourg, Malaysia, Malta, Mauritius, Mexico, Netherlands, New Zealand, Nigeria, North Macedonia, Pakistan, Poland, Portugal, Romania, Russia, Saudi Arabia, Serbia, Singapore, Slovak Republic, Slovenia, South Africa, Spain, Sri Lanka, Switzerland, Thailand, Trinidad and Tobago, Tunisia, Turkey, Ukraine, United Kingdom, United States, Viet Nam and Zambia.

Switzerland

Switzerland has met all aspects of the terms of reference (OECD, 2017[3]) (ToR) for the calendar year 2019 (year in review), except for identifying all past rulings in scope of the transparency framework (ToR I.4.1.2), the timely provision of information on rulings to the Competent Authority (ToR II.5.5) and the timely exchange of information on past and future rulings (ToR II.5.6). Switzerland receives three recommendations on this point for the year in review.

In the prior year report, no recommendations were made. However, as there were new circumstances, recommendations have been made as relevant.

Switzerland can legally issue four types of rulings within the scope of the transparency framework.

In practice, Switzerland issued rulings within the scope of the transparency framework as follows:

- 871 past rulings;
- For the calendar year 2017: 300 future rulings,
- For the calendar year 2018: 228 future rulings, and
- For the year in review: 293 future rulings.

Peer input was received from six jurisdictions in respect of the exchanges of information on rulings received from Switzerland. The input was generally positive, noting that information was complete, in a correct format and almost all received in a timely manner. Some peers noted that the exchange of information on rulings from Switzerland was delayed.

A. The information gathering process

1066. Switzerland can legally issue the following four types of rulings within the scope of the transparency framework: (i) preferential regimes;[1] (ii) cross-border unilateral APAs and any other cross-border unilateral tax rulings (such as an advance tax ruling) covering transfer pricing or the application of transfer pricing principles; (iii) permanent establishment rulings; and (iv) related party conduit rulings.

Past rulings (ToR I.4.1.1, I.4.1.2, I.4.2.1, I.4.2.2)

1067. For Switzerland, past rulings are any tax rulings within scope that are issued on or after 1 January 2010 until 31 December 2016, provided they were still in effect as at 1 January 2018.

1068. In the prior years' peer review reports, it was determined that Switzerland's undertakings to identify past rulings and all potential exchange jurisdictions were sufficient to meet the minimum standard. However, during the year in review, the 26 Swiss cantons (which have competence to issue rulings and are each responsible for identifying rulings in accordance with the domestic law) identified an additional 40 past rulings that had not otherwise been identified in the prior year. Although this is a small error relative to the overall volume of past rulings issued by Switzerland, in order to ensure that similar issues are not encountered in future, Switzerland is recommended to strengthen its information gathering process identifying all past rulings in scope of the transparency framework.

Future rulings (ToR I.4.1.1, I.4.1.2, I.4.2.1)

1069. For Switzerland, future rulings are any tax rulings within scope that are issued on or after 1 January 2017, provided they are still in effect on or after 1 January 2018.

1070. In the prior years' peer review reports, it was determined that Switzerland's undertakings to identify future rulings and all potential exchange jurisdictions were sufficient to meet the minimum standard. Switzerland's undertakings in this regard remain unchanged, and therefore continue to meet the minimum standard.

Review and supervision (ToR I.4.3)

1071. In the prior years' peer review reports, it was determined that Switzerland's review and supervision mechanism was sufficient to meet the minimum standard. As noted above, during the year in review, Switzerland identified an addition 40 past rulings. As part of the efforts to strengthen the information gathering process, Switzerland is therefore recommended to strengthen its review and supervision mechanism to ensure that the information gathering process is working effectively.

Conclusion on section A

1072. Switzerland has met all of the ToR for the information gathering process except for identifying all past rulings in scope of the transparency framework (ToR I.4.1.2). Switzerland is recommended to strengthen its information gathering process identifying all past rulings in scope of the transparency framework and its review and supervision mechanism to ensure that the information gathering process is working effectively.

B. The exchange of information

Legal basis for spontaneous exchange of information (ToR II.5.1, II.5.2)

1073. Switzerland has the necessary domestic legal basis to exchange information spontaneously. Switzerland notes that there are no legal or practical impediments that prevent the spontaneous exchange of information on rulings as contemplated in the Action 5 minimum standard.

1074. Switzerland international agreement permitting spontaneous exchange of information is the *Multilateral Convention on Mutual Administrative Assistance in Tax Matters: Amended by the 2010 Protocol* (OECD/Council of Europe, 2011[4]) ("the Convention").[2] The necessary domestic and international legal framework for spontaneous exchange of information entered into force on 1 January 2017, allowing for exchanges from 1 January 2018.

Completion and exchange of templates (ToR II.5.3, II.5.4, II.5.5, II.5.6, II.5.7)

1075. In the prior years' peer review reports, it was determined that Switzerland's process for the completion and exchange of templates were sufficient to meet the minimum standard. However, during the year in review, Switzerland experienced recurring delayed exchanges for both past rulings and future rulings.

1076. Switzerland indicates that rulings may be issued both by cantonal and federal tax authorities. As noted above, during the year in review, Switzerland identified 40 additional past rulings. The Competent Authority exchanged the information on these additional rulings as soon as it received them. In addition, with respect to other rulings, exchanges were delayed because the Competent Authority, had to revert to the cantonal tax authorities in order to guarantee the quality of the text in the summary box in the template for the recipient jurisdictions. In some cases, the cantonal tax authorities needed to revert to the taxpayers, to request additional information in order to complete the template (e.g. to complete the text in the summary box, and/or other additional information on the affected entities, such as their addresses and tax identification numbers). As taxpayers are usually required to fill out the template before a future ruling is approved by the tax authority, this was generally expected to be less of an issue for future rulings than for past rulings, but in practice, the Competent Authority had to revert to the cantonal authorities for both past and future rulings.

1077. Switzerland notes that as more experience is gained with filling out the templates correctly, the need for the Competent Authority to revert to cantons is expected to become less frequent. Switzerland further notes that it considered the additional time taken to be important in order to ensure a better quality of the information transmitted.

1078. Switzerland notes that information on past rulings still may become available from the cantons. Therefore, it cannot guarantee that all information on past rulings has yet been exchanged.

1079. Switzerland is recommended to continue its efforts to strengthen its process and allocation of resources and to ensure the accurate and timely completion of the template summaries, in order to reduce the timelines for providing the information on past and future rulings to the Competent Authority (ToR II.5.5).

1080. For the year in review, the timeliness of exchanges is as follows:

Past rulings in the scope of the transparency framework	Number of exchanges transmitted by 31 December 2019	Delayed exchanges		
		Number of exchanges not transmitted by 31 December 2019	Reasons for the delays	Any other comments

	442[3]	128	See below.	108 exchanges were transmitted by the end of February 2020 and further 20 exchanges were transmitted by mid July 2020.
Future rulings in the scope of the transparency framework	Number of exchanges transmitted within three months of the information becoming available to the competent authority or immediately after legal impediments have been lifted	Delayed exchanges		
		Number of exchanges transmitted later than three months of the information on rulings becoming available to the competent authority	Reasons for the delays	Any other comments
	338	174	Need to substantiate summaries and revert to cantonal tax authorities; number of exchanges for the year in review considerably higher than expected.	N/A
Total	780	302		

Follow up requests received for exchange of the ruling	Number	Average time to provide response	Number of requests not answered
	0	N/A	N/A

1081. Switzerland encountered delays with the exchange of information on both past rulings and future rulings. This was due to issues regarding completion of the templates as described above and also personnel issues. Switzerland indicates that the workload of the Competent Authority has significantly increased over the last few years. This concerns both spontaneous exchange of information on rulings and other forms of exchanges. For spontaneous exchange of information on rulings, the number of exchanges on future rulings for the year in review was considerably higher than initially expected, because of an unexpected demand by taxpayers for rulings. The Competent Authority has internally reorganised in the fall of 2019 to respond to these challenges and have the appropriate human resources and processes in place. New staff has been recruited and new teams have been set up.[4] In order to optimise processes, members of staff have more clearly defined and less diversified tasks, which enables those responsible for spontaneous exchange of information to focus more on this work stream. Furthermore, the IT System has been enhanced so that the steps of the transmission can be monitored more accurately.

1082. Switzerland is recommended to continue to ensure that all information on past and future rulings is exchanged as soon as possible (ToR II.5.6).

Conclusion on section B

1083. Switzerland has met all of the ToR for the information gathering process except for the timely provision of information on rulings to the Competent Authority (ToR II.5.5) and the timely exchange of information on past and future rulings (ToR II.5.6). Switzerland is recommended to continue its efforts to strengthen its process and allocation of resources and to ensure the accurate and timely completion of the summary templates, in order to reduce the timelines for providing the information on future rulings to the

Competent Authority. In addition, Switzerland is recommended to continue to ensure that all information on past and future rulings is exchanged as soon as possible.

C. Statistics (ToR IV)

1084. The statistics for the year in review are as follows:

Category of ruling	Number of exchanges	Jurisdictions exchanged with
Ruling related to a preferential regime	514	Albania, Argentina, Australia, Austria, Azerbaijan, Barbados, Belgium, Brazil, Bulgaria, Canada, Chile, China (People's Republic of), Colombia, Costa Rica, Croatia, Cyprus, Czech Republic, Denmark, Estonia, Finland, France, Germany, Ghana, Greece, Guernsey, Hong Kong (China), Hungary, India, Indonesia, Ireland, Israel, Italy, Japan, Jersey, Kazakhstan, Korea, Latvia, Liechtenstein, Lithuania, Luxembourg, Malta, Mauritius, Mexico, Moldova, Netherlands, New Zealand, Nigeria, Norway, Pakistan, Poland, Portugal, Romania, Russia, Saudi Arabia, Singapore, Slovak Republic, Slovenia, South Africa, Spain, Sweden, Tunisia, Turkey, Ukraine, United Kingdom, Uruguay
Cross-border unilateral advance pricing agreements (APAs) and any other cross-border unilateral tax rulings (such as an advance tax ruling) covering transfer pricing or the application of transfer pricing principles	408	Albania, Argentina, Australia, Austria, Azerbaijan, Barbados, Belgium, Brazil, Bulgaria, Canada, Chile, China (People's Republic of), Colombia, Costa Rica, Croatia, Curaçao, Cyprus, Czech Republic, Denmark, Estonia, Finland, France, Germany, Ghana, Greece, Guernsey, Hong Kong (China),Hungary, India, Indonesia, Ireland, Isle of Man, Israel, Italy, Japan, Jersey, Kazakhstan, Korea, Latvia, Liechtenstein, Lithuania, Luxembourg, Malta, Mauritius, Mexico, Moldova, Netherlands, New Zealand, Nigeria, Norway, Pakistan, Panama, Poland, Portugal, Romania, Russia, Saint Kitts and Nevis, Saudi Arabia, Senegal, Singapore, Slovak Republic, Slovenia, South Africa, Spain, Sweden, Tunisia, Turkey, Ukraine, United Kingdom, Uruguay
Permanent establishment rulings	162	Albania, Argentina, Australia, Austria, Azerbaijan, Barbados, Belgium, Brazil, Bulgaria, Canada, Chile, China (People's Republic of), Colombia, Costa Rica, Croatia, Curaçao, Cyprus, Czech Republic, Denmark, Estonia, France, Germany, Ghana, Greece, Guernsey, Hong Kong (China), Hungary, India, Indonesia, Ireland, Israel, Italy, Japan, Jersey, Kazakhstan, Korea, Latvia, Lithuania, Luxembourg, Malaysia, Mauritius, Mexico, Moldova, Netherlands, New

		Zealand, Nigeria, Norway, Poland, Portugal, Romania, Russia, Saudi Arabia, Singapore, Slovak Republic, Slovenia, South Africa, Spain, Sweden, Tunisia, Ukraine, United Kingdom
Related party conduit rulings	3	*De minimis* rule applies
Total	1 087[5]	

D. Matters related to intellectual property regimes (ToR I.4.1.3)

1085. Switzerland offered an intellectual property regime (IP regime)[6] that was amended as of 1 January 2016 and is not subject to the transparency requirements under the Action 5 Report (OECD, 2015[1]), because:

- ***New entrants benefitting from the grandfathered IP regime***: the IP regime is a grandfathered IP regime, but there were no new entrants in the period after the relevant date from which the enhanced transparency obligations apply.
- ***Third category of IP assets***: not applicable as the regime does not allow the third category of IP assets to qualify for the benefits.
- ***Taxpayers making the use of the option to treat the nexus ratio as a rebuttable presumption***: not applicable as the regime does not allow the nexus ratio to be treated as a rebuttable presumption.

Summary of recommendations on implementation of the transparency framework

Aspect of implementation of the transparency framework that should be improved	Recommendation for improvement
Switzerland identified additional past rulings that were not previously captured.	Switzerland is recommended to strengthen its information gathering process identifying all past rulings in scope of the transparency framework and its review and supervision mechanism to ensure that the information gathering process is working effectively.
Switzerland experienced delays in the provision of rulings to the Competent Authority, as additional steps were required in order to ensure the summary templates provided to the Competent Authority were complete and correct.	Switzerland is recommended to continue its efforts to strengthen its process and allocation of resources and to ensure the accurate and timely completion of the summary templates, in order to reduce the timelines for providing the information on past and future rulings to the Competent Authority.
Switzerland experienced some delays in exchanging information on past and future rulings.	Switzerland is recommended to continue to ensure that all information on past and future rulings is exchanged as soon as possible.

References

OECD (2017), *BEPS Action 5 on Harmful Tax Practices - Terms of Reference and Methodology for the Conduct of the Peer Reviews of the Action 5 Transparency Framework*, OECD Publishing, Paris, http://www.oecd.org/tax/beps/beps-action-5-harmful-tax-practices-peer-review-transparency-framework.pdf. [3]

OECD (2015), *Countering Harmful Tax Practices More Effectively, Taking into Account Transparency and Substance, Action 5 - 2015 Final Report*, OECD/G20 Base Erosion and Profit Shifting Project, OECD Publishing, Paris, https://dx.doi.org/10.1787/9789264241190-en. [1]

OECD/Council of Europe (2011), *The Multilateral Convention on Mutual Administrative Assistance in Tax Matters: Amended by the 2010 Protocol*, OECD Publishing, Paris, https://dx.doi.org/10.1787/9789264115606-en. [4]

Notes

[1] With respect to the following preferential regimes: 1) Auxiliary company regime (previously referred to as domiciliary company regime, 2) Mixed company regime, 3) Commissionaire ruling regime, 4) Holding company regime (cantonal level), 5) Licence box (Canton of Nidwalden).

[2] Parties to the Convention are available here: www.oecd.org/tax/exchange-of-tax-information/convention-on-mutual-administrative-assistance-in-tax-matters.htm.

[3] The 2018 peer review report noted a total number of 352 delayed exchanges by 31 December 2018. The difference between the total delayed exchanges of past rulings in 2018 and the total exchanges of past rulings in 2019 is due to the fact that during the year in review, Switzerland exchanged further past rulings already identified by the end of 2018 and identified additional past rulings that led to additional exchanges.

[4] Switzerland notes that it has a federalist structure and that the cantons therefore have organisational autonomy. Hence, the Competent Authority has no insight into the specific (re-)organisations in the cantons.

[5] Switzerland explained that in some cases the ruling templates identified in the statistics on exchanges above fall in two or more categories (42 in two categories, 1 in three categories) which has led to some multiple counting in this table. For the year in review, 815 individual exchanges took place.

[6] Canton of Nidwalden – License box.

Thailand

Thailand has met all aspects of the terms of reference (OECD, 2017[3]) (ToR) for the calendar year 2019 (year in review) and no recommendations are made, except for having the domestic legal framework for spontaneous exchange of information on rulings (ToR II.5.1) and the timely exchange of information on past and future rulings (ToR II.5.6). Thailand receives two recommendations on these points for the year in review.

In the prior year report, Thailand had received one recommendation. As it has not been addressed, the recommendation remains in place.

Thailand can legally issue one type of ruling within the scope of the transparency framework.

In practice, Thailand issued rulings within the scope of the transparency framework as follows:

- 182 past rulings;
- For the calendar year 2018: 36 future rulings, and
- For the year in review: 157 future rulings.

As no exchanges took place, no peer input was received in respect of the exchanges of information on rulings received from Thailand.

A. The information gathering process

1086. Thailand can legally issue the following type of rulings within the scope of the transparency framework: preferential regimes.[1]

1087. For Thailand, past rulings are any tax rulings within scope that are issued either: (i) on or after 1 January 2016 but before 1 April 2018; or (ii) on or after 1 January 2014 but before 1 January 2016, provided they were still in effect as at 1 January 2016. Future rulings are any tax rulings within scope that are issued on or after 1 April 2018.

1088. In the prior year's peer review report, it was determined that Thailand's undertakings to identify past and future rulings and all potential exchange jurisdictions were sufficient to meet the minimum standard. In addition, it was determined that Thailand's review and supervision mechanism was sufficient to meet the minimum standard. Thailand's implementation remains unchanged, and therefore continues to meet the minimum standard.

1089. Thailand has met all of the ToR for the information gathering process and no recommendations are made.

B. The exchange of information

Legal basis for spontaneous exchange of information (ToR II.5.1, II.5.2)

1090. In the previous year's peer review report, it was noted that Thailand has the necessary domestic legal basis to exchange information spontaneously. However, Thailand has corrected this information and indicated that there is a legal impediment that prevents the spontaneous exchange of information on rulings as contemplated in the Action 5 minimum standard, meaning that no such domestic legal basis exists. The Revenue Department is currently not permitted by law to exchange information with respect to tax rulings. The reason for this is that under Section 10 of the Revenue Code, taxpayers' information is protected from disclosure to any other persons unless there is a power to do so under the law. As tax rulings concern the information of taxpayers, Thailand is prohibited to exchange them to treaty partners without requests.

1091. Thailand is in the process of implementing a new legal provision with respect to exchange of information to address this issue for the purposes of complying with the transparency framework. This will involve an amendment to Section 10 of the Revenue Code. This Exchange of Information Bill is currently undergoing the legislative process and is expected to enter into force by mid-2021. Thailand is recommended to finalise the amendments to put the domestic legal basis in place to commence exchanges as soon as possible.

1092. Thailand has international agreements permitting spontaneous exchange of information, including bilateral agreements in force with 60 jurisdictions.[2]

Completion and exchange of templates (ToR II.5.3, II.5.4, II.5.5, II.5.6, II.5.7)

1093. In the prior year peer review report, it was determined that Thailand's process for the completion and exchange of templates were sufficient to meet the minimum standard. Although Thailand could not legally exchange the information, Thailand is preparing the templates to be in a position to complete the exchanges as soon as the legal basis is in force. However, Thailand notes that although the appropriate process for the completion and exchange of templates has been implemented, in practice, the Revenue Department lacked the appropriate resources to be able to complete all templates in accordance with the timelines under the transparency framework. Therefore, Thailand is recommended to ensure that all information on past and future rulings is exchanged as soon as possible after the legal basis is in force.

1094. For the year in review, the timeliness of exchanges is as follows:

Past rulings in the scope of the transparency framework	Number of exchanges transmitted by 31 December 2019	Delayed exchanges		
		Number of exchanges not transmitted by 31 December 2019	Reasons for the delays	Any other comments
	0	182	See previous paragraph.	N/A
Future rulings in the scope of the transparency framework	Number of exchanges transmitted within three months of the information becoming available to the competent authority or immediately after legal impediments have been lifted	Delayed exchanges		
		Number of exchanges transmitted later than three months of the information on rulings becoming available to the competent authority	Reasons for the delays	Any other comments
	0	193	See previous paragraph.	N/A
Total	0	375		

Follow up requests received for exchange of the ruling	Number	Average time to provide response	Number of requests not answered
	0	N/A	N/A

Conclusion on section B

1095. Thailand is recommended to finalise the amendments to put the domestic legal basis in place to commence exchanges and to ensure that all information on past and future rulings is exchanged as soon as possible (ToR II.5.1 and II.5.6).

C. Statistics (ToR IV)

1096. As there was no information on rulings exchanged by Thailand for the year in review, no statistics can be reported.

D. Matters related to intellectual property regimes (ToR I.4.1.3)

1097. In the previous year in review, Thailand offered three non-nexus compliant IP regimes.[3] During the year in review, Thailand abolished these regimes without providing grandfathering and as such, no enhanced transparency requirements apply.

1098. In addition, Thailand offers an intellectual property regime (IP regime)[4] that is not subject to the transparency requirements under the Action 5 Report (OECD, 2015[1]), because:

- ***New entrants benefitting from the grandfathered IP regime***: as this is a new IP regime rather than a grandfathered IP regime, transparency on new entrants is not relevant.
- ***Third category of IP assets***: not applicable as the regime does not allow the third category of IP assets to qualify for the benefits.
- ***Taxpayers making use of the option to treat the nexus ratio as a rebuttable presumption***: not applicable as the regime does not allow the nexus ratio to be treated as a rebuttable presumption.

Summary of recommendations on implementation of the transparency framework

Aspect of implementation of the transparency framework that should be improved	Recommendation for improvement
Thailand does not yet have the necessary legal framework in place for exchanging information on rulings.	Thailand is recommended to finalise the amendments to put the domestic legal basis in place to commence exchanges as soon as possible.
Thailand did not undertake spontaneous exchange of information on all tax rulings within scope of the transparency framework during the year in review.	Thailand is recommended to ensure that all information on past and future rulings is exchanged as soon as possible after the domestic legal basis is in force. This recommendation remains unchanged since the prior year's peer review report.

References

OECD (2017), *BEPS Action 5 on Harmful Tax Practices - Terms of Reference and Methodology for the Conduct of the Peer Reviews of the Action 5 Transparency Framework*, OECD Publishing, Paris, http://www.oecd.org/tax/beps/beps-action-5-harmful-tax-practices-peer-review-transparency-framework.pdf. [3]

OECD (2015), *Countering Harmful Tax Practices More Effectively, Taking into Account Transparency and Substance, Action 5 - 2015 Final Report*, OECD/G20 Base Erosion and Profit Shifting Project, OECD Publishing, Paris, https://dx.doi.org/10.1787/9789264241190-en. [1]

OECD/Council of Europe (2011), *The Multilateral Convention on Mutual Administrative Assistance in Tax Matters: Amended by the 2010 Protocol*, OECD Publishing, Paris, https://dx.doi.org/10.1787/9789264115606-en. [4]

Notes

[1] With respect to the following preferential regimes: 1) International headquarters and treasury centre, 2) International trading centre and 3) International business centre.

[2] Parties to the Convention are available here: www.oecd.org/tax/exchange-of-tax-information/convention-on-mutual-administrative-assistance-in-tax-matters.htm. Thailand also has bilateral agreements with Armenia, Australia, Austria, Bangladesh, Belarus, Belgium, Bulgaria, Cambodia, Canada, Chile, China (People's Republic of), Cyprus, Czech Republic, Denmark, Estonia, Finland, France, Germany, Hong Kong (China), Hungary, India, Indonesia, Ireland, Israel, Italy, Japan, Korea, Kuwait, Laos, Luxembourg, Malaysia, Mauritius, Myanmar, Nepal, Netherlands, New Zealand, Norway, Oman, Pakistan, Philippines, Poland, Romania, Russia, Seychelles, Singapore, Slovenia, South Africa, Spain, Sri Lanka, Sweden, Switzerland, Chinese Taipei, Tajikistan, Turkey, Ukraine, United Arab Emirates, United Kingdom, United States, Uzbekistan and Viet Nam.

[3] 1) International headquarters and treasury centre, 2) Regional operating headquarters 1 and 3) Regional operating headquarters 2.

[4] International business centre.

Turkey

Turkey has met all aspects of the terms of reference (OECD, 2017[3]) (ToR) for the calendar year 2019 (year in review) except for identifying and exchanging information on new entrants to the grandfathered IP regime and exchanging information on all taxpayers benefitting from the third category of assets in the IP regime (ToR I.4.1.3). Turkey receives one recommendation on this point for the year in review.

In the prior year report, as well as in the 2017 peer review, Turkey received the same recommendation. As it has not been addressed, the recommendation remains in place.

Turkey can legally issue one type of rulings within the scope of the transparency framework.

In practice, Turkey issued rulings within the scope of the transparency framework as follows:

- Three past rulings;
- For the period 1 April 2016 - 31 December 2016: no future rulings;
- For the calendar year 2017: eight future rulings,
- For the calendar year 2018: no future rulings, and
- For the year in review: no future rulings.

As no exchanges took place, no peer input was received in respect of the exchanges of information on rulings received from Turkey.

A. The information gathering process

1099. Turkey can legally issue the following type of ruling within the scope of the transparency framework: cross-border unilateral APAs and any other cross-border unilateral tax rulings (such as an advance tax ruling) covering transfer pricing or the application of transfer pricing principles; (iii) rulings providing for unilateral downward adjustments

1100. For Turkey, past rulings are any tax rulings within scope that are issued either: (i) on or after 1 January 2014 but before 1 April 2016; or (ii) on or after 1 January 2010 but before 1 January 2014, provided they were still in effect as at 1 January 2014. Future rulings are any tax rulings within scope that are issued on or after 1 April 2016.

1101. In the prior years' peer review reports, it was determined that Turkey's undertakings to identify past and future rulings and all potential exchange jurisdictions were sufficient to meet the minimum standard. In addition, it was determined that Turkey's review and supervision mechanism was sufficient to meet the minimum standard. Turkey's implementation remains unchanged, and therefore continues to meet the minimum standard.

1102. Turkey has met all of the ToR for the information gathering process and no recommendations are made.

B. The exchange of information

1103. In the prior years' peer review reports, it was determined that Turkey's process for the completion and exchange of templates were sufficient to meet the minimum standard. With respect to past rulings, no further action was required. Turkey's implementation in this regard remains unchanged and therefore continues to meet the minimum standard.

1104. Turkey has international agreements permitting spontaneous exchange of information, including being a party to the (i) *Multilateral Convention on Mutual Administrative Assistance in Tax Matters: Amended by the 2010 Protocol* (OECD/Council of Europe, 2011[4]) ("the Convention") and (ii) bilateral agreements in force with 86 jurisdictions.[1]

1105. As Turkey did not issue any rulings in scope of the transparency framework in the relevant period, Turkey was not required to exchange any information on rulings in the year in review and no data on the timeliness of exchanges can be reported.

1106. Turkey has the necessary legal basis for spontaneous exchange of information, a process for completing the templates in a timely way and has completed all exchanges. Turkey has met all of the ToR for the exchange of information process and no recommendations are made.

C. Statistics (ToR IV)

1107. As there was no information on rulings exchanged by Turkey for the year in review, no statistics can be reported.

D. Matters related to intellectual property regimes (ToR I.4.1.3)

1108. Turkey offers two intellectual property regimes (IP regime) that are subject to transparency requirements under the Action 5 Report (OECD, 2015[1]).[2] It states that the identification of the benefitting taxpayers will occur as follows:

Technology development zone regime:

- ***New entrants benefitting from the grandfathered IP regime***: Transparency obligations apply for the regime, because grandfathering is provided to entrants that entered the regime after the relevant date from which enhanced transparency obligations apply. In addition, the regime has been found to be actually harmful to the extent of extended grandfathering to taxpayers that entered the regime between 1 July 2016 and 19 October 2017. Therefore, the period for enhanced transparency for new entrants on the grandfathered regime is from 6 February 2015 until 19 October 2017. Turkey has obliged taxpayers to declare their exempted IP income earned in this period in a temporary tax return, in order to be able to identify both new taxpayers and new IP assets of existing taxpayers entering the regime in the relevant period. However, during the year in review, Turkey was not able to identify and exchange information on new entrants to the grandfathered IP regime and no information has yet been exchanged. Therefore, Turkey is recommended to continue its efforts to identify and exchange information on new entrants to the grandfathered IP as soon as possible. Additional steps have been taken to address this, as noted below in "Jurisdiction's response and recent developments".
- ***Third category of IP assets***: In order for taxpayers to benefit from the third category of IP assets, the Ministry of Industry and Technology issues project completion documents, after the research-development project is completed and the assets have been created. A company requests the completion document electronically and the Ministry of Industry and Technology assesses the application to determine whether the relevant IP assets have been created in the zone and the resulting income is therefore eligible for the tax benefit. After the document is approved and issued electronically by the Ministry, it is provided to the taxpayer. Turkey has also obliged taxpayers to declare their exempted IP income for the third category of IP assets in the temporary tax return. However, during the year in review, Turkey has not exchanged information on these taxpayers and therefore, it is recommended to exchange information on taxpayers benefitting from the third category of IP assets as soon as possible. Additional steps have been taken to address this, as noted below in "Jurisdiction's response and recent developments".
- ***Taxpayers making use of the option to treat the nexus ratio as a rebuttable presumption***: not applicable as the regime does not allow the nexus ratio to be treated as a rebuttable presumption.

5/B regime:

- ***New entrants benefitting from the grandfathered IP regime***: as this is a new IP regime rather than a grandfathered IP regime, transparency on new entrants was not required.
- ***Third category of IP assets***: not applicable as the regime does not allow the third category of IP assets to qualify for the benefits.
- ***Taxpayers making use of the option to treat the nexus ratio as a rebuttable presumption***: not applicable as the regime does not allow the nexus ratio to be treated as a rebuttable presumption.

Summary of recommendations on implementation of the transparency framework

Aspect of implementation of the transparency framework that should be improved	Recommendation for improvement
During the year in review, Turkey was not able to identify and exchange information on new entrants to the grandfathered IP regime or to exchange information on all taxpayers benefitting from the third category of assets in the IP regime.	Turkey is recommended to identify and exchange information on new entrants to the grandfathered IP regime and to exchange information on taxpayers benefitting from the third category of IP assets as soon as possible. This recommendation remains unchanged since the 2017 and 2018 peer review reports.

Jurisdiction's response and recent developments

1109. Turkey indicates that it has completed its first round of identifying new entrants to the grandfathered IP regime, but that additional work on the identification of the taxpayer is needed. The second part of this work has been initiated, but is still ongoing and has been impeded by the Covid-19 pandemic. Turkey indicates that all new entrants will be identified by the end of 2020 and information will be exchanged. In addition, Turkey notes that it expects that a little number of new taxpayers will be identified for exchange of information as most of the taxpayers benefitting from the regime are pure domestic taxpayers. With respect to the third category of IP assets, Turkey notes that it has identified the taxpayers for the year 2018 and 2019 and made exchanges in September 2020. This will be assessed during next year's peer review.

References

OECD (2017), BEPS Action 5 on Harmful Tax Practices - Terms of Reference and Methodology for the Conduct of the Peer Reviews of the Action 5 Transparency Framework, OECD Publishing, Paris, http://www.oecd.org/tax/beps/beps-action-5-harmful-tax-practices-peer-review-transparency-framework.pdf. [3]

OECD (2015), Countering Harmful Tax Practices More Effectively, Taking into Account Transparency and Substance, Action 5 - 2015 Final Report, OECD/G20 Base Erosion and Profit Shifting Project, OECD Publishing, Paris, https://dx.doi.org/10.1787/9789264241190-en. [1]

OECD/Council of Europe (2011), The Multilateral Convention on Mutual Administrative Assistance in Tax Matters: Amended by the 2010 Protocol, OECD Publishing, Paris, https://dx.doi.org/10.1787/9789264115606-en. [4]

Notes

[1] Parties to the Convention are available here: www.oecd.org/tax/exchange-of-tax-information/convention-on-mutual-administrative-assistance-in-tax-matters.htm. Turkey also has bilateral agreements with Albania, Algeria, Australia, Austria, Azerbaijan, Bahrain, Bangladesh, Belarus, Belgium, Bosnia and Herzegovina, Brazil, Bulgaria, Canada, China (People's Republic of), Croatia, Czech Republic, Denmark, Egypt, Estonia, Ethiopia, Finland, France, Gambia, Georgia, Germany, Greece, Hungary, India, Indonesia, Iran, Ireland, Israel, Italy, Japan, Jordan, Kazakhstan, Korea, Kosovo, Kuwait, Kyrgyzstan, Latvia, Lebanon, Lithuania, Luxembourg, Malaysia, Malta, Mexico, Moldova, Mongolia, Montenegro, Morocco, Netherlands, New Zealand, North Macedonia, Norway, Oman, Pakistan, Philippines, Poland, Portugal, Qatar, Romania, Russian Federation, Saudi Arabia, Serbia, Singapore, Slovak Republic, Slovenia, South Africa, Spain, Sudan, Sweden, Switzerland, Syria, Tajikistan, Thailand, Tunisia, Turkish Republic of Northern Cyprus, Turkmenistan, Ukraine, United Arab Emirates, United Kingdom, United States, Uzbekistan, Viet Nam and Yemen.

[2] These regimes are: 1) Technology development zone regime and 2) 5/B regime.

Ukraine

Ukraine has met all aspects of the terms of reference (OECD, 2017[3]) (ToR) for the calendar year 2019 (year in review) that can be met given in the absence of rulings being issued.

Ukraine can legally issue one type of ruling within the scope of the transparency framework. In practice, Ukraine has issued no rulings within the scope of the transparency framework. Ukraine notes that as of the end of 2019, it has received four requests for unilateral APAs (two requests received in 2018 and two in 2019) which are under review.

As no exchanges were required to take place, no peer input was received in respect of the exchanges of information on rulings received from Ukraine.

A. The information gathering process

1110. Ukraine can legally issue the following type of ruling within the scope of the transparency framework: cross-border unilateral APAs and any other cross-border unilateral tax rulings (such as an advance tax ruling) covering transfer pricing or the application of transfer pricing principles.

1111. For Ukraine, past rulings are any tax rulings within scope that are issued either: (i) on or after 1 January 2016, but before 1 April 2018; and (ii) on or after 1 January 2014, but before 1 January 2016, provided still in effect as at 1 January 2016. Future rulings are any tax rulings within scope that are issued on or after 1 April 2018.

1112. In the prior years' peer review report, it was determined that Ukraine's undertakings to identify past and future rulings and all potential exchange jurisdictions were sufficient to meet the minimum standard. In addition, it was determined that Ukraine's review and supervision mechanism was sufficient to meet the minimum standard. Ukraine's implementation remains unchanged, and therefore continues to meet the minimum standard. In the previous year peer review report, Ukraine noted that it was working to have in place a more formal procedure with respect to its review and supervision mechanism. During the year in review, Ukraine clarified that the existing APA procedure, formalised in the tax code, is able to ensure that all relevant information related to APAs rulings is captured adequately.

1113. Ukraine has met all of the ToR for the information gathering process and no recommendations are made.

B. The exchange of information

1114. In the prior year' peer review report, it was determined that Ukraine's process for the completion and exchange of templates were sufficient to meet the minimum standard. With respect to past rulings, no action was required. Ukraine's implementation in this regard remains unchanged and therefore continues to meet the minimum standard.

1115. Ukraine has international agreements permitting spontaneous exchange of information, including being a party to the (i) *Multilateral Convention on Mutual Administrative Assistance in Tax Matters: Amended by the 2010 Protocol* (OECD/Council of Europe, 2011[4]) ("the Convention") and (ii) bilateral agreements in force with 75 jurisdictions.[1]

1116. As no rulings have been issued, no exchanges were required for the year in review and no data on timeliness can be reported.

1117. Ukraine has the necessary legal basis for spontaneous exchange of information and a process for completion of templates and exchange of information on rulings. Ukraine has met all of the ToR for the exchange of information process and no recommendations are made.

C. Statistics (ToR IV)

1118. As no rulings have been issued, no statistics can be reported.

D. Matters related to intellectual property regimes (ToR I.4.1.3)

1119. Ukraine does not offer an intellectual property regime for which transparency requirements under the Action 5 Report (OECD, 2015[1]) were imposed.

Summary of recommendations on implementation of the transparency framework

Aspect of implementation of the transparency framework that should be improved	Recommendation for improvement
	No recommendations are made.

References

OECD (2017), *BEPS Action 5 on Harmful Tax Practices - Terms of Reference and Methodology for the Conduct of the Peer Reviews of the Action 5 Transparency Framework*, OECD Publishing, Paris, http://www.oecd.org/tax/beps/beps-action-5-harmful-tax-practices-peer-review-transparency-framework.pdf. [3]

OECD (2015), *Countering Harmful Tax Practices More Effectively, Taking into Account Transparency and Substance, Action 5 - 2015 Final Report*, OECD/G20 Base Erosion and Profit Shifting Project, OECD Publishing, Paris, https://dx.doi.org/10.1787/9789264241190-en. [1]

OECD/Council of Europe (2011), *The Multilateral Convention on Mutual Administrative Assistance in Tax Matters: Amended by the 2010 Protocol*, OECD Publishing, Paris, https://dx.doi.org/10.1787/9789264115606-en. [4]

Notes

[1] Parties to the Convention are available here: www.oecd.org/tax/exchange-of-tax-information/convention-on-mutual-administrative-assistance-in-tax-matters.htm. Ukraine also has bilateral agreements with Algeria, Armenia, Austria, Azerbaijan, Belarus, Belgium, Brazil, Bulgaria, Canada, China (People's Republic of), Croatia, Cyprus, Czech Republic, Denmark, Egypt, Estonia, Finland, France, Georgia, Germany, Greece, Hungary, Iceland, India, Indonesia, Iran, Ireland, Israel, Italy, Japan, Jordan, Kazakhstan, Korea, Kuwait, Kyrgyzstan, Latvia, Lebanon, Libya, Lithuania, Luxembourg, Malaysia, Malta, Mexico, Moldova, Mongolia, Montenegro, Morocco, Netherlands, North Macedonia, Norway, Pakistan, Poland, Portugal, Qatar, Romania, Russia, Saudi Arabia, Serbia, Singapore, Slovak Republic, Slovenia, South Africa, Spain, Sweden, Switzerland, Syria, Tajikistan, Thailand, Turkey, Turkmenistan, United Arab Emirates, United Kingdom, United States, Uzbekistan and Viet Nam.

United Kingdom

The United Kingdom has met all aspects of the terms of reference (OECD, 2017[3]) (ToR) for the calendar year 2019 (year in review) and no recommendations are made.

The United Kingdom can legally issue three types of rulings within the scope of the transparency framework.

In practice, the United Kingdom issued rulings within the scope of the transparency framework as follows:

- 599 past rulings;
- For the period 1 April 2016 - 31 December 2016: 71 future rulings;
- For the calendar year 2017: 16 future rulings,
- For the calendar year 2018: 20 future rulings,[1] and
- For the year in review: 14 future rulings.

No peer input was received in respect of the exchanges of information on rulings received from United Kingdom.

A. The information gathering process

1120. The United Kingdom can legally issue three types of rulings within the scope of the transparency framework: (i) preferential regimes;[2] (ii) cross-border unilateral APAs and any other cross-border unilateral tax rulings (such as an advance tax ruling) covering transfer pricing or the application of transfer pricing principles; and (iii) permanent establishment rulings.

1121. For the United Kingdom, past rulings are any tax rulings within scope that are issued either: (i) on or after 1 January 2014 but before 1 April 2016; or (ii) on or after 1 January 2010 but before 1 January 2014, provided they were still in effect as at 1 January 2014. Future rulings are any tax rulings within scope that are issued on or after 1 April 2016.

1122. In the prior years' peer review reports, it was determined that the United Kingdom's undertakings to identify past and future rulings and all potential exchange jurisdictions were sufficient to meet the minimum standard. In addition, it was determined that The United Kingdom's review and supervision mechanism was sufficient to meet the minimum standard. The United Kingdom's implementation remains unchanged, and therefore continues to meet the minimum standard.

1123. The United Kingdom has met all of the ToR for the information gathering process and no recommendations are made.

B. The exchange of information

1124. In the prior years' peer review reports, it was determined that the United Kingdom's process for the completion and exchange of templates were sufficient to meet the minimum standard. With respect to past rulings, no further action was required. The United Kingdom's implementation in this regard remains unchanged and therefore continues to meet the minimum standard.

1125. The United Kingdom has international agreements permitting spontaneous exchange of information, including being a party to the (i) *Multilateral Convention on Mutual Administrative Assistance in Tax Matters: Amended by the 2010 Protocol* (OECD/Council of Europe, 2011[4]) ("the Convention"), (ii) the Directive 2011/16/EU with all other European Union Member States and (iii) double tax agreements in force with 121 jurisdictions.[3]

1126. For the year in review, the timeliness of exchanges is as follows:

Future rulings in the scope of the transparency framework	Number of exchanges transmitted within three months of the information becoming available to the competent authority or immediately after legal impediments have been lifted	Delayed exchanges		
		Number of exchanges transmitted later than three months of the information on rulings becoming available to the competent authority	Reasons for the delays	Any other comments
	17	0	N/A	N/A

Follow up requests received for exchange of the ruling	Number	Average time to provide response	Number of requests not answered
	0	N/A	N/A

1127. The United Kingdom has the necessary legal basis for spontaneous exchange of information, a process for completing the templates in a timely way and has completed all exchanges. The United Kingdom has met all of the ToR for the exchange of information process and no recommendations are made.

C. Statistics (ToR IV)

1128. The statistics for the year in review are as follows:

Category of ruling	Number of exchanges	Jurisdictions exchanged with
Ruling related to a preferential regime	*De minimis rule* applies	N/A
Cross-border unilateral advance pricing agreements (APAs) and any other cross-border unilateral tax rulings (such as an advance tax ruling) covering transfer pricing or the application of transfer pricing principles	16	China (People's Republic of), Guernsey, Hungary, Hong Kong (China), Jersey, Japan, Luxembourg, Switzerland, United States
Permanent establishment rulings	0	N/A
De minimis rule	1	
IP regimes: total exchanges on taxpayers benefitting from the third category of IP assets, new entrants benefitting from grandfathered IP regimes; and taxpayers making use of the option to treat the nexus ratio as a rebuttable presumption	0	N/A
Total	17	

D. Matters related to intellectual property regimes (ToR I.4.1.3)

1129. The United Kingdom offers an intellectual property regime (IP regime)[4] that is subject to the transparency requirements under the Action 5 Report (OECD, 2015[1]). It states that the identification of the benefitting taxpayers occurs as follows:

- ***New entrants benefitting from the grandfathered IP regime***: in the prior year peer review report, it was determined that the United Kingdom's process for identifying and exchanging information on new entrants to the grandfathered IP regime were sufficient to meet the minimum standard. The United Kingdom's implementation in this regard remains unchanged and therefore continues to meet the minimum standard.
- ***Third category of IP assets***: not applicable as the regime does not allow the third category of IP assets to qualify for the benefits.
- ***Taxpayers making use of the option to treat the nexus ratio as a rebuttable presumption***: The United Kingdom recorded three elections to use the rebuttable presumption during the year in review. However, the companies which elected to use the rebuttable presumption were all wholly domestic companies (and where the nexus ratio was in any event a ratio of 1) and therefore no exchanges were required for the year in review.

Summary of recommendations on implementation of the transparency framework

Aspect of implementation of the transparency framework that should be improved	Recommendation for improvement
	No recommendations are made.

References

OECD (2017), *BEPS Action 5 on Harmful Tax Practices - Terms of Reference and Methodology for the Conduct of the Peer Reviews of the Action 5 Transparency Framework*, OECD Publishing, Paris, http://www.oecd.org/tax/beps/beps-action-5-harmful-tax-practices-peer-review-transparency-framework.pdf. [3]

OECD (2015), *Countering Harmful Tax Practices More Effectively, Taking into Account Transparency and Substance, Action 5 - 2015 Final Report*, OECD/G20 Base Erosion and Profit Shifting Project, OECD Publishing, Paris, https://dx.doi.org/10.1787/9789264241190-en. [1]

OECD/Council of Europe (2011), *The Multilateral Convention on Mutual Administrative Assistance in Tax Matters: Amended by the 2010 Protocol*, OECD Publishing, Paris, https://dx.doi.org/10.1787/9789264115606-en. [4]

Notes

[1] The prior year peer review report noted that 19 future rulings were issued in 2018. During the course of this year's review, a correction was made to reflect one additional ruling issued late in 2018. The information on this ruling was exchanged on time in early 2019.

[2] With respect to the following preferential regimes: 1) Patent box and 2) Shipping regime.

[3] Parties to the Convention are available here: www.oecd.org/tax/exchange-of-tax-information/convention-on-mutual-administrative-assistance-in-tax-matters.htm. The United Kingdom also has bilateral agreements with Albania, Algeria, Antigua and Barbuda, Argentina, Armenia, Australia, Azerbaijan, Bahrain, Bangladesh, Barbados, Belarus, Belize, Bolivia, Bosnia and Herzegovina, Botswana, British Virgin Islands, Brunei, Bulgaria, Cayman Islands, Chile, China (People's Republic of), Colombia, Côte d'Ivoire, Croatia, Cyprus, Czech Republic, Denmark, Egypt, Estonia, Ethiopia, Falkland Islands, Faroe Islands, Fiji, Finland, Gambia, Georgia, Ghana, Greece, Grenada, Guernsey, Guyana, Hong Kong (China), Hungary, Iceland, India, Indonesia, Ireland, Isle of Man, Israel, Jamaica, Japan, Jersey, Jordan, Kazakhstan, Kenya, Kiribati, Korea, Kosovo, Kuwait, Latvia, Lesotho, Libya, Lithuania, Malawi, Malaysia, Malta, Mauritius, Mexico, Moldova, Mongolia, Montenegro, Montserrat, Morocco, Myanmar, Namibia, New Zealand, Nigeria, North Macedonia, Norway, Oman, Pakistan, Panama, Papua New Guinea, Philippines, Poland, Portugal, Qatar, Romania, Russia, Saudi Arabia, Senegal, Serbia, Sierra Leone, Singapore, Slovak Republic, Slovenia, Solomon Islands, South Africa, Spain, Sri Lanka, Saint Kitts and Nevis, Sudan, Swaziland, Chinese Taipei, Tajikistan, Thailand, Trinidad and Tobago, Tunisia, Turkey, Turkmenistan, Tuvalu, Uganda, Ukraine, United Arab Emirates, United States, Uruguay, Uzbekistan, Venezuela, Viet Nam, Zambia and Zimbabwe.

[4] Patent box.

United States

The United States has met all aspects of the terms of reference (OECD, 2017[3]) (ToR) for the calendar year 2019 (year in review) and no recommendations are made.

The United States can legally issue four types of rulings within the scope of the transparency framework.

In practice, the United States issued rulings within the scope of the transparency framework as follows:

- 114 past rulings;
- For the period 1 April 2016 - 31 December 2016: 21 future rulings;
- For the calendar year 2017: 30 future rulings;
- For the calendar year 2018: 27 future rulings; and
- For the year in review: 30 future rulings.

Peer input was received from one jurisdiction in respect of the exchanges of information on rulings received from the United States. The input was positive, noting that information was complete, in a correct format and received in a timely manner.

A. The information gathering process

1130. The United States can legally issue three types of rulings within the scope of the transparency framework: (i) cross-border unilateral APAs and any other cross-border unilateral tax rulings (such as an advance tax ruling) covering transfer pricing or the application of transfer pricing principles; (ii) permanent establishment rulings; and (iii) related party conduit rulings.

1131. For the United States, past rulings are any tax rulings within scope that are issued either: (i) on or after 1 January 2014 but before 1 April 2016; or (ii) on or after 1 January 2010 but before 1 January 2014, provided they were still in effect as at 1 January 2014. Future rulings are any tax rulings within scope that are issued on or after 1 April 2016.

1132. In the prior years' peer review reports, it was determined that the United States' undertakings to identify past and future rulings and all potential exchange jurisdictions were sufficient to meet the minimum standard. In addition, it was determined that the United States' review and supervision mechanism was sufficient to meet the minimum standard. The United States' implementation remains unchanged, and therefore continues to meet the minimum standard.

1133. The United States has met all of the ToR for the information gathering process and no recommendations are made.

B. The exchange of information

1134. In the prior years' peer review reports, it was determined that the United States' process for the completion and exchange of templates were sufficient to meet the minimum standard. With respect to past rulings, no further action was required. The United States' implementation in this regard remains unchanged and therefore continues to meet the minimum standard.

1135. The United States has international agreements permitting spontaneous exchange of information, including being a party to the (i) *Multilateral Convention on Mutual Administrative Assistance in Tax Matters*[1] ("the Convention") and (ii) bilateral agreements in force with 49 jurisdictions.[2]

1136. For the year in review, the timeliness of exchanges is as follows:

Future rulings in the scope of the transparency framework	Number of exchanges transmitted within three months of the information becoming available to the competent authority or immediately after legal impediments have been lifted	Delayed exchanges		
		Number of exchanges transmitted later than three months of the information on rulings becoming available to the competent authority	Reasons for the delays	Any other comments
	37	1	This delay was due to the U.S. government shutdown, and was exchanged as soon as possible and within the year in review.	N/A

Follow up requests received for exchange of the ruling	Number	Average time to provide response	Number of requests not answered
	0	N/A	N/A

1137. The United States has the necessary legal basis for spontaneous exchange of information, a process for completing the templates in a timely way and has completed all exchanges. The United States has met all of the ToR for the exchange of information process and no recommendations are made.

C. Statistics (ToR IV)

1138. The statistics for the year in review are as follows:

Category of ruling	Number of exchanges	Jurisdictions exchanged with
Ruling related to a preferential regime	0	N/A
Cross-border unilateral advance pricing agreements (APAs) and any other cross-border unilateral tax rulings (such as an advance tax ruling) covering transfer pricing or the application of transfer pricing principles	38	Argentina, Brazil, Canada, China (People's Republic of), Finland, France, Germany, Israel, Italy, Japan, Luxembourg, Mexico, Netherlands, New Zealand, South Africa, United Kingdom
Permanent establishment rulings	0	N/A
Related party conduit rulings	0	N/A
Total	38	

D. Matters related to intellectual property regimes (ToR I.4.1.3)

1139. The United States does not offer an intellectual property regime for which transparency requirements under the Action 5 Report (OECD, 2015[1]) were imposed.

Summary of recommendations on implementation of the transparency framework

Aspect of implementation of the transparency framework that should be improved	Recommendation for improvement
The United States experienced some delays in exchanging information on one future ruling.	No recommendation is made because the United States completed the exchange on the delayed future ruling quickly after the issues were identified and resolved, and this is not a recurring issue.

References

OECD (2017), BEPS Action 5 on Harmful Tax Practices - Terms of Reference and Methodology for the Conduct of the Peer Reviews of the Action 5 Transparency Framework, OECD Publishing, Paris, http://www.oecd.org/tax/beps/beps-action-5-harmful-tax-practices-peer-review-transparency-framework.pdf. [3]

OECD (2015), Countering Harmful Tax Practices More Effectively, Taking into Account Transparency and Substance, Action 5 - 2015 Final Report, OECD/G20 Base Erosion and Profit Shifting Project, OECD Publishing, Paris, https://dx.doi.org/10.1787/9789264241190-en. [1]

OECD/Council of Europe (2011), The Multilateral Convention on Mutual Administrative Assistance in Tax Matters: Amended by the 2010 Protocol, OECD Publishing, Paris, https://dx.doi.org/10.1787/9789264115606-en. [4]

Notes

[1] The United States is a Party to the original Convention but not the amended Convention. The United States signed the Protocol in 2010 which amends the original Convention but the Protocol has not yet entered into force.

[2] Parties to the Convention are available here: www.oecd.org/tax/exchange-of-tax-information/convention-on-mutual-administrative-assistance-in-tax-matters.htm. The United States also has bilateral agreements with Australia, Austria, Barbados, Belgium, Bulgaria, Canada, China (People's Republic of), Czech Republic, Denmark, Egypt, Estonia, Finland, France, Germany, Greece, Hungary, Iceland, India, Indonesia, Ireland, Israel, Italy, Jamaica, Japan, Kazakhstan, Latvia, Lithuania, Luxembourg, Malta, Mexico, Netherlands, New Zealand, Norway, Pakistan, Poland, Portugal, Romania, Russia, Slovak Republic, Slovenia, South Africa, Spain, Sri Lanka, Sweden, Switzerland, Thailand, Turkey, Ukraine and the United Kingdom.

Uruguay

Uruguay has met all aspects of the terms of reference (OECD, 2017[3]) (ToR) for the calendar year 2019 (year in review) and no recommendations are made.

Uruguay can legally issue one type of rulings within the scope of the transparency framework.

In practice, Uruguay issued rulings within the scope of the transparency framework as follows:

- One past ruling; and
- no future rulings.

Peer input was received from one jurisdiction in respect of the exchanges of information on rulings received from Uruguay. The input was positive, noting that information was complete, in a correct format and received in a timely manner.

A. The information gathering process

1140. Uruguay can legally issue the following type of ruling within the scope of the transparency framework: cross-border unilateral APAs and any other cross-border unilateral tax rulings (such as an advance tax ruling) covering transfer pricing or the application of transfer pricing principles

1141. For Uruguay, past rulings are any tax rulings within scope that are issued either: (i) on or after 1 January 2016 but before 1 April 2018; or (ii) on or after 1 January 20114 but before 1 January 2016, provided they were still in effect as at 1 January 2016. Future rulings are any tax rulings within scope that are issued on or after 1 April 2018.

1142. In the prior year's peer review report, it was determined that Uruguay's undertakings to identify past and future rulings and all potential exchange jurisdictions were sufficient to meet the minimum standard. In addition, it was determined that Uruguay's review and supervision mechanism was sufficient to meet the minimum standard. Uruguay's implementation remains unchanged, and therefore continues to meet the minimum standard.

1143. Uruguay has met all of the ToR for the information gathering process and no recommendations are made.

B. The exchange of information

1144. In the prior year's peer review report, it was determined that Uruguay's process for the completion and exchange of templates were sufficient to meet the minimum standard. With respect to past rulings, no further action was required. Uruguay's implementation in this regard remains unchanged and therefore continues to meet the minimum standard.

1145. Uruguay has international agreements permitting spontaneous exchange of information, including being a party to the (i) *Multilateral Convention on Mutual Administrative Assistance in Tax Matters: Amended by the 2010 Protocol* (OECD/Council of Europe, 2011[4]) ("the Convention") and (ii) bilateral agreements in force with 20 jurisdictions.[1]

1146. As Uruguay did not issue any rulings in scope of the transparency framework in the relevant period, Uruguay was not required to exchange any information on rulings in the year in review and no data on the timeliness of exchanges can be reported.

1147. Uruguay has the necessary legal basis for spontaneous exchange of information, a process for completing the templates in a timely way and has completed all exchanges. Uruguay has met all of the ToR for the exchange of information process and no recommendations are made.

C. Statistics (ToR IV)

1148. As there was no information on rulings exchanged by Uruguay for the year in review, no statistics can be reported.

D. Matters related to intellectual property regimes (ToR I.4.1.3)

1149. In the year of review, Uruguay offered three intellectual property regimes (IP regime).[2] However, these are not subject to the transparency requirements under the Action 5 Report (OECD, 2015[1]), because:

- ***New entrants benefitting from the grandfathered IP regime***: not applicable for the (i) Benefits under law 16.906 for biotechnology and (ii) Free zones regimes, as these regimes were abolished and amended without grandfathering. For the Benefits under lit S art. 52 for biotechnology and for software regime, no enhanced transparency requirements apply as follows. Uruguay amended the IP regime by implementing the nexus approach. The previous regime has been closed-off, and although grandfathering was provided, it is not available to new entrants that entered more recently and for which enhanced transparency obligations would apply.
- ***Third category of IP assets***: not applicable as the regimes do not allow the third category of IP assets to qualify for the benefits.
- ***Taxpayers making use of the option to treat the nexus ratio as a rebuttable presumption***: not applicable as the regimes do not allow the nexus ratio to be treated as a rebuttable presumption.

Summary of recommendations on implementation of the transparency framework

Aspect of implementation of the transparency framework that should be improved	Recommendation for improvement
	No recommendations are made.

References

OECD (2017), BEPS Action 5 on Harmful Tax Practices - Terms of Reference and Methodology for the Conduct of the Peer Reviews of the Action 5 Transparency Framework, OECD Publishing, Paris, http://www.oecd.org/tax/beps/beps-action-5-harmful-tax-practices-peer-review-transparency-framework.pdf. [3]

OECD (2015), Countering Harmful Tax Practices More Effectively, Taking into Account Transparency and Substance, Action 5 - 2015 Final Report, OECD/G20 Base Erosion and Profit Shifting Project, OECD Publishing, Paris, https://dx.doi.org/10.1787/9789264241190-en. [1]

OECD/Council of Europe (2011), The Multilateral Convention on Mutual Administrative Assistance in Tax Matters: Amended by the 2010 Protocol, OECD Publishing, Paris, https://dx.doi.org/10.1787/9789264115606-en. [4]

Notes

[1] Parties to the Convention are available here: www.oecd.org/tax/exchange-of-tax-information/convention-on-mutual-administrative-assistance-in-tax-matters.htm. Uruguay also has bilateral agreements with Belgium, Chile, Ecuador, Finland, Germany, India, Korea, Liechtenstein, Luxembourg, Malta, Mexico, Paraguay, Portugal, Romania, Singapore, Spain, Switzerland, United Arab Emirates, United Kingdom and Viet Nam.

[2] These are: (i) Benefits under law 16.906 for biotechnology, (ii) Benefits under lit S art. 52 for biotechnology and for software and (iii) Free zones regimes.

Viet Nam

Viet Nam has met all aspects of the terms of reference (OECD, 2017[3]) (ToR) for the calendar year 2019 (year in review), except for having in place a process for completion of templates and exchange of information on rulings (ToR II.5). Viet Nam receives one recommendation on this point for the year in review.

In the prior year report, as well as in the 2017 peer review, Viet Nam had received the same recommendation. As it has not been addressed, the recommendation remains in place.

Viet Nam can legally issue one type of ruling within the scope of the transparency framework. In practice, Viet Nam issued no rulings within the scope of the transparency framework.

As no exchanges were required to take place, no peer input was received in respect of the exchanges of information on rulings received from Viet Nam.

A. The information gathering process

1150. Viet Nam can legally issue the following type of rulings within the scope of the transparency framework: cross-border unilateral APAs and any other cross-border unilateral tax rulings (such as an advance tax ruling) covering transfer pricing or the application of transfer pricing principles.

1151. For Viet Nam, past rulings are any tax rulings within scope that are issued either: (i) on or after 1 January 2015 but before 1 September 2017; or (ii) on or after 1 January 2012 but before 1 January 2015, provided they were still in effect as at 1 January 2015. Future rulings are any tax rulings within scope that are issued on or after 1 September 2017. In last year's report, Viet Nam indicated it had received three requests for unilateral APAs which were at a preliminary stage. During the year in review, Viet Nam put the APA program on a hold due to the new assessment requirements set out in the revised Tax Administration Law for 2019. As a result, none of the APA requests previously received were approved, and no APAs were issued during the year in review.

1152. In the prior years' peer review reports, it was determined that Viet Nam's undertakings to identify past and future rulings and all potential exchange jurisdictions were sufficient to meet the minimum standard. In addition, it was determined that Viet Nam's review and supervision mechanism was sufficient to meet the minimum standard. Viet Nam's implementation remains unchanged, and therefore continues to meet the minimum standard.

1153. Viet Nam has met all of the ToR for the information gathering process and no recommendations are made.

B. The exchange of information

Legal basis for spontaneous exchange of information (ToR II.5.1, II.5.2)

1154. Viet Nam has the necessary domestic legal basis to exchange information spontaneously. Viet Nam notes that there are no legal or practical impediments that prevent the spontaneous exchange of information on rulings as contemplated in the Action 5 minimum standard.

1155. Viet Nam has international agreements permitting spontaneous exchange of information, including being a party to bilateral agreements in force with 76 jurisdictions.[1]

Completion and exchange of templates (ToR II.5.3, II.5.4, II.5.5, II.5.6, II.5.7)

1156. In the prior years' peer review reports, it was determined that Viet Nam's process for the completion and exchange of templates met all the ToR, except for the completion and exchange of templates (ToR II.5). Therefore, Viet Nam was recommended to continue to put in place a process to complete the templates for all relevant rulings and to ensure the timely exchange of information on rulings in the form required by the transparency framework.

1157. During the year in review, Viet Nam continued to work on the development of a process to complete the templates on relevant rulings, to make them available to the Competent Authority for exchange of information, and to exchange them with relevant jurisdictions. Viet Nam also indicated its intention to develop internal guidance covering the timelines for the transmission of the template to the Competent Authority and for the completion of exchanges, including appropriate training for the relevant tax officers. The process described above is yet to be completed, as new legal instruments accompanying the implementation of the Tax Administration Law for 2019, including new guidance for transfer pricing as well as for APAs, is yet to become effective. Therefore, the prior year recommendation remains.

1158. As no rulings within the scope of the transparency framework have been issued in practice, Viet Nam was not required to complete any exchanges of information and there is no data to report on the timeliness of exchanges.

Conclusion on section B

1159. Viet Nam has the necessary legal basis for spontaneous exchange of information. Viet Nam is currently putting in place a process for completion of templates and exchange of information on rulings (ToR II.5). Viet Nam is recommended to develop a process to complete the templates on relevant rulings and to ensure that the exchanges of information on rulings occur in accordance with the form and timelines under the transparency framework.

C. Statistics (ToR IV)

1160. As there was no information on rulings required to be exchanged by Viet Nam for the year in review, no statistics can be reported.

D. Matters related to intellectual property regimes (ToR I.4.1.3)

1161. Viet Nam does not offer an intellectual property regime for which transparency requirements under the Action 5 Report (OECD, 2015[1]) were imposed.

Summary of recommendations on implementation of the transparency framework

Aspect of implementation of the transparency framework that should be improved	Recommendation for improvement
Viet Nam is currently putting in place a process for completion of templates and exchange of information on rulings.	Viet Nam is recommended to develop a process to complete the templates on relevant rulings and to ensure that the exchanges of information on rulings occur in accordance with the form and timelines under the transparency framework. This recommendation remains unchanged since the 2017 and 2018 peer review reports.

References

OECD (2017), BEPS Action 5 on Harmful Tax Practices - Terms of Reference and Methodology for the Conduct of the Peer Reviews of the Action 5 Transparency Framework, OECD Publishing, Paris, http://www.oecd.org/tax/beps/beps-action-5-harmful-tax-practices-peer-review-transparency-framework.pdf. [3]

OECD (2015), Countering Harmful Tax Practices More Effectively, Taking into Account Transparency and Substance, Action 5 - 2015 Final Report, OECD/G20 Base Erosion and Profit Shifting Project, OECD Publishing, Paris, https://dx.doi.org/10.1787/9789264241190-en. [1]

OECD/Council of Europe (2011), The Multilateral Convention on Mutual Administrative Assistance in Tax Matters: Amended by the 2010 Protocol, OECD Publishing, Paris, https://dx.doi.org/10.1787/9789264115606-en. [4]

Notes

[1] Viet Nam has bilateral agreements with Australia, Austria, Azerbaijan, Bangladesh, Belarus, Belgium, Brunei Darussalam, Bulgaria, Cambodia, Canada, China (People's Republic of), Croatia, Cuba, Czech Republic, Democratic People's Republic of Korea, Denmark, Estonia, Finland, France, Germany, Hong Kong (China), Hungary, Iceland, India, Indonesia, Iran, Ireland, Israel, Italy, Japan, Kazakhstan, Korea, Kuwait, Lao People's Democratic Republic, Latvia, Luxembourg, Macau (China), Malaysia, Malta, Mongolia, Morocco, Mozambique, Myanmar, Netherlands, New Zealand, Norway, Oman, Pakistan, Palestinian Authority, Panama, Philippines, Poland, Portugal, Qatar, Romania, Russia, San Marino, Saudi Arabia, Serbia, Seychelles, Singapore, Slovak Republic, Spain, Sri Lanka, Sweden, Switzerland, Chinese Taipei, Thailand, Tunisia, Turkey, Ukraine, United Arab Emirates, United Kingdom, Uruguay, Uzbekistan and Venezuela.

www.ingramcontent.com/pod-product-compliance
Ingram Content Group UK Ltd.
Pitfield, Milton Keynes, MK11 3LW, UK
UKHW051456290926
15471UKWH00008B/1236

9 789264 705647